Redefining the Future of Digital Marketing With Virtual Influencers

Ricardo Correia
Polytechnic Institute of Bragança, Portugal & Applied Management Research Unit (UNIAG), Portugal

Dominyka Venciute
ISM University of Management and Economics, Lithuania

IGI Global
Scientific Publishing
Publishing Tomorrow's Research Today

Vice President of Editorial	Melissa Wagner
Director of Acquisitions	Mikaela Felty
Director of Book Development	Jocelynn Hessler
Production Manager	Mike Brehm
Cover Design	Phillip Shickler

Published in the United States of America by
IGI Global Scientific Publishing
701 East Chocolate Avenue
Hershey, PA, 17033, USA
Tel: 717-533-8845
Fax: 717-533-7115
Website: https://www.igi-global.com E-mail: cust@igi-global.com

Library of Congress Cataloging-in-Publication Data

Names: Correia, Ricardo Fontes, 1978- editor | Venciūtė, Dominyka, 1990- editor
Title: Redefining the future of digital marketing with virtual influencers / edited by: Ricardo Correia, Dominyka Venciute.
Description: Hershey, PA : IGI Global Scientific Publishing, [2025] | Includes bibliographical references and index. | Summary: "This book delves into the emerging phenomenon of Virtual Influencers (VIs) and their growing influence on marketing strategies across diverse industries, such as fashion, tourism, and consumer goods. By blending artificial intelligence (AI), computer-generated imagery (CGI), and human-like personas, Virtual Influencers offer brands a unique opportunity to engage audiences in new and powerful ways"-- Provided by publisher.
Identifiers: LCCN 2025000069 (print) | LCCN 2025000070 (ebook) | ISBN 9798337302553 hardcover | ISBN 9798337302560 paperback | ISBN 9798337302577 ebook
Subjects: LCSH: Internet marketing | Virtual humans (Artificial intelligence) | Influence (Psychology) | Consumers' preferences | Artificial intelligence--Marketing applications
Classification: LCC HF5415.1265 .R428 2025 (print) | LCC HF5415.1265 (ebook) | DDC 658.8/72--dc23/eng/20250410
LC record available at https://lccn.loc.gov/2025000069
LC ebook record available at https://lccn.loc.gov/2025000070

British Cataloguing in Publication Data
A Cataloguing in Publication record for this book is available from the British Library.

Table of Contents

Detailed Table of Contents

This chapter explores the growing phenomenon of Virtual Influencers (VIs) in digital advertising and their transformative impact on brand communication. As artificial intelligence and computer-generated imagery enable the creation of lifelike digital personas, VIs offer marketers a new set of tools to engage consumers across global markets. The chapter examines the theoretical foundations of parasocial interaction and source credibility to understand how audiences respond to these non-human figures.

Traditional marketing has been affected by the rise of virtual influencers (VIs). Traditionally, products were marketed by celebrities or human influencers. Influencer marketing has been a strategy for connecting with audiences through credible and engaging social media figures and celebrities. This chapter explores the rise of VIs as they reshape the marketing landscape. Unlike human influencers, VIs offer unparalleled consistency, innovative engagement methods, and cost efficiency, revolutionizing marketing strategies across platforms like Instagram, TikTok, and virtual reality environments. This chapter also examines the rise of VIs, popular VIs, the cultural effects of VIs on Filipinos, popular VIs, and the ethical and operational implications of VIs. By integrating these insights, this chapter underscores how VIs exemplify digital disruption's transformative power, redefining traditional marketing practices while influencing the future of marketing and consumer engagement.

Virtual influencers, digitally created personas powered by artificial intelligence and computer graphics, have emerged as a transformative force in marketing. Unlike traditional influencers, virtual influencers are entirely controlled by their creators, enabling brands to design highly customized, consistent, and engaging narratives. This paper explores the impact of virtual influencers on contemporary marketing strategies, focusing on their unique advantages, such as cost efficiency, creative flexibility, and the ability to transcend physical limitations. It also examines their potential challenges, including authenticity concerns, audience trust, and ethical considerations. Through case studies and industry examples, this research highlights how brands leverage virtual influencers to enhance consumer engagement, build brand identity, and drive sales. By analyzing the interplay between technology and human-like branding, this study sheds light on how virtual influencers are reshaping the marketing landscape and paving the way for innovative digital campaigns.

The advent of social media has ushered in a new age of communication, information sharing and marketing. The recent phenomenon of influencers, both human and virtual, on social media has transformed our modern society. Human influencers have led the way in using their power of influence on social platforms, providing brands with a powerful way to reach their target audience in a precise, authentic and engaging way. Virtual influencers, created digitally, are also gaining prominence on online platforms, mainly on Instagram. Created for brands, these characters generated by Artificial Intelligence (AI) have the realistic characteristics, personalities, thoughts and feelings of real human beings. This chapter explores the similarities and differences between human influencers (HI) and virtual influencers (VI) in the context of influencer marketing, in order to understand the reasons for the success of these new imaginary characters. We will present the evolution and current context of marketing, including the appearance of human influencers and then that of virtual influencers,

The emerging trend of using virtual influencers in tourism is transforming how companies engage with travelers, becoming a mass phenomenon among younger digital audiences. These characters, crafted using CGI (Computer-Generated Imagery) by digital marketing teams, are not only used to promote destinations but also serve as virtual guides, assisting users in planning their trips. Thanks to their ability to adapt and emphasize brand values, virtual influencers can produce unlimited, engaging content without geographic or temporal restrictions. This chapter analyzes the impact of using virtual influencers in the tourism sector, addressing both the benefits and the ethical challenges they present. To this end, a content analysis was conducted on seven virtual influencers, two of whom focus exclusively on tourism and travel. In conclusion, virtual influencers represent an innovative tool for tourism, with the potential to enhance engagement and sustainability in destination promotion, though challenges of authenticity and trust must be addressed to maximize their impact.

This chapter explores the emergence and impact of Virtual Influencers (VIs) in the Indian digital marketing landscape, focusing on their ability to engage consumers and redefine brand interactions through AI-driven personas. By examining case studies of prominent Indian virtual influencers like Kyra and Naina Avtr, the chapter analyzes their roles in consumer engagement, cultural relevance, and brand partnerships. The discussion highlights the unique strengths of VIs, including their consistency, scalability, and ability to operate across diverse platforms, while also addressing challenges related to authenticity, emotional connection, and regional adaptation. Drawing on theories of social influence and digital marketing, the chapter provides insights into the opportunities and limitations of VIs in India's culturally diverse and technology-driven market. It concludes by exploring the future of virtual influencers as dynamic tools for brands aiming to balance technological innovation with human-like relatability in a competitive digital ecosystem.

Preface

INTRODUCTION

The digital marketing landscape is undergoing a seismic transformation, and at the forefront of this evolution are Virtual Influencers (VIs). As editors of *Redefining the Future of Digital Marketing With Virtual Influencers*, we are excited to present this volume, which explores a dynamic and increasingly influential facet of modern marketing. Virtual Influencers, powered by artificial intelligence, computer-generated imagery, and carefully crafted human-like personas, are not only reshaping how brands connect with audiences but are also redefining what it means to be an "influencer" in the digital age.

This book represents a multidisciplinary collaboration, uniting insights from marketing, technology, communication, and ethics. We have curated chapters that investigate the technical processes behind VI creation, the psychological and social dimensions of their appeal, and the strategic advantages they offer to industries such as fashion, tourism, and consumer goods. At the same time, we recognize the inherent challenges of this emerging phenomenon—questions of authenticity, transparency, and ethical responsibility are woven throughout our discussions.

The goal of this book is not just to inform, but to provoke thoughtful dialogue and equip readers with a practical understanding of how VIs can be deployed effectively and responsibly. Whether it is through case studies of pioneering brands or theoretical discussions on parasocial interactions, our contributors have delivered insights that are both academically rigorous and practically relevant.

We envision this book as a critical resource for a diverse readership:

- For marketing professionals, it offers a forward-looking lens on a trend that is already shaping consumer engagement strategies.

- For academics and researchers, it provides a foundational framework for understanding the implications of VIs on digital communication and brand dynamics.
- For students, it delivers contemporary and accessible insights into a fast-evolving field.
- And for business leaders, it opens up new possibilities for innovation at the intersection of technology, creativity, and consumer psychology.

As Virtual Influencers continue to gain traction, their presence raises profound questions and opens exciting opportunities. We hope this book serves as a roadmap to navigating this complex and fascinating terrain, and that it inspires readers to explore the potential of VIs with both curiosity and critical thought.

ORGANIZATION OF THE BOOK

In *Redefining the Future of Digital Marketing With Virtual Influencers*, each chapter offers a unique lens on the evolving landscape of virtual influencer (VI) marketing, presenting both theoretical insights and practical applications to guide scholars, professionals, and students through this digital transformation.

Chapter 1, *From Human to Posthuman: The Strategic Role of Virtual Influencers in Contemporary Marketing*, introduces readers to the theoretical underpinnings of Virtual Influencers. Drawing on parasocial interaction and source credibility theories, this chapter lays the groundwork for understanding how lifelike digital personas are strategically employed in global marketing campaigns. The chapter outlines how brands use these AI-driven figures to reshape consumer engagement and redefine authenticity in digital branding.
Chapter 2, *Digital Disruption: Virtual Influencers Transforming Traditional Marketing*, highlights the disruptive potential of virtual influencers in replacing or complementing traditional human influencers. With particular attention to platforms like Instagram, TikTok, and emerging virtual environments, this chapter explores how VIs provide consistent messaging, cost efficiency, and new creative formats. Cultural implications, including insights from the Filipino market, bring added depth to the analysis of how VIs are reshaping brand communication and influencing consumer behavior.
Chapter 3, *Virtual Influencer Marketing and Its Impact on Marketing Strategies*, delves into how virtual influencers are fundamentally transforming digital marketing. Through real-world examples and industry case studies, the chapter illustrates how brands leverage VIs for enhanced storytelling, cost-effective

campaigns, and scalable content production. It also reflects on the ethical and trust-related challenges that emerge when audiences engage with digital rather than human personas.

Chapter 4, *Human Versus Virtual Influencers in the Context of Influencer Marketing: A Comparative Analysis*, investigates the strengths and limitations of both human and virtual influencers. By exploring their evolution in the context of modern marketing, this chapter offers a comparative lens to assess how VIs mimic human characteristics and emotional appeal. It raises key questions about the authenticity of influence and how these synthetic figures compete—or collaborate—with their human counterparts.

Chapter 5, *Virtual Influencers vs Human Influencers: Crossing the Roads or Going Together*, extends this comparative dialogue with a focus on coexistence. This chapter presents a compelling case for synergy between human and virtual influencers rather than competition. Drawing on extensive literature review, it outlines strategic pathways where both entities can align to enhance brand storytelling and market reach, advocating for a collaborative future in influencer marketing.

Chapter 6, *Parasocial Interaction and Virtual Influencers: Building Connections in a Digital World*, returns to theory to examine how VIs establish emotionally resonant connections with followers. Using Horton and Wohl's parasocial interaction framework, this chapter investigates the dynamics of audience attachment, particularly among Generation Z. It critically examines ethical concerns such as manipulation, unrealistic standards, and transparency, urging marketers to consider the psychological implications of deploying VIs in campaigns.

Chapter 7, *The Use of Virtual Influencers in the Tourism Sector*, focuses on the tourism industry's adoption of virtual influencers as digital brand ambassadors and travel guides. By analyzing case studies of tourism-specific VIs, the chapter discusses how these digital personas offer immersive, scalable engagement. It also addresses challenges of trust and authenticity, ultimately framing VIs as sustainable marketing tools capable of transforming destination promotion.

Chapter 8, *Virtual Influencers in India: Transforming Digital Marketing in the AI Era*, shifts the spotlight to India, a fast-evolving digital marketplace. With case studies of virtual personas like Kyra and Naina Avtr, this chapter explores how VIs resonate with culturally diverse Indian audiences. It highlights both opportunities and limitations, including technological adaptability and emotional resonance, offering a detailed view of how VIs are reshaping marketing in one of the world's largest consumer economies.

Chapter 9, *Practical Strategies for Brands Using Virtual Influencers: A Brand's Guide to Success*, serves as a pragmatic guide for marketers. It outlines actionable strategies for selecting, designing, and deploying virtual influencers across sectors. The chapter discusses how brands can build believable and engaging VI personalities, align them with campaign goals, and maximize their digital reach. It emphasizes the versatility of VIs and offers tools for effective brand integration in a competitive digital space.

Together, these chapters map the contours of an emerging marketing paradigm shaped by artificial intelligence, synthetic personas, and human-like storytelling. As editors, we believe this volume provides a critical and timely contribution to both marketing scholarship and practice, equipping readers with the theoretical depth, empirical evidence, and strategic guidance needed to navigate the virtual influencer revolution.

CONCLUSION

As editors of this volume, we are pleased to present a compelling exploration into the rapidly evolving domain of virtual influencers—a phenomenon that not only reflects the future of digital marketing but actively shapes it. Across these diverse chapters, our contributors have dissected the strategic, psychological, technological, and ethical dimensions of virtual influencers, offering a nuanced and multidisciplinary perspective that addresses both their potential and their limitations.

From the theoretical foundations of parasocial interaction to practical strategies for brand implementation, this book demonstrates how virtual influencers are no longer a speculative trend but a legitimate and transformative force in global marketing practices. Whether examining their role in reshaping traditional marketing, enhancing tourism experiences, or breaking ground in culturally complex markets like India, the chapters collectively emphasize that virtual influencers are not replacing human touch—they are redefining how it is created, simulated, and perceived in the digital age.

We hope this volume equips academics, practitioners, and students alike with the insights necessary to navigate this new frontier. As artificial intelligence and immersive technologies continue to develop, virtual influencers will only grow in influence and sophistication. It is our hope that the work presented here will serve as a foundational reference for future research and innovation, while encouraging ethical reflection and creative thinking in the ever-evolving landscape of digital communication.

Chapter 1
From Human to Posthuman:
The Strategic Role of Virtual Influencers in Contemporary Marketing

Ricardo Correia
https://orcid.org/0000-0002-0132-4002
Polytechnic Institute of Bragança, Portugal & Applied Management Research Unit (UNIAG), Portugal

Ruta Fontes
https://orcid.org/0000-0001-8697-1323
Fundação para a Ciência e Tecnologia, Portugal

Dominyka Venciute
ISM University of Management and Economics, Lithuania

ABSTRACT

This chapter explores the growing phenomenon of Virtual Influencers (VIs) in digital advertising and their transformative impact on brand communication. As artificial intelligence and computer-generated imagery enable the creation of lifelike digital personas, VIs offer marketers a new set of tools to engage consumers across global markets. The chapter examines the theoretical foundations of parasocial interaction and source credibility to understand how audiences respond to these non-human figures.

DOI: 10.4018/979-8-3373-0255-3.ch001

1. INTRODUCTION

The rapid evolution of digital technologies has reshaped the advertising landscape, catalyzing novel forms of consumer engagement and communication. One of the most significant developments in this digital transformation is the emergence of virtual influencers (VIs), computer-generated characters powered by artificial intelligence and designed to emulate human behavior across social media platforms. While influencer marketing has traditionally relied on human influencers to promote brands through authentic, relatable content (Lou & Yuan, 2019), the rise of virtual influencers marks a paradigm shift in how brands conceptualize identity, trust, and communication in digital environments.

Historically, human influencers have dominated the social media marketing domain, capitalizing on their ability to form parasocial relationships with followers, foster emotional resonance, and provide relatable narratives rooted in real-life experiences (Venciute et al., 2023). However, recent advances in artificial intelligence, machine learning, and computer-generated imagery have facilitated the rise of virtual influencers. These digital characters, ranging from hyper-realistic avatars to stylized figures, are increasingly deployed by global brands across industries such as fashion, technology, automotive, and entertainment (Shin & Lee, 2023).

Unlike their human counterparts, virtual influencers offer marketers complete creative control over appearance, messaging, and behavior. They do not age, fatigue, or face reputational risks associated with personal scandals or erratic behavior, making them a stable and scalable marketing asset (Ju et al., 2024). Their content is meticulously designed to align with brand identity, maintain aesthetic coherence, and engage target audiences in culturally and linguistically diverse markets. Furthermore, VIs can be programmed to interact with audiences in real-time, allowing brands to maintain a 24/7 online presence and responsiveness.

The increasing prevalence of VIs is also reflective of shifting consumer behavior, particularly among younger digital-native cohorts such as Generation Z and Millennials. These generations exhibit a heightened openness to AI-driven interactions and are habituated to engaging with virtual environments and gamified digital experiences. In this context, VIs serve as culturally resonant figures capable of curating aspirational lifestyles, championing brand values, and driving curiosity and engagement through their novelty and artificiality (Ameen et al., 2023; Appel et al., 2020).

Nevertheless, the integration of virtual influencers in advertising raises critical questions about authenticity, trust, and ethical responsibility. While some consumers perceive VIs as engaging and aesthetically appealing, others critique their artificial nature, limited emotional depth, and lack of spontaneity. Concerns have also emerged regarding consumer deception, transparency in disclosure, and the potential reinforcement of unrealistic beauty ideals. Regulatory bodies have begun to examine the ethical implications of VIs, advocating for clear guidelines on disclosure and authenticity in digital advertising practices (Lou et al., 2022).

Despite their increasing visibility, academic inquiry into virtual influencers remains in its early stages. There is limited empirical understanding of how consumers perceive and respond to AI-generated personas, particularly in relation to trust, parasocial engagement, and purchase intention. Existing literature has predominantly focused on human influencers, leaving a notable gap in understanding the psychological, behavioral, and ethical dynamics underpinning consumer interactions with virtual influencers (Kate & Sun, 2023).

Therefore, this chapter seeks to explore the role of virtual influencers in contemporary advertising, with a particular focus on their effectiveness in brand communication, their psychological and behavioral impact on consumers, and the ethical considerations surrounding their use. By analyzing current practices, theoretical frameworks, and empirical evidence, this research contributes to the evolving discourse on AI in marketing and provides strategic insights into the future of influencer-based advertising in a digitally mediated world.

2. CONCEPTUAL FOUNDATIONS AND LITERATURE REVIEW

2.1 Influencer Marketing

Influencer marketing has become an indispensable tool in digital marketing, transforming how brands communicate with consumers by leveraging the credibility, expertise, and social influence of individuals on social media platforms (Kozinets et al., 2023). Traditional influencers capitalize on authenticity, emotional connections, and personal narratives, often engaging audiences through relatable content grounded in their real-life experiences (Lou & Yuan, 2019; Tanwar et al., 2022). Brands utilize influencers to enhance visibility, strengthen brand image, and directly influence consumer purchase intentions, with the global influencer marketing industry expected to exceed $32.5 billion in 2023 (Nasrin, 2022).

However, the emergence of Vis has introduced a significant paradigm shift (Ju et al., 2024). These digital personas, such as Lil Miquela, Shudu, and Noonoouri, offer unprecedented control and consistency, enabling brands to craft meticulously aligned messages and visual aesthetics without human limitations or ethical risks (Kate & Sun, 2023). Despite their controlled nature, virtual influencers maintain high engagement rates, particularly with digitally native younger demographics, due to their innovative and culturally resonant appeal (Rossi & Rivetti, 2023).

2.2 Theoretical Foundations

The effectiveness of VIs in digital advertising can be explained using several established theoretical frameworks, including Parasocial Interaction (PSI) and Source Credibility. Parasocial Interaction theory (Horton & Wohl, 1956) highlights how individuals develop one-sided emotional bonds with media personas, perceiving these interactions as genuine relationships despite their artificial nature. VIs, through consistent character portrayal and immersive narratives, foster a sense of intimacy, familiarity, and emotional engagement, mirroring real-life influencer-follower dynamics. PSI has been demonstrated to enhance consumer trust, loyalty, and receptivity to recommendations (Venciute et al., 2023), which is essential for the sustained impact of influencer marketing campaigns.

Source Credibility theory (Hovland et al., 1953) emphasizes the importance of perceived trustworthiness, expertise, and attractiveness of communicators. In the context of VIs, credibility is maintained through accurate and consistent information delivery, transparency about the VI's artificial nature, and strategic aesthetic design (Xie-Carson et al., 2023a). Although VIs inherently face challenges related to authenticity, strategically crafted narratives and expertly managed personas can significantly mitigate these limitations, enhancing their persuasive power (Kim & Park, 2024).

2.3 Audience Reactions to Virtual Influencers

Audience reactions to VIs demonstrate complexity, marked by both enthusiasm and skepticism. Younger audiences, particularly those accustomed to digital environments and gaming cultures, display higher receptivity towards virtual influencers, perceiving them as innovative and entertaining (Ameen et al., 2023; Franke et al., 2023). Gender differences are also evident; women may engage more positively with VIs in contexts such as fashion and beauty, likely due to their visually appealing nature and safe, aspirational portrayals (Barari, 2023).

Moreover, cultural factors significantly influence VI acceptance. Regions with high technological integration, such as East Asia, show greater affinity toward virtual influencers compared to regions emphasizing personal authenticity and real-life connections (Angmo et al., 2023). Audience acceptance and engagement are critically dependent on content authenticity, narrative quality, and coherence, emphasizing the need for genuine, resonant content to bridge the emotional and psychological gap inherent in VI interactions (Suprawan & Pojanavatee, 2022).

2.4 Ethical Considerations and Consumer Trust

The integration of virtual influencers also brings forth ethical concerns related to transparency, consumer deception, and unrealistic beauty standards. Regulatory bodies, such as the Federal Trade Commission (FTC), advocate explicit disclosures regarding the artificial nature of VIs to preserve consumer trust and prevent misleading practices (Lou et al., 2022). Trust in digital marketing is critically dependent on transparency, authenticity, and ethical responsibility, demanding that brands find a balanced approach between creative control and spontaneous authenticity to maintain credible and effective communication (Zhu & Chen, 2012).

2.5 Comparative Analysis: Virtual vs. Human influencers

The proliferation of VIs has precipitated a paradigmatic shift in digital marketing, raising substantive questions about the comparative value and effectiveness of virtual versus human influencers. This shift is particularly consequential in light of the growing strategic adoption of AI-generated personas across sectors ranging from fashion and beauty to tourism and technology (Conti et al., 2022; Hofeditz et al., 2022). While human influencers have historically dominated the influencer economy through emotionally resonant storytelling, spontaneous communication, and parasocial intimacy (Lou & Yuan, 2019), VIs offer distinct advantages in message control, visual perfection, and scalability (Xie-Carson et al., 2023a).

At the core of this comparative tension lies the construct of authenticity, a key driver of consumer trust and engagement in influencer marketing. Human influencers derive their credibility from real-life narratives, affective transparency, and perceived sincerity (Kim & Park, 2024). Their ability to share personal experiences fosters parasocial interactions (PSI) that deepen consumer-brand relationships (Venciute et al., 2023; Cynthia & Bradley, 2024). In contrast, virtual influencers, although capable of simulating emotion and routine, are fundamentally scripted entities whose perceived authenticity remains fragile, often hinging on narrative coherence and transparency regarding their artificial nature (Lou et al., 2022; Liu & Lee, 2024).

While VIs lack the spontaneous affectivity of human influencers, they compensate through precision, consistency, and controllability. Their algorithmically designed personas allow for meticulous alignment with brand identity and campaign goals, free from the reputational volatility of human personalities (Ju et al., 2024). Moreover, VIs can transcend temporal, geographic, and linguistic limitations, making them particularly effective in globalized, cross-cultural campaigns (Belova, 2021; Rossi & Rivetti, 2023). In tourism marketing, for instance, virtual figures such as VenereItalia and Marija have emerged as compelling ambassadors, demonstrating how VIs can embody cultural narratives and promote destinations in visually immersive ways (Pfalz, 2022; Xie-Carson et al., 2023b).

Nonetheless, the emotional engagement gap remains a fundamental limitation of VIs. Their inability to generate genuine emotion or spontaneous interaction may impair their effectiveness in high-involvement categories where trust, relatability, and warmth are paramount. Hofeditz et al. (2022) found that while virtual influencers are perceived as visually appealing and innovative, they are often evaluated as less trustworthy than their human counterparts. Similarly, Liu and Lee (2024) demonstrated that perceived authenticity is significantly lower for VIs, although congruence between the product type and influencer format can mitigate these deficits.

This insight aligns with the match-up hypothesis (Kamins, 1990), suggesting that the effectiveness of an influencer depends on the compatibility between their image and the endorsed product or destination. For instance, Li (2023) shows that VIs are more effective in promoting destinations associated with competence (e.g., innovation-driven cities), whereas human influencers perform better when warmth and social connection are central (e.g., romantic or heritage-focused locales). Such findings point to the necessity of strategic congruence in influencer selection, aligning the influencer archetype with the symbolic identity of the brand or destination.

The source credibility theory (Hovland et al., 1953) further elucidates these dynamics. Trustworthiness, expertise, and attractiveness constitute the tripartite foundation of persuasive communication. While VIs often excel in visual aesthetics and consistent expertise portrayal (e.g., curated knowledge of tourist destinations or product features), their trustworthiness is contingent on clear AI disclosure and narrative transparency (Kim et al., 2022). The risk of consumer deception—particularly when VIs are hyper-realistic or inadequately disclosed, remains a significant ethical and regulatory concern (Lou et al., 2022).

In parallel, consumer engagement, a critical determinant of digital marketing efficacy, is closely tied to emotional salience and interactivity (Obilo et al., 2020; Vivek et al., 2012). Studies show that VIs such as Imma or Miquela, which adopt interactive formats (e.g., video diaries, Q&A sessions, cross-platform storytelling), foster stronger engagement metrics than more static figures such as VenereItalia (Xie-Carson et al., 2023b). As consumer expectations evolve toward real-time responsiveness and conversational authenticity, the ability of VIs to simulate engagement, possibly through generative AI, will become central to their strategic value.

Importantly, hybrid strategies combining human and virtual influencers are increasingly emerging as a best practice. These collaborations allow brands to blend the emotional authenticity of human voices with the aesthetic consistency and scalability of VIs. Kate and Sun (2023) advocate for such synergy, arguing that hybrid models offer a pathway to optimizing trust, relatability, and brand coherence. From a managerial perspective, this approach enables nuanced audience segmentation, deploying human influencers in emotionally driven contexts, while leveraging VIs for innovative, tech-oriented branding efforts.

In conclusion, the comparative analysis reveals that neither virtual nor human influencers hold universal superiority. Rather, their effectiveness is highly context-dependent, shaped by the nature of the product or service, cultural sensibilities, and campaign objectives. As the influencer ecosystem continues to evolve, marketers must adopt a strategically calibrated approach, guided by psychological theory, empirical evidence, and cultural insights. By doing so, they can effectively harness the unique affordances of each influencer type, while navigating the ethical and relational complexities of this rapidly digitizing domain.

3. EMPIRICAL CASES OF VIRTUAL INFLUENCERS IN PRACTICE

The integration of VIs into digital advertising represents a paradigm shift in the construction of brand identity, audience engagement, and message control. Designed through computer graphics and artificial intelligence, VIs function as programmable personas who deliver curated content across social media platforms. Their appeal lies in their creative flexibility, immunity to scandal, and ability to maintain consistent branding across global markets (Ju et al., 2024; Kate & Sun, 2023). However, the effectiveness of VIs is not monolithic, it is deeply contingent on the symbolic identity, audience segmentation, and strategic objectives underpinning their use.

This section offers a comparative case analysis of six leading virtual influencers: Lil Miquela; Noonoouri, Shudu Gram, Imma, Lu do Magalu, and Venere. These cases illustrate the breadth of strategic possibilities enabled by virtual personas, ranging from aspirational luxury narratives to socially embedded corporate communication. Drawing on relevant theoretical frameworks, this analysis also situates VIs within broader debates surrounding authenticity, parasocial relationships, and symbolic consumption.

3.1 Lil Miquela: Posthuman Identity, Activism, and Hybrid Engagement

Lil Miquela, created in 2016 by Los Angeles-based startup Brud, stands as one of the most iconic and commercially successful virtual influencers to date. Characterized by her freckled face, casual-chic style, and Gen Z-coded activism, Miquela Sousa (@lilmiquela) epitomizes the convergence of digital aesthetics, posthuman identity, and socio-cultural storytelling. Her persona (an AI-generated 19-year-old Brazilian-American robot living in LA) functions not only as a fashion model but also as a cultural interlocutor, engaging audiences through complex narratives involving romance, social justice, and digital selfhood.

Miquela's brand identity is built on a hybridized strategy that fuses aspirational fashion with affective authenticity and socio-political positioning. Her collaborations span global luxury brands such as Prada, Calvin Klein, and Givenchy, as well as mass-market names like Samsung, BMW and YouTube Music. With over 2.6 million Instagram followers and an engagement rate surpassing many human influencers, Miquela occupies a unique space in the influencer ecosystem: simultaneously artificial and emotionally resonant. Her content strategy integrates high-aesthetic visuals with interactive elements such as reels, video diaries, music tracks, and occasional comment replies, enabling a dynamic and immersive audience experience.

Unlike static or editorially minimalist VIs, Miquela exemplifies a narratively rich and emotionally performative model of virtual influence. Her Instagram feed is structured around a continuous storyline featuring not only fashion campaigns but also interpersonal relationships, fictional dilemmas, and reflections on her synthetic existence. This narrative scaffolding supports parasocial interaction (Horton & Wohl, 1956), allowing followers to develop affective bonds with her as if she were a sentient being (Ju et al., 2024).

From a theoretical perspective, Lil Miquela's success is deeply informed by Source Credibility theory (Hovland et al., 1953). Her perceived expertise is rooted in fashion acumen and cultural fluency; her attractiveness is amplified through photo-realistic CGI design and aspirational styling; and her trustworthiness (despite being an artificial entity), is bolstered by transparency and consistency. Unlike some VIs who obscure their synthetic origins, Miquela's fictional status is openly acknowledged, even woven into her storytelling. This deliberate self-disclosure aligns with emerging scholarship that emphasizes transparency as a crucial moderating factor in VI effectiveness (Lou et al., 2022; Kim & Park, 2024).

Notably, Miquela is positioned not merely as a brand agent but as a cultural actor. She has engaged with progressive causes such as Black Lives Matter, LGBTQ+ rights, and mental health awareness, thereby extending her influence into domains traditionally reserved for human advocates. This performative activism introduces new questions about the role of synthetic voices in public discourse. Scholars such as Appel et al. (2020) argue that virtual influencers can function as symbolic actors within digital culture, shaping values, discourses, and consumer identities in posthuman societies.

However, Miquela's model also reveals critical tensions. While her hybrid authenticity, combining aesthetic perfection with emotional storytelling, has garnered substantial engagement, some critiques highlight the ontological dissonance between her artificiality and her affective performances. Concerns include the potential for consumer deception, the commodification of activism, and the use of a non-human entity to simulate lived experience (Shin & Lee, 2023; Lou et al., 2022). Such critiques resonate with ongoing ethical debates around the authenticity of algorithmically generated narratives and their implications for trust in digital marketing.

In strategic terms, Lil Miquela illustrates the efficacy of a multi-platform, multi-narrative approach to virtual influence. By leveraging the interactive affordances of Instagram, YouTube, and Spotify, she expands beyond static promotional content to foster ongoing relational engagement. Her model exemplifies a new archetype of virtual influencer, what this chapter defines as the "Narrative Hybrid", which combines the scalability and visual coherence of AI design with the emotional cadence and ideological resonance of human storytelling. In doing so, Miquela transcends the functional role of a marketing tool, operating instead as a symbolically rich, culturally embedded figure in the posthuman branding landscape.

3.2 Noonoouri: Stylized Advocacy and Cross-Media Expansion

Noonoouri, created in 2018 by German designer Joerg Zuber, represents a distinctive case within the VI ecosystem, blending stylized aesthetics, ethical branding, and cross-media presence. Characterized by her hyper-stylized, doll-like appearance, with oversized eyes, a petite frame, and an almost anime-inspired elegance, Noonoouri embodies a fantasy-driven persona deeply aligned with luxury fashion and ethical advocacy. Her artificiality is not masked but embraced, positioning her not as a human simulacrum but as a visual symbol of digital couture and aspirational ideals.

Strategically, Noonoouri functions as a transmedia brand ambassador, with an extensive portfolio of over 130 collaborations with global luxury brands such as Dior, Valentino, Balenciaga, and Versace. She is frequently featured in high-fashion campaigns and digital runway shows, where her aesthetic consistency and curated elegance reinforce the symbolic capital of the brands she represents. Unlike hyperrealistic VIs such as Shudu, Noonoouri's stylization becomes a communicative asset, signaling both exclusivity and imaginative distance, thereby preserving a fantasy-oriented brand narrative while avoiding ethical debates around digital realism and racial representation.

What distinguishes Noonoouri is her integration of advocacy into brand aesthetics. Beyond fashion, she consistently promotes social and environmental causes, such as sustainability, animal rights, and mental health, often in collaboration with ethical beauty brands and non-profit campaigns. This fusion of visual glamour with value-based messaging creates a hybrid form of influence that aligns with Generation Z's expectation for activism from digital figures (Kate & Sun, 2023; Appel et al., 2020). The result is a character who operates at the intersection of spectacle and substance, artificial yet morally performative.

Her strategic evolution reached a significant milestone in 2023, when she became the first virtual pop singer signed to Warner Music, launching original songs and music videos. This move marks her transition from a visual icon to a cross-modal entertainment entity, expanding her influence from fashion into the music and entertainment industries. Her first single, created using AI-generated vocals, embodies the convergence of synthetic media and cultural production, challenging traditional notions of celebrity, talent, and authenticity (Angmo et al., 2025).

Despite her aesthetic appeal and brand versatility, Noonoouri's engagement metrics reveal the paradox of stylized influence. With an Instagram engagement rate of approximately 1.4%, she underperforms compared to both human influencers and certain emotionally resonant VIs such as Imma or Lu do Magalu. This suggests that while her brand partnerships and visual narrative are highly curated, her capacity to foster deep parasocial interaction may be constrained by her overt artificiality and limited emotional realism (Ju et al., 2024; Lou et al., 2022). Her fantasy persona, though coherent and aesthetically powerful, operates with a degree of emotional distance, potentially limiting relational intimacy and interactive authenticity.

Nevertheless, Noonoouri's audience, primarily women aged 18–35 in fashion-forward markets such as France, Germany, the United States, and the UK, demonstrates strong brand alignment. These consumers are typically tech-savvy, ethically conscious, and highly engaged with aspirational content, making them receptive to her stylized storytelling. The coherence between her visual identity, ethical values, and brand associations enhances her source credibility within niche markets, especially when framed through Source Credibility Theory's dimensions of expertise (in fashion) and attractiveness (in aesthetics), even if her perceived trustworthiness remains under scrutiny due to her artificial nature (Xie-Carson et al., 2023a; Kim & Park, 2024).

3.3 Shudu Gram: Hyperrealism and Editorial Exclusivity

Shudu Gram, introduced by British fashion photographer Cameron-James Wilson in 2017, is widely regarded as the world's first digital supermodel. Her hyperrealistic design, marked by a deep complexion, symmetrical features, and editorial poise, has positioned her as an emblem of digital beauty and high-fashion sophistication. Shudu's aesthetic is strongly aligned with global luxury brands such as Balmain, Fenty Beauty, Louis Vuitton, and Tiffany & Co., and her content strategy emphasizes photorealistic still images in visually curated, minimalist settings. Unlike more narratively rich VIs like Lil Miquela or Imma, Shudu operates within a framework of editorial exclusivity, engaging audiences primarily through symbolic visual storytelling rather than interactive or dialogical content.

Strategically, Shudu occupies a unique niche in the virtual influencer ecosystem, one grounded in prestige, refinement, and visual perfection. Her Instagram feed resembles that of a traditional supermodel, with high-fashion shoots that reflect elite aesthetic values and cosmopolitan brand affiliations. This approach enhances her symbolic capital and aligns her with the semiotics of aspirational beauty often featured in luxury advertising (Franke et al., 2023). However, Shudu's mode of influence is less about parasocial intimacy and more about visual awe and aspirational projection.

Nevertheless, Shudu's creation has sparked significant controversy and critical discourse around digital representation, racial politics, and cultural appropriation. As a hyperrealistic Black female figure created and controlled by a white male artist, Shudu embodies a complex intersection of posthuman aesthetics and identity politics. Critics argue that her existence reflects a commodification of Black beauty, divorced from lived experience and sociocultural agency. This tension raises ethical concerns regarding digital embodiment and voice: Who has the right to create and profit from marginalized identities in virtual form?

From a theoretical perspective, Shudu's reception challenges the boundaries of authenticity and credibility in digital influence. According to Source Credibility Theory (Hovland et al., 1953), perceived attractiveness and expertise may elevate her persuasive potential, especially in the context of luxury fashion branding. Yet her trustworthiness—another core component of source credibility—is undermined by opacity surrounding her creation and the absence of a personal narrative or voice. The lack of direct interaction also limits her capacity to foster parasocial relationships (Horton & Wohl, 1956), resulting in a lower engagement rate (~0.93%) relative to more emotionally resonant VIs such as Imma or Lu do Magalu.

Despite this, Shudu has been instrumental in foregrounding issues of digital diversity and inclusion, albeit contentiously. While some praise her for expanding representational visibility in the fashion industry, others critique her as a simulacrum that reinforces structural imbalances by substituting digitally perfected Black femininity for real Black voices. This ethical ambiguity underscores the need for critical scrutiny in the deployment of VIs, especially those who visually represent historically marginalized communities.

In terms of strategic deployment, Shudu's value lies in her alignment with high-status branding goals. Her hyperreal aesthetic and visual minimalism render her an effective conduit for editorial campaigns, particularly in sectors where symbolic exclusivity and prestige are paramount. However, the absence of narrative engagement limits her utility in campaigns requiring emotional resonance, interactivity, or social storytelling

3.4 Imma: Cultural Realism and Urban Tech Identity

Imma, launched in 2018 by Tokyo-based Aww Inc., represents one of the most emotionally resonant and culturally embedded virtual influencers currently active. Distinguished by her pink bob haircut, minimalist streetwear, and digitally stylized yet naturalistic appearance, Imma exemplifies a unique form of "augmented realism", a digital persona that blurs the boundary between artificial creation and everyday authenticity. Unlike editorially distant VIs such as Shudu or Venere, Imma's identity is anchored in micro-relatable narratives and urban cultural fluency, particularly within the technologically saturated ecosystems of East Asian metropolises.

Imma's content strategy is rooted in quotidian realism. Her Instagram feed features a blend of lifestyle vignettes, eating at cafes, visiting museums, attending fashion events, and posing in urban environments, constructed with meticulous attention to both aesthetic composition and narrative coherence. These activities simulate the mundanity and affective texture of real life, cultivating a sense of familiarity that fosters parasocial interaction (Horton & Wohl, 1956). Her emotional accessibility, combined with narrative continuity and visual consistency, facilitates the formation of affective bonds with followers, enabling her to function as a believable, emotionally proximate digital companion.

From a strategic standpoint, Imma epitomizes the convergence of cultural identity and technological sophistication. Her brand collaborations, spanning Nike, Ikea, Dior, Porsche Japan, SK-II, and more recently Shiseido, reflect her hybrid positioning as both a fashion-forward tastemaker and a tech-embedded lifestyle ambassador. Her persona resonates strongly with Gen Z and Millennial consumers in Japan, South Korea, the United States, and parts of Europe, demographics that are both digitally native and culturally attuned to urban minimalism, self-expression, and ethical aesthetics.

Imma's success can be interpreted through the lens of Parasocial Interaction (PSI) theory, which posits that sustained exposure to media figures, especially those perceived as authentic, can generate one-sided emotional relationships akin to friendship or companionship. Imma's digitally simulated routines, combined with her perceived sincerity and relatability, offer a strong foundation for these affective bonds, distinguishing her from more abstract or editorially detached VIs (Venciute et al., 2023). Furthermore, Source Credibility theory (Hovland et al., 1953) reinforces her effectiveness: her perceived expertise in lifestyle and fashion, visual attractiveness, and trustworthy presentation, bolstered by consistent messaging and transparent branding, position her as a persuasive figure within both influencer marketing and tech-oriented brand ecosystems.

Crucially, Imma also exemplifies the growing integration of VIs into immersive digital environments. She has been featured in augmented reality (AR) experiences, virtual fashion runways, and metaverse campaigns, reflecting her adaptability to emerging technological interfaces. This multi-platform operability increases her utility in forward-facing brand strategies, particularly in contexts where innovation, interactivity, and youth-oriented engagement are critical.

However, Imma's aesthetic and narrative coherence also present certain limitations. While her authenticity is algorithmically engineered, it remains inherently constructed, a reality that may invite skepticism among more critically conscious consumers. Her success relies heavily on the suspension of disbelief and the strategic use of emotional cues that mimic, but do not originate from, lived experience. Moreover, her reliance on curated urban imagery may limit cross-cultural scalability in regions less attuned to minimalist aesthetics or technologically mediated lifestyles.

3.5 Lu do Magalu: Mass-Market Utility and Corporate Trust

Lu do Magalu, created in 2009 by Brazilian retail giant Magazine Luiza, stands as one of the most commercially successful and operationally integrated virtual influencers in the world. Initially developed as a digital assistant for e-commerce tutorials, Lu has evolved into a multifaceted brand ambassador, content creator, and corporate spokesperson, an exemplar of how virtual influencers can transcend promotional novelty and become institutionalized within a firm's broader brand architecture.

Distinct from aspirational or editorial VIs such as Shudu or Noonoouri, Lu embodies a utilitarian ethos grounded in mass-market accessibility, consumer education, and everyday relevance. Her content, distributed across Instagram, TikTok, YouTube, and WhatsApp, features product reviews, tech tips, CSR campaigns, and real-time brand updates. This function-oriented design aligns her more closely with service marketing and relationship marketing paradigms than with traditional influencer strategies, reflecting a shift from symbolic consumption toward pragmatic engagement and trust-building.

Lu's strategic value lies in her ability to operate as a hybrid agent, simultaneously transactional and relational. She facilitates product discovery, explains technical functionalities, and humanizes corporate messaging in a tone that is both friendly and authoritative. Her visual design, approachable, expressive, and consistently branded, reinforces this relational identity, allowing her to serve as a digital proxy for the brand's personality and values. With over 7 million followers on both Instagram and TikTok, and engagement rates ranging from 5% to 15%, Lu consistently outperforms many human influencers and other VIs in terms of both reach and conversion metrics.

Theoretically, Lu do Magalu represents a compelling case for extending Source Credibility Theory into the domain of corporate virtual agents. Her attractiveness derives not from hyperrealism or fantasy aesthetics, but from design simplicity and brand familiarity. Her expertise is anchored in her perceived role as a knowledgeable guide across product categories, while her trustworthiness is bolstered by years of consistent, transparent communication—characteristics that are often difficult to engineer in more stylized or ambiguous VIs (Hovland et al., 1953; Kim & Park, 2024).

Additionally, Lu exemplifies a form of parasocial engagement distinct from that generated by lifestyle or fashion-oriented VIs. Rather than simulating intimacy through emotional storytelling, she cultivates consumer relationships through routine functionality, predictability, and utility-driven content. This corresponds with Vivek et al.'s (2012) conceptualization of engagement as a multidimensional construct, where cognitive, affective, and behavioral involvement converge to foster long-term brand loyalty. In this regard, Lu serves as a virtual instantiation of corporate trust—reliable, informative, and emotionally neutral, yet embedded in a communicative style that promotes closeness and continuity.

Moreover, Lu's role in corporate social responsibility (CSR) initiatives amplifies her strategic utility. She frequently participates in campaigns addressing digital literacy, sustainability, and social inclusion, demonstrating how virtual influencers can embody ethical commitments and institutional values without the volatility or reputational risks associated with human spokespersons. Her integration into the firm's omnichannel strategy also reflects a unique case of VI scalability, where her presence extends from e-commerce to internal communications, live chat assistance, and even seasonal campaigns, ensuring cohesive brand experience across touchpoints.

Nonetheless, Lu's success is contextually anchored in Brazilian digital culture, where consumer openness to AI-driven interactions is relatively high and where Magazine Luiza holds strong brand equity. Her transferability to other markets may be constrained by differing cultural expectations around authenticity, technology, and the personalization of customer service. In this sense, Lu challenges the assumption that all VIs must emulate human emotion or hyperreal aesthetics to be effective. Her appeal lies not in illusion or fantasy, but in pragmatic trust and consistent brand embodiment

3.6 Venere: Italian Muse with Digital Glamour and Aesthetic Minimalism

Venere, styled as @venereitalia23 on Instagram, represents a novel archetype within the virtual influencer (VI) landscape, strategically developed by the Italian Tourism Commission to embody national heritage through a digital muse. Positioned as a 30-year-old "Worldwide Renaissance icon," Venere is a posthuman reinterpretation of classical Italian beauty, drawing iconographic inspiration from the Roman goddess Venus. Her visual identity is deeply entrenched in a high-aesthetic tradition that fuses neoclassical elegance with contemporary digital minimalism, making her a compelling ambassador for Italy's luxury tourism and cultural diplomacy.

Unlike emotionally expressive or narratively dynamic VIs such as Imma or Lu do Magalu, Venere is constructed as a visually symbolic figure, anchored in still imagery, aesthetic curation, and silent grandeur. Her content emphasizes iconic Italian landmarks (e.g., the Colosseum, Duomo di Milano, Trevi Fountain) and events (e.g., Giro d'Italia), positioning her not as a lifestyle influencer but as a static visual envoy of national identity. This editorial restraint reflects a strategy of image-based semiotic communication rather than engagement through interactivity or affective storytelling.

Venere's brand function is best understood through the lens of symbolic consumption and place branding theory. Her digital persona operates as a conduit for national imaginaries, communicating cultural sophistication, timeless elegance, and territorial prestige through idealized visual representations. Her embodiment of Venus as a mythical figure reconfigures traditional notions of destination branding by blending heritage symbolism with virtual aesthetics, thus expanding the semiotic repertoire of country branding strategies (Pfalz, 2022).

However, her minimal interactivity and absence of narrative personalization limit her capacity to cultivate parasocial relationships (Horton & Wohl, 1956). Unlike other VIs that simulate daily life, emotional expression, or audience dialogue, Venere remains largely non-agentic, her communicative power residing in the spectacle of aesthetic perfection rather than relational intimacy. As a result, her engagement rate lags behind more dialogical VIs, and her emotional resonance remains subdued, despite strong visual appeal.

From a source credibility perspective (Hovland et al., 1953), Venere's attractiveness and perceived expertise in cultural aesthetics are indisputable. Her hyper-stylized elegance aligns seamlessly with high-end cosmetics, fashion, and tourism partnerships, reinforcing the competence and visual authority of the brands she endorses. Yet, her trustworthiness, an essential component of influencer effectiveness, may be undermined by the opacity of her authorship and the abstract nature of her digital persona. As an AI-generated figure with no discernible backstory or voice, her authenticity is purely aesthetic, not relational or experiential (Lou et al., 2022; Kim & Park, 2024).

Nonetheless, Venere's strategic role is not to simulate human realism, but to elevate cultural capital through posthuman spectacle. In this regard, she aligns with contemporary trends in luxury tourism marketing that prioritize iconicity, brand symbolism, and visual prestige over interactivity or relatability. Her presence serves to reframe Italy's national brand through a digitally mediated lens, bridging myth, modernity, and metaverse potential. As the metaverse emerges as a new frontier for destination marketing, figures like Venere offer an opportunity to embed national heritage within immersive digital ecosystems, from virtual tours to gamified cultural experiences (Appel et al., 2020; Angmo et al., 2025).

It is also worth noting that Venere represents a rare case of a public-sector-created VI, signaling the increasing institutionalization of virtual identities in place branding and nation marketing. Her deployment by a governmental agency reflects a growing awareness of the symbolic power of digital aesthetics in shaping international perceptions, particularly in high-involvement sectors such as tourism, heritage, and cultural diplomacy

3.7 Comparative Matrix of Strategic Typologies

To systematically compare the strategic, aesthetic, and psychological dimensions of virtual influencers (VIs) analyzed in this study, a comparative matrix has been developed (Table 1). This matrix synthesizes key characteristics of six prominent Vis (Lil Miquela, Noonoouri, Shudu Gram, Imma, Lu do Magalu, and Venere) highlighting their identity types, engagement styles, aesthetic strategies, and theoretical underpinnings. By mapping these variables, the matrix reveals the heterogeneity of virtual influencer archetypes and their alignment with distinct branding objectives, audience profiles, and levels of parasocial interactivity. Grounded in established frameworks such as Source Credibility Theory and Parasocial Interaction Theory, the matrix provides a conceptual lens through which to evaluate the symbolic and strategic affordances of VIs in digital advertising.

Table 1. VI comparative matrix

VI Name	Identity Type	Aesthetic Strategy	Engagement Style	Strategic Function	Theoretical Anchors	Audience Profile	Key Limitations
Lil Miquela	Narrative Hybrid	Hyper-real, Gen Z-coded	High interactivity, story-driven	Fashion/lifestyle branding + cultural activism	PSI; Source Credibility	Gen Z, fashion-forward, socially engaged	Ontological dissonance; perceived inauthenticity
Noonoouri	Stylized Fantasy Advocate	Stylized, animated doll-like	Low interactivity, visual spectacle	Luxury fashion + ethical and artistic branding	Source Credibility; Symbolic Consumption	Women (18–35), luxury/ethics-conscious	Emotional distance; lower engagement rate
Shudu Gram	Editorial Realist	Hyper-realistic, supermodel aesthetics	Minimal interaction, high fashion focus	Symbolic prestige and racial representation (controversial)	Source Credibility; Ethical representation	Luxury consumers, fashion elites	Cultural appropriation concerns; low parasocial engagement
Imma	Urban Tech Companion	Naturalistic with digital flair	High interactivity, lifestyle realism	Urban lifestyle branding, AR/VR innovation	PSI; Source Credibility	Gen Z & Millennials; tech-savvy, minimalism	Algorithmic authenticity; potential cultural specificity
Lu do Magalu	Corporate Utility Agent	Simplified, brand-friendly	High interaction, pragmatic content	Customer education, CSR, omnichannel integration	Source Credibility; Engagement Theory	Brazilian consumers, mass-market, practical users	Culturally bound appeal; limited aspirational fantasy
Venere	Symbolic Cultural Icon	Classical minimalism, heritage-driven	Static content, visual representation	Nation branding, digital tourism symbolism	Symbolic Consumption; Source Credibility	Tourists, cultural elites, national image-builders	Low parasocial engagement; lack of narrative

Source: The authors

The comparative analysis also reveals that VI effectiveness is context-dependent. VIs designed for editorial minimalism or aesthetic perfection (e.g., Shudu, Venere) are best suited for prestige and aspirational branding, while VIs aligned with cultural or emotional authenticity (e.g., Imma, Lu) are more appropriate for interactive storytelling and brand-customer intimacy.

5. FUTURE TRENDS AND IMPLICATIONS

The evolution of AI continues to disrupt influencer marketing, not only by optimizing influencer selection and performance tracking but also by enabling the creation of autonomous, AI-driven personas. Early applications of AI in influencer marketing focused primarily on predictive analytics and natural language processing (NLP) to match brands with suitable human influencers based on audience segmentation, content relevance, and engagement metrics (Leung et al., 2022). However, with the emergence of generative AI tools such as ChatGPT and DALL·E, the marketing paradigm has shifted toward AI-driven content production, exemplified by the rise of virtual influencers (Kate & Sun, 2023).

VIs increasingly serve as scalable brand ambassadors capable of producing high-quality, personalized, and on-brand content at speed and scale. Their appeal lies in their visual perfection, consistency, and immunity to reputational risk, factors that make them especially attractive in long-term and global campaigns (Ju et al., 2024; Xie-Carson et al., 2023a). Enabled by machine learning algorithms, VIs analyze large volumes of consumer data to tailor content strategies, forecast engagement, and simulate parasocial interactions, thereby enhancing relevance and resonance with target audiences (Appel et al., 2020; Angmo et al., 2025).

Looking forward, the integration of VIs with immersive technologies such as augmented reality (AR), virtual reality (VR), and the metaverse represents a critical frontier for brand engagement. These technologies facilitate multidimensional consumer interactions beyond static social media platforms. In AR and VR contexts, VIs can participate in real-time product demonstrations, offer guided experiences, and act as immersive shopping assistants (Technavio, 2022). For instance, fashion brands may deploy metaverse-exclusive digital avatars to host virtual runway shows or curate immersive brand events, thus enhancing experiential branding (Appel et al., 2020; Shin & Lee, 2023).

Moreover, VIs are poised to revolutionize customer service. As AI systems become more capable of simulating natural conversation and emotional responsiveness, brands may deploy VIs to serve as interactive agents for customer engagement, available around the clock and trained to address queries with predictive accuracy. These digital assistants can bridge transactional and relational objectives, reinforcing brand consistency while enhancing perceived responsiveness (Lou et al., 2022; Obilo et al., 2021).

However, the increasing realism and integration of VIs introduce substantial ethical and regulatory challenges. One of the primary concerns is consumer deception: without proper disclosure, audiences may not realize that they are interacting with AI-generated entities, which raises critical issues surrounding authenticity, trust, and informed consent (Lou et al., 2022; Hofeditz et al., 2022). Regulatory bodies such as the Federal Trade Commission (FTC) in the U.S. and the Advertising Standards Authority (ASA) in the U.K. are expected to issue stricter guidelines, potentially mandating explicit markers such as #VirtualInfluencer or #AIGenerated to ensure transparency.

Data privacy is another pressing issue. Given that VIs rely on real-time analysis of user data to generate personalized content, compliance with data protection regulations such as the General Data Protection Regulation (GDPR) becomes imperative. Firms must ensure that AI-driven personalization does not compromise consumer rights or exploit behavioral data without consent (Zhu & Chen, 2012). Additionally, as VIs gain autonomy in content creation, questions about intellectual property, authorship, and digital personhood will intensify, necessitating new legal and ethical frameworks (Angmo et al., 2025).

From a strategic standpoint, brands must adopt a multifaceted approach to maximize the advantages of VIs while mitigating risks. Transparency is paramount, consumers should be informed about the AI-generated nature of the influencer to preserve trust and ethical integrity (Lou et al., 2022). Furthermore, virtual influencer personas must be closely aligned with brand identity, ensuring consistency in tone, aesthetic, and values across campaigns (Kim & Park, 2024). Continuous monitoring of audience sentiment and performance analytics is essential to adapt content strategies in real time and sustain engagement (Appel et al., 2020; Liu & Lee, 2024).

A hybrid model combining human and virtual influencers may emerge as an optimal strategy. While VIs offer control, scalability, and technological novelty, human influencers remain superior in emotional authenticity, spontaneity, and deep parasocial connectivity (Venciute et al., 2023; Cynthia & Bradley, 2024). Strategic collaboration between human and virtual agents allows for segmentation and balance, positioning VIs in technology-oriented or futuristic campaigns while assigning human influencers to contexts that require warmth and emotional relatability (Li, 2023; Kate & Sun, 2023).

Finally, several research gaps warrant scholarly investigation. First, more empirical work is needed to understand how consumers cognitively and emotionally respond to AI disclosure in influencer interactions. Second, cross-cultural variations in the perception and acceptance of virtual influencers require deeper analysis, particularly as brands expand their global reach. Third, longitudinal studies should assess the impact of VIs on brand equity, consumer loyalty, and trust over time (Leung et al., 2022; Ju et al., 2024).

As virtual influencers become increasingly integrated into posthuman marketing ecosystems, their role will transcend mere promotional functions. They will co-construct digital identities, mediate cultural meanings, and shape consumer-brand relationships in the metaverse and beyond. Navigating this new frontier requires a synthesis of technological innovation, psychological insight, and ethical foresight. By doing so, marketers can responsibly harness the transformative power of AI while maintaining transparency, authenticity, and consumer trust in the digital age.

6. CONCLUSION

The growing integration of VIs into advertising signals a transformative shift in the logic and practice of digital marketing. This paper has examined how Vis, algorithmically designed, visually curated, and strategically managed personas, are reshaping brand communication, consumer engagement, and influencer strategies. Positioned at the intersection of artificial intelligence, media aesthetics, and consumer psychology, virtual influencers embody both the opportunities and the tensions inherent in technologically mediated branding (Appel et al., 2020; Ju et al., 2024; Kate & Sun, 2023).

The findings underscore that virtual influencers offer compelling advantages: they allow for complete creative control, consistent brand alignment, risk mitigation, and scalable content delivery across global markets (Xie-Carson et al., 2023a; Ju et al., 2024). Their aesthetic versatility and programmable behaviors make them especially suitable for brands operating in innovation-driven sectors or those seeking to differentiate through digital sophistication. Moreover, VIs can be crafted to reflect aspirational lifestyles, ethical commitments, or cultural specificity, enhancing symbolic congruence with brand values (Rossi & Rivetti, 2023).

However, these benefits are tempered by significant challenges, chief among them is the issue of perceived authenticity. While some VIs, such as Imma or Lu do Magalu, successfully foster parasocial interactions through relatable narratives and localized content (Franke et al., 2023), others fall short due to limited emotional depth and transparency deficits (Lou et al., 2022). Parasocial interaction theory suggests that perceived authenticity and emotional engagement are essential for fostering trust and behavioral influence (Horton & Wohl, 1956; Venciute et al., 2023), and virtual influencers often struggle to match the spontaneous and affective resonance of human influencers (Kim & Park, 2024).

Ethical and regulatory concerns further complicate the integration of VIs into mainstream marketing. The potential for consumer deception, the reinforcement of unattainable beauty ideals, and the implications for labor displacement in the influencer economy raise critical questions about the responsible design and use of virtual personas (Shin & Lee, 2023; Lou et al., 2022). Regulatory bodies such as the Federal Trade Commission (FTC) have begun to advocate for explicit AI disclosure, underscoring the need for transparent communication to prevent misleading practices.

The strategic value of VIs is thus highly context-dependent. As supported by the match-up hypothesis (Kamins, 1990) and source credibility theory (Hovland et al., 1953), VIs perform best in campaigns where their image, expertise, and symbolic cues align with product attributes—particularly in domains emphasizing innovation, aesthetics, or competence (Li, 2023; Liu & Lee, 2024). In contrast, human influencers remain more effective in contexts demanding emotional authenticity, interpersonal warmth, or culturally grounded storytelling (Hofeditz et al., 2022).

This suggests the increasing relevance of hybrid strategies, where human and virtual influencers are deployed in tandem to leverage the strengths of both formats. Such models allow brands to optimize for both scalability and emotional resonance, enabling nuanced audience segmentation and campaign personalization (Kate & Sun, 2023; Angmo et al., 2025). These developments are further amplified by advances in AI-driven analytics, which empower marketers to dynamically monitor engagement patterns, consumer sentiment, and campaign performance.

Looking ahead, the evolution of VIs will be shaped by continued developments in generative AI, natural language processing, and immersive media technologies such as AR, VR, and the metaverse. As VIs become more interactive and lifelike, capable of simulating emotions, responding in real time, and operating across platforms—their role will expand beyond static brand endorsements toward relational brand ambassadorships (Appel et al., 2020; Angmo et al., 2025; Technavio, 2022). This evolution, however, necessitates critical reflection on digital authenticity, AI ethics, and the boundaries of posthuman branding.

In conclusion, virtual influencers are not merely a marketing novelty but a structural innovation in the digital advertising ecosystem. Their long-term strategic impact will depend on how brands reconcile technological sophistication with ethical responsibility and how they manage the delicate balance between aesthetic control and emotional engagement. Future research should further investigate consumer cognitive responses to AI disclosure, cross-cultural variations in VI reception, and the longitudinal effects of virtual-human collaborations on brand equity and consumer trust

REFERENCES

Ameen, N., Hosany, S., & Taheri, B. (2023). Generation Z's psychology and new-age technologies: Implications for future research. *Psychology and Marketing*, *40*(10), 2029–2040. DOI: 10.1002/mar.21868

Angmo, P., Mahajan, R., & Ranjitha, G. P. (2025). Unveiling the Power of Virtual Influencers: Impact of Content and Credibility on Consumer Engagement and Purchase Intentions. *Journal of Relationship Marketing*, •••, 1–32. DOI: 10.1080/15332667.2025.2471668

Appel, G., Grewal, L., Hadi, R., & Stephen, A. T. (2020). The future of social media in marketing. *Journal of the Academy of Marketing Science*, *48*(1), 79–95. DOI: 10.1007/s11747-019-00695-1 PMID: 32431463

Barari, M. (2023). Unveiling the dark side of influencer marketing: How social media influencers (human vs virtual) diminish followers' well-being. *Marketing Intelligence & Planning*, *41*(8), 1162–1177. DOI: 10.1108/MIP-05-2023-0191

Belova, A. D. (2021). Virtual influencers in multimodal advertising. *The journal of VN Karazin Kharkiv National University*, (93), 14-21.

Conti, M., Gathani, J., & Tricomi, P. P. (2022). Virtual influencers in online social media. *IEEE Communications Magazine*, *60*(8), 86–91. DOI: 10.1109/MCOM.001.2100786

Cynthia, A. H., & Bradley, J. B. (2024). Parasocial relationships, social media, & well-being. *Current Opinion in Psychology*, *45*, 101306. PMID: 35219157

Franke, C., Groeppel-Klein, A., & Müller, K. (2023). Consumers' responses to virtual influencers as advertising endorsers: Novel and effective or uncanny and deceiving? *Journal of Advertising*, *52*(4), 523–539. DOI: 10.1080/00913367.2022.2154721

Hofeditz, L., Nissen, A., Schütte, R., & Mirbabaie, M. "Trust Me, I'm an Influencer! – A Comparison of Perceived Trust in Human and Virtual Influencers" (2022). ECIS 2022 Research-in-Progress Papers. 27. https://aisel.aisnet.org/ecis2022_rip/27

Horton, D., & Richard Wohl, R. (1956). Mass communication and para-social interaction: Observations on intimacy at a distance. *psychiatry, 19*(3), 215-229.

Hovland, C. I., Janis, I. L., & Kelley, H. H. (1953). Communication and persuasion.

Ju, N., Kim, T., & Im, H. (2024). Fake human but real influencer: The interplay of authenticity and human likeness in Virtual Influencer communication? *Fash Text*, *11*(1), 16. DOI: 10.1186/s40691-024-00380-0

Kamins, M. A. (1990). An investigation into the "match-up" hypothesis in celebrity advertising: When beauty may be only skin deep. *Journal of Advertising*, *19*(1), 4–13. DOI: 10.1080/00913367.1990.10673175

Kate, J. B., & Sun, J. A. (2023). A Systematic Review of Virtual Influencers: Similarities and Differences between Human and Virtual Influencers in Interactive Advertising. *Journal of Interactive Advertising*, *23*(4), 293–306. DOI: 10.1080/15252019.2023.2236102

Kim, H., & Park, M. (2024). When digital celebrity talks to you: How human-like virtual influencers satisfy consumer's experience through social presence on social media endorsements. *Journal of Retailing and Consumer Services*, *76*, 103581. DOI: 10.1016/j.jretconser.2023.103581

Kim, J., Merrill, K.Jr, Xu, K., & Kelly, S. (2022). Perceived credibility of an AI instructor in online education: The role of social presence and voice features. *Computers in Human Behavior*, *136*, 107383. DOI: 10.1016/j.chb.2022.107383

Kozinets, R. V., Gretzel, U., & Gambetti, R. (2023). *Influencers and Creators: Business, Culture, and Practice*. Sage.

Leung, F. F., Gu, F. F., & Palmatier, R. W. (2022). Online influencer marketing. *Journal of the Academy of Marketing Science*, *50*(2), 226–251. DOI: 10.1007/s11747-021-00829-4

Liu, F., & Lee, Y. H. (2024). Virtually authentic: Examining the match-up hypothesis between human vs virtual influencers and product types. *Journal of Product and Brand Management*, *33*(2), 287–299. DOI: 10.1108/JPBM-03-2023-4418

Lou, C., Kiew, S. T. J., Chen, T., Lee, T. Y. M., Ong, J. E. C., & Phua, Z. (2022). Authentically Fake? How Consumers Respond to the Influence of Virtual Influencers. *Journal of Advertising*, *52*(4), 540–557. DOI: 10.1080/00913367.2022.2149641

Lou, C., & Yuan, S. (2019). Influencer marketing: How message value and credibility affect consumer trust of branded content on social media. *Journal of Interactive Advertising*, *19*(1), 58–73. DOI: 10.1080/15252019.2018.1533501

Nasrin, N. (2022). Brands will Spend a Whopping $32.5bn on Influencer Advertising in 2023, *Marketing Magazine*, Retrieved from https://marketingmagazine.com.my/brands-will-spend-a-whopping-32-5bn-on-influencer-advertising-in-2023/

Obilo, O. O., Chefor, E., & Saleh, A. (2021). Revisiting the consumer brand engagement concept. *Journal of Business Research*, *126*, 634–643. DOI: 10.1016/j.jbusres.2019.12.023

Pfalz, L. (2022). Malta creates world's first "virtual citizen" to promote tourism. TRAVELPULSE. https://www. travelpulse.com/news/destinations/malta-creates -worlds-first- virtual-citizen-to-promote-tourism.html

Rossi, C., & Rivetti, F. (2023, May). Virtual influencer marketing: Is it effective in engaging younger generations. In ECSM 2023 10th European Conference on Social Media. Academic Conferences and publishing limited.

Shin, Y., & Lee, S. (2023). Issues of virtual fashion influencers' reproduced bodies: A qualitative analysis based on body discourse. *Fashion and Textiles*, *10*(1), 30. DOI: 10.1186/s40691-023-00349-5

Suprawan, L., & Pojanavatee, S. (2022). What causes social media users to engage and mimic virtual influencers? The role of self-congruity. *Innovative Marketing*, *18*(4), 148–160. DOI: 10.21511/im.18(4).2022.13

Tanwar, A. S., Chaudhry, H., & Srivastava, M. K. (2022). Trends in influencer marketing: A review and bibliometric analysis. *Journal of Interactive Advertising*, *22*(1), 1–27. DOI: 10.1080/15252019.2021.2007822

Technavio, 2022. Artificial Intelligence (AI) in Social Media Market by Application and Geography - Forecast and Analysis 2022- 2026. https://www.technavio.com/re port/artificial-intelligence-ai-in-social-media-market-industry-analysis?utm_source =prnewswire&utm_medium=pressrelease&utm_campaign=autov8-vsg_wk43_2022_013_report&utm_content=IRTNTR74206.

Venciute, D., Mackeviciene, I., Kuslys, M., & Correia, R. F. (2023). The role of influencer–follower congruence in the relationship between influencer marketing and purchase behaviour. *Journal of Retailing and Consumer Services*, *75*, 103506. DOI: 10.1016/j.jretconser.2023.103506

Vivek, S. D., Beatty, S. E., & Morgan, R. M. (2012). Customer engagement: Exploring customer relationships beyond purchase. *Journal of Marketing Theory and Practice*, *20*(2), 122–146. DOI: 10.2753/MTP1069-6679200201

Xie-Carson, L., Benckendorff, P., & Hughes, K. (2023a). Keep it# Unreal: Exploring Instagram users' engagement with virtual influencers in tourism contexts. *Journal of Hospitality & Tourism Research (Washington, D.C.)*, •••, 10963480231180940.

Xie-Carson, L., Magor, T., Benckendorff, P., & Hughes, K. (2023b). All hype or the real deal? Investigating user engagement with virtual influencers in tourism. *Tourism Management*, *99*, 104779. DOI: 10.1016/j.tourman.2023.104779

Zhu, Y. Q., & Chen, H. G. (2012). Service fairness and customer satisfaction in internet banking: Exploring the mediating effects of trust and customer value. *Internet Research*, *22*(4), 482–498. DOI: 10.1108/10662241211251006

Chapter 2
Digital Disruption:
Virtual Influencers Transforming Traditional Marketing

Ethelbert Garcia Galang
https://orcid.org/0009-0001-7631-970X
University of the Philippines Dilimam, Philippines

Marie Grace Avelino Gomez
https://orcid.org/0000-0003-0180-9875
University of the Philippines Diliman, Philippines

ABSTRACT

Traditional marketing has been affected by the rise of virtual influencers (VIs). Traditionally, products were marketed by celebrities or human influencers. Influencer marketing has been a strategy for connecting with audiences through credible and engaging social media figures and celebrities. This chapter explores the rise of VIs as they reshape the marketing landscape. Unlike human influencers, VIs offer unparalleled consistency, innovative engagement methods, and cost efficiency, revolutionizing marketing strategies across platforms like Instagram, TikTok, and virtual reality environments. This chapter also examines the rise of VIs, popular VIs, the cultural effects of VIs on Filipinos, popular VIs, and the ethical and operational implications of VIs. By integrating these insights, this chapter underscores how VIs exemplify digital disruption's transformative power, redefining traditional marketing practices while influencing the future of marketing and consumer engagement.

DOI: 10.4018/979-8-3373-0255-3.ch002

INTRODUCTION

Influencer marketing has evolved into a dominant strategy that leverages individuals with significant online followings to promote products and services. Traditionally, brands have partnered with celebrities and human influencers to engage consumers. However, the emergence of VIs created using CGI and artificial intelligence has reshaped this landscape. Unlike their human counterparts, virtual influencers (VIs) are fully controlled by brands, eliminating risks related to scandals or inconsistencies.

This chapter analyzes this shift by applying the 4 Ps of Marketing framework—Product, Price, Place, and Promotion. This framework provides a structured approach to understanding how VIs influence marketing dynamics. This chapter also explores the cultural acceptance of VIs in the Philippines and their implications for career education.

The 4Ps of Marketing—Product, Price, Place, and Promotion—constitute the foundational elements of an organization's growth strategy, with each component playing a crucial role in attaining business objectives (Nicos & Alexander, 2024). The product dimension underscores the quality, characteristics, and benefits of goods or services. For instance, Lululemon's success can be attributed to its innovative product strategy, which features high-quality athletic apparel tailored to meet specific market demands (Wang, 2024). Similarly, Rumah Makan Cahaya Minang emphasizes product quality and flavor for its customers (Niluth, 2024).

Pricing strategies are essential in ensuring products are accessible to various consumer demographics. Lululemon employs strategic pricing to enhance its brand equity and attract a diverse consumer base (Wang, 2024). Conversely, Rumah Makan Cahaya Minang maintains affordable pricing to make its offerings accessible to a broad audience (Niluth, 2024).

The distribution or placement strategy focuses on identifying optimal locations to reach target customers effectively. Lululemon's carefully selected store locations enhance its market presence (Wang, 2024). Similarly, Rumah Makan Cahaya Minang has chosen strategic sites to maximize customer traffic (Niluth, 2024).

Promotion encompasses communication tactics employed to inform and persuade potential customers. Lululemon's promotional efforts are integral to its brand's success (Wang, 2024). This VI has utilized social media and direct marketing strategies to boost sales (Niluth, 2024). In the petroleum sector, effective promotional strategies have been linked to substantial increases in profitability (Yahya, 2024).

The 4Ps framework, remains a cornerstone of marketing strategy, providing businesses with a structured approach to developing and implementing their marketing efforts. However, the COVID-19 pandemic has significantly altered consumer behavior, market conditions, and business operations, necessitating reevaluating and adapting these traditional marketing mix elements. When formulating their marketing strategies, organizations must now consider factors such as increased digital adoption, changing consumer priorities, and supply chain disruptions (Reyes-Carlos et al., 2024).

To maintain relevance and effectiveness in this evolving landscape, businesses must continuously assess and refine their marketing mix. This may involve adjusting product offerings to meet new consumer needs, implementing flexible pricing strategies to accommodate economic uncertainties, expanding digital distribution channels, and adapting promotional tactics to align with shifting media consumption patterns. By proactively modifying the 4Ps in response to market changes, organizations can sustain their competitive advantage and better address consumers' evolving expectations in a post-pandemic world. This ongoing process of evaluation and adaptation is crucial for businesses to remain agile and responsive to future market disruptions and consumer trends.

The internet has had a transformative impact on retail through the emergence of e-commerce, particularly online stores. This new trading method has revolutionized consumer shopping behavior, offering unparalleled convenience and accessibility. Businesses are increasingly adapting their marketing strategies to leverage online platforms, underscoring the critical role of Internet marketing in navigating the digital marketplace. Internet marketing evolution focuses on how retailers can optimize their strategies to thrive in this competitive environment. Essential e-commerce tools significantly influence marketing functions, enabling retailers to engage with customers, manage sales, and enhance their online presence (Rosario & Raimundo, 2021).

VIs are created using digital graphics, computer-generated imagery, and motion capture technology (Moustakas et al., 2020). Many VIs come with backstories and personalities that brands develop to resonate with various audiences (Moustakas et al., 2020). They have an omni-channel presence (Silva et al., 2024; Nguyen, 2023). They are not limited to traditional social media and can appear in video games, virtual reality environments, or live-streamed virtual events (Osiyevskyy et al., 2024). Thus, companies can create ongoing narratives that foster a sense of consumer connection (Paz & Delgado, 2020). This can be a mechanism for consumers to follow and engage with (De Brito Silva, 2023).

These VIs specialize in targeted communication (Arsenyan & Mirowska, 2021; Guthrie, 2001). They can be highly customized to resonate with specific audience demographics, with tailored looks, behaviors, and interests to match the preferences of the targeted group (Kim, 2023). They can directly engage with audiences by commenting, responding to messages, and posting relatable content using advanced technology. Because they are powered by modern technology, they can immediately react to questions posed by consumers.

VIs are less unpredictable than human influencers (Kim & Park, 2023). Brands can control VIs to avoid potential controversies or personal scandals, such as brand ambassadors who can engage in scandalous circumstances (Kim et al., 2023; Gerrath et al., 2024). Some VIs go beyond marketing their products. Some people have raised their awareness of diversity, mental health, and environmental protection.

Further, VIs can reduce operational costs. They do not need to travel, stay, or work cheaply. They can be reused across multiple campaigns at minimal costs. VIs do not demand insurance, healthcare, or other benefits like their human counterparts. They do not become sick and will not suffer from accidents. Therefore, many business owners may see its practicality over human influencers or actor endorsers in the long run.

CHAPTER OBJECTIVES

This chapter has the following objectives:

First, it defines traditional marketing, digital disruption, and VIs. Traditional marketing refers to conventional advertising and brand promotion methods, such as print media, television commercials, radio advertisements, and billboards (Ullah, 2023). These strategies rely on direct consumer engagement through offline channels and have been the foundation of brand communication for decades (Shahid, 2023). However, digital disruption has transformed the marketing landscape by integrating technology-driven innovations that challenge traditional marketing norms. This disruption has paved the way for new marketing techniques, particularly in the digital realm, leading to the rise of VIs (Ogwa et al., 2024). These influencers are AI-generated or computer-created digital personalities designed to engage audiences, promote brands, and shape consumer perceptions like human influencers (Dondapati, 2025). By understanding these concepts, we can analyze how marketing has evolved and how virtual influencers reshape brand engagement strategies.

Second, it explains the shift from traditional to social media influencers to digital influencers. The evolution of marketing strategies has progressed from traditional advertising to influencer-driven content marketing, spurred by the growing influence of social media platforms (Cayla et al., 2025). Initially, businesses relied on celebrity endorsements and traditional advertising channels, but as social media gained prominence, brands turned to social media influencers. These are individuals with large online followings who create authentic and engaging content (Delbaere et al., 2021). Social media influencers have established trust with their audiences and become powerful marketing tools (Vrontis et al., 2021). More recently, the emergence of digital influencers, including AI-generated or computer-animated personalities, has taken this evolution further. Unlike human influencers, digital influencers are entirely controlled by brands or creative teams, ensuring consistency in messaging and eliminating potential controversies (Bishop, 2021). This transition signifies a significant shift in how brands interact with consumers, prioritizing engagement through highly curated and algorithm-driven content (Alam et al., 2024).

Third, it describes the rise of digital influencers. The rise of VIs is a product of technological advancements, changes in consumer behavior, and the increasing reliance on artificial intelligence in marketing (Kopalle et al., 2022).. VIs like Lil Miquela and Imma have gained widespread recognition for their lifelike appearances, unique digital personas, and interactive storytelling. These AI-generated influencers are designed to align with brand narratives and market trends, allowing companies full control over their messaging. The growing acceptance of digital influencers is also fueled by the demand for consistent content production, cost-effective influencer marketing, and novelty appeal in the digital space. As consumers spend more time online, brands leverage these virtual personalities to engage audiences innovatively, marking a new era in digital marketing.

Fourth, it explains how VIs affect digital influencers in the Philippines setting. In the Philippines, where social media usage is among the highest in the world, the introduction of VIs presents a new dimension to influencer marketing (Ibardeloza et al., 2022). Filipino consumers are highly engaged with social media personalities, making the transition to VIs are a significant development (Ines & Tolentino, 2024). Local brands have begun exploring the potential of VIs in advertising, capitalizing on their controlled messaging and ability to reach diverse audiences without the unpredictability of human influencers (Vallespin et al., 2024). Additionally, the cultural dynamics of the Philippine market, where authenticity and relatability play crucial roles in brand engagement, challenge VIs to establish credibility among Filipino consumers (Orencia, 2023). The extent to which VIs can integrate into the Philippine digital ecosystem depends on how well they resonate with local audiences and how brands utilize them to complement human influencers.

Lastly, it explains how VIs can affect career education. VIs have the potential to reshape career education by serving as digital mentors, role models, and educational content creators. With AI and machine learning advancements, VIs can be programmed to provide career advice, simulate real-world job scenarios, and guide students in skill development. These AI-driven personas can offer personalized career insights, helping individuals explore different career paths engagingly and interactively. Furthermore, VIs can be integrated into career education platforms to deliver content on industry trends, workplace expectations, and emerging job opportunities. By leveraging VIs in career education, institutions can create innovative learning experiences that are accessible, visually engaging, and adaptive to students' needs, ultimately bridging the gap between education and career readiness.

VIS AND DIGITAL DISRUPTION

VIs are digital personas crafted by computers to interact with social media audiences and transform the marketing landscape. This phenomenon is driven by their perceived genuineness, creative engagement strategies, and the application of cutting-edge technologies. VIs might be seen as more trustworthy than human influencers, especially by those who have confidence in machine-based decision-making (Lee et al. 2024).

Also known as computer-generated influencers (CGIs), VIs are virtual personas that mimic human traits and actions. They utilize social media platforms like Instagram, Twitter, Facebook, and TikTok to promote products and brands, distinguishing themselves from traditional human influencers (Bambeshwar et al., 2024).

The impact of these elements is heightened by essential qualities such as warmth, interactivity, and responsiveness. Warmth fosters an emotional bond with consumers, enhancing their appreciation and comprehension. Interactivity promotes dynamic communication, encouraging active involvement and deeper engagement. Responsiveness ensures prompt and pertinent replies to consumer questions, preferences, and feedback, cultivating trust and loyalty. Collectively, these attributes work in harmony to engage the audience, enable meaningful interactions, and ultimately positively and enduringly influence consumer behavior (Davlembayeva et al., 2024; Lin et al., 2024).

Digital disruption signifies the significant changes brought about by digital technologies in conventional business models and industry frameworks, reshaping boundaries and challenging established standards. This phenomenon is fueled by innovations like artificial intelligence, blockchains, and the Internet of Things (IoT). Digital disruption boosts operational efficiency, facilitates predictive analytics, and encourages personalization. These technological advancements open up new avenues for innovation and force organizations to reevaluate their strategies to stay competitive (Lei et al., 2023). Due to technological progress, digital innovations have become more evident, leading to the emergence of VIs.

Traditional Marketing (TM) has undergone a significant transformation with the advent of virtual influencers, who have become powerful tools for aligning brand messages, values, and aesthetics with unprecedented precision. These digital personas, created and controlled by brands or marketing agencies, offer a level of consistency and customization that human influencers often struggle to maintain (Kumar & Aravamudhan, 2023). VIs can be tailored to embody specific brand attributes, ensuring that every aspect of their appearance, personality, and content aligns perfectly with the brand's identity and marketing objectives (Ozdemir et al., 2023).

Integrating VIs into marketing strategies has opened up new avenues for brand storytelling and consumer engagement. Unlike their human counterparts, they are not subject to personal controversies, scheduling conflicts, or changes in appearance or opinion that might contradict a brand's image. This level of control allows marketers to create long-term, cohesive narratives that resonate with target audiences across various platforms and campaigns. Additionally, VIs can be easily adapted to different cultural contexts and market segments, providing brands with a flexible and scalable approach to global marketing efforts (Audrezet & Koles, 2023). As a result, traditional marketing practices are being reimagined to leverage the unique advantages offered by these digital brand ambassadors, potentially revolutionizing how companies communicate with and influence their consumers.

The Rise of VIS

The Internet has fundamentally transformed marketing practices, enabling organizations to attract a broader customer base, enhance profitability, and optimize long-term operations. This transformation delineates a clear distinction between businesses that implement online marketing strategies and those that do not, ultimately enhancing marketing efficacy and fostering greater success (Saeed et al., 2023). The Internet empowers companies to refine their marketing approaches by leveraging various online tools and platforms, reaching a wider audience and tailoring their initiatives more precisely. Notably, the Internet facilitates customer acquisition, providing a significant advantage to firms that adopt digital marketing over their offline counterparts. Furthermore, it enhances time management by streamlining long-term marketing activities, making them less labor-intensive. This increased efficiency allows organizations to reallocate resources to other critical functions while maintaining robust and effective marketing operations (Saeed et al., 2023).

Digital marketing strategies, such as Search Engine Optimization (SEO) and content marketing, are essential for effectively engaging targeted demographics. SEO enhances a brand's visibility by optimizing websites and content to achieve higher rankings in search engine results, thereby reaching audiences actively seeking relevant products and services. Concurrently, content marketing generates customized, valuable content that addresses the audience's needs, cultivates trust, and fosters enduring relationships. When combined, these strategies enhance engagement, drive conversions, and promote brand loyalty by ensuring that brands connect with the appropriate audience at an optimal moment through compelling messaging (Mohamad, 2022).

Virtual influencers are AI-generated avatars that brands and agencies can oversee. They provide a high degree of customization and adaptability in advertising and present fewer ethical concerns than their human counterparts. Consequently, they are gaining recognition as significant assets in marketing strategies (Martin et al., 2023).

The rising prominence within the marketing sector highlights their emerging role as strategic assets for brand promotion. However, there is still a considerable lack of insight into the key factors contributing to this trend and their effects on consumer engagement. This knowledge gap serves as the basis for the study's objective, which seeks to examine the relative effectiveness of VIs compared to human influencers in influencing consumer behavior, while identifying the distinct characteristics and dynamics that render them an attractive option for marketers (Lee et al., 2024).

VIs can be categorized into three main types: mimic-human, animated-human, and non-human. Mimic human influencers closely resemble real individuals by fostering trust and emotional connections through realistic attributes and interactions. Animated human influencers combine human-like traits with artistic or exaggerated features, offering a unique blend of realism and creativity that appeals to audience members who seek distinctiveness. Non-human influencers take imaginative or abstract forms, such as robots or animals, engaging audiences through novelty and innovation (Arsenyan & Mirowska, 2021; Yan et al., 2024).

Each category influences consumer attachment differently, with mimic-human influencers building stronger trust because of their realistic resemblance to actual people. In contrast, animated human and non-human influencers captivate consumers through entertainment, escapism, and their contribution to imaginative brand storytelling. The perceived realism of these influencers plays a critical role in shaping consumer responses, impacting purchasing decisions, and fostering brand loyalty (Yan et al., 2024).

The rise of VIs signifies a notable transformation in digital marketing by merging elements of real-world interactions with innovative virtual technologies. Nonetheless, their existence prompts critical discussions surrounding authenticity and ethical considerations, as their realistic appearances and behaviors challenge the conventional views of influencers, igniting debates about transparency and accountability in marketing practices. Examples such as Lil Miquela and Kyra illustrate how brands use virtual figures to create engaging stories and reach specific audience segments. While they offer benefits such as constant availability and creative adaptability, they are also subject to criticism regarding their authenticity and the ethical implications of employing such technology, particularly concerning the promotion of unrealistic ideals or distortions of reality (Khan, 2024; Rhythm, 2024).

Impact of VIS on Traditional Marketing

The shift from conventional social media influencers to VIs marks a significant transformation in influencer marketing propelled by technological advancements, changing consumer behaviors, and the emergence of parasocial relationships. VIs are digitally constructed entities with distinct advantages, including consistent branding, managed narratives, and effortless integration into immersive platforms like the metaverse. These characteristics allow them to cultivate robust parasocial relationships through meticulously designed personas and captivating content, thus enhancing their credibility and acceptance among audiences. The fashion, technology, tourism, and healthcare sectors increasingly utilize VIs to harness these advantages, align themselves with contemporary digital marketing trends, and appeal to consumers. Technological progress and psychological engagement highlight their transformative capacity to redefine the marketing landscape and foster deeper connections with consumers (Kumar & Varshney, 2023).

The immersive capabilities of the metaverse have significantly shaped the shift from traditional social media influencers to virtual influencers. These digital realms provide brands with novel and captivating methods for engaging with consumers. Within the metaverse, brands can design interactive virtual environments, such as showrooms and events, where users can discover products, participate in experiences, and interact with VIs in real time. This enhanced level of engagement transcends conventional platforms, enabling consumers to co-create content, customize products, and actively influence brand narratives. Such immersive interactions cultivate stronger emotional bonds, rendering the brand experience more significant, as consumers view themselves as active contributors rather than mere spectators. User-generated content enhances a brand's authenticity within virtual landscapes. When consumers share their creations or experiences, it serves as social validation, bolstering the brand's credibility and fostering a sense of community. This collective content establishes trust and elevates VIs' perceived authenticity of VIs, positioning them as integral elements of a vibrant, collaborative ecosystem. By harnessing these interactive and participatory elements, brands can develop personalized, immersive, and highly engaging marketing strategies that resonate with digitally literate audiences. (Yadav et al., 2024).

Technological advancements, the integration of artificial intelligence, and the evolving dynamics of consumer culture drive the shift from social media influencers to VIs. These elements have redefined notions of identity and representation, allowing VIs to contest and reinforce societal standards across multiple digital platforms (Miyake, 2024).

VIs attain their effectiveness by embodying characteristics that resonate profoundly with their audiences. A significant aspect of this resonance is relatability. VIs mirror their target demographics' interests, values, and behaviors and are more likely to establish strong emotional bonds. This bond is further enhanced by visual appeal, where high-quality imagery, engaging designs, and aesthetically pleasing content are crucial, particularly in sectors such as fashion, where visual presentation is paramount. Although digitally created, they bolster their authenticity by crafting relatable backstories or personality traits, contributing to their credibility and fostering trust. Their capacity to actively engage with audiences through likes, comments, and shares nurtures a sense of community and enhances follower loyalty. Consistency and innovation are vital to the success of VIs. Upholding a coherent brand image and messaging ensures they remain aligned with the brand's identity, reinforcing recognition over time. Concurrently, innovative content strategies, such as creative storytelling, interactive posts, and collaborations, enable them to distinguish themselves in a saturated digital landscape. VIs can significantly influence consumer perceptions and purchasing behaviors by customizing their styles, personalities, and product presentations to resonate with audience preferences. These meticulously developed traits and strategies empower VIs to enhance brand visibility and effectively impact consumer behavior (Masri et al., 2023).

Cultural Acceptance of VIS Among Filipinos

Filipino buying behavior can be influenced by family, friends, relatives, and colleagues (Castillo, 2018). Filipino millennials purchase products that are positively framed and bring instant gratification (Tengco-Pacquing et al., 2019). Positively framed products demonstrate the benefits of consumption (Lee et al., 2018). In making purchases, the expertise and trustworthiness of the endorser are the most influential factors in predicting the brand attitude of Filipino consumers (Singco et al., 2023). Filipino Instagram macro-influencers with millions of followers significantly affect purchase intention, decision-making, consumer trust, and positive electronic word-of-mouth about skincare products (Libunao et al., 2022). Social media macro-influencers are more effective brand ambassadors than celebrity endorsers in predicting skin care product purchases compared to celebrity endorsers (Lim et al., 2022). Influencers who establish honesty and trustworthiness can change Filipino consumers' behavior and purchase intentions (Dalangin et al., 2021).

Filipinos have yet to fully accept the use of VIs. There may be concerns about authenticity and trust, and skepticism about the digital persona may disengage Filipinos from them. Bernila, a Filipino-developed VI, received criticism from social media users for her appearance, as she did not look like a typical Filipina (Wong, 2023). She had big eyes, overly fair skin, and an extremely slender figure, which

Filipinos tended to view as typical (Wong, 2023; Borlongan, 2023). She is viewed more as an artificial intelligence model than a VI (Borlongan, 2023). Therefore, this VI is yet to receive product endorsement projects.

Effects of VIS on Traditional Marketing

Online shopping offers consumers exceptional convenience, facilitating rapid price comparisons across various platforms and granting access to an extensive range of products from diverse brands. This capability for swift comparison equips consumers to make well-informed purchasing choices, ensuring they secure optimal value for their expenditures. Additionally, direct engagement between manufacturers and consumers removes the necessity for intermediaries, contributing to lower distribution costs and enhancing service delivery. By circumventing conventional retail pathways, online shopping fosters a more streamlined supply chain, resulting in expedited shipping, tailored services, and improved customer satisfaction (Nia and Nia, 2021).

Influencer marketing, mainly through the innovative application of VIs, is acknowledged as a highly effective and economically viable approach for engaging a broad audience. VIs can embody various demographic subgroups, providing brands a distinctive opportunity to enhance their relatability and expand their appeal across diverse populations. By capitalizing on the novelty and creativity inherent in VIs, brands can develop impactful campaigns that ignite curiosity and foster organic word of mouth, extending their reach. This heightened engagement cultivates deeper emotional connections with consumers, positively affecting their intention to follow and purchase. Ultimately, this strategic implementation enhances brand perception, strengthens customer loyalty, and promotes sustainable business growth (Carla et al., 2024).

VIs offer a budget-friendly option in marketing compared to their human counterparts. They utilize their distinctive traits to captivate audiences and improve brand perception. Being entirely digital enables more precise management of branding and communication, thereby minimizing the risks linked to human influencers. The subsequent sections detail the essential features of VIs as economical marketing resources.

VIs represent a cost-efficient and innovative alternative to traditional human influencers (HIs) in advertising. Unlike HIs, VIs are digitally generated entities that grant brands comprehensive control over their image, conduct, and messaging. This capability to design customized personas and narratives renders VIss particularly appealing to brands, aiming for adaptable and contemporary advertising approaches. Furthermore, VIs mitigate the typical expenses linked to human influencers, including fees for appearances, travel costs, and the complexities of personal brand management. Their ability to foster interactive experiences and engage audiences in real-time significantly amplifies their attractiveness, offering brands a distinctive and scalable solution to maintain relevance and connect with a broad audience (Byun & Ahn, 2023).

By utilizing digital platforms and online marketing techniques, companies can access a worldwide market, overcome geographical barriers, and broaden their customer base on a global scale. This extensive reach allows organizations to attract new clients from various regions, increasing their market presence and promoting growth. Furthermore, a global footprint enables businesses to connect with diverse customer segments, allowing them to customize their products or services to align with different cultures or demographics' distinct preferences and requirements. The capacity to serve a larger audience also improves customer retention, as companies can sustain ongoing engagement and deliver personalized experiences that build loyalty. With effective digital tools, businesses can optimize customer interactions, provide prompt support, and craft memorable brand experiences that enhance long-term relationships and encourage repeated patronage (Saeed et al. 2023).

While the internet provides numerous shopping benefits but also presents challenges that can impact consumer trust and satisfaction, misinformation regarding products, including deceptive reviews and inaccurate descriptions, can result in consumer dissatisfaction and diminish confidence in online transactions. Furthermore, inconsistencies in product quality, in which items fail to align with their advertised representations, can lead to adverse experiences and weaken customer loyalty. Many consumers attracted by the convenience and extensive variety offered by online shopping tend to allocate a substantial portion of their income to e-commerce, with some even opting to borrow funds to support their purchases. This behavior underscores a significant reliance on online shopping and the considerable market potential of e-commerce enterprises, highlighting the critical need for trust, transparency, and dependable customer service to sustain consumer loyalty (Chen & Shen, 2023; Wilfred, 2023).

One notable discovery is that 46.15% of those who frequently watch live-streaming platforms are driven to purchase because they trust bloggers who promote products (Chen & Shen, 2023). This trust does not happen overnight; it is built over time through influencers' repetitive and strategic marketing efforts to engage their audiences. As influencers consistently showcase products and create relatable content, they gradually establish credibility and connections, ultimately motivating their followers to take action.

The Pygmalion effect, or "self-fulfilling prophecy," plays a key role in influencer marketing by shaping how followers perceive the value of products (Romney et al., 2024). When influencers consistently promote certain products through content, such as reviews and tutorials, they influence their audience's perception, gradually enhancing the product's perceived worth. This repetitive endorsement builds trust as followers internalize the positive attributes the influencer associates with the product. Over time, this increased trust in the influencer's judgment leads consumers to view the product as more desirable and of higher quality, thereby influencing their purchasing decisions. Ultimately, the Pygmalion effect fosters consumer trust and drives purchases by creating the belief that the endorsed product will meet or exceed expectations (Chen & Shen, 2023).

Information technology (IT) advancements have profoundly altered marketing methodologies, providing a diverse array of platforms and techniques to improve consumer brand awareness. Digital marketing approaches, including online advertising, social media engagement, content creation, email outreach, and website promotion, have gained widespread acceptance and are being employed across multiple sectors in response to the swift pace of technological change. These digital marketing techniques facilitate brand recognition (Karen & Zai, 2022; Minclute & Olar, 2018).

A notable positive correlation between Internet advertising and brand recognition emphasizes its efficacy in enhancing consumer awareness of brands. Furthermore, additional digital marketing strategies, such as social media, content, and email marketing, are crucial in fostering brand awareness. (Hollebeek & Mackey, 2019; Karen & Zai, 2022). Internet advertising and other digital marketing strategies effectively boost brand awareness, particularly in the current digital landscape, where online consumer engagement is on the rise (Karen & Zai, 2022).

The rise of VIs has significantly reshaped the digital marketing landscape, with figures such as Lil Miquela leading the way. These computer-generated avatars, which combine human-like features and artificial intelligence, enable brands to engage audiences in innovative and unique ways.

Popular VIS and Impact on Marketing Mix

Popular VIs are significant for redefining the marketing and branding landscape in the digital age. These computer-generated personas transcend traditional influencer boundaries by offering unmatched consistency, scalability, and creative flexibility (Zhao, 2022). Their curated personalities and flawless aesthetics appeal to niche audiences, creating deeper engagement and loyalty (Roy & Chakraborty, 2023). They reduce the risks associated with human influencers, such as controversies or inconsistencies, while giving brands precise control over messaging. By bridging technology and human-like relatability, successful VIs can enhance brand visibility and pave the way for innovative, cost-effective marketing strategies that resonate with tech-savvy consumers (Sands et al., 2022).

Miquela Sousa, popularly recognized as Lil Miquela, stands out as a prominent VI, boasting around 2.5 million followers on Instagram. Developed by *Brud*, she seamlessly integrates elements of fashion, activism, and digital creativity, exerting considerable influence on virtual influence and marketing. Miquela has gained acclaim for her partnerships with high-end brands such as Prada, Calvin Klein, and Balmain, allowing these brands to exercise control over her representation while preserving a lifelike appearance. In addition to her fashion endeavors, she champions various social issues, including racial equality, LGBTQ+ rights, and environmental sustainability, which enrich her digital identity and enhance her emotional resonance with her audience. Lil Miquela is at the forefront of transforming the concept of VIs, skillfully intertwining fashion with social advocacy within a wholly digital environment (Neri, 2022; Claire, 2018; Gerrath, 2024).

Noonoouri is also one of the prominent VIs with 454,000 followers on Instagram, recognized for her AI-generated persona embodying musical talent and a commitment to sustainability. The brainchild of Joerg Zuber, a 43-year-old graphic designer based in Munich, Noonoouri, was conceived seven years ago, although Zuber initially faced challenges in securing support for the initiative. In late 2017, he opted to launch Noonoouri independently and has since established herself as a significant presence in digital marketing. Noonoouri has partnered with esteemed brands such as Marc Jacobs, Dior, and Versace, in addition to endorsing Kim Kardashian's cosmetics line. Furthermore, she is regarded as a 'friend' of renowned supermodels like Naomi Campbell, solidifying her status in fashion and influencer domains (Iglhaut, 2019; Gerrath, 2024).

Shudu Gram is a pioneering VI designed as a digital model, exhibiting lifelike human traits. She symbolizes the intersection of virtual and physical realms, aligning with brand initiatives to captivate consumers through innovative marketing strategies within the metaverse. Recognized as the "world's first digital supermodel,' Shudu has collaborated with prestigious brands such as Balmain and was featured in prominent publications like Vogue and Cosmopolitan. Originating in South Africa, she champions sustainable fashion and advocates for a virtual human community. Created by Cameron James, the founder of T*he Digitals Agency*, Shudu presents striking fashion in an enchanting setting while consistently maintaining an impeccable appearance. James also developed other virtual personas, including Koffi, Brenn, Galaxia, and Dagny (Mona, 2019; Gerrath, 2024).

Lu do Magalu emerged as the most-followed virtual influencer in 2022, amassing over six million followers on Instagram, 14 million on Facebook, and nearly three million subscribers on YouTube, with her primary audience in Brazil (Carrillo-Durán et al., (2024). She debuted more than ten years ago through collaboration with *Magazine Luiza*, one of Brazil's leading retail enterprises. Since then, Lu has established herself as a significant brand ambassador, producing unboxing videos, product reviews, and promotional materials for companies on various digital platforms. Her achievements underscore VIs' extensive reach and cultural versatility of VIs, illustrating their capacity to engage with diverse audiences across multiple markets. (Durán et al., 2024; Denise et al 2024). These examples highlight the growing influence and potential of VIs in modern marketing strategies.

VIss have impacted marketing by offering brands-controlled representation and engaging audiences. Lil Miquela connects with millennials through luxury fashion and music, while Noonoouri features in Dior and Versace campaigns. Shudu Gram, the first digital supermodel, sparks diversity discussions in fashion, and Lu do Magalu is vital in Brazil's e-commerce by merging influencer marketing with retail. These influencers ensure consistent messaging but raise ethical concerns about authenticity and consumer influence. As digital marketing evolves, virtual influencers' roles are expected to grow, challenging brands to balance innovation and transparency.

Product

These VIs are pioneering a new era in digital marketing and brand representation, each establishing a distinct presence in the online world. Lil Miquela and Noonoouri have strategically positioned themselves at the crossroads of fashion, beauty, and social advocacy, partnering with renowned luxury brands while participating in wider social and cultural discussions. This strategy helps them stay relevant and attract a varied audience. Shudu Gram has developed a niche in high fashion and photography, collaborating with top-tier brands to present their products in a carefully curated and visually appealing way. Lu do Magalu distinguishes itself by concentrating on e-commerce and technology, acting as both a brand ambassador and a customer service representative for Magazine Luiza. This role enables Lu do Magalu to bridge the gap between consumers and the brand, promoting sales and improving customer experience. By integrating into their respective brand ecosystems, these VIs provide companies with unparalleled control over their digital portrayal, allowing for tailored messaging and imagery that reflect brand values and marketing goals. This control, along with the VIs' capacity to engage audiences across various platforms and contexts, highlights the potential of digital personas as practical tools for brand communication and customer interaction in the ever-changing digital marketplace.

Price

VIs allow brands to manage their messaging and image precisely, potentially lowering expenses associated with human influencers. Although the initial investment in VIs can be substantial, particularly in high-fashion and luxury industries like Lil Miquela, Noonoouri, and Shudu Gram, these digital figures require sophisticated 3D modeling, animation, and consistently high-quality content to sustain their elite status and allure. Once they are established, they can be utilized in numerous campaigns without the human constraints of scheduling issues or controversies. Their cost-effectiveness extends beyond just financial considerations. Brands can tailor these digital representatives to reflect values, aesthetics, and demographics that resonate with their target audience, facilitating more focused marketing strategies. Moreover, virtual influencers like Lu do Magalu demonstrate how they can seamlessly integrate into e-commerce platforms, directly linking influencer marketing to sales. This direct connection provides a more straightforward way to assess ROI than traditional influencer partnerships concentrating on brand awareness and engagement metrics.

Place

VIs have established distinct roles in the digital realm, utilizing various platforms and tactics to engage with their audiences. Lil Miquela and Noonoouri are active on Instagram, TikTok, and YouTube, where they blend storytelling with brand collaborations, merging lifestyle content with commercial partnerships. Shudu Gram, on the other hand, maintains a carefully curated presence, emphasizing high-fashion visuals on Instagram and in digital campaigns, consistent with her image as a digital supermodel. Lu do Magalu differentiates herself through her strong connections to e-commerce and the Brazilian retail sector. Her influence extends beyond social media, actively participating in Magazine Luiza's shopping ecosystem. This integration enables Lu do Magalu to entertain and guide consumers in their shopping experiences, setting her apart from VIs who focus solely on entertainment. This functional role highlights how virtual personas can fulfill specific business goals while maintaining an engaging character.

Promotion

In recent years, these digitally crafted personas have become increasingly popular, offering brands fresh ways to connect with audiences and showcase their products.

Lil Miquela and Noonoouri are at the forefront of digital fashion marketing. They collaborate with prestigious brands, appearing in carefully curated content that merges the lines between reality and digital artistry. Their lifelike appearances and engaging personalities allow them to showcase clothing, accessories, and lifestyle products in a way that appeals to younger, tech-savvy consumers.

Noonoouri expands her influence by incorporating music collaborations into her repertoire. This approach extends her reach beyond fashion enthusiasts, tapping into the vast and passionate music audience. By partnering with famous artists and music events, Noonoouri creates a multi-faceted appeal that attracts a diverse demographic, making her an attractive option for brands looking to boost their visibility across various interest groups.

Shudu Gram takes a different approach, focusing on visual aesthetics rather than interactive engagement. As a virtual supermodel, Shudu's striking appearance and flawless features make her ideal for showcasing products through still images. This strategy appeals to brands that prioritize visual impact and aim to create memorable, artistic campaigns that stand out in a crowded digital space.

Lu do Magalu represents a more specialized approach to virtual influencer marketing. Unlike her counterparts who work with multiple brands, Lu is dedicated solely to promoting products for a single retail company. This focus allows for a more targeted and cohesive marketing strategy, effectively driving direct sales for the company's extensive product range. Lu's persona is carefully crafted to align with the brand's identity.

VIs generally offer brands an unprecedented level of control over their marketing efforts. Unlike human influencers, these digital characters can be precisely tailored to perfectly match a brand's image and messaging, ensuring consistency across all promotional endeavors. They are available 24/7, can appear in multiple places simultaneously, and are not subject to the unpredictability of human behavior or personal controversies.

Furthermore, VIs allow brands to implement various strategies to connect with and engage their audience. Whether through collaborations in high fashion, partnerships in music, visually striking photoshoots, or direct product endorsements, these digital personas provide versatility in content creation and audience interaction. This adaptability enables brands to experiment with different marketing approaches and determine the most effective ways to reach their target audience.

As technology continues to advance, the role of VIs in marketing is anticipated to expand. Brands may explore innovative methods to integrate these digital figures into their campaigns, potentially leveraging augmented reality or interactive virtual environments. This evolving landscape presents exciting opportunities for creative marketing strategies, broadening how brands can engage with consumers in the digital realm.

IMPLICATIONS FOR PHILIPPINE CAREER EDUCATION

The Philippine Republic Act 11206, known as the Secondary School Career Guidance and Counseling Act, enables Grades 7 to 12 Filipino students to receive instructional materials to develop their capabilities to access tertiary education, the labor market, and the requirements and expectations of the government, industry, and economy (Philippine Congress, 2018). Senior high schools also provide specific educational tracks to strengthen students' competencies in their chosen fields.

Some Philippine schools offer Accountancy, Business, and Management (ABM) as a senior high school strand in preparation for university entrance. Senior high school students majoring in ABM must understand the growing significance of VIs in shaping modern business strategies to boost sales, even if local VI have not yet gained acceptance. Technological advances may enable computer specialists to develop effective VI in the future.

As digital marketing evolves, VIs are transforming how brands engage with audiences (Lou et al., 2023). Teaching students about influencers' ability to create cost-effective, customizable, and highly engaging campaigns can broaden their entrepreneurial pursuits (Teixeira et al., 2023). Moreover, senior high school students should learn how virtual influencers cater to specific target markets, leverage data-driven insights, and enhance their brand credibility. They should also recognize that VIs are more predictable and cost-effective than their human counterparts. By integrating this knowledge into the ABM strand, students will be equipped to harness VIs' potential and stay competitive in an increasingly digital marketplace.

CONCLUSIONS AND RECOMMENDATIONS

The growing presence of VIs raises important ethical and social issues that need careful consideration. One concern is transparency, as audiences may not always realize they engage with digital personas instead of real people. This confusion can further obscure the line between genuine content and manipulation in advertising, especially since some VIs look very much like humans.

From a societal viewpoint, VIs might also promote unattainable beauty standards or ideals, as their perfect appearances are entirely crafted. This could potentially impact the self-esteem and body image of impressionable viewers. Moreover, the existence of these flawlessly designed figures might lead to the replacement of human influencers (HIs) and experienced celebrity endorsers, who could find themselves excluded from product promotions. Consequently, job loss in this field could become a pressing issue.

The use of VIs also raises questions about accountability: Who is responsible for their actions or statements if they mislead or offend? Who is liable for any infractions they commit? Will developers or brand owners be held accountable for any wrongdoings by VIs? At present, many countries have yet to establish laws or guidelines for VIs.

From a marketing standpoint, VIs are revolutionizing the conventional 4Ps framework:

VIs represent an innovative marketing tool, offering brands a novel method to engage with consumers. Unlike human influencers, VIs provide controlled and consistent brand representation, free from the unpredictability associated with personal opinions or behavior. Their seamless integration with artificial intelligence and virtual reality renders them an invaluable digital asset for brands aiming to create immersive storytelling experiences. As digital constructs, VIs can be fully customized to align with a brand's identity, values, and marketing objectives. Companies have the capability to design these influencers with specific aesthetics, personalities, and messaging strategies tailored to appeal to targeted demographics.

In contrast to human influencers, who may evolve in ways that do not always align with brand values, VIs maintain consistency in their messaging and image. This reliability enables brands to develop long-term marketing strategies with minimal risk of reputational damage. Moreover, VIs can be optimized for various platforms, allowing brands to utilize them across different media formats, ranging from static advertisements to interactive virtual experiences.

The cost effectiveness of VIs makes them appealing to brands. Unlike human influencers, who require contracts, salaries, insurance, and other compensations, VIs eliminate these costs. Although the initial investment in their creation and ongoing content production can be significant, their scalability ensures long-term cost-effectiveness.

Beyond direct financial savings, VIs offer brands greater control over their marketing budgets. Instead of the variable costs associated with human influencers—who may demand higher fees as their popularity increases—VIs maintain a consistent cost structure, making campaign planning more predictable. Additionally, brands can reuse and modify digital influencers without additional negotiation or increased fees. This financial stability allows companies to allocate resources to other areas of their marketing strategy, such as enhancing engagement tools or expanding digital campaigns.

VIs are digital entities capable of operating globally across a multitude of online platforms, including social media, e-commerce sites, and virtual reality environments. Their ability to transcend geographical limitations enables brands to maintain a consistent presence across diverse markets. Nevertheless, cultural perceptions and regulatory frameworks may affect consumer acceptance in various regions.

Due to their lack of physical constraints, VIs facilitate brands in reaching international audiences concurrently, thereby enhancing the efficiency of cross-border marketing efforts. In contrast to human influencers, who may encounter language barriers or cultural misalignments, VIs can be tailored to accommodate regional preferences. By utilizing AI-driven language translation and localization tools, VIs can engage with consumers in multiple languages and cultural contexts, thereby fostering deeper engagement. However, brands must navigate regulatory and ethical considerations in different regions with caution to uphold credibility and consumer trust.

VIs are transforming the landscape of influencer marketing by enabling brands to uphold an impeccable image and execute campaigns with meticulous precision. Their flexibility allows for programming that aligns seamlessly with brand values and aesthetics, thereby mitigating risks associated with human influencers. Nonetheless, transparency remains imperative; consumers must be informed that they interact with AI-generated entities to cultivate trust and credibility.

The promotional capabilities of VIs extend beyond conventional advertising, as they can engage dynamically with audiences through AI-driven personalization. Brands can program VIs to address consumer inquiries, participate in live virtual events, and facilitate user-generated content collaborations. This level of engagement enhances brand-consumer relationships and fosters long-term loyalty. However, it is essential to ensure that audiences are aware of the digital nature of VIs to prevent potential backlash related to deceptive marketing practices. Ethical guidelines and clear disclosure policies will be crucial in maintaining consumer confidence.

Adopting VIs represents a significant evolution in marketing strategies, blending cutting-edge technology with the human-centric approach that has long been the cornerstone of successful brand engagement. This innovative fusion allows companies to create digital personas that can resonate with audiences across various demographics, potentially transcending cultural and linguistic barriers more easily than traditional human influencers. The flexibility and controllability of VIs offer brands unprecedented opportunities to tailor their messaging and visual representation to specific market segments, while maintaining a consistent brand image across diverse platforms and campaigns.

However, the effectiveness of VIs in driving long-term brand loyalty and sales remains a subject of ongoing research and debate. While initial consumer responses have been largely positive, particularly among younger, tech-savvy demographics, questions persist about the depth and authenticity of connections formed with these digital entities. As the technology behind VIs continues to advance, incorporating more sophisticated AI and machine learning algorithms, marketers will need to navigate complex ethical considerations and potential regulatory challenges. Additionally, the success of VI campaigns will likely depend on striking a delicate balance between leveraging the unique advantages of digital personas and maintaining a sense of authenticity that consumers have come to expect from brand interactions. Ongoing market research and consumer behavior analysis will be crucial in refining VI strategies and understanding their impact on brand perception, engagement metrics, and ultimately, product sales in various industry sectors.

REFERENCES

Al Masri, Y., Hamadneh, S., Al-Dmour, R., & Al-Okaily, M. (2023). *Can Computer Virtual Influencers Replace Human Influencers in the Future? An Empirical Investigation in the Age of Digital Transformation.* Jordan Journal of Business Administration., DOI: 10.35516/jjba.v19i4.1430

Alam, S., Susbiyantoro, S., Yuwantiningrum, S. E., Suwastika, I. W. K., & Muhdaliha, E. (2024). The Influence of Social Media Algorithms on Consumer Behavior: A Strategic Analysis for Brand Positioning. *The Journal of Academic Science, 1*(7), 832–841.

Anuradha, Y., Vijaya, K., Manda., M., Rao, J. (2024). Influencer Marketing in the Age of Metaverse. Advances in marketing, customer relationship management, and e-services book series, DOI: 10.4018/979-8-3693-4167-4.ch008

Arsenyan, J., & Mirowska, A. (2021). Almost human? A comparative case study on the social media presence of virtual influencers. *International Journal of Human-Computer Studies, 155*, 102694. DOI: 10.1016/j.ijhcs.2021.102694

Audrezet, A., & Koles, B. (2023). Virtual influencer as a brand avatar in interactive marketing. In *The Palgrave handbook of interactive marketing* (pp. 353–376). Springer International Publishing. DOI: 10.1007/978-3-031-14961-0_16

Bambeshwar, A., Kamble, N.S., Singh, S., Soni, N. A.(2024). Real vs virtual influencer: impact on youngster's perception. DOI: 10.58532/V3BFMA16P1CH4

Baso Soriano, E. E., & Matthews, R. (2024). Marketing social para minimizar daños ambientales, utilizando las 4P. *Entrelíneas, 3*(2), e030202. DOI: 10.56368/Entrelineas322

Bishop, S. (2021). Influencer management tools: Algorithmic cultures, brand safety, and bias. *Social Media + Society, 7*(1), 20563051211003066. DOI: 10.1177/20563051211003066

Borlongan, M. (2023). *First-ever Filipina virtual model earns negative reactions for her 'not-so-Filipino' features.* https://pop.inquirer.net/339527/first-ever-filipina-virtual-model-earns-negative-reactions-for-her-not-so-filipino-features

Byun, K. J., & Ahn, S. J. (2023). A Systematic Review of Virtual Influencers: Similarities and Differences between Human and Virtual Influencers in Interactive Advertising. *Journal of Interactive Advertising, 23*(4), 293–306. DOI: 10.1080/15252019.2023.2236102

Carrillo-Durán, M. V., García, M. G., & Cortés, L. C. (2024). Influencers virtuales de apariencia humana como forma de comunicación online: El caso de Lil Miquela y Lu do Magalu en Instagram. *Revista De Comunicación, 23*(1), 119–140. DOI: 10.26441/RC23.1-2024-3453

Castillo, F. G.Jr. (2018). Consumer buying behavior: The multicultural influence in the Philippines. *The International Journal of Business Management and Technology, 2*(2), 71–75.

Cayla, J., Bhatnagar, K., Nanarpuzha, R., & Dey, S. (2025). From social feeds to market fields: How influencer stories drive market innovation. *International Journal of Research in Marketing*. Advance online publication. DOI: 10.1016/j.ijresmar.2025.03.001

Chang, W., & Chang, H. (2023). The Impact of Digital Disruption: Influences of Digital Media and Social Networks on Forming Digital Natives' Attitude. *SAGE Open, 13*(3), 21582440231191741. Advance online publication. DOI: 10.1177/21582440231191741

Dalangin, J. J. G., McArthur, J. M. B., Salvador, J. B. M., & Bismonte, A. B. (2021). The impact of social media influencers purchase intention in the Philippines. *Jurnal Studi Komunikasi, 5*(3). Advance online publication. DOI: 10.25139/jsk.v5i3.3708

Davlembayeva, D., Simos, C., & Savvas, P. (2024). Virtual Influencers in Consumer Behaviour: A Social Influence Theory Perspective. *British Journal of Management*. Advance online publication. DOI: 10.1111/1467-8551.12839

De Brito Silva, M. J., Delfino, L., Alves Cerqueira, K. A., & de Oliveira Campos, P. (2022). Avatar marketing: A study on the engagement and authenticity of virtual influencers on Instagram. *Social Network Analysis and Mining, 12*(1), 130. DOI: 10.1007/s13278-022-00966-w

Delbaere, M., Michael, B., & Phillips, B. J. (2021). Social media influencers: A route to brand engagement for their followers. *Psychology and Marketing, 38*(1), 101–112. DOI: 10.1002/mar.21419

Dondapati, A. (2025). Maximizing the Consumer Connection: Avatars, Emotions, and Effective Virtual Influencer Advertising. *Review of Marketing Science*, (0).

Elfadel, M. W., Othman, R. B., Mat, N. H. B. N., Hamad, F. F., Mohadis, H. M., & Ahmed, M. (2024). The relationship between e-marketing mix framework (4Ps) and customer satisfaction with electronic information services: An empirical analysis of Jordanian university libraries. *Information Services & Use, 44*(2), 139–164. DOI: 10.3233/ISU-240230

Ferraro, C., Sands, S., Zubcevic-Basic, N., & Campbell, C. (2024). Diversity in the digital age: How consumers respond to diverse virtual influencers. *International Journal of Advertising*, *43*(8), 1342–1365. DOI: 10.1080/02650487.2023.2300927

Gerrath, M. (2024). Meet five virtual influencers inspiring climate action; The Conversation. University of Leeds; https://theconversation.com/meet-five-virtual-influencers-inspiring-climate-action-230898

Gerrath, M. H., Olya, H., Shah, Z., & Li, H. (2024). Virtual influencers and pro-environmental causes: The roles of message warmth and trust in experts. *Journal of Business Research*, *175*, 114520. DOI: 10.1016/j.jbusres.2024.114520

Hollebeek, L. D., & Macky, K. (2019). Digital content marketing's role in fostering consumer engagement, trust, and value: Framework, fundamental propositions, and implications. *Journal of Interactive Marketing*, *45*(1), 27–41. DOI: 10.1016/j.intmar.2018.07.003

Hubble, C. (2018). Miquela Sousa and the rise of fake influencers. Eureka street. https://www.semanticscholar.org/paper/Miquela-Sousa-and-the-rise-of-fake-influencers-Hubble/0e41b0698fd13d3216598767d6767860ba0cd7ae

Ibardeloza, K. B., Badillo, L. T., Macatangay, J. M. H., Cruz, K. R. D., & Malabanan, M. P. (2022). Students' exposure to social media and their radical involvement on the societal issues in the Philippines. *International Review of Social Sciences Research*, *2*(1), 47–60. DOI: 10.53378/352878

Iglhaut, C. (2019). The influencers of tomorrow will be virtual. https://www.deutschland.de/en/topic/culture/who-is-noonoouri-fashion-avatar-conquers-the-fashion-world

Ines, J., & Tolentino, M. Q. (2024). Beyond likes and shares: Exploring the influence of social media on brand choices among college of business students at a private higher education institution in the Philippine. *American Journal of Economics and Business Innovation*, *3*(2), 66–74. DOI: 10.54536/ajebi.v3i2.2545

Jhawar, A., Prashant, K., Sanjeev, V. (2023). The emergence of virtual influencers: a shift in the influencer marketing paradigm. Young Consumers: Insight and Ideas for Responsible Marketers, DOI: 10.1108/YC-05-2022-1529

Jing, W. (2024). Research On Marketing and Business Management Strategy of Sports Commercial Brand Based On 4ps Theory: A Case Study of Lululemon. Highlights in business, economics and management, 37:351-357. DOI: 10.54097/wv3efn51

Karen, K., & Zai, I. (2022). Analyzing the effects of digital marketing on brand awareness among internet users. [Management and Business Review]. *MBR*, *6*(2). Advance online publication. DOI: 10.21067/mbr.v6i2.7298

Khan, S. A. (2024). Virtual influencers: Crafting the future of marketing. https://yourstory.com/2024/02/virtual-influencers-rise-2024

Kim, E., Kim, D. E. Z., & Shoenberger, H. (2023). The next hype in social media advertising: Examining virtual influencers' brand endorsement effectiveness. *Frontiers in Psychology*, *14*, 1089051. DOI: 10.3389/fpsyg.2023.1089051 PMID: 36949930

Kopalle, P. K., Gangwar, M., Kaplan, A., Ramachandran, D., Reinartz, W., & Rindfleisch, A. (2022). Examining artificial intelligence (AI) technologies in marketing via a global lens: Current trends and future research opportunities. *International Journal of Research in Marketing*, *39*(2), 522–540. DOI: 10.1016/j.ijresmar.2021.11.002

Kumar, S., & Aravamudhan, S. (2023). Investigating the Effects of Virtual Personas on Brand Image. In *Brand Awareness-Recent Advances and Perspectives*. IntechOpen.

Lee, H., Shin, M., Yang, J., & Chock, T. M. (2024). Virtual Influencers vs. Human Influencers in the Context of Influencer Marketing: The Moderating Role of Machine Heuristic on Perceived Authenticity of Influencers. *International Journal of Human-Computer Interaction*, •••, 1–18. DOI: 10.1080/10447318.2024.2374100

Lee, H. C., Liu, S. F., & Cheng, Y. C. (2018). Positive or Negative? The Influence of Message Framing, Regulatory Focus, and Product Type. *International Journal of Communication*. https://ijoc.org/index.php/ijoc/article/viewFile/7601/2266

Lei, J., Indiran, L., Kohar, U. H. A., Liu, H., & Khatib, S. F. A. (2023). Examining the Role of Digital Technology as an Enabler of Digital Disruption: A Systematic Review. *Research Square*. DOI: 10.21203/rs.3.rs-3657875/v1

Libunao, F. M., Martinez, J. D., Rodriguez, M. K., & Castaño, M. C. (2022). Consumers Attitude towards Skincare Products Endorsed by Filipino Macro-Influencers on Instagram. *Journal of Business and Management Studies*, *4*(2), 123–135. DOI: 10.32996/jbms.2022.4.2.10

Lim, R. L., Rosales, M. Z., Salazar, A. T., & Pantoja, E. (2022). Perception of Filipino Skincare Product Users on the Effectiveness of Social Media Influencers vs Celebrity Endorsers as Brand Ambassadors. *Journal of Business and Management Studies*, *4*(1), 131–139. DOI: 10.32996/jbms.2022.4.1.16

Lou, C., Kiew, S. T. J., Chen, T., Lee, T. Y. M., Ong, J. E. C., & Phua, Z. (2023). Authentically fake? How consumers respond to the influence of virtual influencers. *Journal of Advertising*, *52*(4), 540–557. DOI: 10.1080/00913367.2022.2149641

Minculete, G., & Olar, P. (2018). Approaches to the modern concept of digital marketing. In *International conference Knowledge-based organization* (Vol. 24, No. 2, pp. 63-69). DOI: 10.1515/kbo-2018-0067

Miyake, E. (2024). *Virtual Influencers.* Doi: DOI: 10.4324/9781003433170

Moustakas, E., Lamba, N., Mahmoud, D., & Ranganathan, C., C. (2020). "Blurring lines between fiction and reality: Perspectives of experts on marketing effectiveness of virtual influencers," *2020 International Conference on Cyber Security and Protection of Digital Services (Cyber Security)*, Dublin, Ireland, 2020, pp. 1-6, DOI: 10.1109/CyberSecurity49315.2020.9138861

Neri, F. C. (2022). Artificial Intelligence or a Neoliberal Marketing Scheme? The Performative Nature of Lil Miquela's Racialized Design and Politics on Instagram. *The IJournal: Student Journal of the Faculty of Information* 7 (2). Toronto, Canada:52–59. https://doi.org/.DOI: 10.33137/ijournal.v7i2.38617

Nguyen, H. (2023). Omnichannel marketing strategy for fashion retailers. https://www.theseus.fi/bitstream/handle/10024/796801/Nguyen_Hue.pdf?sequence=2

Nicos, A., & Alexander, B. (2024). The 4Ps Marketing Strategy as a Driver of Dynamic Capabilities: Path to Consumer/Voter Satisfaction. *Review of Marketing Science*, *0*(0), 117–132. Advance online publication. DOI: 10.1515/roms-2023-0125

Niluth, N. (2024). Konsep 4P Sebagai Strategi Rumah Makan Cahaya Minang Dalam Mempertahankan Usahanya (Studi Kasus pada Kampung Hambulu Kabupaten Bogor). *Wiratani Jurnal Ilmiah Agribisnis*, *7*(1), 12. DOI: 10.33096/wiratani.v7i1.316

Ogwa, A. L., Rabiu, M. S., & Ogande, A. (2024). Interactive Electronic Billboard as A Tool for Advertising in the Modern-Day Nigerian Society. *Nasarawa Journal Of Multimedia And Communication Studies*, *6*(1), 140–151.

Oliveira, D. C., Ventura, J. B. S., & Silva, P. C.Da Costa Oliveira. (2024). Narrativas de consumo de moda, inteligência artificial e emoções: O riso de Lu do Magalu. *Organicom*, *21*(44), 133–146. DOI: 10.11606/issn.2238-2593.organicom.2024.220272

Orencia, A. J. (2023). Authenticity, Relatability, and Cultural Influences in Contemporary Marketing Strategies: A Qualitative Inquiry. *Psychology and Education: A Multidisciplinary Journal, 15*, 675-679.

Osiyevskyy, O., Umantsiv, Y., & Kavun, O. (2024). Strategy for striking the omnichannel balance in Retail 4.0. *Strategy and Leadership*, *52*(3/4), 7–19. DOI: 10.1108/SL-12-2023-0120

Ozdemir, O., Kolfal, B., Messinger, P. R., & Rizvi, S. (2023). Human or virtual: How influencer type shapes brand attitudes. *Computers in Human Behavior*, *145*, 107771. DOI: 10.1016/j.chb.2023.107771

Paz, M. D. R., & Delgado, F. J. (2020). Consumer experience and omnichannel behavior in various sales atmospheres. *Frontiers in Psychology*, *11*, 1972. DOI: 10.3389/fpsyg.2020.01972 PMID: 32849155

Philippine Congress. (2018). Republic Act 11206 (An Act Establishing a Career Guidance and Counseling Program for All Secondary Schools and Appropriating Funds Therefore). https://lawphil.net/statutes/repacts/ra2019/ra_11206_2019.html

Qiaoling, L., Imm, Ng. S. I., Basha., N.K. Luo. X. Li, Y. (2024). Impact of virtual influencers on customer engagement of Generation Z consumers: a presence perspective. Young Consumers: Insight and Ideas for Responsible Marketers, DOI: 10.1108/YC-01-2024-1958

Rhythm (2024). The Rise of AI-Generated Influencers. https://rhythmagency.com/blog/may-2024/the-rise-of-ai-generated-influencers

Romney, A., Harrison, J. T., & Benson, S. (2024). Looking back to predict the future: A review of empirical support for the self-fulfilling prophecy. *Management Research Review*, *47*(2), 245–260. DOI: 10.1108/MRR-01-2022-0051

Rosário, A., & Raimundo, R. (2021). Consumer marketing strategy and E-commerce in the last decade: A literature review. *Journal of Theoretical and Applied Electronic Commerce Research*, *16*(7), 3003–3024. DOI: 10.3390/jtaer16070164

Roy, D., & Chakraborty, J. (2023). "Forever young, beautiful, and scandal-free": Exploring the Ethical Frames and Crafted Authenticity in the Animated Images of Female Virtual Influencers. *Global Media Journal. Indian Edition, 15*(1), 1-23.

Sands, S., Ferraro, C., Demsar, V., & Chandler, G. (2022). False idols: Unpacking the opportunities and challenges of falsity in the context of virtual influencers. *Business Horizons*, *65*(6), 777–788. DOI: 10.1016/j.bushor.2022.08.002

Sarkar, A., Saeed, S., Rezhan, A., Nada, B, A.. (2023). Effect of the Internet on Enhancing Marketing among Business Organizations. DOI: 10.31098/ijmadic.v1i2.1751

Shahid, S. (2023). From traditional marketing to digital marketing: Digital Sign Media Ltd.

Silva, R., Pereira, I., Nicola, S., & Madureira, A. (2024). Exploring Virtual Reality in Omnichannel Marketing: A Systematic Review. In *International Conference on Marketing and Technologies* (pp. 865-880). Springer, Singapore DOI: 10.1007/978-981-97-1552-7_58

Singco, M. Y. A., Lopez, I. D. A., & Cabauatan, R. R. (2023). The Effect of Influencer Marketing on Purchase Intentions and Brand Attitude of Consumers in the Philippines. *International Journal of Research in Engineering Science and Management*, *6*(12), 50–62. https://journal.ijresm.com/index.php/ijresm/article/view/2881

Soni, S. & Yadav, U. (2024). Statistical analysis of consumer attitudes towards virtual influencers in the metaverse. DOI: 10.1201/9781003471059-59

Teixeira, S., Teixeira, S., Oliveira, Z., & Souza, E. (Eds.). (2023). *Using Influencer Marketing as a Digital Business Strategy*. IGI Global. DOI: 10.4018/979-8-3693-0551-5

Tengco-Pacquing, M. C. M., Bustamante, R. N., Cabanban, A. P. E., Cosare, M. B. M., Gamez, C. C., & Andre, V. (2019). Positive Framing Effect: A Mixed Method Study on the Buying Behavior of Filipino Millennials. *North American Journal of Psychology*, *21*(1).

Tolani, K., Saraiya, A., Manohar, S. (2024). T*he Digital Disruption of Distribution. Advances in web technologies and engineering book series*, DOI: 10.4018/979-8-3693-1762-4.ch007

Ullah, S. (2023). The Semantics Analysis of the Selected Billboards. *University of Chitral Journal of Linguistics and Literature*, *7*(II), 12–21.

Vallespin, M. R., Bodiongan, J. K., Banabana, V., Dacut, A., Gloria, V., Roa, S., & Tapungot, E. M. (2024). Exploring the Impact of Social Media Marketing on Customer Engagement and Purchasing Involvement among Grade 12 Students in a Private Sectarian School in Cagayan de Oro City, Misamis Oriental, Philippines: A Quantitative Analysis. *Misamis Oriental, Philippines: A Quantitative Analysis (May 9, 2024)*.

Vrontis, D., Makrides, A., Christofi, M., & Thrassou, A. (2021). Social media influencer marketing: A systematic review, integrative framework and future research agenda. *International Journal of Consumer Studies*, *45*(4), 617–644. DOI: 10.1111/ijcs.12647

Wilfred, E. (2023). *Influence of digital marketing platforms on customer purchasing behaviours in Moshi municipality*(Doctoral dissertation, Moshi Co-operative University (MoCU))

Wong, D. J. (2023). Philippines' First-Ever Virtual Model Gets Flack for Not Looking Filipino Enough. *Mashable Southeast Asia*. https://sea.mashable.com/tech/22481/philippines-first-ever-virtual-model-gets-flack-for-not-looking-filipino-enough

Xurui, C., & Shangshang, S. (2023). *The Impact of New Media Marketing to Peoples Consumption Behaviour*. Lecture Notes in Education Psychology and Public Media., DOI: 10.54254/2753-7048/4/2022842

Yahya, M.A. (2024). Effects of 4Ps Marketing Mix Strategies on Profitability Enhancement of Petroleum Companies in Afghanistan – A Case Study. Istanbul management journal, DOI: 10.26650/imj.2024.96.1372899

Zhao, X. (2022). *Virtual Fashion Influencers: towards a more sustainable consumer behaviour of Generation Z?* (Master's thesis).

Zhou, Q., Li, B., Li, H., & Lei, Y. (2024). Mere copycat? The effects of human versus human-like virtual influencers on brand endorsement effectiveness: A moderated serial-mediation model. *Journal of Retailing and Consumer Services, 76*, 103610. DOI: 10.1016/j.jretconser.2023.103610

Wang, C. [illegible]

[illegible] (2023). [illegible] Psychology and [illegible] Media. DOI: 10.1 [illegible]

[illegible] M. A. (2024). Effects of [illegible] strategies on [illegible] Pakistan: A Case Study [illegible] DOI: [illegible]

Zhao, Y. (2022). *Virtual Presence* [illegible]

Zhao, [illegible] (2023). The effects of human versus human-like virtual influencers on brand endorsement effectiveness: A moderated serial mediation model. *Journal of Retailing and Consumer Services*, 76, 103610. DOI: 10.1016/j.jretconser.2023.103610

Chapter 3
Virtual Influencer Marketing and Its Impact on Marketing Strategies

Nandini Goyal
https://orcid.org/0009-0006-6074-9795
Maharishi Markandeshwar Institute of Management, Maharishi Markandeshwar University, India

Komal Bhardwaj
https://orcid.org/0000-0002-9378-5542
Maharishi Markandeshwar Institute of Management, Maharishi Markandeshwar University, India

Garima
Maharishi Markandeshwar Institute of Management, Maharishi Markandeshwar University, India

ABSTRACT

Virtual influencers, digitally created personas powered by artificial intelligence and computer graphics, have emerged as a transformative force in marketing. Unlike traditional influencers, virtual influencers are entirely controlled by their creators, enabling brands to design highly customized, consistent, and engaging narratives. This paper explores the impact of virtual influencers on contemporary marketing strategies, focusing on their unique advantages, such as cost efficiency, creative flexibility, and the ability to transcend physical limitations. It also examines their potential challenges, including authenticity concerns, audience trust, and ethical considerations. Through case studies and industry examples, this research highlights how brands leverage virtual influencers to enhance consumer engagement, build brand identity, and drive sales. By analyzing the interplay between technology and

DOI: 10.4018/979-8-3373-0255-3.ch003

human-like branding, this study sheds light on how virtual influencers are reshaping the marketing landscape and paving the way for innovative digital campaigns.

1. INTRODUCTION

In the digital age, social media has revolutionized how brands connect with their audiences, with influencer marketing becoming a dominant strategy. Traditionally, influencer marketing has relied on real individuals to promote products and services. However, the advent of virtual influencers—computer-generated characters designed to emulate human behaviour—has introduced a groundbreaking shift in this space. These virtual personas are powered by advanced artificial intelligence (AI) and computer graphics, enabling them to interact with audiences in ways that are both engaging and innovative.

Virtual influencers are often indistinguishable from real humans in appearance, behaviour, and communication, making them compelling representatives for brands. From fashion to technology, industries are increasingly leveraging these digital entities to create highly curated content and deliver precise messaging. Unlike human influencers, virtual influencers do not age, require time off, or encounter personal controversies, offering brands unparalleled control over their image and activities.

Despite their advantages, virtual influencers raise questions about authenticity, trust, and ethical considerations. How do audiences perceive these digital characters? Can they establish the same level of trust and relatability as their human counterparts? Moreover, the rise of virtual influencers challenges marketers to rethink traditional strategies, blending creativity with cutting-edge technology to craft impactful campaigns.

This study delves into the rise of virtual influencers and their implications for marketing strategies. It explores their unique benefits, potential drawbacks, and the broader transformation they bring to the marketing landscape. By examining real-world examples and industry trends, this research aims to provide a comprehensive understanding of how virtual influencers are reshaping the way brands engage with their audiences in the digital era.

2. LITERATURE REVIEW

The emergence of virtual influencers has drawn considerable attention from academics and practitioners alike, prompting discussions on their role, effectiveness, and implications in marketing. Scholars have highlighted the unique capabilities of virtual influencers that differentiate them from human influencers. According to Miao et al. (2021), virtual influencers are designed with precision to align with brand values and maintain a consistent persona, offering brands complete control over their messaging. Their ability to create engaging and visually appealing content, often leveraging advanced AI and CGI technologies, enhances their appeal across diverse demographics (Wirtz et al., 2020). Unlike human influencers, virtual influencers are immune to scandals, personal biases, and the unpredictability of human behaviour, making them a reliable choice for brands (Le, 2022).

Consumer trust is a cornerstone of influencer marketing, and virtual influencers challenge traditional notions of authenticity. A study by Chahal and Raina (2021) found that younger audiences, particularly Generation Z, are more accepting of virtual influencers, viewing them as innovative and futuristic. However, other research has raised concerns about the perceived lack of authenticity, which could undermine trust among more sceptical consumer groups (Sundar et al., 2020). To counter this, brands often integrate storytelling and human-like interactions to foster emotional connections with audiences (Knoll & Matthes, 2022).

The effectiveness of virtual influencers in driving consumer engagement and sales has been a significant area of focus. Virtual influencers have been shown to outperform traditional influencers in terms of adaptability and scalability, as they can operate across multiple platforms and cultures without geographical or logistical constraints (Bae & Kim, 2021). Additionally, brands utilizing virtual influencers often see higher engagement rates due to the novelty factor and the seamless integration of virtual characters into digital environments (Huang et al., 2023).

As virtual influencers gain prominence, ethical and regulatory challenges have come to the forefront. Researchers such as Millan and Singh (2021) have emphasized the need for transparency in virtual influencer marketing. They argue that audiences must be informed when interacting with digital personas to avoid misleading consumers. Furthermore, ethical concerns about the creation and use of virtual influencers, including issues related to representation and diversity, have been widely debated (Brady et al., 2022).

The advancement of AI and CGI technologies continues to expand the potential of virtual influencers. Studies by Kim et al. (2022) highlight the growing integration of machine learning algorithms that enable virtual influencers to analyse audience preferences and deliver personalized content. This technological evolution is expected to further blur the lines between virtual and human influencers, enhancing their effectiveness while raising questions about the future of human-centric marketing.

The reviewed literature underscores the transformative potential of virtual influencers in marketing; while also highlighting the challenges they pose in terms of authenticity, trust, and ethical considerations. Although research in this domain is still evolving, the existing studies provide a robust foundation for exploring the impact of virtual influencers on marketing strategies. This paper builds upon these insights to analyse real-world applications and offer recommendations for brands seeking to navigate the rapidly changing landscape of influencer marketing.

3. RESEARCH METHODOLOGY

This study adopts a mixed-methods approach to comprehensively analyse the impact of virtual influencers on marketing strategies. The methodology is designed to capture both quantitative data, which provides measurable insights, and qualitative data, which offers a deeper understanding of consumer perceptions and industry practices. The following steps outline the research process:

Research Design

The research employs an exploratory and descriptive design. The exploratory aspect aims to identify emerging trends and patterns in virtual influencer marketing, while the descriptive component focuses on analysing their impact on consumer engagement, brand loyalty, and overall marketing strategies.

4. OBJECTIVES

1. To establish a clear understanding of what virtual influencers are, distinguishing their unique identity and role from traditional human influencers.
2. To analyse the defining features, characteristics, and personas of virtual influencers, with a focus on how they are crafted and represented online.
3. To explore how virtual influencers are integrated into marketing strategies and their impact on audience engagement and brand promotion.

5. HISTORICAL EVOLUTION OF INFLUENCER MARKETING

The concept of influencer marketing has evolved significantly over time, shaped by advancements in technology, cultural shifts, and changing consumer behaviours. From the early days of celebrity endorsements to the rise of social media influencers and now virtual influencers, the journey highlights the dynamic interplay between brands, individuals, and audiences.

In its earliest form, influencer marketing relied on traditional celebrities—actors, athletes, and musicians—who leveraged their fame to promote products. During the 20th century, advertisements featuring celebrities were ubiquitous in print media, television, and radio, as their endorsements lent credibility and aspirational value to brands. Companies recognized the persuasive power of celebrity appeal in shaping consumer perceptions and driving sales.

The advent of social media in the early 2000s marked a turning point, democratizing the concept of influence. Platforms like YouTube, Instagram, and Twitter enabled everyday individuals to amass large followings and establish themselves as influential figures in niche areas such as fashion, fitness, gaming, and travel. These social media influencers differed from traditional celebrities in that their appeal lay in relatability and authenticity. Consumers were drawn to their personal stories and recommendations, often perceiving them as more genuine and trustworthy than corporate advertising.

As social media platforms grew, brands began to harness the power of influencers to reach targeted audiences more effectively. Influencers became integral to marketing strategies, driving engagement and fostering direct connections with consumers. This period also saw the emergence of micro-influencers—individuals with smaller but highly engaged followings—who offered brands access to specific communities and subcultures.

In recent years, technological advancements have introduced a new paradigm: virtual influencers. Unlike human influencers, these computer-generated personas are meticulously crafted by teams of designers and marketers to exhibit human-like appearances and behaviours. The emergence of virtual influencers can be traced back to the rise of artificial intelligence (AI) and computer-generated imagery (CGI), which enabled the creation of lifelike characters capable of interacting with audiences in real-time.

Lil Miquela, one of the first widely recognized virtual influencers, debuted in 2016, signalling a new era in influencer marketing. As digital personas began to gain traction, brands quickly recognized their potential for delivering consistent messaging, avoiding the unpredictability associated with human influencers, and creating immersive storytelling experiences. Virtual influencers represent the culmination of a decades-long evolution in marketing, where the focus has shifted from broad celebrity endorsements to hyper-targeted and digitally optimized campaigns.

This historical progression underscores the adaptability of influencer marketing to technological and cultural changes. From leveraging the star power of celebrities to embracing the authenticity of social media influencers and now exploring the creative possibilities of virtual personas, the journey reflects the ongoing quest to engage consumers in meaningful and innovative ways.

6. UNDERSTANDING VIRTUAL INFLUENCERS

Virtual influencers are computer-generated characters created using advanced technologies such as artificial intelligence (AI) and computer-generated imagery (CGI). These digital personas are designed to exhibit human-like appearances, emotions, and behaviours, allowing them to interact with audiences as if they were real individuals. Unlike human influencers, virtual influencers are entirely controlled by their creators—typically brands, marketing agencies, or creative studios—offering unparalleled consistency and precision in delivering curated content.

At their core, virtual influencers are a blend of artistry and technology. They are crafted to embody specific traits, lifestyles, and narratives that align with the values of the brands they represent. Their creators use sophisticated CGI techniques to make them visually appealing and lifelike, often indistinguishable from real humans. Beyond their appearance, AI technologies enable virtual influencers to engage in interactive communication, respond to comments on social media, and even adapt their content based on audience preferences.

One of the most compelling features of virtual influencers is their versatility. They can be tailored to resonate with diverse audiences, transcending geographical, cultural, and demographic boundaries. For instance, virtual influencers can easily adopt different languages, styles, and interests, making them highly adaptable to global marketing campaigns. Their ability to seamlessly integrate into digital environments, such as social media platforms, virtual reality spaces, and gaming worlds, further enhances their appeal.

Several virtual influencers have gained significant popularity in recent years, setting industry benchmarks. Lil Miquela, created by the company Brud, is a virtual influencer known for her activism and fashion collaborations. Shudu Gram, described as the world's first digital supermodel, represents luxury brands with her striking photorealistic appearance. These examples demonstrate how virtual influencers can capture public attention and create engaging narratives that rival or even surpass their human counterparts.

Despite their growing popularity, virtual influencers face unique challenges. One critical issue is the question of authenticity and trust. While audiences may appreciate their visual appeal and creative content, some consumers are sceptical about engaging with non-human entities, particularly when it comes to product endorsements. Transparency about their virtual nature is essential to maintain credibility and avoid misleading audiences.

Moreover, virtual influencers raise ethical considerations, such as representation and diversity. Since they are designed by humans, they may inadvertently reflect the biases or stereotypes of their creators. Brands and creators must ensure that virtual influencers promote inclusive and positive messages to avoid reinforcing harmful societal norms.

Understanding virtual influencers involves recognizing their potential as a powerful marketing tool and acknowledging their limitations. As technology continues to evolve, virtual influencers are expected to become increasingly sophisticated, offering brands innovative ways to connect with audiences while challenging traditional notions of influence and authenticity.

7. ADVANTAGES OF VIRTUAL INFLUENCERS

Virtual influencers have emerged as a transformative force in modern marketing, offering several distinct advantages over traditional human influencers.

1. **Complete Creative Control**

One of the most significant advantages of virtual influencers is the ability to maintain complete creative control. Brands and creators can script every aspect of a virtual influencer's persona, behaviour, and messaging, ensuring alignment with the brand's identity and goals. This control eliminates the unpredictability associated with human influencers, such as controversies or personal missteps, and allows for consistent, on-brand communication.

2. **Cost Efficiency and Longevity**

While creating a virtual influencer involves an initial investment in design and technology, their long-term costs are often lower compared to human influencers. Virtual influencers do not require salaries, travel expenses, or accommodations, and they can "work" 24/7 without fatigue. Additionally, their digital nature allows them to remain ageless, providing brands with a long-term asset that can be updated and adapted over time.

3. **Customizable and Adaptable**

Virtual influencers can be designed to target specific demographics, cultures, and preferences, offering unparalleled customization. They can seamlessly adopt different styles, languages, and personas to resonate with diverse audiences. Their adaptability makes them ideal for global campaigns, where cultural and linguistic nuances are crucial.

4. **Visual and Creative Appeal**

Virtual influencers often stand out due to their visually stunning and hyper-realistic appearances. They can be designed with extraordinary aesthetics or even fantastical elements that capture attention and intrigue. Their creators can experiment with innovative storytelling and immersive experiences that would be challenging or impossible with human influencers.

5. **Data-Driven Personalization**

Powered by artificial intelligence, virtual influencers can analyse audience data to create highly personalized content. This capability ensures that campaigns are tailored to the preferences and behaviours of target audiences, increasing engagement and effectiveness.

6. **Seamless Integration with Emerging Technologies**

Virtual influencers are inherently digital, making them well-suited for integration with emerging technologies such as augmented reality (AR) and virtual reality (VR). These integrations enable brands to create interactive and immersive experiences, further enhancing audience engagement and brand recall.

7. **Novelty Factor and Engagement**

The novelty of virtual influencers often generates curiosity and excitement among audiences, leading to higher engagement rates. Their futuristic and innovative appeal makes them particularly attractive to younger demographics, such as Generation Z and Millennials, who value creativity and technological innovation.

8. **Reduced Logistical Challenges**

Virtual influencers eliminate many logistical hurdles associated with human influencers, such as scheduling conflicts, location constraints, and physical limitations. This efficiency allows brands to execute campaigns quickly and with greater flexibility.

By leveraging these advantages, virtual influencers provide brands with a versatile and forward-thinking tool for connecting with modern audiences. Their unique blend of creativity, control, and adaptability positions them as a compelling alternative to traditional influencer marketing.

8. CHALLENGES AND LIMITATIONS

While virtual influencers present numerous advantages, they also come with distinct challenges and limitations that brands must consider when incorporating them into marketing strategies. These issues revolve around authenticity, ethical concerns, technological complexities, and consumer trust.

1. **Authenticity and Trust Issues**

A significant challenge for virtual influencers is the perception of authenticity. Unlike human influencers, virtual influencers are not "real," which can make it difficult for some consumers to relate to them. While younger, tech-savvy audiences may embrace virtual influencers for their creativity, others may question the credibility of product endorsements coming from artificial personas. This scepticism can affect consumer trust and engagement, particularly in industries where personal experiences and emotional connections are critical.

2. **Transparency and Ethical Concerns**

Transparency is essential when brands use virtual influencers. If audiences are unaware that they are interacting with a virtual persona, it could lead to accusations of deception, damaging the brand's reputation. Ethical concerns also arise around the representation of diversity, body image, and cultural appropriation. Since virtual influencers are created by teams of developers, they may inadvertently reflect biases or stereotypes, leading to criticisms about inclusivity and fairness.

3. **High Initial Costs and Technical Expertise**

Developing a virtual influencer requires a substantial investment in AI, CGI, and design technologies. These costs can be prohibitive for smaller brands. Additionally, maintaining and updating a virtual influencer demands ongoing technical expertise and resources, which may not be readily available to all organizations.

4. **Limited Emotional Depth**

Virtual influencers, despite their realistic appearances, lack genuine emotions and lived experiences. This limitation can hinder their ability to connect with audiences on a deeper, more personal level. While storytelling and scripting can partially address this issue, it is challenging to replicate the spontaneity and relatability of human influencers.

5. **Regulatory and Legal Challenges**

The use of virtual influencers raises complex legal questions, such as intellectual property rights and disclosure requirements. Regulatory bodies in various countries are still catching up with the evolving landscape of virtual influencer marketing. For instance, it is crucial to disclose that a virtual influencer is not a real person when endorsing products, but the guidelines around such disclosures are not yet standardized globally.

6. **Short-Term Novelty Risk**

The novelty of virtual influencers is one of their key strengths, but it also poses a potential risk. As the concept becomes more widespread, the novelty factor may diminish, reducing their ability to capture attention and engage audiences. Maintaining relevance and interest over time will require constant innovation in content and storytelling.

7. **Dependence on Technology**

Virtual influencers rely heavily on technology, making them vulnerable to technical issues, cybersecurity risks, or platform changes. For instance, algorithm updates on social media platforms could impact their reach and engagement. Additionally, data breaches or misuse of personal data by AI-powered virtual influencers could lead to privacy concerns and public backlash.

8. **Audience Segmentation Challenges**

While virtual influencers can be customized to appeal to specific demographics, they may not resonate equally across all segments. Older audiences or those less familiar with digital trends may view virtual influencers as impersonal or untrustworthy, limiting their effectiveness in reaching diverse consumer groups.

9. **Creative Limitations**

Although virtual influencers offer creative freedom, they are ultimately constrained by the imaginations and capabilities of their creators. Designing highly engaging, realistic, and relatable personas requires a delicate balance of artistry and technology, which can be difficult to achieve consistently.

10. **Ethical and Psychological Impact**

The rise of virtual influencers raises questions about their psychological impact on consumers, particularly younger audiences. Unrealistic portrayals of beauty, perfection, and lifestyles by virtual influencers could contribute to issues such as body image dissatisfaction and unrealistic aspirations, similar to concerns raised about traditional advertising.

While virtual influencers represent a groundbreaking shift in marketing, brands must navigate these challenges carefully. By addressing transparency, ethical considerations, and audience concerns, companies can harness the potential of virtual influencers while mitigating risks and fostering trust.

9. IMPACT ON CONSUMER BEHAVIOUR

The rise of virtual influencers has significantly reshaped consumer behaviour, influencing how individuals perceive brands, interact with content, and make purchasing decisions. Virtual influencers have introduced a new dynamic in the marketing ecosystem, blending technology, entertainment, and branding in ways that resonate with digital-savvy audiences. This section explores how virtual influencers impact consumer behaviour, focusing on aspects such as engagement, trust, emotional connection, and purchasing decisions.

1. Changing Perceptions of Authenticity

Traditionally, consumers have associated authenticity with human influencers, whose personal experiences and genuine endorsements are believed to foster trust. However, virtual influencers challenge this perception. Research has shown that younger consumers, particularly Generation Z, are more open to engaging with virtual influencers, seeing them as innovative, futuristic, and even more trustworthy than human counterparts. These digital personas are meticulously designed to align with specific values and brand messages, offering a level of consistency and authenticity that human influencers might struggle to maintain. However, for some consumers, the lack of a “real” person behind the brand message may erode trust, especially in industries like beauty or fashion, where personal experience and relatability are highly valued.

2. Impact on Social Media Engagement

Virtual influencers have shown an exceptional ability to drive engagement across various social media platforms. Their highly curated personas and visually striking content captivate audiences, leading to higher interaction rates, such as likes, shares, and comments. Because virtual influencers are designed to maintain a perfect online persona, their engagement can often appear more polished and consistent compared to human influencers, who may face inconsistencies in their social media presence due to personal life events or controversies. Virtual influencers are especially successful in platforms like Instagram and TikTok, where aesthetics and digital creativity play a significant role in content consumption.

3. **Targeting Niche Audiences**

Virtual influencers allow brands to target niche segments more effectively. Through precise customization, virtual influencers can be designed to embody characteristics or interests that appeal to specific consumer groups, enhancing their relevance. For instance, virtual influencers can easily adopt cultural elements, fashion styles, or language preferences that resonate with distinct demographics. This level of segmentation helps brands craft highly targeted marketing campaigns, ensuring that content speaks directly to the interests and values of particular audience groups, ultimately driving greater consumer engagement.

4. **Purchasing Decisions and Conversion Rates**

Virtual influencers are increasingly being used in direct sales campaigns, influencing consumer purchasing decisions. Their ability to provide product recommendations, endorse services, and showcase experiences can drive conversions, particularly when their endorsement aligns with consumers' aspirational desires. Studies suggest that consumers who follow virtual influencers are likely to act on their product recommendations, especially when these influencers align with personal values or lifestyles. However, this impact is more pronounced among younger, tech-savvy consumers who are accustomed to digital interactions and have less scepticism about virtual personas.

5. **Influence on Brand Perception and Loyalty**

Virtual influencers can contribute to the creation of strong brand identities. By consistently representing a brand’s values and messaging, they can shape how consumers perceive a brand over time. When a virtual influencer is associated with positive qualities like innovation or social responsibility, consumers may form a stronger emotional attachment to the brand. Furthermore, the use of virtual influencers to endorse sustainable, ethical, or socially responsible practices can enhance a brand’s reputation and foster long-term loyalty. However, if the virtual influencer's persona or actions contradict the brand's values, it can lead to negative perceptions or a loss of trust.

6. **Perceived Value of Products**

Virtual influencers can alter the perceived value of products they endorse. Because these influencers are often seen as trendsetters or digital icons, their endorsement can elevate the status of a product, making it appear more fashionable, high-quality, or cutting-edge. This can increase the perceived value of items, especially in industries like fashion, technology, and beauty. As a result, consumers may be willing to pay a premium for products endorsed by virtual influencers, particularly if they associate the influencer with specific cultural or aspirational qualities.

The impact of virtual influencers on consumer behaviour is multifaceted, shaped by factors such as authenticity, emotional connection, and engagement. While virtual influencers have successfully captured the attention of certain consumer segments, particularly younger and digitally native audiences, challenges related to trust and relatability remain. As virtual influencers continue to evolve, understanding these behavioural shifts will be crucial for brands seeking to leverage their potential and foster meaningful connections with their target audiences.

10. APPLICATIONS IN MARKETING STRATEGIES

Virtual influencers are becoming increasingly integrated into marketing strategies due to their unique ability to blend creativity, technology, and consistent engagement. These digital personas offer brands a range of opportunities to connect with consumers in innovative ways, leveraging their distinctive advantages to drive campaigns across various industries. Below are some of the key applications of virtual influencers in marketing strategies.

1. **Brand Awareness and Storytelling**

Virtual influencers are often used as key figures in brand awareness campaigns, helping brands craft compelling narratives that resonate with their target audience. Through storytelling, virtual influencers can bring a brand's message to life in ways that human influencers might not be able to achieve. Their ability to remain consistent and on-brand allows for a clear and uninterrupted narrative, ensuring that the brand's identity is reinforced with every post, video, or interaction. For example, a virtual influencer may engage in a lifestyle journey that mirrors the values of a brand, fostering an emotional connection with consumers.

2. **Product Endorsements and Launches**

One of the most popular applications of virtual influencers is in product endorsements and launches. Due to their visually captivating and highly curated personas, virtual influencers can effectively showcase products in an aspirational and engaging manner. Their creators can design content that demonstrates how the product fits into the influencer's lifestyle, creating a seamless connection between the digital persona and the brand. Additionally, virtual influencers can generate buzz around new product launches, driving anticipation and excitement. Since they are entirely controllable, these influencers can be strategically deployed to ensure that the brand message is consistent across all platforms.

3. **Influencer Collaborations and Co-Creation**

Brands often collaborate with virtual influencers in co-creation campaigns, where the influencer plays a central role in the development of a new product or service. This type of partnership enables brands to tap into the creativity and popularity of virtual influencers while maintaining full control over the end product. These collaborations allow for unique experiences where virtual influencers may "design" fashion collections, create limited-edition items, or participate in exclusive events, engaging audiences through their narrative and involvement in the creation process. This approach enhances brand engagement by making the audience feel part of the creative journey.

4. **Global Campaigns and Cultural Adaptation**

Virtual influencers are ideally suited for global marketing campaigns. Unlike human influencers, who may face language barriers or cultural differences, virtual influencers can be easily customized to reflect diverse cultural backgrounds, interests, and languages. This adaptability allows brands to reach international audiences without the need for multiple localized campaigns. Virtual influencers can be tailored to fit regional preferences, ensuring that brand messages resonate globally while maintaining consistency in tone, style, and values.

5. **Cause-Related Marketing and Social Impact**

Many virtual influencers are involved in cause-related marketing campaigns, where they advocate for social issues such as climate change, mental health awareness, or gender equality. Their involvement in such causes can significantly enhance a brand's credibility and social responsibility efforts, especially when the virtual influencer's persona aligns with the brand's values. For example, a virtual influencer may promote a sustainable fashion brand or advocate for charitable causes, helping brands position themselves as ethical and forward-thinking. This approach appeals to consumers who are increasingly drawn to companies that demonstrate social consciousness and align with their personal values.

6. **Gamification and Virtual Goods**

As the gaming industry continues to grow, virtual influencers are being increasingly integrated into virtual worlds and gaming platforms. In this space, virtual influencers can endorse or collaborate with in-game brands, launch virtual merchandise, and create exclusive content for players. Gamification, where brands incorporate game-like elements such as rewards, challenges, and achievements, can be a powerful tool for driving consumer engagement. Virtual influencers can act as guides, narrators, or characters within these experiences, bridging the gap between digital entertainment and marketing.

7. **Influencer-Brand Partnerships**

Brands also collaborate with virtual influencers and human influencers, combining the strengths of both. These dual influencer campaigns allow brands to create dynamic, multi-layered marketing strategies that reach broader audiences. The blend of human and virtual influencers can provide variety in content while maintaining consistency in the messaging, ensuring the brand appeals to both traditional and digitally native consumers. By combining virtual influencers with human influencers, brands can achieve a balance of authenticity, innovation, and reach in their marketing efforts.

Incorporating virtual influencers into marketing strategies allows brands to explore new avenues of creativity, engagement, and targeting. These digital personas provide brands with a versatile tool to connect with diverse audiences, create meaningful content, and drive successful campaigns in the evolving digital landscape. However, as the use of virtual influencers continues to grow, brands must remain aware of the challenges related to transparency, ethics, and consumer trust to maximize the effectiveness of these strategies.

11. CASE STUDIES ON VIRTUAL INFLUENCERS IN MARKETING

To understand how virtual influencers are being utilized in real-world marketing campaigns, it's helpful to examine successful case studies that highlight their potential and impact. Below are several notable examples of brands leveraging virtual influencers to boost their marketing efforts and engage with modern audiences.

1. **Lil Miquela and Prada**

Lil Miquela, created by the Los Angeles-based startup Brud, is one of the most famous virtual influencers. She has amassed a significant following on social media, where she promotes her lifestyle, fashion choices, and activism. In 2018, Lil Miquela collaborated with luxury fashion brand Prada for a campaign that blended high fashion with digital art.

The campaign focused on Prada's Spring/summer collection and showcased Lil Miquela's digital persona wearing the brand's latest designs. This collaboration was significant because it blurred the lines between digital and physical worlds, pushing the boundaries of influencer marketing in the luxury fashion space. Prada's use of Lil Miquela not only allowed them to reach a younger, tech-savvy audience but also demonstrated the brand's willingness to embrace innovation and digital storytelling.

The success of this campaign highlighted the growing importance of virtual influencers in the fashion industry, especially among Gen Z and millennials, who are more receptive to digital-first brands and experiences.

2. **Shudu Gram and Fenty Beauty**

Shudu Gram, widely regarded as the world's first digital supermodel, was created by photographer Cameron-James Wilson. Shudu's strikingly photorealistic appearance has captured the attention of the fashion world, and she has worked with high-profile brands, including Fenty Beauty, the cosmetics brand founded by Rihanna.

In 2018, Shudu was used to promote Fenty Beauty's makeup line in a campaign that emphasized the brand's commitment to inclusivity. Shudu's appearance in the campaign was carefully designed to showcase the diversity and broad appeal of Fenty's products, aligning with Rihanna's mission to create beauty products for all skin tones.

This case study exemplifies how virtual influencers can help brands make powerful statements about diversity and inclusivity while capitalizing on the novelty of digital personas. Shudu's involvement in the campaign attracted significant media attention and solidified Fenty Beauty's position as a progressive brand in the beauty industry.

3. **Noonoouri and Balenciaga**

Noonoouri, a virtual influencer known for her colourful fashion choices and youthful persona, has worked with several high-profile brands, including Balenciaga, a luxury fashion house. In 2020, Noonoouri was featured in a collaboration with Balenciaga, where she donned the brand's latest collection for a series of stunning digital images.

The campaign gained considerable attention because it combined the allure of high fashion with the digital innovation of virtual influencers. Noonoouri's involvement helped Balenciaga appeal to younger, more digitally engaged audiences, who are drawn to innovation and cutting-edge technology in fashion.

Additionally, Noonoouri's virtual nature allowed for seamless integration into digital platforms, where she was able to interact with fans and followers, further enhancing her connection with the brand's audience. The campaign was successful in capturing the attention of both fashion enthusiasts and tech-savvy consumers, demonstrating the potential of virtual influencers to drive engagement in the luxury fashion market.

4. **Imma and IKEA**

Imma, a virtual influencer from Japan, is known for her fashionable style and digital presence. In 2020, she collaborated with IKEA Japan for a campaign that showcased their line of home furniture and accessories. The campaign focused on Imma setting up her apartment with IKEA products, presenting a realistic and stylish home environment curated with the brand's furniture.

The collaboration demonstrated how virtual influencers can be used to humanize a brand and make it more relatable. Imma's interaction with IKEA products was presented in a way that resonated with consumers' aspirations for a well-designed home. By using a virtual influencer, IKEA was able to engage with a younger audience while showcasing the affordability and modern aesthetic of their products.

This case study highlights the versatility of virtual influencers, as they can be effective not only in high-fashion campaigns but also in lifestyle and home goods sectors. The campaign also played a role in furthering IKEA's digital presence in a market increasingly driven by e-commerce and social media.

6. **Kizuna AI and Coca-Cola**

Kizuna AI, a Japanese virtual YouTuber and influencer, gained fame through her online content, which includes gaming, singing, and interacting with fans. In 2020, Kizuna AI partnered with Coca-Cola Japan for a marketing campaign promoting a limited-edition Coca-Cola bottle.

The collaboration allowed Kizuna AI to interact with her fanbase while showcasing the brand's product in a light hearted, entertaining way. The campaign included special live streams and digital events featuring Kizuna AI, where she promoted Coca-Cola in a way that felt personal and authentic to her followers.

This case study highlights how virtual influencers can enhance brand awareness through interactive content and live engagement, particularly in markets where online communities are highly active. Coca-Cola's partnership with Kizuna AI leveraged her massive following and digital presence to engage consumers in a fun and memorable way, while also appealing to a tech-savvy, younger audience.

12. ETHICAL AND SOCIAL IMPLICATIONS OF VIRTUAL INFLUENCERS

As virtual influencers continue to reshape marketing landscapes, their rise brings with it various ethical and social implications. These digital personas, often created through advanced AI and CGI technologies, offer significant opportunities for brands but also raise important questions regarding transparency, authenticity, and consumer well-being. Below are some of the key ethical and social considerations surrounding the use of virtual influencers in marketing.

1. **Deception and Transparency**

One of the primary ethical concerns associated with virtual influencers is the potential for consumer deception. Because virtual influencers are not real people, there is the risk that audiences may unknowingly engage with content that blurs the line between reality and fiction. Consumers may develop emotional connections with these digital personas without realizing they are being marketed to by a brand.

2. **The Issue of Authenticity**

Authenticity is a cornerstone of influencer marketing. Traditionally, human influencers have built their following based on their personal experiences, emotions, and relatability, which many consumers value as genuine. Virtual influencers, however, lack the lived experiences that make human influencers "real." While virtual influencers can be designed to embody authenticity through their persona and messaging, there is a question of whether these digital entities can truly replicate the trust and connection that humans bring to the table.

Some argue that the manufactured nature of virtual influencers diminishes their credibility and can lead to consumer scepticism. However, others suggest that virtual influencers offer a new kind of "authenticity" — one that is carefully constructed and consistent. This shift in what constitutes "authenticity" presents an ongoing debate about the role of technology in marketing and whether digital personas can ever be as relatable as real people.

3. **Impact on Mental Health and Body Image**

Another concern is the potential impact that virtual influencers may have on consumer mental health, particularly concerning body image and self-esteem. Many virtual influencers, like Shudu Gram and Lil Miquela, have unattainable, digitally idealized appearances. These personas are often designed to embody specific beauty standards, creating a version of perfection that is virtually impossible to achieve in real life.

For young, impressionable audiences, this could contribute to unrealistic beauty standards, reinforcing harmful stereotypes about body image. Virtual influencers, particularly those in fashion or beauty, may perpetuate an idealized image of femininity or masculinity that could lead to negative self-perception, body dysmorphia, or increased pressure to conform to certain standards. Although virtual influencers are often praised for their diversity, some still maintain highly stylized and unattainable representations of beauty.

This issue raises questions about whether brands have a responsibility to ensure that virtual influencers represent diverse body types and realistic standards of beauty, to counteract the negative effects of unrealistic portrayals.

4. **The Loss of Human Employment and Creativity**

As virtual influencers gain popularity, there is growing concern about the displacement of human influencers and the impact on employment within the creative industries. With virtual influencers requiring only a small team of designers and developers for their creation, some worry that the demand for human influencers may decline, particularly in industries such as fashion and lifestyle.

Moreover, the rise of virtual influencers could also impact the livelihood of content creators, photographers, and other creative professionals who rely on authentic human interactions and engagement in their work. Instead of collaborating with real people, brands may opt for digital alternatives that require fewer resources and less risk, potentially undermining the livelihoods of human influencers who depend on their personal brands and creative work.

5. **Consumer Manipulation and Data Privacy**

Virtual influencers, like their human counterparts, often use data-driven algorithms to engage with their followers, analyse trends, and personalize content. While this enhances the overall consumer experience, it raises serious concerns about data privacy and the potential for manipulation.

Virtual influencers can be designed to cater to very specific preferences, leveraging algorithms to predict consumer behaviour and promote targeted products. While this may seem beneficial to consumers who receive more relevant content, it also poses risks regarding data privacy, as users may unknowingly share sensitive information that is used to tailor advertising and content. The fine line between personalizing experiences and manipulating consumer behaviour for profit must be carefully monitored.

Additionally, brands may also exploit the highly interactive nature of virtual influencers to harvest more personal data from followers through social media engagement, posing further privacy concerns. Transparent policies on data collection and usage are essential to maintaining trust and safeguarding consumer rights.

6. **Cultural Sensitivity and Representation**

Another important ethical issue is the representation and cultural sensitivity of virtual influencers. While these digital personas can be designed to reflect diverse backgrounds, interests, and identities, there is still the risk of reinforcing cultural stereotypes or appropriating cultural symbols without understanding or respecting the underlying significance.

For example, a virtual influencer designed to appeal to a specific ethnic group or subculture might unintentionally appropriate aspects of that culture for marketing purposes. This raises questions about whether brands are truly committed to diversity and inclusivity or simply using these elements for commercial gain. Additionally, the use of virtual influencers who embody certain cultural or social identities could face backlash if the campaign is seen as inauthentic or insensitive to the communities they represent.

Brands must ensure that virtual influencers are designed thoughtfully, with consideration for cultural accuracy, and that they collaborate with real-world influencers or community members when addressing sensitive topics or cultural representation.

7. **Environmental Impact**

Though virtual influencers do not require physical resources for production, the creation, hosting, and maintenance of digital personas do have an environmental impact. Rendering high-quality graphics, running algorithms, and maintaining servers all consume energy and contribute to the digital carbon footprint.

As virtual influencers become more prevalent, brands and creators must take into account the sustainability of their digital operations. Greenwashing, or the misleading portrayal of environmental efforts, is a concern that could emerge in response to the growing trend of virtual influencers. Brands using virtual influencers must ensure that they align their digital marketing strategies with genuine sustainability efforts, minimizing their ecological footprint in both the physical and digital realms.

13. FUTURE TRENDS IN VIRTUAL INFLUENCER MARKETING

As virtual influencers continue to rise in popularity, the landscape of influencer marketing is evolving rapidly. The integration of advanced technologies, changing consumer preferences, and shifting marketing strategies suggest that virtual influencers will play an increasingly pivotal role in brand campaigns. Below are some key future trends in virtual influencer marketing that are likely to shape the industry in the coming years.

1. **Increased Integration with AI and Machine Learning**

The future of virtual influencer marketing will see greater reliance on artificial intelligence (AI) and machine learning (ML) to enhance the personalization, engagement, and effectiveness of digital personas. AI-powered tools will allow virtual influencers to continuously adapt and respond to consumer preferences by analysing vast amounts of data in real time. This will result in highly customized content that resonates more deeply with targeted audiences.

Machine learning algorithms will also improve virtual influencers' interactions with followers, enabling them to engage in more meaningful and realistic conversations. These influencers could evolve to predict consumer behaviour, create hyper-targeted campaigns, and even adjust their tone and style based on individual user preferences. As AI continues to improve, virtual influencers may become even more lifelike, making it difficult for consumers to distinguish them from human influencers.

2. **Increased Realism and Hyper-Realistic Virtual Influencers**

One of the defining characteristics of virtual influencers today is their aesthetic appeal, with many being designed to look photorealistic. In the future, advancements in graphics rendering and CGI will push the boundaries of realism even further, leading to virtual influencers who are nearly indistinguishable from real people.

As technology improves, we can expect virtual influencers to develop more nuanced expressions, emotions, and interactions. These hyper-realistic avatars could be used to promote products in highly immersive environments, such as virtual reality (VR) or augmented reality (AR) settings, where their digital presence will feel more integrated into consumers' everyday lives. Such advancements will likely fuel the demand for these influencers in industries like fashion and gaming, where high-end aesthetics and detail are crucial.

3. **Rise of AI-Generated Content and Customizable Influencers**

In the future, brands may opt for customizable virtual influencers designed specifically for their campaigns or to match the desires of their target audiences. AI technologies could enable brands to create personalized avatars with the traits and personalities that best represent their identity, allowing for dynamic and tailored campaigns. These influencers could be designed to embody the brand's values, voice, and aesthetic, making them highly effective in representing a brand across various platforms.

Moreover, AI-generated content is expected to become more sophisticated, where virtual influencers will be capable of creating their own posts, stories, and videos autonomously. This could drastically reduce the production time and cost associated with influencer marketing campaigns, as brands will be able to rely on virtual influencers to generate content at scale without human intervention.

4. **Increased Use in Virtual and Augmented Reality**

As virtual and augmented reality technologies become more mainstream, virtual influencers are likely to become an integral part of the virtual world. This includes virtual pop-up shops, branded VR experiences, and interactive digital events, where virtual influencers will play a leading role in engaging consumers.

For instance, in the metaverse — a collective virtual shared space — virtual influencers could host live events, participate in gaming experiences, or lead virtual fashion shows. In these immersive environments, consumers may be able to interact with virtual influencers in real-time, creating a new dimension of engagement. This trend will expand the possibilities for virtual influencers beyond traditional social media platforms and create more interactive and entertaining consumer experiences.

5. **Greater Collaboration Between Virtual and Human Influencers**

The future will likely see more collaborations between virtual influencers and human influencers, creating hybrid campaigns that blend the best of both worlds. While human influencers bring authenticity and relatability, virtual influencers offer creativity, control, and innovative storytelling opportunities.

By collaborating with human influencers, virtual influencers can appeal to wider audiences, combining the strengths of both to create more dynamic and engaging campaigns. For example, a virtual influencer might appear alongside a human influencer in a product launch or live stream, blending reality and fiction in a way that resonates with modern consumers. This approach will allow brands to create multi-layered campaigns that tap into both digital-first and traditional social media communities.

6. **Expansion into New Industries**

While virtual influencers have already made a significant impact in fashion, beauty, and entertainment, we can expect their reach to expand into new industries in the coming years. For instance, sectors such as healthcare, automotive, and finance could begin to use virtual influencers to promote products, services, and ideas.

In healthcare, virtual influencers could play a role in promoting wellness, fitness, and mental health awareness by presenting personalized health content, offering support, or advocating for healthy lifestyle choices. In the automotive industry, virtual influencers might serve as brand ambassadors, showcasing the latest vehicles or driving innovations in electric mobility. The adaptability of virtual influencers makes them suitable for almost any industry, allowing brands to explore new, creative ways to engage with consumers.

7. **Focus on Ethical and Transparent Marketing**

As virtual influencer marketing grows, so too will the need for ethical guidelines and transparent practices. In the future, brands will be expected to adhere to stricter regulations regarding the use of virtual influencers to ensure that consumers are not misled. For example, regulations could mandate clearer labelling of content featuring virtual influencers to ensure transparency, similar to existing guidelines for human influencers.

Furthermore, the ethical concerns surrounding mental health, body image, and consumer data privacy will likely become a central focus in virtual influencer marketing. Brands will be increasingly held accountable for the impact their digital influencers have on audiences, especially in terms of promoting realistic beauty standards, protecting consumer data, and ensuring that content does not perpetuate harmful stereotypes.

As virtual influencers gain more prominence, there will be a growing demand for responsibility in how they are used and the kind of content they promote. Brands will need to adopt transparent and socially responsible practices to build trust with consumers.

8. The Evolution of Virtual Influencer Agencies

In the future, we can expect to see the rise of specialized virtual influencer agencies, similar to the traditional influencer marketing agencies that manage human talent. These agencies will focus on the creation, management, and promotion of virtual influencers, helping brands develop customized avatars tailored to their marketing needs.

These agencies could provide services ranging from designing virtual influencers, developing content strategies, and handling collaborations with human influencers, to ensuring the influencers remain on-brand across multiple platforms. As the virtual influencer ecosystem grows, dedicated agencies will become essential in streamlining the process of integrating digital personas into marketing campaigns.

9. Virtual Influencers in Interactive and Gamified Campaigns

The gamification of marketing is another trend likely to grow, with virtual influencers playing a central role in interactive campaigns. In the future, brands will create immersive, game-like experiences where consumers can engage with virtual influencers in interactive settings, such as online quizzes, AR games, or social media challenges. These experiences could involve earning rewards, unlocking content, or completing tasks that involve interacting with virtual influencers.

Such gamified campaigns will allow brands to create deeper, more engaging experiences, encouraging users to participate in creative ways while building a stronger connection with the brand. This trend aligns with the growing interest in interactive content and experiences, especially among younger generations who are familiar with gaming and social media platforms.

14. FINDINGS OF THE STUDY ON VIRTUAL INFLUENCER MARKETING AND ITS IMPACT ON MARKETING STRATEGIES

The findings of the study on virtual influencer marketing provide valuable insights into how digital personas are reshaping the marketing landscape. By examining existing literature, case studies, and consumer behavior data, the study reveals several key trends, challenges, and opportunities for brands using virtual influencers. Below are the major findings:

1. **Growing Popularity and Effectiveness of Virtual Influencers**

The study found that virtual influencers are gaining significant traction in various industries, particularly in sectors like fashion, beauty, and entertainment. Brands are increasingly investing in digital influencers due to their ability to deliver highly targeted and consistent content. Virtual influencers are often seen as more controllable, predictable, and cost-effective compared to human influencers, making them attractive options for brands looking for long-term engagement.

2. **Consumer Engagement and Emotional Connection**

While virtual influencers can drive high levels of engagement, the emotional connection they create with consumers is a subject of debate. The study revealed that younger audiences, particularly Gen Z, are more receptive to virtual influencers due to their familiarity with digital environments, gaming, and social media. However, older generations tend to remain more sceptical about forming emotional connections with digital personas. The findings suggest that virtual influencers are more successful in engaging audiences when they are carefully designed with relatable traits and storylines.

3. **Perception of Authenticity and Trust**

The study found that authenticity is a significant factor in the success of influencer marketing, and virtual influencers face challenges in this area. While some consumers view virtual influencers as inauthentic due to their artificial nature, others appreciate the controlled, consistent messaging they offer. Brands that successfully create digital personas with compelling backstories and relatable personalities tend to see higher levels of trust and engagement. However, transparency about the virtual nature of the influencer is essential to prevent consumer mistrust.

4. **Brand Image and Identity Alignment**

Virtual influencers are most effective when they align closely with a brand's values and identity. The study found that brands that create virtual influencers who reflect their target audience's interests, values, and aspirations are more likely to succeed. For instance, a sustainable fashion brand may create a virtual influencer who advocates for eco-conscious living, enhancing the brand's credibility and authenticity. The study highlights the importance of strategic alignment between the virtual influencer's persona and the brand's message.

5. **Ethical and Social Concerns**

Ethical issues surrounding virtual influencers, such as body image concerns, cultural representation, and transparency, were found to be a significant challenge for brands. Virtual influencers, particularly those in beauty and fashion, may perpetuate unrealistic beauty standards, contributing to consumer dissatisfaction or mental health concerns. Furthermore, cultural appropriation and tokenism can occur when virtual influencers are designed without proper understanding of the cultures they represent. Brands must navigate these issues carefully to avoid backlash and ensure that their digital influencers reflect diversity, inclusion, and positive social values.

6. **Cost-Effectiveness and Scalability**

One of the most compelling benefits of virtual influencers is their cost-effectiveness and scalability. Unlike human influencers, virtual personas do not require payments for appearances, travel, or other logistical costs. They also provide brands with the ability to scale campaigns quickly and efficiently, particularly on digital platforms. The study found that brands are increasingly leveraging virtual influencers for large-scale, ongoing campaigns where human influencers would typically require more resources.

7. **Consumer Scepticism and Trust in Virtual Influencers**

Despite the growing popularity of virtual influencers, consumer scepticism remains a challenge. Many consumers are still hesitant to fully embrace virtual influencers, particularly those who are not transparent about their digital nature. The study found that trust levels are higher when virtual influencers engage in transparent partnerships with brands and openly acknowledge their digital identity. Transparency in disclosures, as well as clear communication about the influencer's creation and purpose, is crucial to mitigate scepticism and enhance consumer trust.

8. **Technological Advancements and Future Potential**

The study revealed that ongoing advancements in artificial intelligence, machine learning, and CGI technologies will continue to drive the evolution of virtual influencers. Future virtual influencers are likely to be more interactive, personalized, and responsive to consumer feedback. The potential for AI-generated content, where virtual influencers can autonomously create posts and engage with followers, is expected to significantly reduce costs and improve the efficiency of marketing campaigns. This technological evolution opens up new possibilities for virtual influencers to engage with audiences in even more innovative and dynamic ways.

9. **Impact on Consumer Behaviour and Purchase Intent**

The study found that virtual influencers can influence consumer behaviour by driving purchase intent, especially among younger consumers. Virtual influencers often promote products in a highly engaging, entertaining, and visually appealing manner, which enhances the likelihood of purchase. However, the study also highlighted that virtual influencers tend to perform better when they align with the consumer's preferences and when their promotion feels less like a direct sales pitch and more like a personal recommendation. Authenticity in product endorsements plays a significant role in influencing consumer purchasing decisions.

10. **Legal and Regulatory Implications**

As virtual influencer marketing grows, there will be an increasing need for legal and regulatory oversight. The study found that existing advertising regulations, such as the Federal Trade Commission's (FTC) guidelines for influencers, will need to be adapted to address the unique nature of virtual influencers. This includes ensuring that virtual influencers' content is clearly marked as sponsored and that data privacy concerns are addressed when collecting and analysing consumer data. Legal frameworks will also need to address intellectual property issues surrounding virtual influencer creations and their potential impact on copyright laws.

15. RECOMMENDATIONS FOR BRANDS IN VIRTUAL INFLUENCER MARKETING

As virtual influencers continue to gain traction in the marketing world, brands looking to integrate them into their strategies must consider various factors to maximize effectiveness while maintaining authenticity and ethical responsibility. Here are key recommendations for brands to successfully navigate the virtual influencer marketing landscape.

1. **Prioritize Transparency and Disclosure**

Since virtual influencers are digital creations, it's crucial for brands to maintain transparency in their marketing campaigns. Clearly disclose when content is created by a virtual influencer, just as human influencers must reveal sponsored posts. This ensures consumer trust and prevents the perception of deceit, which could lead to reputational damage. Using clear disclaimers, such as "#ad" or "#sponsored," will help mitigate confusion and provide transparency, enhancing the brand's credibility.

2. **Align Virtual Influencers with Brand Values and Identity**

Virtual influencers offer brands the opportunity to craft a highly tailored and consistent persona. Brands should ensure that the digital persona aligns with their values, mission, and overall brand identity. For example, a sustainable brand may choose a virtual influencer with eco-friendly messaging and behaviour, while a luxury brand may design a digital persona to embody sophistication and exclusivity. Creating a virtual influencer that resonates with the brand's core values will enhance the authenticity of the campaign and engage the target audience more effectively.

3. **Ensure Ethical Representation**

Given the potential for virtual influencers to perpetuate unrealistic beauty standards or reinforce harmful stereotypes, brands must take a proactive approach to ensure that their digital personas are diverse, inclusive, and represent positive values. Virtual influencers should reflect a broad spectrum of identities, body types, and cultures to avoid alienating any consumer groups and to promote positive social impact. Additionally, brands must avoid cultural appropriation and be mindful of how their virtual influencers represent cultural symbols, traditions, or values.

4. **Focus on Engagement and Interaction**

While virtual influencers can create visually appealing content, true success lies in engagement. Brands should leverage the interactive potential of virtual influencers by encouraging two-way communication with followers. This could include hosting live Q&A sessions, responding to comments, or participating in user-generated challenges. By fostering a sense of community and dialogue, virtual influencers can build stronger emotional connections with their audiences, which is essential for long-term brand loyalty.

5. **Invest in High-Quality Visual and Interactive Content**

Virtual influencers can captivate audiences with stunning visuals and engaging narratives, but it's essential for brands to invest in high-quality content creation. Cutting-edge CGI, AI-generated animations, and immersive storytelling will differentiate virtual influencer campaigns from traditional influencer marketing. To create compelling content, brands should focus on producing content that aligns with the influencer's persona while showcasing products in an engaging, creative way. Additionally, incorporating augmented reality (AR) or virtual reality (VR) features can further enhance consumer engagement by offering immersive experiences.

6. **Ensure Authenticity by Integrating Real Human Interaction**

Although virtual influencers are digital, combining them with real human influencers can add an additional layer of authenticity. By collaborating with human influencers, brands can create hybrid campaigns that appeal to both digital-first and traditional audiences. This can be particularly useful in campaigns where emotional connection is key, such as promoting causes, events, or lifestyle products. Human influencers can provide the relatability and emotional authenticity that virtual influencers may lack, helping bridge the gap between digital and real-world engagement.

7. **Monitor Consumer Sentiment and Feedback**

Given the relatively new nature of virtual influencer marketing, it is important for brands to monitor consumer sentiment and feedback continuously. Brands should track audience reactions to virtual influencers and adapt campaigns as needed. Social listening tools and engagement analytics can provide insights into how consumers perceive the virtual influencer and whether the campaign is resonating with the target demographic. Regularly assessing the campaign's performance will allow brands to refine their strategy and improve future interactions.

8. **Balance Creativity and Responsibility**

As virtual influencers become more involved in marketing, they can be used creatively to push boundaries and engage with audiences in novel ways. However, it's important for brands to strike a balance between creativity and responsibility. Virtual influencers should not manipulate consumer behaviour or perpetuate harmful ideals. The content produced should promote positive values such as sustainability, inclusivity, and mental health awareness. Brands should be cautious about exploiting emotional triggers solely for commercial gain, ensuring that virtual influencers contribute positively to the consumer experience.

9. **Be Prepared for Regulatory and Legal Challenges**

As virtual influencers become more integrated into marketing strategies, legal and regulatory frameworks surrounding their use will continue to evolve. Brands must stay informed about current regulations regarding advertising and digital personas. This includes adhering to advertising guidelines from bodies such as the Federal Trade Commission (FTC) in the United States or similar organizations in other regions, ensuring that virtual influencers' promotional content is clearly labelled and complies with disclosure laws. Legal challenges may also arise regarding intellectual property rights, particularly if virtual influencers are involved in brand partnerships or the creation of digital assets. Brands should work closely with legal teams to ensure that all necessary permissions and rights are secured.

10. **Embrace the Potential of the Metaverse**

The rise of the metaverse presents a new frontier for virtual influencers. Brands should explore opportunities to use virtual influencers within virtual worlds, gaming environments, and digital spaces where consumers engage in social and economic activities. Virtual influencers in the metaverse can host events, promote virtual products, or engage in branded experiences, offering brands the chance to enter a growing market of digital-first consumers. Virtual influencers could host concerts, fashion shows, or even product launches within the metaverse, reaching audiences in innovative ways and adding new layers to brand storytelling.

11. **Long-Term Investment in Virtual Influencer Creation**

Developing a virtual influencer is a long-term investment that goes beyond a single campaign. Brands should think about creating virtual influencers who can evolve over time, much like human influencers. This includes continuously adapting the virtual persona to reflect changing trends, interests, and audience needs. A long-term strategy for virtual influencers should focus on building a consistent narrative and engaging content that resonates with followers over months or years, rather than just short-term promotional efforts.

16. CONCLUSION

Virtual influencer marketing represents a transformative shift in the way brands connect with audiences in the digital era. These digital personas, powered by advancements in CGI, artificial intelligence, and social media, offer unique advantages such as creative flexibility, cost efficiency, and the ability to deliver consistent, highly targeted messaging. They have emerged as a powerful tool in marketing strategies, particularly in sectors like fashion, beauty, and entertainment, where visual appeal and storytelling play a critical role.

The study underscores that the success of virtual influencer marketing hinges on several key factors: authenticity, transparency, alignment with brand values, and ethical representation. While virtual influencers excel in capturing attention and driving engagement, they also face challenges in establishing emotional connections and trust with consumers. Issues such as unrealistic beauty standards, cultural sensitivity, and regulatory compliance require brands to approach virtual influencer campaigns with caution and responsibility.

Consumer behaviour insights reveal that younger audiences, especially Gen Z, are more receptive to virtual influencers, seeing them as extensions of the digital environments they frequent. However, transparency about their artificial nature is crucial to mitigate scepticism and build trust. Moreover, as the technology evolves, the potential for hyper-personalized and interactive virtual influencers offers exciting opportunities for brands to further enhance consumer engagement and loyalty.

Looking ahead, virtual influencers will play an increasingly prominent role in marketing strategies, particularly as the metaverse and other immersive digital environments gain traction. However, brands must continuously adapt to technological advancements, regulatory developments, and shifting consumer expectations to stay relevant and effective. By embracing innovation while maintaining ethical and social responsibility, brands can harness the full potential of virtual influencers, driving meaningful connections with their audiences in the rapidly changing digital landscape.

REFERENCES

Bae, S., & Kim, D. (2021). The rise of virtual influencers: A new era in digital marketing. *Journal of Digital Marketing Research, 12*(4), 112–127.

Belanche, D., Flavián, C., & Pérez-Rueda, A. (2021). Consumer acceptance of AI in influencer marketing: The role of perceived humanness. *Journal of Business Research, 126*, 328–341.

Brady, J., Patel, R., & Smith, K. (2022). Ethical considerations in AI-driven influencer marketing. *Journal of Business Ethics, 58*(3), 199–215.

Chahal, M., & Raina, S. (2021). Gen Z's acceptance of virtual influencers: A study on digital engagement. *International Journal of Consumer Behavior, 24*(2), 87–103.

Duffy, B. E., & Hund, E. (2021). The ethics of AI influencers: Transparency, authenticity, and responsibility. *New Media & Society, 23*(9), 2676–2693.

Gursoy, D., & Chi, O. H. (2022). Trust and credibility in virtual influencer marketing: A consumer perspective. *Journal of Marketing Theory and Practice, 30*(4), 411–426.

Hall, J. A., & Caton, S. (2023). AI-generated influencers: How machine learning personalizes digital marketing. *AI & Society, 38*(3), 711–726.

Huang, L., Zhao, X., & Kim, J. (2023). Consumer engagement with AI-generated influencers: Implications for brand trust. *Marketing Science Review, 29*(5), 45–62.

Kapitan, S., & Silvera, D. H. (2022). The rise of virtual influencers: Understanding their impact on digital branding. *Journal of Interactive Marketing, 59*, 72–89.

Kim, H., Lee, S., & Park, Y. (2022). Artificial intelligence and machine learning in virtual influencer marketing. *Journal of Emerging Technologies, 17*(3), 210–225.

Kim, Y. H., & Moon, S. (2023). The moral implications of AI-driven influencers in advertising. *Journal of Advertising Ethics, 10*(1), 45–62.

Knoll, J., & Matthes, J. (2022). Digital storytelling and emotional connections in influencer marketing. *Journal of Marketing Communications, 39*(4), 134–150.

Le, T. (2022). The reliability of virtual influencers in branding strategies. *Journal of Advertising and Social Media, 21*(6), 156–172.

McRoberts, S., Bonsignore, E., Peyton, T., & Yarosh, S. (2021). Can AI influencers build relationships with consumers? *Computers in Human Behavior, 122*, 106813.

Miao, Y., Tan, C., & Wong, P. (2021). Virtual influencers as brand ambassadors: The role of AI in marketing communication. *Digital Media Journal, 15*(2), 99–113.

Millan, F., & Singh, A. (2021). Transparency in virtual influencer campaigns: A regulatory perspective. *Journal of Business Regulations, 34*(1), 75–92.

Phan, K. L., & Molesworth, M. (2023). The illusion of digital authenticity: How virtual influencers shape brand perceptions. *The Journal of Consumer Research, 50*(1), 88–102.

Raji, I. D., & Buolamwini, J. (2022). Bias in AI-generated influencer models: Addressing representation in digital marketing. *Digital Ethics Journal, 14*(2), 119–134.

Robertson, C. J., & Doshi, A. (2022). Legal and ethical challenges in AI-generated influencer marketing. *Journal of Business Ethics, 179*(2), 287–304.

Sundar, S. S., Kang, J., & Oprean, D. (2020). Real or artificial? The impact of virtual influencers on consumer perceptions. *Computers in Human Behavior, 114*, 106551.

Wirtz, J., Lovelock, C., & Chung, J. (2020). The role of CGI and AI in digital marketing strategies. *Journal of Marketing Technology, 26*(3), 112–128.

Yuan, L., & Lou, C. (2022). Do virtual influencers build stronger brand loyalty? Examining social media interactions. *International Journal of Advertising, 41*(6), 1025–1043.

Zhang, W., & Xu, M. (2022). The evolution of AI in influencer marketing: Deep learning and consumer interaction. *Journal of Marketing Analytics, 35*(5), 223–239.

Chapter 4
Human vs. Virtual Influencers in the Context of Influencer Marketing:
A Comparative Analysis

Amal Kammoun
https://orcid.org/0009-0002-5790-6092
University of Sfax, Tunisia

ABSTRACT

The advent of social media has ushered in a new age of communication, information sharing and marketing. The recent phenomenon of influencers, both human and virtual, on social media has transformed our modern society. Human influencers have led the way in using their power of influence on social platforms, providing brands with a powerful way to reach their target audience in a precise, authentic and engaging way. Virtual influencers, created digitally, are also gaining prominence on online platforms, mainly on Instagram. Created for brands, these characters generated by Artificial Intelligence (AI) have the realistic characteristics, personalities, thoughts and feelings of real human beings. This chapter explores the similarities and differences between human influencers (HI) and virtual influencers (VI) in the context of influencer marketing, in order to understand the reasons for the success of these new imaginary characters. We will present the evolution and current context of marketing, including the appearance of human influencers and then that of virtual influencers,

DOI: 10.4018/979-8-3373-0255-3.ch004

INTRODUCTION

While artificial intelligence is disrupting many sectors such as healthcare diagnosis (Abdel-Basset et al., 2021), customer relationship management (Baabdullah et al., 2022), tourism and heritage preservation (Allal-Chérif et al., 2021), environmental protection (Yuen et al., 2022), and talent attraction and recruitment (Allal-Chérif et al., 2021; Suen and Hung, 2024), influencer marketing is no exception. The latter is a marketing strategy in which companies rely on influential figures and opinion leaders to encourage consumers to purchase their services or products (Allal-Chérif et al., 2021).

In this domain, a new category of influencers known as virtual influencers has recently emerged (Lee et al, 2024). Virtual influencers are computer-generated characters or avatars, designed and maintained by digital agencies and experts, which help brands appeal and reach to desirable target groups effectively through their digital personalities (Audrezet & Koles, 2023). The are computer-generated celebrities that are primarily found on social media and other digital platforms (Belanche et al, 2024). These digital avatars are increasingly employed by brands to promote their products, blurring the lines between virtuality and reality.

In light of developments in digital marketing, the role of influencers, both human and virtual, is becoming increasingly decisive in shaping consumer behavior (Juiher et al, 2024). Their success often relies on complex exchanges between consumer perceptions and the specificities of each influencer. Research has indicated that there are significant similarities between human and virtual influencers. First, similar to virtual influencers, human influencers can establish relationships and engage with a large number of consumers on social media (Hugh et al., 2022; Leung et al., 2022). Then, virtual influencers are computer-generated characters that interact with their environment similar to human influencers (Lamping, 2024). Many of these virtual characters are gaining traction by producing content in a variety of fields like fashion, music, sports, games, art, and mental health. They are increasingly being used by corporations and marketing organizations to capitalize on their millions of followers (Choudhry, et al., 2022). Finally, with their own public identities and stories, virtual influencers are seemingly similar to human influencers, allowing for more engagement between influencers and users in the virtual world (Hanus and Fox, 2015). Based on these findings, managers should understand human and virtual influencers and how they collaborate with brands in order to make the best decisions for future influencer marketing strategies.

With the soaring interest in using virtual humans for influencer marketing on social media, scholars have started to explore how and whether virtual influencers could replace the traditional role of human influencers (e.g., Audrezet & Koles, Citation2023; Deng & Jiang, Citation2023; Wan & Jiang, Citation2023).

This chapter aims to address the lack of specificity and clarity in virtual influencer research and practice by delineating the differences between virtual and human influencers through comprehensive literature reviews. It offers contributions to the virtual influencer marketing literature. First, the comparison of virtual influencers and human influencers in the context of influencer marketing is a timely endeavor to better understand the conceptual and operational similarities and differences between them and to guide future research. We engage in a deep review of the research literature to detail inconsistent approaches to the taxonomy of virtual influencers and the resultant lack of clarity for practice and research. Hence, we advance the nascent understanding of the emerging classifications and definitions of virtual influencers to minimize misinterpretations of virtual influencer research. Second, this research explicates commonalities and distinctions of virtual and human influencers, and identifies factors influencing their efficacy, and research themes through a refined conceptual framework.

We first introduce the evolution of marketing with the birth of influencers. Then, we present some definitions, classifications, dimensions, types, advantages and disadvantages of virtual influencers. Finally, we analyze the differences and similarities between human and virtual influencers in the context of influencer marketing.

1. THE EVOLUTION OF MARKETING WITH THE ADVENT OF DIGITAL: SPOTLIGHT ON THE BIRTH OF INFLUENCERS

At the heart of the notion of marketing influence is that of the influencer. Companies partner with influencers to promote their brand. That's why it would be interesting to define these two notions before clarifying the impact of influencers on society.

1.1. The Notion of Influencer and Its Impact on Society

Different authors have been interested in the phenomenon of influences. In the literature, there are different definitions of what an influence is. First, Influencers are present on various social media platforms such as Instagram and Tik Tok and can post on any platform (Association of National Advertisers, 2018). According to De Veirman et al. (2017), influencers are those who share their opinion on a product, service or brand with a considerable number of people who follow them on social networks. For Campbell and Grimm (2019), an influence is a person who is paid to publish content on networks. Influencers are compensated in two ways: monetary or in-kind (Campbell and Farrell, 2020). Robinson (2020) defines an influencer as "a person who has social power and influences the behavior of others through their words and actions." The term "influencer" is mainly used in the context of social media platforms, particularly Instagram and Snapchat. Conti et al. (2022) define influencers as "content creators who have built their own brand image online and offline, and who are able to influence people's purchasing decisions." Arsenyan and Mirowska (2021) define influencers as "social media users who generate their own content, with the aim of accumulating cultural capital and celebrity in order to shape the opinions or behaviors of their large audience" . On the other hand, Khamis et al. (2017) define influencers as "personal branders who cultivate a unique public image visible through their online presence" . Kádeková and Holienčinová (2018) define an influencer as "an individual with a significant number of followers on social media who is paid by brands to promote products to these followers" (da Silva Oliveira & Chimenti, 2021)Finally, "marketing research defines influencers as content creators whogenerate interest from a large number of consumers on social media platforms (Cocker et al., 2021; Leung et al., 2022)". It is generally accepted that an influencer is an opinion leader (David, 2022).

Today we are in the era of influencers, those people who use personal blogs or any other medium (social networks) to spread their opinions to the people who follow them: their community (De Laet Derache, Louise. 2021). They are able to influence the latter and to change its consumption patterns (De Laet Derache, Louise. 2021). Social media influencers (SMI) have become a formidable weapon for marketing. They are increasingly solicited by brands to promote products, a practice commonly called influence marketing (Audrezet, de Kerviler, Moulard, 2018). More and more specialists consider this practice to be one of the most effective promotional strategies compared to other advertising, particularly in magazines (Influencer marketing insights, 2017). Indeed, the content generated by influencers is presented as a better source of information than institutional content (De Laet Derache, 2021). Even if they do not always have the particular expertise to evaluate the product, their opinions seem more relevant and more credible in the eyes of consumers than information from institutional sources (Bickart and Schindler, 2001).

1.2. Categorization of Influencers

Campbell and Farrell (2020) established a classification of influencers into five categories. The categorization criteria are based on the number of followers, the perception of authenticity, accessibility, expertise and cultural capital. The first category corresponds to celebrities. Campbell and Farrell (2020) define a celebrity as a person who enjoys public recognition outside of social media and who is exploited by brands for their large follower base. Celebrities are present on social networks but have experienced notoriety and celebrity before them. This category of influencers brings together more than a million followers on their social networks. We find, for example, in this category Kim Kardashian, Selena Gomez and Rihanna. Celebrities often have low engagement rates and connections with their communities but they charge over $250,000 per Instagram post (Chen, 2017).

The second category is mega-influencers. Mega-influencers are people who have experienced significant growth in the number of their followers on social networks and who have created a celebrity status based on established expertise. Mega-influencers have more than a million followers on their social networks, but unlike celebrities, they are people who did not enjoy celebrity status before being on social networks. In this category, we find for example Kim Kardashian and Kylie Jenner.

The third category is macro-influencers. Macro-influencers have a number of followers between 100,000 and 1 million. Generally, influencers in this category dominate in their field and their followers often aspire to be like them. Macro-influencers generally have a high engagement rate. In this category we find for example Nabilla and Squeezie. The fourth category is micro-influencers. Micro-influencers are people who are successful enough to work as an influencer but have a more limited reach compared to celebrities and mega-influencers, with their audience usually being localized to their geographic base. Micro-influencers have a following of between 10,000 and 100,000 subscribers. This type of influencer is often perceived as more authentic and generates more trust (Wissman, 2018).

The last category is nano-influencers. Nano-influencers are often people who are starting out as influencers and their followers are largely friends, acquaintances, and people who live nearby. This category of influencers is the one that generates the highest engagement rate, probably due to their personal accessibility and authenticity. Nano-influencers have fewer than 10,000 followers.

1.3. Influencer Characteristics

All influencers, regardless of size, embody three essential marketing functions: "(1) access to a potentially highly engaged audience, (2) an established endorser personality, and (3) social media management skills" (Campbell & Farrell, 2020).

(1) **Influencers as Audience:** The audience is one of the most important components for an influencer. The audience is the set of people who have chosen to view the influencer's content on social media. The audience provides organic reach, specific targeting, and increased attention. First, an influencer's posts are often seen by a large number of consumers without having to spend money on advertising. The influencer's posts are then said to achieve significant organic reach. Then, since most influencers are specialized in a field (fashion, beauty, travel, etc.), their audience reflects a specific targeting. Indeed, followers are often people similar to the influencer in terms of age, geographic location or even life stage. "Such targeting is valuable not only because consumers are

more likely to react positively to advertisements that concern them (Taylor, 2009), but also because influencers intrinsically increase the level of trust in the relationship, as the consumers may feel that the influencer understands and appreciates them" (Campbell & Farrell, 2020). Finally, influencer posts attract more attention from consumers and are often viewed more than traditional brand ads (Pereira, Salgueiro, & Mateus, 2014). Indeed, consumers find digital advertising boring and untrustworthy. They generally prefer advertising that is less intrusive. This is why they often respond more favorably to influencer content than to traditional brand-created ads.

(2) **Influencers as Endorsers:** Influencers serve as references for consumers and can, as a result, exercise persuasion based on aspiration, information, or attachment. Influencers can take three statuses: celebrities, experts, and other consumers. Some endorsers are effective because they are seen as celebrities. It should be noted that not all endorsers are influencers categorized as "celebrity." The persuasive power of these influencers stems from the fact that their followers like them and sometimes even want to imitate them. Many followers watch influencers daily for entertainment. Many influencers are experts in a field or product categories. "An endorser's credibility in a given field affects their informational influence on consumers (Lin, Bruning, & Swarna, 2018), and this effect is all the more important when a product corresponds to the endorser's domain of expertise (Till & Busler, 2000) (Campbell and Farrell, 2020). Influencers often present themselves as "mere consumers" which makes them more persuasive. Indeed, word-of-mouth reviews are considered by consumers as more credible and trustworthy (Nielsen, 2015).

(3) **Influencers as Social Media Managers:** The third component of an influencer is their role as social media managers. "On the one hand, a brand may want an influencer to do very little other than show up for a photoshoot and post images on their social media that the brand has created and approved. In other cases, a brand may expect an influencer not only to strategize and create the content they post, but also to manage interactions with their followers (Campbell and Farrell, 2020). One of the most visible aspects of the influencer's role is content production. Influencers are often skilled at producing and editing content on their social networks, particularly for partner brands as part of a partnership. This is particularly useful for small businesses that do not know how to create content. By combining knowledge of their audience and the needs of the brand they work with, influencers can play the role of content strategist. Indeed, having a good knowledge of their followers, influencers know what content will appeal to their followers and will be perceived as more authentic and they can then create compelling content. Finally, influencers also play the role of community manager. Indeed, after publishing content on their social networks, the influencer

often interacts with their followers, particularly through likes and comments. "This not only encourages and amplifies engagement, which increases organic reach, but also provides a support function1 (Campbell and Farrell, 2020).

The influencer must also share the company's values because individuals are attached to this idea of consistency between the influencer and the brand. If this is not the case, the advertising message will be poorly received, because there will be a lack of credibility on the part of the influencer which will be reflected on the brand (Belanche et al, 2020). Generally influencers help to increase brand awareness, generate trust and customer loyalty and strengthen brand engagement. The success of influencers with brands can be explained by their ability to build a strong relationship and inspire trust in consumers by creating a sense of interactive communication and sharing personal information so that consumers can identify with them (Penttinen et al., 2022; Mouritzen et al., 2023).

Influencers, representatives of their community, can increase and strengthen consumer loyalty to a brand, and save time in launching and improving a tailored customer strategy (Ouahi. and Melghagh, 2020). Companies can integrate influencers into their marketing strategy while limiting potential risks to their image. Product launches are when the role of influencers is most important to promote them (Ouahi. and Melghagh, 2020). Influencers play a key role in digital marketing by creating engaging content on social media that influences consumer behavior. Thanks to their credibility and trust with their audience, influencers can effectively promote brands and products. Their engaging content captures consumers' attention and encourages them to interact and share, thus reinforcing their power of influence. If a company wants to develop its communication through influencer marketing, it must find an influencer to promote it.

2. HUMAN INFLUENCERS AT THE SERVICE OF INFLUENCER MARKETING

2.1. The Notion of Influencer Marketing

Influencer marketing is the sponsored collaboration or partnership between brands and influencers (Hennessy, 2018). It is "a form of communication in which brands collaborate with individuals who have a large community of followers on social media in order to promote a product, service or campaign" (Renard and Vachaudez, 2022). Leung et al. (2022) define influencer marketing as "a strategy in which a company selects and incentivizes online influencers to engage their followers on social media with the goal of leveraging the unique resources of these influencers to promote the company's offerings, with the ultimate goal of improving company performance2."

For their part, Conti et al. (2022) define influencer marketing as "a phenomenon in which companies approach famous or highly influential people on social media to endorse a brand or product, thus extending the "word-of-mouth" marketing strategy." Furthermore, influencer marketing is a significant phenomenon with a diversity of different influencer profiles. These are distinguished according to the number of followers, engagement rate, budgetary requirements, area of expertise, etc. (Campbell and Farrell, 2020). This type of marketing, due to the popularity of the influencer on social media, consists of using this popularity to promote products or brands to the consumer (Doyle, 2020). The expansion of social networks, such as Instagram, has seen the development of sponsored content, and its strong use by influencers and marketers (Doyle, 2020). According to Doyle (2020), this influencer marketing is illustrated by stories, photo or video publications, hashtags created by influencers on their accounts.

2.2. The Role of Human Influencers in Influencer Marketing

Simultaneously with the advent of the social Web, where the Internet has become a social space in which users interact and create content on social platforms, a player with increasing power has established itself in the digital space for several years: the human influencer (HI) (De Laet Derache, 2021). Its effectiveness is now formidable. More and more brands are calling on it to collaborate to achieve their marketing objectives (De Laet Derache, 2021). Human influencers express their opinions on products, services or other elements that make up our lifestyle such as art, sport, fashion, beauty, etc (De Laet Derache, 2021). These people, endowed with considerable power of influence, are capable of mobilizing and generating behaviors in the individuals who follow them on the social platforms where they are active.

Human marketing influencers are people, with a significant level of followers, who post messages on a social media account in exchange for compensation but remain independent of the brand (Campbell, C and Grimm, P.E, 2019; Kádeková & Holienčinová, 2018). They are therefore paid by companies to promote the brand's products by posting content on social networks such as Instagram. Human influencers have an authentic approach and share their private and/or professional lives by expressing their opinions and exposing their experiences (De Veirman et al, 2017). A human influencer or digital opinion leader is someone who, through their fame, lifestyle or social status, influences the opinions and decisions of those around them (Shanahan, Tran, Taylor, 2019; Belwaere, 2020). Influencers have managed to take their place thanks to the arrival of the Web, social networks and the democratization of the Internet around the world. Followed by thousands, even millions of people, they exercise their power of influence daily and can thus impact the opinions and decisions of their subscribers (Belwaere, 2020).

3. NEW ERA OF INFLUENCER MARKETING: VIRTUAL INFLUENCERS

Recently, a new type of influencer has emerged: the virtual influencer (VI) (De Laet Derache, 2021). A digital character created from scratch in computer graphics software, with a personality defined by a first-person view of the world and made accessible on social platforms for influence purposes (De Laet Derache, 2021). A virtual influencer can exist on physical media such as derivative products, magazines, comics, etc., but it is above all on digital platforms, such as Instagram, that they are mainly active (De Laet Derache, 2021).

Brands still have to collaborate with virtual influencers, also known as digital influencers. Today, virtual influencers represent a new way of reinventing external communication. They are created from scratch with design and 3D modeling, animation and virtual reality. Artificial intelligence allows them to have a personality and simulate real life. Thus, they look like human beings and are able to interact with their audience. They are present on social media, streaming platforms, blogs and even in virtual spaces. It is therefore not surprising that they also have millions of subscribers like their human counterparts.

3.1. The Origin of the Concept of Virtual Influencers

Virtual influencers were born from the growth of interest in video games, virtual avatars and anime (ContenteEngine LLC, 2021). It was in Asia that the Japanese company Horipro created a completely virtual idol in 1995. A decade later, in 2007, Hatsune Miku was born, the first virtual avatar star (Irma, 2020). They are complex individuals created to share realistic content, in the image of their community, or humanized (Gammoh, Jiménez & Wergin, 2018). But this is not the first time that we have been able to observe the influencer as a fictional entity. Indeed, this can extend to the brand icon like Mr. Clean or Michelin Man. Brands often use icons to foster relationships with consumers (Lin & Wang, 2012). This observation led us to question the place of the virtual influencer in the spectrum of the real influencer and the virtual avatar. From a marketing perspective, the avatar has been used as a virtual model for online shopping and allows the consumer to, for example, visualize clothes (Garnier & Poncin, 2013; Salem & Earl, 2000). According to Salem & Earl (2000), there are three types of avatars: realistic avatars (resembling the user), abstract avatars (referring to fictional cartoon characters or fictional spokespersons) and finally naturalistic avatars (strongly resembling humans).

Avatar is defined as "a computer-generated graphical representation of the user in a virtual environment" (Andersson & Sobek, 2020, p1). According to Gammoh, Jiménez & Wergin (2018), the avatar is a complex individual created to share realistic virtual content and visually represents users in an online community. The virtual avatar, by mirroring the virtual influencer, has a visual personality and character reflecting that of the human; in doing so, it becomes a naturalistic avatar (Gammoh, Jiménez & Wergin, 2018; Salem & Earl, 2000). The avatar attempts to be a virtual replica of a human that can present under a static or animated image in a virtual or real world (Garnier & Poncin, 2013; Salem & Earl, 2000).

3.2. History of Virtual Influencers

It is difficult to define what or who a virtual influencer is without first having reviewed the definition of a so-called "classic" influencer. The definition has now evolved to include the notion of digital platforms: A person who influences opinion and consumption through their audience on social networks.

The virtual influencer is only a subcategory of what we call "digital characters", which we distinguish as follows:

- The entirely fictional character representing a brand, a company or other. It is created by a brand or a creative studio to become a virtual ambassador.
- The entirely fictional character called "virtual influencer" who brings together a community on digital platforms around common interests. Therefore, we will look at the history of a few fictional celebrities who have already existed and how they set the stage for the success of contemporary virtual influencers:

3.2.1. Cynthia (The Gaba Girl) - 1930

In 1932, designer Lester Gaba introduced Cynthia to the public, a plastic mannequin with realistic measurements for the time. Cynthia's uniqueness was her incredibly detailed and lifelike appearance, even displaying human imperfections such as freckles and slightly inward-turned feet. Her presence was so remarkable that Gaba dared to take her into public spaces, attracting the attention of passersby and the media. Cynthia quickly became a fictional media icon, receiving clothing and jewelry from famous brands such as Tiffany and Cartier. However, her career ended tragically when she fell from a salon chair and shattered into pieces, ending her fame (Cole, 2020).

3.2.2. Alvin and the Chipmunks - 1930

Ross Bagdasarian created the Chipmunks trio with a high-pitched parody voice, which became a commercial success with "The Chipmunk Song". Their popularity spawned a media empire that is still active, including commercial collaborations with McDonald's (Rasmussen, 2022).

3.2.3. Hatsune Miku - 2007

It was in 2007 that the first virtual idol known to the general public appeared. It was Hatsune Miku, a young girl with a graphic designer inspired by Japanese manga and comics, voice mascot for the software "Vocaloid 2". Developed in 2004, this software allows people to create music using artificially generated voices. By entering the lyrics on the computer keyboard and the tune of the song on a synthesizer keyboard or with its computer systems, the user can create a song, to which it is possible to attach a melody. Hatsune Miku quickly became the ambassador

3.2.4. Ami Yamato - 2010

Ami Yamato became the first animated videographer to create vlogging content, a precursor to modern VTubers and virtual streamers (Rasmussen, 2022).

3.2.5. Lil Miquela - 2016

Lil Miquela's appearance on Instagram in 2016 marked the beginning of a new era in the world of virtual influencers. With a striking human appearance, she sparked debates about her reality, which helped increase her interest among the public. Her enigmatic content, posted in the first person, fueled the mystery that'surrounded her, helping her quickly accumulate millions of followers on social media. Miquela, as a virtual influencer par the quintessential, embodies the classic image of the influential girl from Los Angeles, but with a unique advantage: her status as a robot. This singularity attracts an engaged audience, who are also invited to participate in her story, thereby reinforcing her impact and notoriety in the social media landscape (Krehl, 2021). She had 3.6 million followers on TikTok and 3 million followers on Instagram in August 2022 (Statista, 2022).

3.3. Definitions of Virtual Influencers

Before 2012, studies on "influencers" and "influencer marketing" mainly adopted a traditional approach, where companies collaborated with celebrities recognized for their advertisements or campaigns (Khuat, 2023). However, since 2012, with the rise of social media influencers, fueled by the popularity of platforms such as Instagram, TikTok, and streaming sites like Twitch, research has focused on social media influencers by viewing these platforms as enablers (Haenlein et al., 2020). In 2019, the term "influencer" was officially added to the English dictionary (Castro et al., 2021, p.62). The definition of influencers and their reach have also evolved with the emergence of artificial intelligence, where the term "virtual influencers" was first cited in a scientific paper by Kadekova (2018).

There is still no single definition of what a virtual influencer is. Arsenyan and Mirowska (2021) define virtual influencers as "agents augmented by digital avatars, designed to look like humans". Seymour et al. (2018) define a virtual influencer as "an entity, human or not, autonomously controlled by AI. A virtual influencer is presented visually as an interactive entity, rendered in real time in a digital environment." Conti et al. (2022) further define a virtual influencer as "a person or object created by software that can influence others, primarily through marketing collaborations or participation in social campaigns, and that is solely created and consumed through digital media." Finally, Mouritzen et al. (2023) define a virtual influencer as "digital personas assigned to particular social media profiles created andmanaged by individuals, digital agencies or brands" (Guthrie, 2020; Sands et al., 2022).

A state-of-the-art review was carried out by Khuat (2023) on the different definitions of virtual influencers, highlighting both the similarities and divergences in the way of defining the concept. In this context, it is worth noting the different perspectives brought by researchers in the development of these definitions. As presented in the table below, the authors do not agree on a unified definition of virtual influencers. Some studies focus on the technical aspects of the artificial intelligence of a virtual influencer (Thomas & Fowler, 2021), while others take a more commercial or marketing approach, considering these characters as the property of brands (Kadekova, 2018). In addition, there is a variation in the degree of realism attributed.

Table 1. Evolution of definitions of virtual influencers

Author(s)	Definition
Kádeková & Holienči-nová (2018)	A brand-owned influencer created to promote selected brands. Successful and appealing to millions of fans on Insta-gram. Do not exist in real life.
Thomas & Fowler (2021)	A digitally created artificial human who is associated with Internet fame and uses software and algorithms to perform tasks like humans
Zhang & Wei (2021)	Computer-generated artificial charac-ters with a strong social media presence/fame
Batist & Chimenti (2021)	Virtual robots that can emulate human appearance and behaviour have become a trend in marketing
Wibawa et al (2022)	Virtual Influencers are human avatars created by computers with a large social media following. Computer-generated influencers (CGI) or artificial intelligence influencers (AII) with a social media presence are known as Virtual Influencers.
Michaelsen et al. (2022)	Virtual, artificial (or AI), digital, or computer-generated 5imagery (CGI) influencers are computer-generated characters resembling a human active on social media.
Conti et al. (2022)	A person or thing created by software that can influence others, primarily through marketing collaborations or participation in social campaigns, and is solely created and consumed via digital mediums
Stein et al. (2022)	Artificial media personas that are created by single programmers or whole media agencies, who often decide to remain anonymous.
Mouritzen et al. (2023)	Digital personas assigned to particular social media profiles created and managed by individuals, digital agencies or brands.

3.4. Classification of Virtual Influencers According to Their Attributes

Virtual influencers, although distinct from their human counterparts by their digital and artificial nature, nevertheless share similar classification criteria. These criteria include audience size, areas of expertise, social media platforms used, and types of content offered, elements that are also relevant for human influences. However, virtual influences add to this classification an additional set of specific criteria related to their technological nature. Despite this, research on this specific categorization remains limited. Nevertheless, our documentary study, supplemented by the observation of the different virtual influencers, made it possible to identify three other classification criteria specific to them: their appearance, their design, as well as their mode of management, whether it is provided by individuals or by artificial intelligence (Khuat, 2023).

3.4.1. Appearance

Virtual influencers can be classified into two main categories based on their physical appearance. First, humanoid virtual influencers are designed to closely resemble human beings, with similar physical and aesthetic traits. These avatars can be based on human models real, imaginary or hybrid. For example, Lil Miquela and Shudi embody humanoid avatars that share content related to fashion, music and popular culture. In contrast, non-humanoid virtual influencers take on forms different from humans, such as anthropomorphized animals or fantastical creatures. The Chipmunks are one example, offering an alternative perspective through distinct animated characters.

3.4.2. Creation Process

Virtual influencers are also differentiated by the way they are created. On the one hand, some are generated by algorithms and artificial intelligence (AI) technologies. These virtual influencers, such as Shudu Gram, have their autonomous characteristics, behaviors and interactions generated by advanced computer systems. On the other hand, hand-designed virtual influencers are created by individuals or human teams, shaping every aspect of their personality and appearance. Seraphine, the result of the collaboration between Riot Games and artists, illustrates this artisanal and intentional approach to creation.

3.4.3. Management

Finally, virtual influencers are distinguished by the way their activities are managed. Some are managed by human teams or individuals, who create content, make decisions, and interact with followers. Noonoouri is one example, where although her interactions and appearance are digital, her content is orchestrated by a team of human creators. On the other hand, other virtual influencers are almost entirely managed by artificial intelligence systems. Although supervised by human creators, a significant part of their content and interactions is determined by algorithms and AI software, as is the case for Miquela.

3.5. Dimensions of Virtual Influencer

Moustakas, Lamba, Mahmoud & Ranganathan (2020) outline the potential challenges of using virtual influencers and they have identified the factors likely to ensure their success and therefore the important dimensions for the virtual influencer. According to these authors and Andersson and Sobek (2020), virtual influencers must have a motivation, a precise and clear goal. As we will see with the presentation of the virtual influencers chosen for our research, most are activists and have accounts either lifestyle or related to a fashion or offbeat universe assuming their identity. In addition, the authors explain that they must have authenticity which can be associated with a certain transparency and honesty on the part of the account. Andersson and Sobek (2020) explain more precisely that the transparency of the virtual influencer depends on its origin but also on its content. According to them, the creator's transparency on the origin of the virtual influencer must be highlighted as knowing where they come from, how it was made and why it was created, joining the precise goal explained by Moustakas, Lamba, Mahmoud & Ranganathan (2020). But transparency also passes into the perception of communications of the content of virtual influencers but also of collaborations (Andersson & Sobek, 2020).

Virtual influencers must have a humanized personality that is sincere and realistic; this humanized personality helps develop trust in the influencer (Andersson & Sobek, 2020; Moustakas, Lamba, Mahmoud & Ranganathan, 2020). All these dimensions allow the virtual influencer to be accepted, to respond to the challenges of authenticity and fear associated with their own nature. Authenticity according to Morhart et al., (2015) is described by 4 factors that an influencer must possess. First, continuity represents surviving over time without drastic change. Credibility is then the second factor that corresponds to giving what is due; the fundamental pillars of credibility of sources lie in the reliability and expertise of the messenger (Morhart et al, 2015; Hovland & al, 1953). Subsequently, integrity is a value that is communicated and which is transcribed through intentions that must be transparent. Finally, symbolism is developed by the influencer with the brand by building its identity. Authenticity is the key with human influencers (Lou & Yuan, 2019); the authenticity of virtual influencers is threatened because of their non-existence. Virtual influencers to be authentic must be consistent, transparent and passionate (Audrezet & al, 2018). Continuity, as explained by Andersson & Sobek (2020), is the fact of being exposed on news feeds and allows one to be accepted, to overcome the refusal or fear associated with virtual influencers. To do this, Andersson & Sobek (2020) explain that it is necessary to develop multiple interactions and collaborations that last over time.

3.6. Types of Virtual Influencers

There are several types of virtual influencers. Some look like cartoon characters and others are so realistic that it is almost impossible to distinguish them from human influencers (Mouritzen et al., 2023). Existing studies distinguish between computer-generated imagery (CGI) influencers and artificial intelligence (AI) influencers. The term CGI is associated with virtual influencers that are created with CGI technology and whose appearance is similar or identical to that of human influencers (Ahn et al., 2022; Mrad et al., 2022; Mouritzen et al., 2023). The term AI is used to refer to virtual influencers that are created with AI technologies to create content and interact with consumers (Sands et al., 2022; Thomas and Fowler, 2021; Mouritzen et al., 2023). Furthermore, Mouritzen et al. (2023) identify four types of influencers according to their degree of anthropomorphism and their position on the reality-virtuality continuum.

1) **Hyperrealistic Non-Human Virtual Influencers:** Hyperrealistic non-human virtual influencers are created using computer-generated image technologies and can take different forms of animals (e.g. a bee or a dog) and creatures (e.g. a monster) that may or may not exist in the physical world. They usually have a low degree of anthropomorphism that is, they do not really look like humans. The content of this type of influencers presents their personal and social life and often depicts the physical world, sometimes including human (influencers). Hyperrealistic non-human virtual influencers can blur the boundaries between the real and virtual world for consumers.
2) **Hyperrealistic Human Virtual Influencers:** Hyperrealistic human virtual influencers are created, just like hyperrealistic non-human virtual influencers, using CGI technologies. Their degree of anthropomorphism is high and it is sometimes even difficult to distinguish this type of influencer from human influencers. The content of this type of influencer is focused on their personal and social life and shows them in the physical world performing human tasks (e.g. attending events or going out with friends) often with real-life human influencers. Hyper-realistic virtual human influencers make the boundaries between reality and virtuality extremely blurred, if not non-existent.
3) **Unrealistic Non-Human Virtual Influencers:** Unrealistic non-human virtual influencers can take various forms such as animals, realistic creatures (e.g. a unicorn) or humanized objects (e.g. a cupcake). Their degree of anthropomorphism is low, they usually resemble cartoons. The content shared by this type of influencer is most of the time related to certain topics or themes. Unrealistic non-human virtual influencers assume clear boundaries between the real and virtual worlds.
4) **Unrealistic Human Virtual Influencers:** Unrealistic human virtual influencers look like cartoon characters. However, their degree of anthropomorphism is high, meaning they have a very strong resemblance to humans. The content of this type of influencer demonstrates their expertise in a particular field (e.g. travel, fashion, cooking, etc.). Unrealistic human virtual influencers establish clear boundaries between the physical world and the virtual world despite their high

degree of anthropomorphism. It is possible that this type of virtual influencer sometimes appears in the real world, especially to attend events.

3.7. Advantages and Disadvantages

In this point, we discuss the advantages and disadvantages that virtual influencers or their use by brands can have.

3.7.1. Advantages

The employment of virtual influencers offers distinct benefits (Koles et al., 2024). They are not affected by feelings (Sookkaew and Saephoo, 2021) or physical limitations (Koles and Nagy, 2016), so they remain stable and consistent (Belanche et al, 2024). Just like human influencers, virtual influencers can build relationships and engage with a large number of consumers on social media. As influencers become increasingly popular and consumers interact with them, many brands, including Balenciaga, Samsung, and KFC, are interested in using influencers as brand ambassadors (Mouritzen et al., 2023). Virtual influencers meet a need for diversion and entertainment because they offer a view into a different world. The presented life of the virtual influencer allows followers to escape from their mundane lives. While this is also possible with human influencers, the virtual influencer has the advantage of bridging the real and imaginary worlds, which can provide additional entertainment or escapism benefits (Arsenyan and Mirowska, 2021).

The appeal of virtual influencers is that the public relations risk can be completely controlled. In fact, all the actions of this type of influencer are controlled and chosen by a group of people and therefore the risk that the influencer will say something that could lead to a scandal is almost zero (Robinson, 2020). The phenomenon of virtual influencers is not new. Indeed, virtual characters, a phenomenon that has existed since the 1990s, can be considered the predecessors of virtual influencers (Conti et al., 2022). Nowadays, virtual influencers have reached a level of relevance as significant as their human counterparts. In short, artificial intelligence has reshaped the marketing landscape by enabling companies to better understand their customers, personalize interactions, automate tasks, and predict trends. Virtual Influencers have become key players in the contemporary influencer marketing landscape, attracting the attention of marketing researchers and practitioners. The increasing integration of social media into everyday life has amplified their impact on consumer behavior, particularly regarding their purchase intention.

As consumers navigate a constantly changing digital landscape, the influence of social media actors is growing. The specific characteristics of virtual influencers play a crucial role in shaping consumers' attitudes and their purchase intent. Research explores the various attributes that influence the relationship between virtual influencers and consumers' purchase intent, while highlighting the complexity of this dynamic and its impact on contemporary marketing strategies. Two variables often emerge, namely credibility and authenticity:

- **Credibility:** Various elements of success are highlighted in the literature on the positive impact of social media on influencer marketing and brand communication. According to current work, perceived credibility emerges as one of the determining factors of influencers' success (Khuat, 2023; Bouvier, 2022; Chiu, 2023). Source credibility is based on the trust and recognition given by the public to this source, based on its expertise, honesty, and intentions (Charles R. Berger, 1995). It stems from the audience's positive evaluation of the expertise, sincerity, and relevance of the source (Chaiken, 1987). Many studies have revealed that the perception of credibility of a source also influences the perception of credibility of the message conveyed by the source (Qureshi et al, 2021; Riquelme and Gonzalez-Cantergiani, 2016). Credibility is a complex and multidimensional concept (Qureshi et al, 2021). A widely recognized model highlighting the relationship between influencer characteristics and purchase intention is the source of credibility model (Ohanian, 1991). The credibility source model, developed by Ohanian (1991), highlights two essential attributes of virtual influencers: expertise and trust. Both play a crucial role in the perception of the credibility of these influencers and have a direct impact on consumers' purchase intention (Khuat, 2023). The expertise of influencers, stemming from their competence and knowledge in a specific domain, is decisive for the acceptance of the messages they convey. At the same time, the trust perceived by the public in these influencers positively influences their attitude towards the brand and their propensity to purchase (Reinikainen et al., 2021). This trust is often established through authentic, transparent and consistent communication strategies, although the controllers of virtual influencers usually remain anonymous, seeking to maintain a certain transparency through disclosure and interactivity techniques (Khuat, 2023).
- **Authenticity:** Authenticity of virtual influencers is a central topic in current research, as evidenced by the work of Khuat (2023). This concept refers to the sincerity of the influencers' personality, expressed through their actions and communications. Opinions differ regarding the authenticity of virtual influencers: some researchers, such as Robinson (2020), argue that the difference between the authenticity of humans and that of virtual influencers is not significant, while others, such as Conti et al. (2022) and Batist & Chimenti (2021), highlight the challenges that virtual influencers face in being per-

ceived as authentic. An influencer's authenticity is often associated with their ability to share intimate moments and personal reflections that resonate with their audience, as highlighted by the work of Driel & Dumitrica (2020) and Lee & Eastin (2021). This authenticity has been shown to have a positive impact on purchase intent and the favorable perception of sponsored posts (Pöyry et al., 2019). However, maintaining authenticity is a challenge for virtual influencers, especially when promoting commercial products, which can be perceived as inauthentic by their audience, as highlighted by Driel & Dumitrica (2020). In addition, questions persist regarding the identity of the owners of virtual influencer accounts and the technology underlying them, which fuels concerns about the authenticity of their content (Robinson, 2020).

As virtual influencers are managed and created by digital technologies such as artificial intelligence technology or computer graphics, companies (e.g., brands) can meticulously control the appearance of virtual influencers to be favorable for audiences (Yu et al., 2024). Companies can also control interactions with consumers to prevent potential risks of scandals or public relations issues (Sands et al., 2022; Thomas and Fowler, 2021).

Virtual influencers can be much more than just brand ambassadors as they can be designed to closely represent a brand's values and image (Bradley, 2020). Furthermore, for Thomas and Fowler (2021), virtual influencers also have positive effects on brands.

1) **Virtual influencers enable leverage for mainstream and native advertising:** The possibilities in the advertising field are broad for virtual influencers. Brands have long used virtual entities as spokespeople, which allows many customers to identify with them. In recent years, virtual influencers have proliferated on social networks and have extended their influence to other advertising formats. "One of the most notable advertising partnerships is the one between Lil Miquela and Samsung, in which she appears as the only virtual influencer among human celebrities such as Steve Aoki and Millie Bobby Brown " (Sands et al., 2022). For Samsung, including a virtual influencer in its advertising shows that the brand is innovative in terms of culture and technology. In addition, the use of virtual influencers allows brands to engage in more effective native advertising. Native advertising is a type of advertising that seeks to disrupt the user's experience of the platform as little as possible (Campbell and Marks, 2015). Indeed, consumers do not appreciate that content they thought was authentic is in fact sponsored by a human influencer (Sands et al., 2022). However, by voluntarily interacting with a virtual influencer, who they know is a commercial

entity, consumers can be more sensitive and less annoyed by sponsored content (Hanus and Fox, 2015).

2) **Influencers attract and manage brand communities:** Virtual influencers are particularly effective in building a community and gathering consumers around a brand thanks to their higher engagement rate than that of human influencers but also their ability to gain consumers' attention through different means (Sands et al., 2022). By using virtual influencers, it allows brands to integrate into the communities of these influencers (Arsenyan and Mirowska, 2021).
3) **Developing brand-specific virtual influencers:** Virtual influencers can be either owned by the original creators or by a brand (Mouritzen et al., 2023). To be true to the brand identity, values, and target audience, brands can create their own virtual influencer. Through this, they can ensure that the influencers' story, tone of voice, language, values, personality, and beliefs reflect those of the brand and thus create a strong emotional connection between the brand and the influencer (Guthrie, 2020). In addition, brand-specific virtual influencers provide the brand with reputational security (Sands et al., 2022). Typically, branded virtual influencers only promote and collaborate with that brand, while non-branded virtual influencers, like human influencers, collaborate with multiple different brands. Collaborating with virtual influencers allows for greater control over influencer reputations andbrands they collaborate with (da Silva Oliveira and Chimenti, 2021; Thomas and Fowler, 2021; Mouritzen et al., 2023).
4) **Virtual influencers can be personalized:** Since virtual influencers are created digitally and from scratch, all their physical aspects (skin color, height, weight, etc.), their behaviors, or even their specific backgrounds (origin and location) can be decided and modified freely. In addition, those in charge of creating virtual influencers can choose which content will be published as well as the influencer's area of expertise (travel, fashion, cooking, etc.) (Mouritzen et al., 2023). "As a result, personalization allows for the design of virtual influencers with attributes that attract specific consumers or that match the values and image of the brands being promoted (Conti et al., 2022; Thomas and Fowler, 2021; Mouritzen et al., 2023). For example, a brand may decide to create a virtual influencer with the goal of attracting women interested in cosmetics. Brands can tailor virtual influencers to match the brand's image and values (Conti et al., 2022).
5) **Virtual influencers are highly flexible:** Virtual influencers are highly flexible given their digital nature. Unlike human influencers, virtual influencers are not tired, hungry, or sick (Appel et al., 2020). In addition, virtual influencers are not tied to a geographical location, meaning they can be anywhere, at any time (Mouritzen et al., 2023). During the Covid-19 pandemic, this flexibility allowed them to remain active on their social networks by posting innovative content

while human influencers were confined to their homes (Conti et al., 2022). 6) Brand innovation Brands that partner with or create virtual influencers are perceived by consumers as being more innovative (Conti et al., 2022).

3.7.2. Disadvantages

Virtual influencers are also notable draw backs due to their virtual nature. Managed and developed by companies, their motivation for endorsements is inher ently profit-driven (lee et al, 2024). Associated with their deficiency of tangible existence, such motivation for endorsement raises concerns about the authenticity of their recommendations (Wong, 2018). As a result, the lack of transparency regarding their commercial motives and their virtual identity can diminish their perceived trust worthiness (Choudhry et al., 2022). Also, disclosing the virtual influencer's origin has been found to diminish perceptions of parasocial relationships, adversely impacting their credibility (Lim and Lee, 2023). Despite being controlled by artificial intelligence, virtual influencers are also vulnerable to consumer sabotage and subversion when their identity violates consumer expectations (Sands et al., 2022), as seen in the collaboration between Calvin Klein and Lil Miquela (Cusumano, 2019).

The disadvantages of using virtual influencers as well as the challenges they can create.

1) **Neutralize consumers' reservations:** As the boundaries between the virtual and real worlds gradually fade, some consumers feel uncomfortable with the human resemblance of some virtual influencers. In some cases, the resemblance is so strong that it is almost impossible to distinguish whether the influencer is human or virtual (Bradley, 2020). Since virtual influencers are not real, they cannot perform their own tasks (publishing content, responding to comments, etc.). Teams of professionals are then in charge of performing these tasks or this is automated using AI (Sands et al., 2022).

The automation of these tasks can be problematic. Indeed, some consumers do not want to interact and engage with virtual influencers whose communications are managed by AI technologies (Kamoonpuri and Sengar, 2023; Rajaobelina et al., 2021: Mouritzen et al., 2023). In addition, consumers have difficulty fully engaging and interacting withvirtual influencers. Indeed, beyond physical appearance, virtual influencers cannot tell emotional stories, which creates a sense of unease for consumers (Bradley, 2020).

2) **Avoid unrealistic notions of beauty:** Virtual influencers have been identified as a potential risk for the future of culture and media because they create unrealistic expectations about what constitutes beauty, style, and culture (Wong, 2018). Virtual influencers redefine expectations about appearance, style, and culture. This could have a negative impact on the mental and physical health of the public, especially the younger ones, as consumers may feel compelled to imitate the influencer (Conti et al., 2022). As we have seen above, the personalization of virtual influencers is an advantage for brands. However, it can sometimes be problematic. The physical appearance of virtual influencers can sometimes represent unrealistic beauty standards (flawless skin, skinny body, etc.), which can create anxiety in some consumers who would compare themselves to these influencers (Mouritzen et al., 2023). These unrealistic representations can be even more problematic if consumers are unable to distinguish virtual influencers from human influencers (Franke et al., 2022). Indeed, this would mean that consumers, without realizing it, compare themselves to an entity that is not human (Mouritzen et al., 2023).
3) **Be authentic and avoid falsehood:** Consumers demand more authenticity and transparency from influencers, especially since it is increasingly difficult to distinguish human influencers from virtual influencers (Sands et al., 2022). The problem that arises is the following: is it really possible for a virtual influencer to recommend a product that he or she has not physically tested? This can create doubts about the reliability and authenticity of virtual influencers (Conti et al., 2022).
4) **The flexibility of virtual influencers can sometimes be a problem:** As we have seen above, flexibility is one of the advantages of virtual influencers. However, this flexibility can create problems. Indeed, due to their digital nature, virtual influencers can be anywhere, anytime, which can create unrealistic representations of human life and capabilities (Mouritzen et al, 2023). Users may then feel like they are missing out (Dinh and Lee, 2022) when they see the number of trips virtual influencers make and the number of events they attend.
5) **The cost of virtual influencers:** Unlike human influencers who can create their own content with minimal effort, virtual influencers need computer graphics experts who obviously have to be paid. It must therefore be taken into account that the generation of content for virtual influencers is very costly (Conti et al., 2022).
6) **Brand-specific influencer:** Although virtual influencers cannot decide to adopt unethical behaviors or trigger scandals, this is not the case for their owner. Another problem may arise when owners of virtual influencers choose to remain anonymous because they could then adopt unethical behaviors without being identified or punished (Mouritzen et al., 2023).

4. KEY DIFFERENCES BETWEEN VIRTUAL AND HUMAN INFLUENCERS IN THE CONTEXT OF INFLUENCER MARKETING

4.1. Comparison and Theoretical Challenges

Taking into account the identified disadvantages and advantages of virtual influencers, previous studies have delved into a comparative investigation of virtual and human influencers, assessing the viability of virtual influencers as effective alternatives to human counterparts (lee et al, 2024). Virtual influencers offer distinct advantages over human influencers, including controllability, cost-efficiency, customization and flexibility (Deng and Giang, 2022). There do not become enmeshed in scandals, and their messages remain under the complete control of the brand (Rozema, 2023). Humans might lie about products to achieve better impressions (Weiner, 2000), whereas virtual influencers cannot do so unless explicitly programmed to fib (Belanche et al, 2024). Unlike humans, virtual influencers do not suffer from physiological limitations like sickness, aging, and fatigue (Appel et al., 2020), and their images in promotional social media posts are more easily controlled to align with brand interests (Drenten and Brooks, 2020).

Previous studies comparing virtual influencers with human influencers have found that people tend to evaluate virtual influencers as less authentic than humans (Audrezet et al., Citation2020; Choudhry et al., Citation2022; Lou et al., Citation2023; Sands, Ferraro, et al., 2022). Such studies have suggested that virtual influencers should be perceived as less authentic than human influencers as they lack transparency in openly communicating commercial interests (Audrezet et al., Citation2020; Choudhry et al., Citation2022)

Such studies demonstrate that virtual influencers are considered less likable (Bohndel et al., 2023), less human-like (Arsenyan & Mirowska, 2021; Franke et al., 2022; Hofeditz et al., 2022; Molin & Nordgren, 2019; Nissen et al., 2023), less authentic (Arsenyan & Mirowska, 2021; Moustakas et al., 2020; Wan & Jiang, 2023), develop weaker parasocial relationships (Lim & Lee, 2023; Zhou et al., 2024), and perceived less credible (Li et al., 2023; Ozdemir et al., 2023; Yang et al., 2023), and trust worthy (Hofeditz et al., 2022; Nissen et al., 2023; Sands, Campbell, et al., 2022; Wan & Jiang, 2023) than human influencers, resulting them being generally less persuasive (for detailed findings, see Table 1). According to Thomas and Fowler (2021), may perceive virtual influencers as more appealing to collaborate with than human influencers. Employing virtual influencers allows brands the autonomy to hold their representatives in alignment with their creative concepts and represent a brand's values (Arsenyan & Mirowska, 2021), while human influencers aspire to cultivate cultural influence and garner recognition by sharing content on their social profiles (Audrezet, de Kerviler, & Moulard, 2020). Moreover, virtual influencers offer cost benefits over time since traditional influencer marketing necessitates specific organizational endeavors and budget allocations (Tan & Liew, 2020; Arsenyan & Mirowska, 2021).

However, other studies have found that, while virtual influencers generally form weaker parasocial relationships, virtual influencers in a video modality, as compared to those in images, can strengthen these relationships (Zhou et al, 2024). Additionally, the perceived credibility of virtual influencers was found to diminish when they engage in active interaction with users (Yang et al., 2023), or when they use rational language, rather than emotional language (Ozdemir et al., 2023). Furthermore, the study of Mirowska and Arsenyan (2023) demonstrates that people with low emotional disassociation and high cognitive empathy may find virtual influencers to be more socially attractive than human influencers. This research specifically suggests that the attributes found to be weaker in virtual influencers, such as trustworthiness, credibility, and parasocial relationship, can be enhanced depending on the personality traits of individuals (e.g., empathy; Mirowska & Arsenyan, 2023), the degree of interaction from the virtual influencers (Yang et al., 2023), their language (Ozdemir et al., 2023), and the modality of communication they employ (Zhou et al., 2024).

Table 2. Characteristics of human influencers and virtual influencers

Characteristics	Human Influencers	Virtual Influencers
Origin	Activity developed to achieve social notoriety, disseminate information, for commercial purposes (i.e. supporting brands), etc.	Created mainly by organizations seeking new ways of contacting their stakeholders or consumers.
Social links and history	They have a history, live in a certain place, have family, friends and other emotional ties.	They do not have these links. However, they can be incorporated at a later date.
Availability	Their availability is limited by other work or commitments or by their own fatigue (other physical indications).	They are always available and have no physical limitations. They could perform several tasks simultaneously.
Physical appearance	Limited by the characteristics of each person.They age with the course of time (for example, losing physical attractiveness is a very serious problem for influencers in the fashion world, etc.). They can get sick, suffer accidents or have other problems that limit or prevent the development of their activities.	Highly diverse thanks to the graphical possibilities offered by artificial intelligence. They do not age. They do not suffer from diseases, accidents or physical limitations that prevent them from carrying out their activities.
Emotions	Have a person's own emotions Can be driven by positive or negative emotional behaviors.	They lack their own emotions. Their behavior is more stable and is not guided by positive or negative emotions. May show emotion-driven behavior.
Credibility	It is conditioned by their degree of knowledge and by the independence of their opinions. Global data shows that about half of Instagram influencers were involved in scams (Dencheva, 2023).	It is conditioned by the degree of information processing and elaboration associated with artificial intelligence and by its possible dependence on a brand, etc. Virtual influencers eliminate the risk of being associated with harmful content.
Efficiency	Its effectiveness is conditioned by the capacity of the person.	Its efficiency in information processing, calculation capacity, etc. is determined by the programs on which it relies.

(Belanche et al, 2024, p2)

Compared to human influencers, virtual influencers follow the same logics of identifying and presenting a brand's products in their visuals. Some present the brand more directly than others. Indeed, as with the three categories of influencers, the world of Instagram for human influencers also presents different categories of people: lifestyle, fashion, sports influencers, etc. Influencers, in general, differ considerably in terms of brand image, orientation, number of followers, engagement rates and opportunities to offer for brand collaborations (Campbell and Farell, 2020). It is therefore quite natural that distinctions are made on how they present sponsored brands according to the range of characteristics defining influencers. However, virtual influencers have an easier time being positioned in fictitious visuals and as we have seen, this is often what the visuals play on.

The consistency between the product and the visual is present in all influencers. Influencer ads appear online and generally blend into their environment while corresponding to the content of the brand to be displayed (Campbell and Farell, 2020). Indeed, in the advertising field, visuals are important and must be appealing, but also remain consistent. Virtual influencers resemble human influencers in their staging and become a marketing influence option, a new tool. The virtual influencer therefore becomes a new form of marketing influencer, as we were able to visualize in our literature review, adapted in an increasingly digitalized period. The staging between virtual influencer and brand is based on the same logic as the relationships between human influencers and brands. However, these virtual influencers have a complete editing and animation team in the creation of visuals. In addition, their virtual and fictitious identity allows for more freedom in the development of sponsored publications.

The virtual influencer being similar to the human influencer as explained by Kádeková, & Holienčinová (2018), they have the same dimensions relating to attractiveness. However, given the fictitious existence of virtual influences, certain dimensions of the human influencer are complex to obtain for human avatars, such as the emotional connection, the challenge of authenticity (Moustakas et al, 2020; Kádeková, & Holienčinová, 2018). There is a need for transparency on the identity of the virtual influencer in order not to mislead consumers (ContenteEngine LLC, 2020). According to a report by Klear on influencer marketing, emotional connection, authenticity and transparency make influencer marketing powerful with modern consumers and therefore necessary. Indeed, consumers with little experience in gaming mainly with avatars will be more likely to have a negative opinion on the virtual influencer who seems less authentic bringing a real challenge for them (Andersson & Sobek, 2020).

The distinctions between human and virtual influencers primarily reside in (1) their nature and representation, (2) forms of content and narrative delivery, and (3) type of engagement with audiences (Sorosrungruang et al, 2024). First, human influencers bring their personal life trajectories (invented or real) to their online personae, which creates a basis for projective identification for their audience target group and determines their distinctions in those three areas (Sorosrungruang et al, 2024). In contrast, virtual influencers' technological mechanisms (visual rendering, designed mixed-reality content, and pre- programmed responses) and creators (interests, expertize, creative content direction) influence these distinctive aspects. Virtual influencers' appearance can be assessed for homophily and attractiveness similar to humans (Sorosrungruang et al, 2024). However, technological factors and the role of creators complicate direct applications of human-centric theories, such as source credibility, to examine virtual influencers' engagement, credibility, and endorsement efficacy (Sorosrungruang et al, 2024). This complexity arises for the reason that virtual influencers inherently lack the personal life experience that would lend authority to their expressed views (Meng et al., 2024).

A lack of life experience also renders problematic the applicability of the brand match-up hypothesis to brands' links with virtual influencers (Sorosrungruang et al, 2024). With human influencers, the efficacy of the match-up can be influenced by the link history with the user (Kim et Kim, 2021), but with virtual influencers the effects are ambiguous across a range of contexts and industries (Sorosrungruang et al, 2024). Additionally, there might be obscurity in the source of virtual influencers' efficacy and impact attribution (Zhao et al., 2024). Moreover, the explanations of audience-virtual influencer pseudo- or para-relationships may be distorted due to their creators' influence, deficient tailored interactions and preprogrammed interactions (Yan et al., 2024).

Hence, there are numerous contextual issues that potentially distort the quasi-relationship or basis for engagement between virtual and user influencer (Sorosrungruang et al, 2024). There are theorizations that might obviate the potential contradictions in audience responses to virtual and human influencers (Sorosrungruang et al, 2024).

4.2. Factors Influencing the Persuasion Efficacy of Virtual and Human Influencers

Hovland et al (1953) indicated five factors that similarly or differently limit or enhance the influence, consumer engagement, and persuasion efficacy of human and virtual influencers namely: (1) communicator, (2) communication, (3) audience, (4) responses, and (5) underlying mechanisms.

4.2.1. Communicator

Human influencers' credibility is formed through perceived trustworthiness, social identity and expertize by sharing personal interests that resonate with their audience (Ye et al., 2021). Leveraging anthropomorphic realism to appear trustworthy and expert (Igarashi et al., 2024), virtual influencers construct their influences through (1) nuanced forms, (2) identity positioning, (3) operational mechanisms, and (4) technological advancements (Sorosrungruang et al, 2024). For nuanced forms, high degrees of homophily and realism in virtual influencers enhance credibility and persuasiveness (Wan et al., 2024) but can also cause discomfort if overly or unsettlingly humanlike due to cognitive dissonance (Sorosrungruang et al, 2024). Notably, the large numbers of followers and high engagement rates observed in some virtual influencers with low form-relatedness (see typology of virtual influencers) suggest that beyond the degree of humanness, unknown factors may contribute to persuasion (Sorosrungruang et al, 2024). For example, recent study suggest that anime- and nonhumanlike virtual influencers elicit higher emotional attachment and authenticity benefit-seeking than humanlike virtual influencers (Yan et al., 2024).

Regarding operational agencies and identity positioning, human authenticity is perceived through genuine interest in specific topics and autonomy (Leung et al., 2022). Conversely, virtual influencers are managed by creators, which can limit their personalized responses perceived authenticity, and spontaneity (Sorosrungruang et al, 2024). Virtual influencers have restricted sensory capabilities (Li et al., 2023), which reduces their efficacy (Lou et al., 2023) when endorsing products that need a sensory experience (Sorosrungruang et al, 2024). However, exposure to a well-constructed identity and narrative that fits virtual influencers' appearance may raise their authenticity (Lee & Yuan, 2023). Technological advancement, like a more autonomous or artificial intelligent enhancement, may enable virtual influencers to cultivate pseudo- relationships by responsively engaging with followers and posting consistently (Yan et al., 2024).

4.2.2. Communication

Human influencers leverage self-disclosure, rhetoric, and emotional content to build social presence and credibility (Zhou et al., 2021). Emulating humans, virtual influencers employ rational, warm (Gerrath et al., 2024), and flattering messages (Quach et al., 2024) to increase credibility, prosocial behaviors, engagement, and trust (Ameen, Cheah, et al., 2023). These message strategies can enhance virtual influencers' approachability and social presence (Yan et al., 2024) and mitigate perceptions of lack of humanness and inauthenticity (Meng et al., 2024).

4.2.3. Audiences

Both virtual and human influencers can enhance persuasion by aligning their self-concept with target audiences (Wan et al., 2024). Arguably, there are some groups that are more receptive to virtual influencers and their endorsement, including younger consumers, especially younger women, and some cultures and audiences with personality types and certain motivations like promotion- focused (Ham et al., 2023; Muniz et al., 2023). For example, highly empathetic consumers are more willing to engage and follow empathetically with a virtual influencer as a comforting substitute for the complexities of human interaction (Mirowska & Arsenyan, 2023).

Audiences' engagement is motivated by the virtual influencer's novelty, advanced technological features, aesthetic appeal (Lou et al., 2023), and engaging storytelling (Zelenskaya & Rundle-Thiele, 2022).

4.2.4. Responses

Consumer reactions to virtual influencers are inconsistent (Sorosrungruang et al, 2024). Some researchs found negative effects of virtual influencer's unrelatability and appearances (Lou et al., 2023; Mouritzen et al., 2023), while others reported no impact in certain contexts (Kim & Park, 2023; Yan et al., 2024). This implies that although the authenticity and anthropomorphic realism of a virtual influencer matter to some consumers in some contexts, it does not matter in all circumstances (Sorosrungruang et al, 2024). However, both human and virtual influencers are scrutinized over ethical issues such as unattainable standards and misinformation (Sands, Ferraro, et al., 2022; Zhao et al., 2024).

4.2.5. Underlying Mechanisms

Human influencer literature highlighted mechanisms underlying endorsement efficacy in addition to the four elements indicated in the persuasive communication concept (Chen et al., 2023): (1) the relationship between audiences and sources, and (2) the congruence between sources and their recommendations. Attachments and parasocial relationships stimulate influencers' persuasion (Aw & Chuah, 2021). Virtual influencers, particularly nonhumanlike, can leverage advanced artificial intelligence (Meng et al., 2024) to respond interactively and induce emotional attachment, fostering connections similar to human influencers (Yan et al., 2024). Concerning endorser-brand fit, incongruence between the brand and the endorser can damage the human influencer's credibility and worsen consumer attitudes toward the endorsed product (Kim & Kim, 2021). Virtual influencers are further effective for brands that involve innovations or do not need sensory engagement (Franke et al., 2023), and their faulty endorsement elicits lower negative responses than human counterparts due to virtual influencers' low mind perception (i.e. lack of conscionsness and autonomous cognitive processes) (Zhao et al., 2024).

CONCLUSION

Today, influencers represent a real novelty when it comes to publicizing and increasing the desire to consume brands and products from different sectors, and current projections indicate that brands' marketing budgets dedicated to social media will grow. This chapter aims to to elucidate human and virtual influencers' distinctions and their implications in the Context of Influencer Marketing through comprehensive literature reviews.

This study-based analysis and research theme map ping advance understanding of key perspectives in which virtual and human influencers diverge. It offers contributions to the virtual influencer marketing literature. First, the comparison of virtual influencers and human influencers in the context of influencer marketing is a timely endeavor to better understand the conceptual and operational similarities and differences between them and to guide future research. We engage in a deep review of the research literature to detail inconsistent approaches to the taxonomy of virtual influencers and the resultant lack of clarity for practice and research. Hence, we advance the nascent understanding of the emerging classifications and definitions of virtual influencers to minimize misinterpretations of virtual influencer research. Second, this research explicates commonalities and distinctions of virtual and human influencers, and identifies factors influencing their efficacy, and research themes through a refined conceptual framework.

Human influencers are perceived as more authentic, credible, socially present, and generating more parasocial interaction than virtual influencers. That said, given the immense progress in graphic design and editing tools, it is becoming increasingly complicated for an Internet user to distinguish whether they are dealing with one or the other. In any case, human influencers are appreciated, still seem to have a bright future ahead of them and, in our opinion, deserve the full attention of brands.

As for virtual influencers, collaborating with these imaginary characters could attract visibility for the brand. Virtual influencers are a necessary element to understand the evolution of advertising communication in the current digital context. They now work mainly with high-end brands and engage with agencies that monetize them and create new opportunities to increase their notoriety. The success of virtual influencers does not lie solely in rational reasons but is rather explained by the irrational (De Laet Derache, 2021). It lies above all in storytelling, the universe that influencers manage to create, whether they have a virtual aspect or not. If Internet users follow these characters and buy the products they offer, it is not always because they think that the influencers like the product, they buy mainly because these influencers present an inspiring and innovative universe that they want to be a part of.

REFERENCES

Allal-Chérif, O., Simón-Moya, V., & Ballester, A. C. C. (2021). Intelligent purchasing: How artificial intelligence can redefine the purchasing function. *Journal of Business Research, 124*, 69–76.

Andersson, V., & Sobek, T. (2020). Virtual avatars, virtual influencers & authenticity, [doctoral thesis], Gothenburg, University of Gothenburg.

Arsenyan, J., & Mirowska, A. (2021). Almost human? A comparative case study on the social media presence of virtual influencers. *International Journal of Human-Computer Studies, 155*, 102694. DOI: 10.1016/j.ijhcs.2021.102694

Audrezet, A., De Kerviler, G., & Moulard, J. G. (2020). Authenticity under threat: When social media influencers need to go beyond self presentation. *Journal of Business Research, 117*, 557–569. DOI: 10.1016/j.jbusres.2018.07.008

Audrezet, A., & Koles, B. (2023). Virtual Influencer as a Brand Avatar in Interactive Marketing. In Wang, C. L. (Ed.), *The Palgrave Handbook of Interactive Marketing* (pp. 353–376). DOI: 10.1007/978-3-031-14961-0_16

da Silva Oliveira, A. B., & Chimenti, P. (2021). Humanized Robots": A Proposition of Categories to Understand Virtual Influencers. *AJIS. Australasian Journal of Information Systems*, •••, 25.

Belanche, D., Casaló, L., Flavián, M., & Ibáñez-Sánchez, S. (2021). Understanding influencer marketing: The role of congruence between influencers, products and consumers. *Journal of Business Research, 132*, 186–195. DOI: 10.1016/j.jbusres.2021.03.067

Bohndel, M., Jastorff, M., & Rudeloff, C. (2023). AI-driven influencer marketing: Comparing the effects of virtual and human influencers on consumer perceptions. SSRN *Electronic Journal,* 2(2), 165-174. DOI: 10.2139/ssrn.4404372

Campbell, C., & Farrell, J. R. (2020). More than meets the eye: The functional components underlying influencer marketing. *Business Horizons, 63*(4), 469–479. DOI: 10.1016/j.bushor.2020.03.003

Choudhry, A., Han, J., Xu, X., & Huang, Y. (2022). "I felt a little crazy following a 'doll'." Investigating real influence of virtual influencers on their followers. Proceedings of the ACM on Human-Computer Interaction, 6(GROUP), 1-28. DOI: 10.1145/3492862

Cocker, H., Mardon, R., & Daunt, K. L. (2021). Social media influencers and transgressive celebrity endorsement in consumption community contexts. *European Journal of Marketing*, *55*(7), 1841–1872. DOI: 10.1108/EJM-07-2019-0567

Conti, M., Gathani, J., & Tricomi, P. P. (2022). Virtual influencers in online social media. *IEEE Communications Magazine*, *60*(8), 86–91. DOI: 10.1109/MCOM.001.2100786

De Veirman, M., Cauberghe, V., & Hudders, L. (2017). Marketing through Instagram influencers: The impact of number of followers and product divergence on brand attitude. *International Journal of Advertising*, *36*(5), 798–828. DOI: 10.1080/02650487.2017.1348035

Deng, F., & Jiang, X. (2023). Effects of human versus virtual human influencers on the appearance anxiety of social media users. *Journal of Retailing and Consumer Services*, *71*, 103233. DOI: 10.1016/j.jretconser.2022.103233

Dinh, T. C. T., & Lee, Y. (2022). "I want to be as trendy as influencers"–how "fear of missing out" leads to buying intention for products endorsed by social media influencers. *Journal of Research in Interactive Marketing*, *16*(3), 346–364. DOI: 10.1108/JRIM-04-2021-0127

Franke, C., Groeppel-Klein, A., & Müller, K. (2022). Consumers' Responses to Virtual Influencers as Advertising Endorsers: Novel and Effective or Uncanny and Deceiving? *Journal of Advertising*, ●●●, 1–17.

Haenlein, M., Anadol, E., Farnsworth, T., Hugo, H., Hunichen, J., & Welte, D. (2020). Navigating the New Era of Influencer Marketing: How to be Successful on Instagram, TikTok, & Co. *California Management Review*, *63*(1), 5–25. DOI: 10.1177/0008125620958166

Hofeditz, L., Nissen, A., Schutte, R., & Mirbabaie, M. (2022). *Trust me, I'm an influencer! A comparison of perceived trust in human and virtual influencers*. ECIS 2022 Research-in-Progress Papers.

Hugh, D. C., Dolan, R., Harrigan, P., & Gray, H. (2022). Influencer marketing effectiveness: The mechanisms that matter. *European Journal of Marketing*, *56*(12), 3485–3515. DOI: 10.1108/EJM-09-2020-0703

Kádeková, Z., & Holienčinová, M. (2018). Influencer marketing as a modern phenomenon creating a new frontier of virtual opportunities. *Communication Today*, *9*, 90–105.

Lee, H., Shin, M., Yang, J., & Chock, T. M. (2024). Virtual Influencers vs. Human Influencers in the Context of Influencer Marketing: The Moderating Role of Machine Heuristic on Perceived Authenticity of Influencers. *International Journal of Human-Computer Interaction*, 1–18. DOI: 10.1080/10447318.2024.2374100

Leung, F. F., Gu, F. F., Li, Y., Zhang, J. Z., & Palmatier, R. W. (2022). Influencer Marketing Effectiveness. *Journal of Marketing*, *86*(6), 93–115. DOI: 10.1177/00222429221102889

Molin, V., Nordgren, S. (2019). Robot or human? The marketing phenomenon of virtual influencers: A case study about virtual influencers' parasocial interaction on Instagram.

Mouritzen, S. L. T., Penttinen, V., & Pedersen, S. (2023). Virtual influencer marketing: The good, the bad and the unreal. *European Journal of Marketing*.

Moustakas, E., Lamba, N., Mahmoud, D., & Ranganathan, C. (2020). Blurring lines between fiction and reality: Perspectives of experts on marketing effectiveness of virtual influencers. International Conference on Cyber Security and Protection of Digital Services (Cyber Security), pp. 1-6. DOI: 10.1109/CyberSecurity49315.2020.9138861

Nissen, A., Conrad, C., & Newman, A. (2023, April). Are you human? Investigating the perceptions and evaluations of virtual versus human Instagram influencers. In *Proceedings of the 2023 chi conference on human factors in computing systems* (pp. 1-14).

Ozdemir, O., Kolfal, B., Messinger, P. R., & Rizvi, S. (2023). Human or virtual: How influencer type shapes brand attitudes. *Computers in Human Behavior*, *145*, 107771.

Pereira, H. G., de Fátima Salgueiro, M., & Mateus, I. (2014). Say yes to Facebook and get your customers involved! Relationships in a world of social networks. *Business Horizons*, *57*(6), 695–702. DOI: 10.1016/j.bushor.2014.07.001

Sands, S., Ferraro, C., Demsar, V., & Chandler, G. (2022). False idols: Unpacking the opportunities and challenges of falsity in the context of virtual influencers. *Business Horizons*, *65*(6), 777–788. DOI: 10.1016/j.bushor.2022.08.002

Shanahan, T., Tran, P., & Taylor, E. C. (2019). Getting to know you: Social media personalization as a means of enhancing brand loyalty and perceived quality. *Journal of Retailing and Consumer Services*, *47*(C), 57–65. DOI: 10.1016/j.jretconser.2018.10.007

Thomas, V. L., & Fowler, K. (2021). Close encounters of the AI kind: Use of AI influencers as brand endorsers. *Journal of Advertising*, *50*(1), 11–25. DOI: 10.1080/00913367.2020.1810595

Yang, J., Chuenterawong, P., Lee, H., Tian, Y., & Chock, T. M. (2023). Human versus virtual influencer: The effect of humanness and inter activity on persuasive CSR messaging. *Journal of Interactive Advertising*, *23*(3), 275–292. DOI: 10.1080/15252019.2023.2189036

Zhou, Q., Li, B., Li, H., & Lei, Y. (2024). Mere copycat? The effects of human versus human-like virtual influencers on brand endorsement effectiveness: A moderated serial-mediation model. *Journal of Retailing and Consumer Services*, *76*, 103610. DOI: 10.1016/j.jretconser.2023.103610

Chapter 5
Virtual Influencers vs. Human Influencers: Crossing the Roads or Going Together

Shiv Shankar Kumar Yadav
https://orcid.org/0000-0002-3825-9101
Bennett University, India

ABSTRACT

With the advancement of digital marketing landscape, the discussions of influencer marketing has also taken a significant leap. As a result, the entity of virtual influencers has come to existence. These are the computer generated entities helping brands in achieving greater audience coverage while keeping their profitability interest at the center. While on one side, engagement of virtual influencers with brands is paying off well, the engagements of human influencers has come to scrutiny. Cursory overview indicates presence of both perspectives i.e. in favor and against. Motivated from the same, this article, with the help of rigorous literature review, examines the role played by virtual and human influencers and whether both can coexist with the brands. Findings present significant inclination towards coexistence. The article also discusses some meaningful strategies which currently are in discussion. The article concludes with the ideology of coexistence of virtual and human influencers in a distinct harmony

DOI: 10.4018/979-8-3373-0255-3.ch005

INTRODUCTION

In recent years, the concept of influencer marketing has evolved considerably. It has grown into a dynamic ecosystem due to its acceptance in the business world.

In early days, the promotion of products was based on the practice of celebrity endorsements, with the message of living the dream lifestyle of the respective celebrities. Over time, a new category of influencers as "social media influencers" came into existence through leading social networking platforms and has attracted a large number of viewers and followers through their real-life content. Influencers also build a unique bond with their audiences due to their ability to connect with a particular group of society and influence their ideologies. A recent study cites that over 93% organizations engage influencer marketing practice for capitalizing on their ability to spread brand awareness and enrich on customer numbers (Eran, 2022). Over time, the growing practice of influencer marketing has given rise to the entity called "virtual influencer". Virtual influencers, by entity, are cyber-personalities with motive to provide new avenues for social media engagement or related matters. This ability provides them with a competitive edge in marketing strategies that facilitate brand acceptance. Virtual personalities such as 'Lil Miquela' and 'Imma' are such close replica of their human counterparts that it is difficult to distinguish between what is real and what is simulated, because of advance technologies. This helps them in connecting with their audiences while promoting products or brands and positioning brand attributes in customers' psyche. Their presence opens up an unmatchable business dynamics through which organizations can curate the brand's message and presence. This results in seamless connectivity outweighing the uncertainties associated with humans (Ferrai, 2024). Although, this also presents as a paradox about authenticity, connection and emotional bond established by virtual personalities. Human influencers are trusted for their ability to extend authenticity, relatability and emotionally connect with prospects or followers. These abilities help them in enhancing their social contributions being a reliable source of lifestyle inspirations and recommendations while establishing the sense of communalism among their followers. On the contrary, virtual influencers are presented as entities, possessing digital creativity, controller content distribution, and round-the-clock availability. They generally are charming by appearance and attract customers through curated online presence tough lack in microscopic emotional conversations. While human influencers rely on personal tours, struggles, and realistic tales to establish the connection, virtual influencers depend on fully and compactly sequentialized specifications and brand assistance which results in the formation of limited emotional depth. This hurts the trust of consumers which is an important reason for successful business. Human influencers always focus on a strong relationship which results in enhanced trust and connection and also proliferates the sense of belongingness among followers (Kim & Kim, 2021). Brands get benefited from this advantage because proven agreements get transformed into higher conversion rates. Contrary to this, virtual influencers bring unique capabilities that often attract modern business strategies; their abilities of cost excellence, complete control of content, and data-driven strategy deduction help brands reach the targeted population count (Ferrai, 2024). Still, challenges such as authenticity and consumer doubt raise question that whether they can coexist with traditional influencer or it is customary to part ways?

LITERATURE REVIEW

The emergence of Influencer marketing reflects changing consumer behavior, technological augmentations across different verticals, and transformation in the marketing landscape. The extant academic literature vividly showcases this transformation (Wang & Liu, 2022). The initial operandi was centralized around the effectiveness of celebrity endorsements highlighting how old strategies were reliant on traditional mass media (Freberg et al., 2011). The advancements in technological infrastructure and the emergence of social media platforms gained the attention of scholars and they started investigating the impact of influencers. In the early years of 2010 influencer marketing established itself as an important research area and seminal research proved consumer acceptance of the impact made by influencers (Hudders & Lou, 2022). Since then examining the impact made by influencers in distinct markets or product categories became one of the research trends. Over the recent years, researchers have observed the discussions of virtual influencers, specially with Gen Z which are considered to be more awakened towards digital advancements. Many studies vouch for virtual influencer's role in establishing prospect's connect (Kim & Kim, 2021; Koles et al., 2024; Lim & Lee, 2023; Mouritzen et al., 2023; Venciute et al., 2023; Yu et al., 2024).

The essence of influencer marketing is the promotion of brands through influential personalities. Celebrity marketing can be traced back to Roman times when important individuals endorsed products. However, the term 'influencer' entered the modern business lexicon in the 2010s (Suciu, 2021). Since then, the practice of formally using celebrities in marketing strategies has gained momentum, with prominent names including Coco Chanel and brands such as Coca-Cola (Ferrai, 2024). During the 1980s, radio and television emerged as new mediums for product endorsement, and soap operas and sitcoms in particular added a great deal of dimension to the impact of celebrity influence. The advent of social media in the 2000s brought the practice of influencer marketing to a whole new level. Year after year, this evolution gave rise to platforms such as YouTube, Instagram, and TikTok that democratized the practice of celebrity marketing, allowing everyday people to follow it without hindrance. (Influence insider, 2024). This provoked organizations to reevaluate their brand strategies in order to serve the diverse customer bases. In the course the importance of the engagement of microinfluencers and niche content creators was also observed considerably. Very recent emerging studies are spawning the ideas of how influencers foster and engage in personalized discussions which form a stronger bong with the follower's purchase intention (Hudders & Lou, 2022)

Human Influencers, who are known as following entities on social media platforms, are known for traits such as authenticity, relatability, and emotional echo. They share their personal experiences and perspectives which helps them connect well with their followers. This practice gives rise to a parasocial bond whereby these influencers are seen as pillars of trust. As a result, the influencer's inclination towards a product or brand helps their followers to develop a positive opinion about it as well. The bonds created by human influencers help them in increasing their popularity across marketing campaigns.

Virtual influencers, on the other side, may be defined as "*digitized entities with anthropomorphized appearances that have human bodies, social roles, and their own identity; they can play the role of HIs by interacting with other humans, controlled either by humans or computer algorithms*" (Byun & Ahn, 2023). Their engagements are on the rise amid their reasons for high 'fitability' in various requirement forms (Campbell & Farrell, 2020; Kim & Park, 2023; Stein et al., 2024). However, despite the increasing interest in virtual influencers in influencer marketing literature and practices, several gaps warrant further investigation.

a. Longstanding effectiveness of virtual influencers in comparison to their human counterparts
b. Perception of the audience and their emotional engagement threshold regarding virtual vs human influencers.
c. Ethical implications and authenticity challenges

The human influencer inherent promotional engagements are rich in quantity across industries and virtual influencer triggered engagements are on the rise for various reasons such as ease in implementing corrections, round the clock availability, significant costs savings (long time perspective) and greater control (Hwang et al., 2024). Many of these are present as 'difficulty' in cases of human influencers. However, along with these goodness factors about virtual entities, there lies some concerns, such as -

a. Will nearly full control on the persona of virtual influencers, lead to the creation of a crafted world related to organizational offerings?
b. What kind of relationships this human-computer association will lead to?

c. Will these engagements be deeply rooted in the sentiment of consumer good?

Motivated from these issues this article, with the help of rigorous literature survey (of both scholarly and practice domain) and comparative analyses, delves into the exploration of positives and negatives of virtual and human influencers. The article contributes through the changes observed in consumer behavior, purchase intentions, ethical considerations and exploration of other hidden pattern.

APPROACH

To gauge the relevant literature research was performed through SCOPUS and Google Scholar databases using the root keyword virtual influencer and human influencer using different combinations of Boolean operators. This resulted in a total of 132 articles. The further refining criteria for these articles involved relevance to influencer marketing discussion in conjunction with human influencers. Consideration of successful and unsuccessful influencer marketing aspects was also on the list, resulting in a comprehensive discussion data set concerning both influencer types. Additionally, to cover on practitioner's perceptions, trends and practices, websites of concerned leading organizations were considered for analysis. This is how a well-concentrated dataset of 41 articles on the mutual dynamics of human and virtual influencers, all in the marketing context was obtained for further investigation.

This research, in the form of methodology uses a combination of both manual (for accurate and meaningful interpretation) and computer aided content analysis (for validating the findings) as used in (Yadav and Bansal (2021); Yadav and Dubey (2023); Yadav and Mishra (2022), (2024a), (2024b)) studies and has enhanced focus on factors such as perceptions for both entities, engagement rates, overall emotional reflection, ethics and authenticity. To provide rich perspectives to scholarly interventions, this article strengthens on the research's depth and clarity, particularly on *'how can the coexistence of virtual and human influencers be leveraged or if there is a strong need to plan the marketing activities keeping diverged routes for both types.'* The outcomes help by producing actionable recommendations for scholars and key decision-makers so that easy navigation through the influencer marketing landscape can be ensured.

ANALYSIS

All the 41 papers have been published in 23 journals and 1 handbook. Table 1 below shows the source wise distribution of scholarly articles. The interest of virtual influencer, that too in conjunction with human influencer has been covered by a variety of journal groups ranging from administrative science to Information systems to Business to Marketing & Advertising to Hospitality to Retailing to Psychology and to Tourism.

Table 1. Source wise distribution of scholarly articles

Source	Title
Administrative Sciences	1
Australasian Journal of Information Systems	1
Current Issues in Tourism	1
International Journal of Business and Society	1
International Journal of Internet Marketing and Advertising	1
Jordan Journal of Business Administration	1
Journal of Advertising	1
Journal of Business Research	5
Journal of Current Issues and Research in Advertising	1
Journal of Hospitality and Tourism Research	2
Journal of Interactive Advertising	4
Journal of Marketing	1
Journal of Organizational Change Management	1
Journal of Product and Brand Management	1
Journal of Research in Interactive Marketing	2
Journal of Retailing and Consumer Services	7
Journal of Theoretical and Applied Electronic Commerce Research	1
Journal of Vacation Marketing	1
Marketing Intelligence and Planning	1
Psychology and Marketing	3
Technological Forecasting and Social Change	1
The Palgrave Handbook of Interactive Marketing	1
Tourism Management	1
WSEAS Transactions on Business and Economics	1

As evident from the table the maximum number of publications keeping virtual and human influencer-related discussion has been covered by the *Journal of Retailing and Consumer Services* with 7 records, the *Journal of Business Research* with 5 records, the *Journal of Interactive Advertising* with 4 records, the *Psychology and Marketing* with 3 records, the *Journal of Hospitality and Tourism Research* and the *Journal of Research in Interactive Marketing* with 2 records each and remaining other journals with one record each. The year-wise range of publications is 2021-2025. A detailed and collective look can be taken in Figure 1.

Figure 1. Range of publication

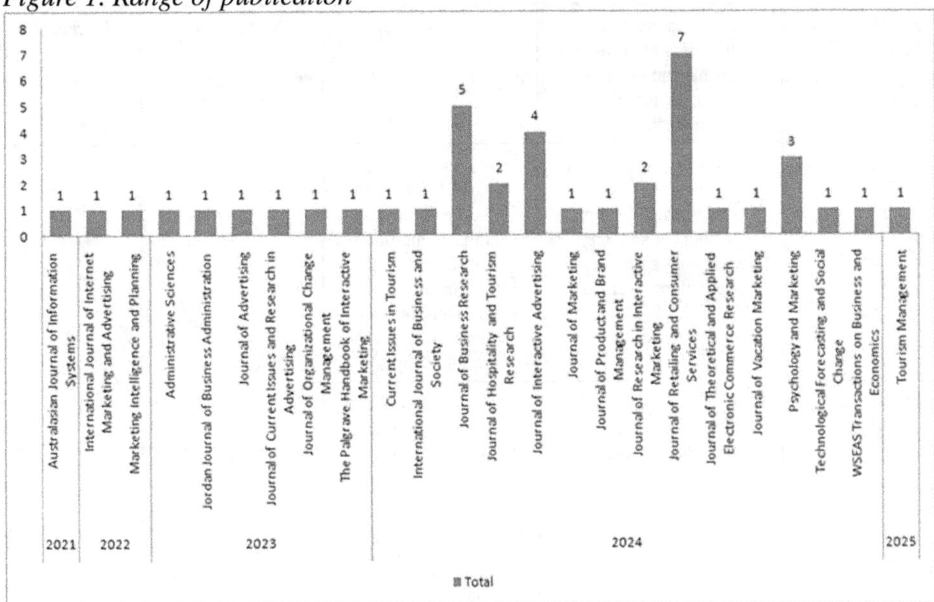

This is worth mentioning that there are other studies covering the discussions of Human and virtual influencer interactions however the discussion is either from a perspective that is not aligned with this article's interest or the discussion is very minute in existence. All such studies though not included in the main dataset however, have been acknowledged in the ensuing discussions. The main dataset includes studies where discussions of human and virtual influencer dynamics are, in comparative tone and attracts significant traction. Table 2 mentioned below are the studies with research context and what they say in the context of human and virtual influencers.

Table 2. Studies in focus

Studies	Research context	Virtual	Human	Coexist (Researcher's Inference)
Xin et al. (2024)	To explore the approach of decision making about Virtual Vs Human Influencer	+ (Low Risk)	+ (To beat competition)	Yes
Belanche et al. (2024)	Comparative study of virtual vs human influencer in the context of utilitarian vs hedonic product	+ (Utilitarian Product)	+ (Hedonic Product)	Yes
Hernández-Méndez et al. (2024)	Assessment of effectiveness of destination promotion in cases of human and virtual influencers	+ (Effective)	+ (More Effective)	Uncertain
Jiang et al. (2024)	Effectiveness of virtual influencer's green endorsement using influencer's image, emotional appeal and product involvement	+ (Human Like Virtual Influencers – Strengthened endorsement, pride appeal and high involvement product) + (Anime Like Virtual Influencers – good for gratitude appeal)		No
Zhou et al. (2024)	Examination of consumer responses on virtual influencer's sensory endorsements	- (products involving proximal sensory experiences such as haptic, olfactory and gustatory) + (when proximal sensory experiences are augmented by technology) + (products offering distal sensory experiences such as visual and auditory)		
Liu and Lee (2024b)	Examination of consumer' attribution of responsibility towards virtual influencers	- (less or no attribution of responsibility)	+ (consumers attribute (responsibility) human influencers for success or failure of endorsements	
Gerlich (2023)	Examination of the impact of virtual influencers on customers and of their rise on human influencers	+ (more trustworthy, credible and relevant)		

continued on following page

Table 2. Continued

Studies	Research context	Virtual	Human	Coexist (Researcher's Inference)
Li et al. (2024)	Examination of the role of human nature and charm perception and mediation effect of trust		+ (higher degree of trust)	
Zheng et al. (2024)	exploration of the relationships between consumers' perceived autonomy of virtual influencers, their purchase intentions, and brand attitudes	- (low autonomy) + (preferred in the category of lowly autonomous influencers)	+ (high autonomy)	
Xie-Carson et al. (2023)	examination of nonhuman influences including both living and non living entities on users in social media setup	+ (emotional connect with both living (animal, plants) and non living entities, same engagement as human)		Yes
Sorosrungruang et al. (2024)	Examinations of AI generated virtual influencers and the concerned dynamics with human responses	+ (brand engagement)	+ (credibility and social presence)	Yes
Meng et al. (2024)	Examining how effective the virtual influencers are while promoting self improvement products	+ (high in case of self improvement product preference)	- (low in case of self improvement product preference	
Igarashi et al. (2024)	Aligned in answering how can marketers increase the effectiveness of virtual influencers in promoting prosocial causes?	- (prosocial behavior)	+ (prosocial behavior)	
Deng and Jiang (2023)	Examination of appearance dissatisfaction being caused due to differences between virtual and human image differences	- (lower appearance anxiety)	+(high appearance anxiety)	
Wasti et al. (2024)	Investigation of the virtual influencer's influence on consumer behaviour	+ (Human like virtual influencer)		
Gerrath et al. (2024)	Study about individual's reaction on virtual influencers promoting proenvironmental behaviour	+(acceptance to learn on proenvironmental subjects)		

continued on following page

Table 2. Continued

Studies	Research context	Virtual	Human	Coexist (Researcher's Inference)
Mo and Wang (2024)	Exploration about how influencer type (human vs virtual) luxury brand consumption	+ (Virtual Influencer +Present luxury narration)	+ (Huam Influencer +Past luxury narration)	Yes
Wang et al. (2025)	Study about the intensity of language arousal and influencer type on customer responses	+ (High arousal language leads to stronger purchase intention)	- (High arousal language leads to weaker purchase intention)	
Li et al. (2023)	To assess the effectiveness of virtual influencer	- (less effective in endorsing in terms of brand attitude and purchase intention)	+ (more effective in endorsing in terms of brand attitude and purchase intention)	
Shao (2024)	Aims to develop an asymmetric framework on consumer's switching intentions to virtual influencers	+(virtual influencer)		
Deng et al. (2024)	Study about the investigation of ad recognition effective in cases of virtual and human influencers	+ (strengthen the ability of ad recognition in consumer)	- (weaker impact on ad recognition ability)	Yes
Meng et al. (2025)	Study about the investigation of the effectiveness of human and virtual influencers' endorsements of natural and cultural destinations	+ (boost visit intentions for cultural destinations)	+ (boost visit intentions for natural destinations	Yes
Liu and Lee (2024a)	Investigations of the rising trend of characters having human like attributes digitally created by influencers	- (less or non authentic across all product types) - (adverse effect on brand attitude and purchase intention)	+ (comparatively authentic across all product types)	Yes
Allal-Chérif et al. (2024)	Study to assess the popularity and limits of selected virtual influencers	+(being non human is advantageous) +(seem more authentic than human) + (Good Story tellers than engagement drivers)	+ (credibility)	Yes
Wang et al. (2024)	Study assessing the congruence effect of influencer (human and virtual both) and tourism activities congruence on tourist's willingness	+ (tourist willingness increases when virtual influencer promote challenging tourism activities	+ (tourist willingness increases when human influencer promote relaxing tourism activities	Yes

continued on following page

Table 2. Continued

Studies	Research context	Virtual	Human	Coexist (Researcher's Inference)
de Boissieu and Baudier (2023)	To understand the perception of luxury consumers of human like virtual influencers	+ (perception according to physical or content attractiveness, expertise, similarities and trustworthiness		
Mo and Zhou (2024)	assessment of effectiveness of virtual (vs human) influencers in conveying public service announcements focusing on consumer's attitudes towards influencers and the acceptance therof	- (less favor to wards virtual influencer when it comes to PSAs)	+ (more facor to human influencers when it comes to PSAs)	Yes
Cheng and Wang (2024)	Study about the effect of 'speciesism' on influencer-product attractiveness transference in AI-powered fashion marketing.	- (speceisism againt AI reduces effectiveness of virtual influencers)	+ (attractive human influencer drive strong purchase intention)	Yes
Choi et al. (2024)	Exploration about how trust of Gen Z travelers on Instagram marketplace gets shifted to trust in tour program sellers and purchase intentions with influencer type (human vs. virtual) and post type (sponsored vs. non-sponsored) as potential moderators	+(high trust on sellers when post is sponsored in platform (Instagram) and endorsed by virtual influencer)	+ (high trust on sellers when post is non sponsored and human influencer is engaged)	Yes
Xie-Carson et al. (2024)	Exploration of the Instagram user' perception towards virtual influencers and factors impacting engagements in tourism contexts	+ (Instagram users are responsive when VIs are engaged ethically)		
Looi and Kahlor (2024)	Study about virtual influencer's ability to foster greater creative control and enhanced engagement	+ (less engagement)	+ (more engagement)	Yes
Byun and Ahn (2023)	Study on the comparative contest of human and virtual influencers in the interactive advertising context	+ (intensity of virtual influencer is is increasing		

continued on following page

Table 2. Continued

Studies	Research context	Virtual	Human	Coexist (Researcher's Inference)
Masri et al. (2023)	Investigation about the impact of computer-generated virtual influencers on a new fashion brand associations and buying intentions	+ (engagement in case of unfamiliar brands)	+ (Human influnecers for newer fashion brands for strong positioning)	
Wan and Jiang (2023)	Investigation of adoption attitude of practitioners and consumers towards replacement of human influencer by virtual influencers in live-streaming e-commerce (LSC)	- (less positive attitudes and lower levels of perceived warmth, trust, usefulness, and dialogue) - (less enjoyable, easier to use, less distant, and less likely to generate purchase intention	+ (more positive attitudes and lower levels of perceived warmth, trust, usefulness, and dialogue) + (consumers did not perceive virtual influencers as more enjoyable, easier to use, more distant, and more likely to generate purchase intention)	Yes
Yang et al. (2023)	Study of the humanness and interactivity on the CSR engagements	+ (enhanced credibility and effectiveness by active interactions)	+ (comparatively moderated effectiveness and credibility by interactions)	
Mrad et al. (2022)	Identification of the key factors affecting Computer-Generated Influencer's (CGI's) identity and corresponding relationship between the CGI and its digital environment	+ (more authentic and trustworthy when positioned with nonhidden creater and has anthropomorphic traits, also when they exhibit human like features)		
Yap and Ismail (2022)	Study of the factors in virtual influencer marketing field affecting the purchase intentions of Generation Y consumers	+ (Successful VIs when known for entertaining yet informative content, attractive with accepted human like attributes, foster connect and parasocial relationships)		
da Silva Oliveira and Chimenti (2021)	Analysis on how non-human influencers affect marketing communications	+ (greater controllability, scalability and reduced risk of scandals	+ (HI bring authenticity and personal touch)	Yes

continued on following page

Table 2. Continued

Studies	Research context	Virtual	Human	Coexist (Researcher's Inference)
Ham et al. (2023)	examining the impact of a mixed reality social media on perceived anthropomorphism and authenticity and effects on advertising perceptions and implicit behavior thereof	+ (VI engagement triggers product selection through endorsers and adds to brand credibility and attitude however too much realism in a single media post attenuate the effect significantly)		
Franke et al. (2023)	Investigates whether consumers find virtual influencers appealing compared to human influencers and whether they are real or computer generated.	+ (difficult to identify whether real or computer generated)	+ (consumers are more positive towards human endorsers)	Yes
Audrezet and Koles (2023)	to offer a detailed presentation of virtual influencers within their ecosystem, taking into consideration their human influencer counterparts as well as consumer perceptions	+ (tech-savvy, excellent targeting and greater control on content and communication, success intensifies when able to humanize in significant capacity)	+ (authencity and emotional connect, foster development and growth) -(Challenges in maintaining authenticity and trustworthiness when collaborate with too many brands)	

DISCUSSION

The analysis of discussions from these articles has highlighted several points where virtual and human influencers differ from each other. Though, certain differences are such where organization can leverage both the entities. Table 3 below covers such points in significant details.

Table 3. Points where virtual and human influencer differ from each other

Points of differences	Virtual Influencers	Human Influencers
Origin	Created by computers for marketing purposes	Secure social presence through personal branding
Authenticity	Scripted based interactions, deficient in emotions	Real life experiences
Brand Control	Thorough control both on delivery and content	random behavior or controversy
Credibility	Perceived as more crafted, less credible	Higher trust and credibility
Audience Connection	No or false emotional depth, no bonding so no or weak connect	Strong personal and emotional bonding, stronger connect
Global Reach	Multilingual in tune with diverse cultures	Comparative language barrier and other cultural constraints
Product experience	no expression of products experience	provide authentic product feedback and testimonials
Demographic Appeal	Popular among Gen Y & Z	Appeals wider age group
Marketing Effectiveness	Less persuasive due to weal emotional connect	comparatively more persuasive due to strong connection
Reliability	Depends on creator's ideology	Independent and empathetic

These differences can provide better clarity to the practitioners/organizations and researchers and can act as guiding stones when it comes to devising marketing campaigns and promotional policies. Presence of both entities may also widen the idea consideration sets for individuals and they can consider combination of parameters in order to make up their mind for a particular product or services consideration.

The data analysis helped in findings answers to the questions which have been discussed below.

1. Will nearly full control on the persona of virtual influencers, lead to the creation of a crafted world related to organizational offerings?

Certainly Yes! While on one side, for individuals, it has the perceived negativeness associated with the word 'crafted', on the other side, for organizations, it can provide immense opportunities for strategically devising the curated personas which are highly aligned with the organizational offerings, thus enabling the organization to maximize the advertising impact and leverage these benefits in boosting sales by following means -

1. Organizations can create persuasive messages resonating with their target segments in terms of brand identity, attitude, and values, enhancing the completeness of marketing communications (Byun & Ahn, 2023; Zheng et al., 2024).
2. With the versatile ability of controlling from computer systems, virtual influencers can be deployed on numerous platforms, thus maintaining the consistency and helping in firm brand identity. This ability can cope up with the changing micro market demands while maintaining the core communication (Deng & Jiang, 2023).
3. Despite the perceived resistance from small random portions of market segments, virtual influencers, with the help of appealing narratives and manipulations in the promoting environment, synchronize deeply and drive engagements from consumers (Audrezet & Koles, 2023).
4. Due to their technologically rich backing, the application of advanced graphics and emotional cues in establishing connection with the audience is quite frequent and this helps in generating stronger and long lasting brand appeal thereby enhancing brand association(Agnihotri et al., 2024; Davlembayeva et al., 2024).
5. Another benefit of technological backing is the ability to transform their personas based on the feedback communicated from the consumers. This agile transformation enables organizations in crafting and applying strategies which develop deeper association with the targeted segments(Lopez et al., 2023).

    2. What kind of relationships this human-computer association will lead to?

The human-computer association can progress towards several dimensions depending on how organizations want to prosper and how it is being received by the audience.

1. Virtual influencers, when humanized significantly, can be considered trustworthy however this trust is different from the one built by the presence of human influencers. Trust triggered by virtual influencers remains conditional i.e. subject to the consumers' receipt of contributing factors like authenticity, acceptability, relatability and engagements(da Silva Oliveira & Chimenti, 2021).
2. By virtue of their nature, humans often engage in peer or social comparison or may be driven by the feeling, 'What others will think if I buy or react on some product-related cue'. Standardized or usual answers to this may lead to the feeling of inadequacy, left out. Organizations may infuse enough 'warmth' (Davlembayeva et al., 2024; El Hedhli et al., 2023; Gerrath et al., 2024; Wan & Jiang, 2023) as often evident from human conversations and behaviors which may console such feelings and simultaneously strengthening the emotional bond by offering desired emotional reflections while maintaining the overall goal of quantitative conversion.

3. Non dependence on humans leads organizations and brand in spawning innovative interactions. In the situations mentioned in above point, carefully craft sentiment sequence can result in desired emotional response most similar to humans. This provokes human mind deep down to accept the virtual character. If done effectively this may maximize engagements manifold across channels and platforms(Lou et al., 2023).
4. With the help of meticulous multifold sentiment analysis at the back end, virtual influencers can facilitate social grouping by aggregating like-minded people. Such grouping begets peer considerations and a sense of belongingness and helps immensely in fostering brand loyalty, with minimal effort and for a longer duration (Shao, 2024).

    3. Will these engagements be deeply rooted in the sentiment of consumer good?

Undoubtedly! Though such engagements may lead to both positive as well as negative results. Such as:

1. With the ability to mimic human gestures and emotions virtual influencers become successful to most extent in crafting aspirational imagery and messages which resonates with the consumers' ideology. As a result organizations are able to touch the consumer sentiments resulting into positive bond associations (Yan et al., 2024; Zhou et al., 2024).
2. Successful engagement strategies trigger consumer participation acquisiting customers in ongoing virtual discussions and narratives, prospering the long-lasting deeper emotional connect, by making consumers feel themselves part of the brand story(Allal-Chérif et al., 2024; Block & Lovegrove, 2021).
3. To establish consumer acceptance and trust, organizations need to create and position their influencer's persona very cleverly so that perception in consumer minds goes positive and a sense of reliability can be developed(Cheng & Wang, 2024; Davlembayeva et al., 2024; De Cicco et al., 2024; Mo & Zhou, 2024).
4. By crunching the ongoing discussions both qualitatively and quantitatively, organizations can assess the inclination of sentiments. Accordingly, they can devise strategies to cater to all clusters of emotions in order to boost engagement levels and positive sentiments(Block & Lovegrove, 2021).
5. Some segments of consumers negatively perceive the immersive experience provided by virtual influencers. They may reflect the same with feelings of emotional distress, anxiety and satisfaction void. These cases should be carefully treated to ensure soothing and adequately balanced promotional narratives(Deng & Jiang, 2023).

By careful planning and implementation of these elements and strategies organizations can make very satisfying use of virtual influencers ensuring profitable and meaningful engagements and fostering of a mutually beneficial promotional landscape.

On the Coexistence of Virtual and Human Influencers

The explorations above clearly indicate an inclination towards coexistence between human and virtual influencers, evident from the cases where organizations are leveraging both entities in order to achieve market coverage and consumer good. Whereas scholarly discussions support this consideration strongly (refer Table 2), practitioner's discussions do not present stated coverage. However, some strategies are in vogue. Table 4 below shows other studies (apart from Table 2 above), which significantly endorse the coexistence of human and virtual influencers.

Table 4. Additional studies supporting the coexistence of human and virtual influencers

Citation	Virtual influencer
Lee et al. (2024)	Some perceive VIs as more authentic, Rest consider humans for credibility and trust so coexist.
De Cicco et al. (2024)	Users do not differentiate, can coexist in a complementary relationship
Zhao et al. (2024)	Can coexist to leverage higher forgiveness and positive response during service failures
Böhndel et al. (2023)	No significant difference so can coexist but are less liked as compared to humans
Landgrebe (2024)	With visual framing, can match human presence so coexist to enhance the consistency of brand

Referring to table 2 and 4 there are significant scholarly evidences when human and virtual influencers can coexist. However this coexistence is in proportions, different for different industries. Similarly in the practice domain coexisting endeavors are in progress under different industries. Table 5 covers many of such meaning strategies.

Table 5. Strategies in line with human and virtual influencer coexistence

Coexistence Strategies	Virtual Influencer Advantages	Human Influencer Advantages
Hybrid promotional campaigns	Round the clock availability	Authenticity and emotional connect
Content Augmentation	easily customizable	Experiences from real life
Targeted market segmentation	Seamless, with no limits	Personalized storytelling

continued on following page

Table 5. Continued

Coexistence Strategies	Virtual Influencer Advantages	Human Influencer Advantages
Multiple platform interactions	Greater creativity and variety	Genuineness
Character development alliance	Absence of constraints	Emotional bonding
Storytelling integration	Unhindered brand visibility	creativity
Digital experience creation	suitable for digital platforms	Tech-savvy only
Interactive content creation	Vivid characters designing	Innovative content
Technical collaborations	Scalable availability	problem-solving

CONCLUSION

This research upon analyzing the human versus virtual influencers literature presents the complex dynamics of authenticity, engagement, and relatability. On one side where human influencers prove their mettle by establishing emotional bonds with the help of concerned narratives, trust, and loyalty across target markets, virtual influencers on the other side propagate political instances to cater to target markets and equip brands with a greater amount of differentiation by the use of technology.

However with the increase of technology enabled promotion in virtual market domain, amid skeptical viewpoints about the authenticity of the virtual influencers, ideology of coexistence seems wise and getting stronger day by day. With the help of both these entities brands can promote transparency and leverage communication power effectively.

The even more evolution of AI day by day will only add to the capabilities of virtual influencers, allowing them to touch newer heights of creativity and innovation. Along with this progress, the existence and importance of human influencers will also grow manifold. The only possible change may be the shift in their contribution areas from mundane and repetitive tasks to more authentic, creative, and human behavior dominated areas in conformance with different market requirements. To close, virtual and human influencers can coexist in harmony in order to add greater competence to existing market strategies which can ultimately drive audience engagement and returns.

Limitations

1. Consideration of other similar keywords for example avatar, digital etc has been willfully ignored because in earlier researches, it did not result in relevant papers and was diluting the dataset.

2. The shortlisted studies also had discussions about some other affecting (moderating and mediating) variables which play role in above, though in smaller portions. The discussion has considered parameters which are relevant as per researcher's understanding of the relevance to this research.

REFERENCES

Agnihotri, D., Chaturvedi, P., & Tripathi, V. (2024). "Virtual bonds and actual transactions": Investigating the impact of virtual influencers' credibility on buying behavior through virtual engagement [Article]. *Journal of Communication Management (London)*. Advance online publication. DOI: 10.1108/JCOM-02-2024-0035

Allal-Chérif, O., Puertas, R., & Carracedo, P. (2024). Intelligent influencer marketing: How AI-powered virtual influencers outperform human influencers [Article]. *Technological Forecasting and Social Change*, *200*, 123113. Advance online publication. DOI: 10.1016/j.techfore.2023.123113

Audrezet, A., & Koles, B. (2023). Virtual Influencer as a Brand Avatar in Interactive Marketing. In *The Palgrave Handbook of Interactive Marketing* (pp. 353–376). Springer International Publishing., DOI: 10.1007/978-3-031-14961-0_16

Belanche, D., Casaló, L. V., & Flavián, M. (2024). Human versus virtual influences, a comparative study. *Journal of Business Research*, *173*, 114493. Advance online publication. DOI: 10.1016/j.jbusres.2023.114493

Block, E., & Lovegrove, R. (2021). Discordant storytelling, 'honest fakery', identity peddling: How uncanny CGI characters are jamming public relations and influencer practices [Article]. *Public Relations Inquiry*, *10*(3), 265–293. DOI: 10.1177/2046147X211026936

Böhndel, M., Jastorff, M., & Rudeloff, C. (2023). AI-driven influencer marketing: Comparing the effects of virtual and human influencers on consumer perceptions. *Journal of AI. Robotics & Workplace Automation*, *2*(2), 165–174. DOI: 10.69554/WBSJ7931

Byun, K. J., & Ahn, S. J. (2023). A Systematic Review of Virtual Influencers: Similarities and Differences between Human and Virtual Influencers in Interactive Advertising [Article]. *Journal of Interactive Advertising*, *23*(4), 293–306. DOI: 10.1080/15252019.2023.2236102

Campbell, C., & Farrell, J. R. (2020). More than meets the eye: The functional components underlying influencer marketing. *Business Horizons*, *63*(4), 469–479. DOI: 10.1016/j.bushor.2020.03.003

Cheng, J., & Wang, J. (2024). Influencer-product attractiveness transference in interactive fashion marketing: The moderated moderating effect of speciesism against AI [Article]. *Journal of Research in Interactive Marketing*. Advance online publication. DOI: 10.1108/JRIM-06-2024-0299

Choi, M., Choi, Y., & Lee, H. (2024). Gen Z Travelers in the Instagram Marketplace: Trust, Influencer Type, Post Type, and Purchase Intention. *Journal of Hospitality & Tourism Research (Washington, D.C.)*, *48*(6), 1020–1034. DOI: 10.1177/10963480231180938

da Silva Oliveira, A. B., & Chimenti, P. (2021). "Humanized Robots": A Proposition of Categories to Understand Virtual Influencers. *AJIS. Australasian Journal of Information Systems*, *25*, 1–27. DOI: 10.3127/ajis.v25i0.3223

Davlembayeva, D., Chari, S., & Papagiannidis, S. (2024). Virtual Influencers in Consumer Behaviour: A Social Influence Theory Perspective. *British Journal of Management*. Advance online publication. DOI: 10.1111/1467-8551.12839

de Boissieu, E., & Baudier, P. (2023). The perceived credibility of human-like social robots: Virtual influencers in a luxury and multicultural context [Article]. *Journal of Organizational Change Management*, *36*(7), 1163–1179. DOI: 10.1108/JOCM-05-2023-0182

De Cicco, R., Iacobucci, S., Cannito, L., Onesti, G., Ceccato, I., & Palumbo, R. (2024). Virtual vs. human influencer: Effects on users' perceptions and brand outcomes [Article]. *Technology in Society*, *77*, 102488. Advance online publication. DOI: 10.1016/j.techsoc.2024.102488

Deng, F., & Jiang, X. (2023). Effects of human versus virtual human influencers on the appearance anxiety of social media users. *Journal of Retailing and Consumer Services*, *71*, 103233. Advance online publication. DOI: 10.1016/j.jretconser.2022.103233

Deng, F., Tuo, M., Chen, S., & Zhang, Z. (2024). Born for marketing? The effects of virtual versus human influencers on brand endorsement effectiveness: The role of advertising recognition. *Journal of Retailing and Consumer Services*, *80*, 103904. Advance online publication. DOI: 10.1016/j.jretconser.2024.103904

El Hedhli, K., Zourrig, H., Al Khateeb, A., & Alnawas, I. (2023). Stereotyping human-like virtual influencers in retailing: Does warmth prevail over competence?. *Journal of Retailing and Consumer Services*, *75*, 103459. Advance online publication. DOI: 10.1016/j.jretconser.2023.103459

Eran, N. (2022). Why Are More Influencers Launching Their Own Brands?Forbes. Retrieved 24 Dec from https://www.forbes.com/councils/forbestechcouncil/2022/06/27/why-are-more-influencers-launching-their-own-brands/

Ferrai, P. (2024). *The new era of influencer marketing*. WeAreBrain. Retrieved 26 Dec from https://wearebrain.com/blog/the-new-era-of-influencer-marketing/

Franke, C., Groeppel-Klein, A., & Müller, K. (2023). Consumers' Responses to Virtual Influencers as Advertising Endorsers: Novel and Effective or Uncanny and Deceiving? [Article]. *Journal of Advertising*, *52*(4), 523–539. DOI: 10.1080/00913367.2022.2154721

Freberg, K., Graham, K., McGaughey, K., & Freberg, L. A. (2011). Who are the social media influencers? A study of public perceptions of personality. *Public Relations Review*, *37*(1), 90–92. DOI: 10.1016/j.pubrev.2010.11.001

Gerlich, M. (2023). The Power of Virtual Influencers: Impact on Consumer Behaviour and Attitudes in the Age of AI [Article]. *Administrative Sciences*, *13*(8), 178. Advance online publication. DOI: 10.3390/admsci13080178

Gerrath, M. H. E. E., Olya, H., Shah, Z., & Li, H. (2024). Virtual influencers and pro-environmental causes: The roles of message warmth and trust in experts [Article]. *Journal of Business Research*, *175*, 114520. Advance online publication. DOI: 10.1016/j.jbusres.2024.114520

Ham, J., Li, S., Shah, P., & Eastin, M. S. (2023). The "Mixed" Reality of Virtual Brand Endorsers: Understanding the Effect of Brand Engagement and Social Cues on Technological Perceptions and Advertising Effectiveness [Article]. *Journal of Interactive Advertising*, *23*(2), 98–113. DOI: 10.1080/15252019.2023.2185557

Hernández-Méndez, J., Baute-Díaz, N., & Gutiérrez-Taño, D. (2024). The effectiveness of virtual versus human influencer marketing for tourism destinations [Article]. *Journal of Vacation Marketing*, 13567667241276212. Advance online publication. DOI: 10.1177/13567667241276212

Hudders, L., & Lou, C. (2022). *A new era of influencer marketing: Lessons from Recent Inquires and Thoughts on Future Directions* (Vol. 41). Taylor & Francis.

Hwang, S., Zhang, S., Liu, X., & Srinivasan, K. (2024). *Should Your Brand Hire a Virtual Influencer?* Harvard Business School Publishing. Retrieved 30 Oct from https://hbr.org/2024/05/should-your-brand-hire-a-virtual-influencer

Igarashi, R., Bhoumik, K., & Thompson, J. (2024). Investigating the effectiveness of virtual influencers in prosocial marketing [Article]. *Psychology and Marketing*, *41*(9), 2121–2135. DOI: 10.1002/mar.22031

Influence insider. (2024). *Social Media Influencer vs. Celebrity: The Key Differences*. Influence Insider. Retrieved 29 Dec from https://influence-insider.com/social-media-influencer-vs-celebrity-the-key-differences/

Jiang, K., Zheng, J., & Luo, S. (2024). Green power of virtual influencer: The role of virtual influencer image, emotional appeal, and product involvement [Article]. *Journal of Retailing and Consumer Services*, *77*, 103660. Advance online publication. DOI: 10.1016/j.jretconser.2023.103660

Kim, D. Y., & Kim, H.-Y. (2021). Trust me, trust me not: A nuanced view of influencer marketing on social media. *Journal of Business Research*, *134*, 223–232. DOI: 10.1016/j.jbusres.2021.05.024

Kim, H., & Park, M. (2023). Virtual influencers' attractiveness effect on purchase intention: A moderated mediation model of the Product–Endorser fit with the brand. *Computers in Human Behavior*, *143*, 107703. DOI: 10.1016/j.chb.2023.107703

Koles, B., Audrezet, A., Moulard, J. G., Ameen, N., & McKenna, B. (2024). The authentic virtual influencer: Authenticity manifestations in the metaverse. *Journal of Business Research*, *170*, 114325. DOI: 10.1016/j.jbusres.2023.114325

Landgrebe, J. (2024). The Rise of Digital Influencer Marketing. *HERMES-Journal of Language and Communication in Business*, (64), 75–102. DOI: 10.7146/hjlcb.vi64.143879

Lee, H., Shin, M., Yang, J., & Chock, T. M. (2024). Virtual influencers vs. human influencers in the context of influencer marketing: The moderating role of machine heuristic on perceived authenticity of influencers. *International Journal of Human-Computer Interaction*, •••, 1–18. DOI: 10.1080/10447318.2024.2374100

Li, H., Lei, Y., Zhou, Q., & Yuan, H. (2023). Can you sense without being human? Comparing virtual and human influencers endorsement effectiveness [Article]. *Journal of Retailing and Consumer Services*, *75*, 103456. Advance online publication. DOI: 10.1016/j.jretconser.2023.103456

Li, L., Liu, S., & Lee, J. Y. (2024). On the Social Media Platform, Virtual Internet Celebrities and Real Idol Brand Spokesmen Perceive Human Nature, Physical Charm, and Study Consumer Reaction Based on Self-Consistency: The Media Effect of Trust [Article]. *WSEAS Transactions on Business and Economics*, *21*, 762–774. DOI: 10.37394/23207.2024.21.64

Lim, R. E., & Lee, S. Y. (2023). "You are a virtual influencer!": Understanding the impact of origin disclosure and emotional narratives on parasocial relationships and virtual influencer credibility. *Computers in Human Behavior*, *148*, 107897. DOI: 10.1016/j.chb.2023.107897

Liu, F., & Lee, Y. H. (2024a). Virtually authentic: Examining the match-up hypothesis between human vs virtual influencers and product types [Article]. *Journal of Product and Brand Management, 33*(2), 287–299. DOI: 10.1108/JPBM-03-2023-4418

Liu, F., & Lee, Y. H. (2024b). Virtually responsible? Attribution of responsibility toward human vs. virtual influencers and the mediating role of mind perception [Article]. *Journal of Retailing and Consumer Services, 77*, 103685. Advance online publication. DOI: 10.1016/j.jretconser.2023.103685

Looi, J., & Kahlor, L. A. (2024). Artificial Intelligence in Influencer Marketing: A Mixed-Method Comparison of Human and Virtual Influencers on Instagram [Article]. *Journal of Interactive Advertising, 24*(2), 107–126. DOI: 10.1080/15252019.2024.2313721

Lopez, C., Chefor, E., & Babin, B. J. (2023). Rethinking Authenticity: An Investigation of Virtual Influencers: An Abstract. In *Developments in Marketing Science: Proceedings of the Academy of Marketing Science* (pp. 95-96). Springer Nature. DOI: 10.1007/978-3-031-24687-6_36

Lou, C., Kiew, S. T. J., Chen, T., Lee, T. Y. M., Ong, J. E. C., & Phua, Z. (2023). Authentically Fake? How Consumers Respond to the Influence of Virtual Influencers [Article]. *Journal of Advertising, 52*(4), 540–557. DOI: 10.1080/00913367.2022.2149641

Masri, Y. A., Hamadneh, S., Al-Dmour, R., & Al-Okaily, M. (2023). Can Computer Virtual Influencers Replace Human Influencers in the Future? An Empirical Investigation in the Age of Digital Transformation [Article]. *Jordan Journal of Business Administration, 19*(4), 498–513. DOI: 10.35516/jjba.v19i4.1430

Meng, L. M., Bie, Y., Yang, M., & Wang, Y. (2024). Watching it motivates me to become stronger: Virtual influencers' impact on consumer self-improvement product preferences [Article]. *Journal of Business Research, 178*, 114654. Advance online publication. DOI: 10.1016/j.jbusres.2024.114654

Meng, L. M., Bie, Y., Yang, M., & Wang, Y. (2025). The effect of human versus virtual influencers: The roles of destination types and self-referencing processes [Article]. *Tourism Management, 106*, 104978. Advance online publication. DOI: 10.1016/j.tourman.2024.104978

Mo, T., & Wang, W. (2024). The virtual new or the real old? The effect of temporal alignment between influencer virtuality and brand heritage narration on consumers' luxury consumption [Article]. *Psychology and Marketing*. Advance online publication. DOI: 10.1002/mar.22132

Mo, Z., & Zhou, M. (2024). Don't Like Them but Take What They Said_ The Effectiveness of Virtual Influencers in Public Service Announcements [Article]. *Journal of Theoretical and Applied Electronic Commerce Research, 19*(3), 2269–2288. DOI: 10.3390/jtaer19030110

Mouritzen, S. L. T., Penttinen, V., & Pedersen, S. (2023). Virtual influencer marketing: the good, the bad and the unreal. *European Journal of Marketing*(ahead-of-print).

Mrad, M., Ramadan, Z., & Nasr, L. I. (2022). Computer-generated influencers: The rise of digital personalities [Article]. *Marketing Intelligence & Planning, 40*(5), 589–603. DOI: 10.1108/MIP-12-2021-0423

Shao, Z. (2024). From human to virtual: Unmasking consumer switching intentions to virtual influencers by an integrated fsQCA and NCA method [Article]. *Journal of Retailing and Consumer Services, 78*, 103715. Advance online publication. DOI: 10.1016/j.jretconser.2024.103715

Sorosrungruang, T., Ameen, N., & Hackley, C. (2024). How real is real enough? Unveiling the diverse power of generative AI-enabled virtual influencers and the dynamics of human responses [Article]. *Psychology and Marketing, 41*(12), 3124–3143. Advance online publication. DOI: 10.1002/mar.22105

Stein, J.-P., Linda Breves, P., & Anders, N. (2024). Parasocial interactions with real and virtual influencers: The role of perceived similarity and human-likeness. *New Media & Society, 26*(6), 3433–3453. DOI: 10.1177/14614448221102900

Suciu, P. (2021). *History Of Influencer Marketing Predates Social Media By Centuries – But Is There Enough Transparency In The 21st Century?* forbes.com. Retrieved 29 Dec from https://www.forbes.com/sites/petersuciu/2020/12/07/history-of-influencer-marketing-predates-social-media-by-centuries--but-is-there-enough-transparency-in-the-21st-century/

Venciute, D., Mackeviciene, I., Kuslys, M., & Correia, R. F. (2023). The role of influencer–follower congruence in the relationship between influencer marketing and purchase behaviour. *Journal of Retailing and Consumer Services, 75*, 103506. https://doi.org/https://doi.org/10.1016/j.jretconser.2023.103506. DOI: 10.1016/j.jretconser.2023.103506

Wan, A., & Jiang, M. (2023). Can Virtual Influencers Replace Human Influencers in Live-Streaming E-Commerce? An Exploratory Study from Practitioners' and Consumers' Perspectives [Article]. *Journal of Current Issues and Research in Advertising, 44*(3), 332–372. DOI: 10.1080/10641734.2023.2224416

Wang, B., Han, Y., Kandampully, J., & Lu, X. (2025). How language arousal affects purchase intentions in online retailing? The role of virtual versus human influencers, language typicality, and trust [Article]. *Journal of Retailing and Consumer Services, 82*, 104106. Advance online publication. DOI: 10.1016/j.jretconser.2024.104106

Wang, L., Li, Y. Q., Ruan, W. Q., & Zhang, S. N. (2024). The congruence effect in tourism activity marketing: The difference between virtual influencers and human influencers [Article]. *Current Issues in Tourism*, 1–19. Advance online publication. DOI: 10.1080/13683500.2024.2400180

Wang, S., & Liu, M. T. (2022). Celebrity endorsement in marketing from 1960 to 2021: A bibliometric review and future agenda. *Asia Pacific Journal of Marketing and Logistics, 35*(4), 849–873. DOI: 10.1108/APJML-12-2021-0918

Wasti, C., Ellizabeth, G., Adhyatma, M. I., & Maulana, A. E. (2024). Anthropomorphism And Authenticity: Exploring The Dynamics Of Virtual Influencers In Contemporary Marketing. *International Journal of Business and Society, 25*(2), 789–809. DOI: 10.33736/ijbs.7631.2024

Xie-Carson, L., Benckendorff, P., & Hughes, K. (2023). Not so different after all? A netnographic exploration of user engagement with non-human influencers on social media [Article]. *Journal of Business Research, 167*, 114149. Advance online publication. DOI: 10.1016/j.jbusres.2023.114149

Xie-Carson, L., Benckendorff, P., & Hughes, K. (2024). Keep it #Unreal: Exploring Instagram Users' Engagement With Virtual Influencers in Tourism Contexts [Article]. *Journal of Hospitality & Tourism Research (Washington, D.C.), 48*(6), 1006–1019. DOI: 10.1177/10963480231180940

Xin, B., Hao, Y., & Xie, L. (2024). Virtual influencers and corporate reputation: From marketing game to empirical analysis [Article]. *Journal of Research in Interactive Marketing, 18*(5), 759–786. DOI: 10.1108/JRIM-10-2023-0330

Yadav, S. S. K., & Bansal, S. (2021). The B2B digital marketing practice-towards an exploration of the'hidden'. *International Journal of Management Practice, 14*(4), 391–410. DOI: 10.1504/IJMP.2021.116585

Yadav, S. S. K., & Dubey, A. (2023). Management innovation: Literature review and research directions. *International Journal of Business and Globalisation, 33*(3), 271–285. DOI: 10.1504/IJBG.2023.129037

Yadav, S. S. K., & Mishra, G. (2022). Corporate Digital Responsibility: Perspectives till date and the way ahead. 2022 5th International Conference on Contemporary Computing and Informatics (IC3I)

Yadav, S. S. K., & Mishra, G. (2024a). Digital Entrepreneurship Ecosystem: An Exploration. 2024 7th International Conference on Contemporary Computing and Informatics (IC3I)

Yadav, S. S. K., & Mishra, G. (2024b). Robotic Process Automation Applications Across Industries: An Exploration. 2024 7th International Conference on Contemporary Computing and Informatics (IC3I)

Yan, J., Xia, S., Jiang, A., & Lin, Z. (2024). The effect of different types of virtual influencers on consumers' emotional attachment. *Journal of Business Research, 177*, 114646. Advance online publication. DOI: 10.1016/j.jbusres.2024.114646

Yang, J., Chuenterawong, P., Lee, H., Tian, Y., & Chock, T. M. (2023). Human versus Virtual Influencer: The Effect of Humanness and Interactivity on Persuasive CSR Messaging [Article]. *Journal of Interactive Advertising, 23*(3), 275–292. DOI: 10.1080/15252019.2023.2189036

Yap, Y. R., & Ismail, N. (2022). Factors of virtual influencer marketing influencing Generation Y consumers' purchase intention in Malaysia [Article]. *International Journal of Internet Marketing and Advertising, 17*(3-4), 437–458. DOI: 10.1504/IJIMA.2022.126735

Yu, J., Dickinger, A., So, K. K. F., & Egger, R. (2024). Artificial intelligence-generated virtual influencer: Examining the effects of emotional display on user engagement. *Journal of Retailing and Consumer Services, 76*, 103560. DOI: 10.1016/j.jretconser.2023.103560

Zhao, T., Ran, Y., Wu, B., Lynette Wang, V., Zhou, L., & Lu Wang, C. (2024). Virtual versus human: Unraveling consumer reactions to service failures through influencer types [Article]. *Journal of Business Research, 178*, 114657. Advance online publication. DOI: 10.1016/j.jbusres.2024.114657

Zheng, X., Miao, M., Zhang, L., & Huang, L. (2024). Standing out or fitting in? How perceived autonomy affects virtual influencer marketing outcomes [Article]. *Journal of Business Research, 185*, 114917. Advance online publication. DOI: 10.1016/j.jbusres.2024.114917

Zhou, X., Yan, X., & Jiang, Y. (2024). Making Sense? The Sensory-Specific Nature of Virtual Influencer Effectiveness [Article]. *Journal of Marketing, 88*(4), 84–106. DOI: 10.1177/00222429231203699

Chapter 6
Parasocial Interaction and Virtual Influencers: Building Connections in a Digital World

Mohd Junaid Akhtar
https://orcid.org/0000-0003-4561-9782
New Delhi Institute of Management, India

Sarita Nagvanshi
https://orcid.org/0009-0007-0442-4213
New Delhi Institute of Management, India

ABSTRACT

In today's digitally driven world, human interaction has transformed significantly, particularly with the emergence of parasocial relationships and virtual influencers. This chapter applies Horton and Wohl (1956) parasocial interaction (PSI) framework to critically analyze how audiences connect with virtual influencers. It examines their appeal to younger demographics like Generation Z, who are more receptive to AI-driven figures, and explores how brands employ these influencers as marketing agents. Ethical concerns are highlighted, including transparency, manipulation, and the promotion of unrealistic standards. The chapter also questions the authenticity of virtual influencers, given their entirely orchestrated personas. Further, the chapter provides a comprehensive exploration of these developments, emphasizing the need for ethical responsibility as technology continues to blur the lines between the virtual and real worlds.

DOI: 10.4018/979-8-3373-0255-3.ch006

1. INTRODUCTION

In the 21st century, the advent of digital technology has fundamentally altered the nature of human interaction, transforming how people connect, communicate, and form relationships (Djarilkanovna & Baxadirovna, 2024). From the earliest days of email and online forums to today's dynamic social media platforms, the evolution of digital communication tools has blurred geographical boundaries, fostering an unprecedented level of global connectivity. The digital age has revolutionized communication, enabling instantaneous interaction across time zones and cultures (Hermawanto & Anggraini, 2020). Traditional media facilitated one-way relationships between celebrities and audiences, but social media platforms have intensified this phenomenon, enabling not only real-life figures but also virtual personas to foster these unique connections (Wikström, 2014; Paul et al., 2022). Unlike traditional communication, which relied heavily on face-to-face or written correspondence, digital platforms provide a hybrid space where individuals can simultaneously consume, share, and produce content (Huttayavilaiphan, 2024). This democratization of communication has amplified the ability of individuals to craft and disseminate their personal narratives, often elevating ordinary people into influencers or public figures with substantial followings. Social media platforms like Instagram, Facebook, TikTok, and YouTube have been at the forefront of this transformation (Hogsnes et al., 2023). They have shifted the focus from one-way communication, exemplified by traditional television and print media, to interactive, multi-directional exchanges. Users are no longer passive recipients of information; they actively engage by liking, commenting, sharing, and creating content. This shift has cultivated a new type of relationship between media figures and audiences, termed "parasocial relationships" (Hoffner & Bond, 2022).

This chapter addresses the theoretical framework of parasocial interaction (PSI) first proposed by Horton and Wohl (1956), which describes the illusionary experience where media consumers feel a personal connection with mediated figures, despite the relationship being one-sided. Originally discussed in the context of traditional television and radio personalities, the concept has since evolved and expanded to include social media influencers, and now, virtual influencers. By applying this framework, this chapter critically analyzes how audiences develop PSI with virtual influencers, drawing from contemporary examples and empirical research in the domains of consumer behavior and media studies. The integration of virtual reality (VR) and augmented reality (AR) technologies promises to deepen parasocial relationships even further, as virtual influencers could become more immersive and interactive, offering real-time, lifelike experiences to their audience (Yu et al., 2024). The boundaries between virtual and real life are likely to blur further with technological advancement, raising important questions about the future of human connection, identity, and interaction in digital spaces (Liu & Lee, 2024). As technology continues to evolve, virtual influencers will likely play an increasingly prominent role in digital marketing and consumer engagement, challenging existing paradigms of social interaction and redefining how connections are formed in the digital age.

Virtual influencers are particularly appealing to younger demographics, such as Generation Z, who have grown up immersed in digital culture and are more open to engaging with AI and CGI-generated figures (Jhawar et al., 2023; Lin et al., 2024). While talking about the dark side of this virtual world, the blurred lines between fiction and reality in the virtual influencer space raise concerns about transparency, manipulation, and the psychological impacts on impressionable audiences (Hwang, 2023). Since virtual influencers are often designed to be aesthetically perfect, there is the risk of promoting unrealistic beauty standards and lifestyles (Ji et al., 2022). Furthermore, the manufactured nature of these influencers can lead to concerns about authenticity, as their behaviors and endorsements are orchestrated entirely by brands or content creators (Sands et al., 2022).

1.1. Purpose of the Chapter

Through an analysis of current trends in marketing and consumer behavior, this chapter examines how virtual influencers act as marketing agents, how brands strategically employ them, and the potential advantages they offer in terms of control, creativity, and adaptability over human influencers. This includes the ability of brands to fully dictate the influencer's persona, interactions, and endorsements without the risk of human error, scandals, or other unpredictable behaviors often associated with real influencers. Additionally, this chapter investigates the ethical challenges of using such influencers for commercial purposes and questions how marketers and platform regulators can ensure ethical responsibility in this new landscape. Further, this chapter also explores the potential future trajectory of virtual influencers and parasocial interaction in a rapidly evolving digital world.

2. THE EVOLUTION OF PARASOCIAL RELATIONSHIPS

Parasocial relationships, originally conceptualized by Horton and Wohl (1956), have undergone a remarkable transformation with the advent of digital technology, becoming a ubiquitous phenomenon in contemporary society. Parasocial relationships defines as the one-sided emotional connections between audiences and mediated figures like television and radio personalities (Loyer, 2015). These relationships can even extend to inanimate objects due to the absence of reciprocated emotion. Unlike human-human interactions, which are typically symmetrical, human-machine interactions are inherently designed to serve human objectives, making them parasocial in nature (Kopecka-Piech & Bolin, 2023). These relationships have expanded and deepened in the digital era, fueled by the unprecedented accessibility and interactivity of social media platforms such as Instagram, YouTube, and TikTok. Unlike traditional media, which offered limited opportunities for engagement, social media allows for continuous, real-time interaction, creating an illusion of reciprocity and intimacy between influencers and their audiences (Paul et al., 2022). This phenomenon is further amplified by the highly curated content influencers share, designed to foster a sense of authenticity and relatability that encourages emotional investment from their followers. As a result, millions of users worldwide feel a deep connection to influencers who, in reality, remain unaware of their existence. These relationships fulfill critical psychological needs, such as companionship, belonging, and validation, making them particularly prevalent among younger demographics like Millennials and Generation Z, who have grown up immersed in a digital-first culture (David, 2019). For them, influencers and digital personas are not just celebrities but also relatable figures who reflect their values, interests, and aspirations. This deep emotional connection has significant implications, particularly in the realms of marketing and consumer behavior, where trust and engagement are key drivers of success (Jarzyna 2021; Zhong et al., 2021).

A key feature of parasocial relationships in the digital age is their significant impact on consumer behavior (Jarzyna 2021). Audiences often view the influencers they follow as trusted friends, valuing their opinions on products, services, and lifestyle choices. This trust has transformed parasocial relationships into a cornerstone of influencer marketing, where brands leverage these connections to drive engagement, and boost sales (Nair & Kumar, 2024). The authenticity perceived in parasocial relationships often makes audiences more receptive to recommendations from influencers than traditional advertising, further highlighting their commercial potential. However, the emergence of virtual influencers has added a new layer of complexity to this dynamic. Unlike human influencers, virtual influencers are entirely manufactured entities, created and controlled by brands or content creators to execute marketing campaigns. Despite their artificial nature, they successfully cultivate parasocial relationships, as audiences emotionally connect with their carefully crafted personalities, narratives, and interactions (Roy & Chakraborty, 2023; Ameen et al., 2024). Their perpetual activity, controversy-free image, and hyper-targeted appeal often make them more effective than their human counterparts in capturing audience attention (Jhawar et al., 2023).

Parasocial relationships are not limited to influencers and celebrities; they extend to fictional characters, political figures, and even organizations, demonstrating their broad applicability across different contexts (Tukachinsky et al., 2020). This versatility has made them a focal point for researchers exploring the intersections of psychology, sociology, marketing, and media studies (Horoub, 2023). As parasocial relationships continue to evolve, they challenge traditional frameworks for understanding human interaction, requiring interdisciplinary approaches to unpack their complexities and implications. The emergence of parasocial relationships represents a profound shift in the dynamics of human interaction, driven by the transformative power of digital technology (Labrecque, 2014). From their origins in traditional media to their current manifestations in social media and virtual influencers, these one-sided connections have redefined how individuals engage with mediated figures, offering both opportunities and challenges in the realms of marketing (Miyake, 2024). As the digital landscape continues to evolve, parasocial relationships are likely to play an increasingly prominent role in shaping the future of human connection, requiring ongoing exploration and critical engagement to navigate their complexities in a rapidly changing world.

3. EVOLUTION OF VIRTUAL INFLUENCERS

Virtual influencers are digitally created characters designed to interact with audiences as human influencers would, yet they are entirely artificial (Stein et al., 2024). Virtual influencers are computer-generated personas, often powered by artificial intelligence (AI) and sophisticated graphic design (Chiu & Ho, 2023; Yu et al., 2024). These influencers are brought to life using a combination of advanced artificial intelligence (AI) and computer-generated imagery (CGI), which allows them to exhibit human-like personalities, emotions, and behaviors (Mrad et al., 2022; Góraj, 2024). Unlike their human counterparts, virtual influencers are not constrained by physical limitations, time, or personal challenges, making them a versatile and controllable tool for brands seeking innovative ways to connect with consumers (Sorosrungruang et al., 2024). By leveraging AI, these digital personas can be programmed to learn and adapt, engaging with audiences through personalized content and interactions that create the illusion of genuine relationships (Bozdağ, (2024). CGI technology, on the other hand, ensures that virtual influencers maintain a polished, aesthetically appealing, and consistent appearance, often surpassing the visual perfection associated with traditional celebrities or influencers (Zhao, 2022). CGI plays a pivotal role in crafting the visual identity of virtual influencers. With advancements in 3D modeling and rendering, these characters can achieve a level of realism that blurs the line between the virtual and the real (Allal-Chérif et al., 2024). This realism is often accompanied by a sense of idealization, as virtual influencers are designed to embody aspirational traits, appearances, and lifestyles.

From high-fashion avatars to relatable "everyday" personas, their versatility enables them to cater to diverse audience preferences and brand strategies (Haukka, 2024).

One of the defining characteristics of virtual influencers is their ability to remain controversy-free. Unlike human influencers, who are subject to personal opinions, biases, or potential scandals, virtual influencers are scripted and managed entirely by their creators, ensuring that their behavior aligns with brand objectives and market expectations (Lou et al., 2023, Koles et al., 2024). This level of control allows brands to mitigate risks associated with traditional influencer marketing while maintaining a dynamic and engaging presence online (Okonkwo & Namkoisse, 2023). The commercial impact of virtual influencers is significant (De Brito Silva et al., 2022). Brands benefit from their cost-effectiveness, as virtual influencers do not require travel, accommodation, or traditional compensation, and their campaigns can be scaled globally with minimal logistical challenges (Teixeira et al., 2023). Furthermore, their scripted nature allows for precise alignment with brand messaging and values, ensuring a cohesive and controlled marketing strategy (Okonkwo & Namkoisse, 2023). In contrast, human influencers, despite their authentic appeal, may introduce unpredictability due to their individual opinions, external commitments, or personal controversies (Koles et al., 2024). Moreover, virtual influencers can be hyper-targeted to specific demographics, with their personas crafted to resonate with particular cultural or consumer niches (Liu et al., 2024). For example, most famous virtual influencer, Lil Miquela, target the Gen Z and millennials interested in fashion, music and social activism (Block & Lovegrove, 2021). Similarly, Shudu Gram make content for the beauty enthusiasts and luxury fashion consumers. Lo Do Magalu target Brazilian online shoppers and tech-savvy consumers. This adaptability makes them particularly valuable in a globalized market where personalization and cultural sensitivity are critical.

The role of AI in virtual influencers extends beyond mere programming; it enables these characters to engage in meaningful, albeit artificial, interactions with their audiences (Looi, 2023). Through natural language processing, AI allows virtual influencers to respond to comments, answer questions, and even participate in trending online conversations, mimicking the behavior of human influencers (Zhou, 2020; Looi & Kahlor, 2024). This capability fosters parasocial relationships, where audiences feel a sense of connection and familiarity with these virtual figures despite the absence of true reciprocity. AI also aids in analyzing audience preferences and behaviors, allowing virtual influencers to optimize their content and remain relevant in an ever-changing digital landscape (Allal-Chérif et al., 2024). The unique blend of AI and CGI allows virtual influencers to transcend the limitations of human influencers, offering brands a reliable, adaptable, and innovative tool for connecting with consumers.

However, this hyper-realism can also lead to ethical concerns as well, such as the promotion of unrealistic beauty standards or the potential manipulation of vulnerable audiences (Ju et al., 2024). Another challenge is the question of authenticity (Sands et al., 2022; Koles et al., 2024). While audiences may admire the creativity and innovation behind virtual influencers, the absence of genuine human experiences can hinder their ability to establish deep emotional connections with certain segments of consumers (Lou et al., 2023). Moreover, the transparency of their artificial nature can lead to skepticism or distrust among audiences who value authenticity over perfection. In response, creators often strive to imbue virtual influencers with relatable backstories, personalities, and narratives, bridging the gap between fiction and reality (Moustakas et al., 2020).

4. VIRTUAL VS REAL INFLUENCERS

When comparing virtual influencers to human influencers, several distinctions emerge. Human influencers draw their appeal from authenticity, relatability, and real-life experiences, which often foster deeper emotional connections with their audiences (Bastrygina et al., 2024; Ebulueme & Vijayakumar, 2024). They build trust through shared values, vulnerabilities, and the perception of being "real people" (Lee, 2020) However, they are also subject to human errors, inconsistencies, and external factors that can impact their reliability and effectiveness as brand ambassadors (Hahl, 2023). Virtual influencers, by contrast, are immune to such limitations. Their appeal lies in their curated perfection, reliability, and the novelty of their digital nature. While they may lack the spontaneity and organic charm of human influencers, they make up for it with consistency, scalability, and the ability to operate 24/7 without fatigue (Dondapati & Dehury, 2024).

The comparison between virtual and real influencers brings to light critical distinctions in their authenticity, adaptability, and impact, significantly shaping contemporary digital marketing strategies. Real influencers, as individuals with personal stories and tangible human experiences, hold an intrinsic ability to forge emotional connections with their audiences (Hund, 2023). Their content, rooted in everyday life, emotions, and genuine interactions, exudes authenticity that often resonates deeply with followers. These connections are further enhanced by their capacity to respond to audience feedback in real-time, navigate cultural nuances, and share personal vulnerabilities that make them relatable (Bastrygina et al., 2024). The trust cultivated by real influencers is a cornerstone of their effectiveness, particularly for campaigns where transparency and credibility are crucial. Virtual influencers, as AI-driven and CGI-crafted digital personas, are free from many of the constraints faced by their human counterparts. These meticulously designed characters are programmed to exhibit human-like traits, including humor, empathy, and charisma, making them appealing to a broad audience (Choudhry et al., 2022). They are immune to human pitfalls such as scandals, fatigue, and unpredictable behavior, providing brands with unparalleled control over their messaging and public image (Sorosrungruang et al., 2024). This precision is particularly advantageous for brands seeking consistency and risk-free representation. Moreover, virtual influencers are capable of maintaining an always-on presence, enabling them to engage audiences across multiple time zones without interruption (Güzel, 2025). Their futuristic appeal and novelty often captivate younger, tech-savvy demographics, particularly Gen Z, who are more open to interacting with AI-driven personas (Ebulueme & Vijayakumar, 2024). Additionally, their ability to hyper-target niche audiences and align seamlessly with brand aesthetics ensures a high degree of customization in marketing campaigns.

However, virtual influencers are not without limitations. Their lack of real-life experience and emotional authenticity often raises skepticism about their ability to genuinely connect with audiences (Lou et al., 2023). While their digital perfection is appealing, it can also appear artificial, leading some consumers to question their reliability and relatability (Koles et al., 2024). This perceived lack of authenticity can be a barrier, particularly in industries where emotional storytelling and genuine engagement are paramount. Moreover, the controlled nature of virtual influencers invites ethical concerns. Critics argue that they often promote unattainable beauty standards and lifestyles, as their flawless appearances are entirely engineered (Gray, 2023; Kauffmann & Vaičiūnaitė, 2024). This can contribute to unrealistic societal expectations, particularly among impressionable audiences. Additionally, because virtual influencers are entirely brand-controlled, their endorsements may lack the spontaneity and transparency typically expected from real influencers, further complicating trust-building efforts (Batinovic et al., 2024; Jhawar, 2024). On the other hand, real influencers bring their own set of challenges. Their human imperfections, while making them relatable, also leave them vulnerable to controversies, inconsistent messaging, and occasional conflicts of interest (Hahl, 2023). For brands, managing partnerships with real influencers requires navigating these potential risks, which can sometimes lead to reputational damage (Cheng & Zhang, 2024). Moreover, real influencers are limited in their capacity to produce content, bound by time, energy, and other personal factors that can affect their consistency and reliability (Backaler & Backaler, 2018).

In a direct comparison, the choice between virtual and real influencers hinges on the specific goals of a marketing campaign. For campaigns emphasizing authenticity, emotional storytelling, and relatability, real influencers offer an unmatched advantage (Liu et al., 2024). Their ability to connect on a human level makes them invaluable for initiatives that require trust and personal engagement. Meanwhile, virtual influencers are ideal for campaigns demanding high precision, consistency, and creative flexibility (Chottechathammanee & Patchimnan, 2024). They excel in scenarios where brands need full control over the narrative or where the futuristic appeal of AI can enhance the campaign's innovative edge. Despite their differences, the convergence of virtual and real influencers is becoming increasingly apparent (You & Liu, 2024). Some brands are experimenting with hybrid strategies, leveraging the strengths of both to maximize their impact. For instance, collaborations between virtual and real influencers can create dynamic campaigns that combine authenticity with innovation, appealing to a diverse audience base (Okonkwo & Namkoisse, 2023). Additionally, the integration of augmented reality (AR) and virtual reality (VR) technologies is blurring the lines between the two, allowing real influencers to adopt virtual elements and virtual influencers to appear more lifelike and interactive (Ju et al., 2024; Sorosrungruang et al., 2024). As technology continues to advance and audience preferences evolve, the interplay between these two forms of influence will likely define the future of digital engagement, offering new opportunities for brands to connect with their audiences in innovative and meaningful ways.

5. VIRTUAL INFLUENCERS IN THE DIGITAL MARKETING ECOSYSTEM

Virtual influencers have rapidly risen as a powerful force in the digital marketing ecosystem, gaining prominence on platforms such as Instagram, YouTube, and TikTok (Gammarano et al., 2024). These virtual influencers are meticulously crafted by teams of developers, marketers, and designers, ensuring that every aspect of their appearance, tone, and behavior aligns seamlessly with the values and objectives of the brands they represent. Platforms like Instagram, with its emphasis on visually captivating and aesthetic-driven content, have become a fertile ground for virtual influencers to showcase their "lives" through posts, stories, and reels, creating an illusion of authenticity and relatability (Teixeira et al., 2023). On YouTube, they engage audiences with long-form content such as vlogs, tutorials, and brand collaborations, while TikTok's dynamic and fast-paced environment is perfect for short, engaging videos that capture the attention of younger audiences, especially Generation Z, who dominate the platform (Pitafi & Awan, 2024).

The rise of virtual influencers is not merely a trend but a reflection of the broader evolution of digital marketing, where brands are constantly seeking innovative ways to connect with an audience that is becoming increasingly selective about how they engage with content (Moustakas et al., 2020; Jhawar et al., 2023). A key factor driving the adoption of virtual influencers is the unparalleled level of control they provide. Unlike their human counterparts, virtual influencers do not have personal lives, controversies, or unpredictable behavior that might jeopardize brand image (Sorosrungruang et al., 2024). Brands can dictate every detail of their content ensuring complete alignment with marketing goals and eliminating risks associated with traditional influencer marketing. This control enables brands to execute campaigns with a level of precision and consistency that is impossible with human influencers, creating a perfect fit for brands that prioritize reputation management and creative storytelling (You & Liu, 2024). Another significant advantage of virtual influencers is their adaptability. These digital personalities can be redesigned or reimagined to fit the needs of a specific campaign, market, or demographic. They can easily adopt new trends, embody diverse cultural identities, or reflect the values of a target audience, making them an ideal tool for brands operating in a rapidly changing market environment (Yu et al., 2024). A virtual influencer can be transformed into an advocate for sustainability, promoting eco-friendly products, or reimagined as a tech-savvy icon championing cutting-edge innovation (Wang et al., 2025). This flexibility allows brands to experiment with bold, imaginative campaigns that push the boundaries of traditional advertising, engaging audiences in fresh and exciting ways.

One of the most compelling reasons for the success of virtual influencers lies in their appeal to younger demographics, particularly Generation Z. Born into the digital age, Gen Z is known for their fluency in technology, affinity for social media, and preference for content that combines authenticity with innovation (Witt & Baird, 2018). Virtual influencers resonate with this demographic because they represent a seamless integration of digital aesthetics, creativity, and relatability (Chiu & Ho, 2023). Despite their artificial nature, many virtual influencers are designed to mimic human emotions, experiences, and values, creating a sense of connection that feels genuine. This is especially effective when these digital personas align with the social causes and values important to Gen Z, such as inclusivity, diversity, and environmental consciousness (Jhawar et al., 2023). By embodying these progressive ideals, virtual influencers position themselves as relatable and aspirational figures, earning the trust and loyalty of younger audiences (Lin et al., 2024). The ability of virtual influencers to engage audiences around the clock further amplifies their value in the digital marketing landscape. Unlike human influencers, who require rest, face physical limitations, and age over time, virtual influencers can remain active and relevant indefinitely (Andersson & Sobek, 2020). They can appear in multiple campaigns simultaneously, across various regions and time zones, providing brands with unmatched scalability and efficiency. Their presence is not limited by geography, language, or physical constraints, allowing them to reach global audiences with ease. This versatility is particularly advantageous for brands looking to expand their international presence or tap into niche markets (Güzel, 2025).

The rise of virtual influencers marks a pivotal moment in the evolution of the digital marketing ecosystem, highlighting the growing importance of creativity, adaptability, and technological innovation in engaging modern consumers (Jhawar et al., 2023). As technology continues to advance, the potential for virtual influencers to transform marketing strategies and redefine consumer engagement is limitless. Their ability to combine precision, scalability, and relatability offers brands an unprecedented opportunity to connect with audiences in meaningful and innovative ways (Allal-Chérif et al., 2024; Melnychuk et al., 2024). While challenges remain, the success of virtual influencers underscores their value as a powerful tool in the arsenal of modern marketing, paving the way for a future where the boundaries between the digital and physical worlds become increasingly blurred.

6. PSYCHOLOGICAL DYNAMICS OF PARASOCIAL RELATIONSHIPS WITH VIRTUAL INFLUENCERS

Virtual influencers are fictional, computer-generated characters crafted specifically for marketing and social engagement activities (Paulovics, 2023). These digital entities exist solely within virtual environments and are designed to emulate human traits, behaviors, and actions without representing any real individuals (Burden & Savin-Baden, 2019). Their primary purpose is to engage audiences by participating in marketing collaborations, raising awareness through social campaigns, and creating interactive content tailored for digital platforms (Paulovics, 2023). While virtual influencers may seem like a modern innovation, the concept dates back to the creation of Kyoko Date in 1996, who was introduced as a virtual Japanese pop star (Nguyen, 2023). However, the phenomenon gained widespread recognition in 2016 with the advent of Lil Miquela, a virtual influencer who captivated audiences through her unique narrative and fashion-forward content (Shieber, 2018). Since then, numerous virtual personas have emerged, each offering distinct aesthetic and thematic elements to capture audience attention. For example, Noonouri's anime-inspired appearance appeals to fans of stylized art, while Shudu, the world's first digital supermodel, showcases the intricacies of photorealistic design and anthropomorphism in virtual agents (Mirowska & Arsenyan, 2023). Virtual influencers actively engage in the practice of microcelebrity (Marwick, 2018), leveraging platforms like Instagram and YouTube to interact with followers and promote brands. A particularly popular subset of virtual influencers is VTubers, or virtual YouTubers, who deliver performances using 3D animated avatars paired with voiceovers (Paulovics, 2023). VTubing gained traction in 2016 but has roots as far back as 2011, with YouTuber Ami Yamato pioneering the use of 3D animated avatars in her content (Rozema,

2022). VTubers often cater to niche interests, further cementing their role as key players in the evolving landscape of influencer marketing.

Recent studies highlight the growing popularity of virtual influencers, showing that users engage with their posts three times more frequently than they do with those of human influencers, an outcome attributed to the novelty and creative flexibility of virtual personas (Conti et al., 2022). This heightened engagement makes them attractive to global brands, as evidenced by notable collaborations with renowned companies like Balmain, Dior, IKEA, and Calvin Klein, underscoring their commercial appeal and adaptability (Morency, 2018). Additionally, during the COVID-19 pandemic, virtual influencers played a pivotal role in raising awareness about social distancing and other preventive measures, showcasing their utility in public service campaigns (Paulovics, 2023). The interactions between audiences and virtual influencers can be understood through the framework of parasocial interactions (PSIs) and parasocial relationships (PSRs). Originally conceptualized by Horton and Wohl (1956) as basic perceptual illusions, PSIs have since been expanded to include cognitive, affective, and conative dimensions, such as thinking about a character's behavior, empathizing with them, or appreciating their humor (Dibble et al., 2016; Schramm & Hartmann, 2008). Repeated interactions may lead audiences to form PSRs, which resemble real-life friendships or romantic bonds to some extent, built on consistent engagement and the sense of familiarity that virtual influencers create through their curated content (Tukachinsky & Stever, 2018). Understanding the motivations behind following virtual influencers requires consideration of the uses and gratifications (U&G) theory, which posits that audiences engage with media for their own benefit (Katz, 1959). Virtual influencers provide entertainment, escapism, and novelty, allowing audiences to connect with content that avoids the complexities often associated with human influencers' personal lives (Arsenyan & Mirowska, 2021). However, their effectiveness is not without challenges. Mori's (1970) uncanny valley theory predicts that as artificial faces become overly realistic, they may evoke unease or distrust among consumers (Lou et al., 2023). There is a delicate balance to maintain, as perceptions of authenticity and transparency significantly impact consumer trust and receptiveness to sponsored content (Molin & Nordgren, 2019; Moustakas et al., 2020).

Despite these concerns, virtual influencers continue to thrive in a competitive digital landscape marked by short attention spans and an abundance of content. Their ability to mimic human emotional sharing and adapt seamlessly to various brand narratives positions them as valuable assets in marketing strategies (Chang, 2010). Moreover, their fully customizable nature enables brands to exert greater control over messaging and content alignment, while their creative flexibility makes them especially appealing to brands seeking innovative marketing approaches (Conti et al., 2022; Morency, 2018). For many, virtual influencers provide a "sweet escape," delivering entertainment without the deep emotional entanglements often linked to human influencers (Mirowska & Arsenyan, 2023). Their lack of personal controversies offers brands a unique advantage, ensuring a consistent and reliable public image. Furthermore, their highly adaptable personas allow them to cater to diverse audience segments, aligning seamlessly with specific marketing objectives or cultural preferences. The versatility of virtual influencers extends beyond traditional marketing, with applications in education, advocacy, and entertainment, exemplifying their potential to influence broader societal narratives (Paulovics, 2023). The evolution of virtual influencers aligns with broader advancements in artificial intelligence, augmented reality, and virtual reality technologies (Mouritzen et al., 2024). These innovations promise to deepen the immersive nature of digital engagement, enabling audiences to experience real-time, lifelike interactions with virtual personas (Morency, 2018). As these technologies mature, virtual influencers may blur the boundaries between fiction and reality, raising critical ethical questions about identity, authenticity, and the nature of human-computer relationships (Rozema, 2022). The potential for virtual influencers to personalize content at scale represents a significant leap forward in audience engagement, but it also underscores the need for responsible design and transparent communication to maintain trust. The emergence of virtual influencers as key players in digital marketing exemplifies the intersection of technology, psychology, and creativity (Kim, E. et al., 2024). Their ability to engage audiences through carefully curated narratives and innovative content strategies has reshaped the influencer landscape, providing brands with novel tools to connect with consumers. However, their success depends on navigating challenges related to authenticity, transparency, and ethical considerations (Gurrieri et al., 2023). By striking a balance between technological innovation and genuine connection, virtual influencers have the potential to redefine how audiences interact with digital media, paving the way for a future where human and virtual elements coexist harmoniously in the pursuit of meaningful engagement.

7. ETHICAL CONSIDERATIONS AND CHALLENGES

Recently, researchers have shown increasing interest in the field of Explainable Artificial Intelligence (XAI), which aims to enhance transparency in intelligent systems and inform users about the decision-making processes behind system behavior, predictions, or recommendations (Wang et al., 2023). XAI initiatives span diverse domains, including recommender systems in educational settings (Karga & Satratzemi, 2019; Zheng & Toribio, 2021), autonomous driving systems (Schneider et al., 2021), clinical decision-support systems (Bussone et al., 2015), and robotics (Kaptein et al., 2017). These applications highlight the critical need for transparency, as complex systems increasingly impact various facets of human life. While XAI is central to this effort, transparency involves more than simply explaining algorithmic decisions. It extends to encompass the explainability of any decisions in online systems that directly or indirectly affect consumers and end users (Wang et al., 2023). In the context of virtual influencers, transparency becomes particularly nuanced and multifaceted, as these artificial entities operate at the confluence of marketing, social interaction, and digital entertainment. The relationship between trust and acceptance of virtual robots has been extensively explored, with findings consistently indicating that trust in these systems depends significantly on social-emotional factors (Molin & Nordgren, 2019). When applied to virtual influencers, the dynamics become even more intricate. These digital personas are not mere participants in interactions but active agents influencing and shaping consumer behavior (Rachmad, 2024). Trust alone is insufficient in this context; the perceived credibility of the virtual influencer is equally critical to their effectiveness (Molin & Nordgren, 2019). This dual emphasis on trust and credibility underscores the challenges these artificial figures face in creating meaningful connections with audiences. Unlike human influencers, who naturally exhibit authenticity and emotional relatability, virtual influencers must rely on carefully curated and algorithmically designed narratives to simulate similar traits (Guthrie, 2020). Authenticity, as a cornerstone of consumer behavior, is particularly influential in purchasing decisions. Research has demonstrated that authenticity serves as the strongest predictor of whether a consumer will purchase a product, even surpassing the role of trustworthiness (Hund, 2023). Virtual influencers, however, often encounter significant hurdles in this domain. Despite leveraging hyper-realistic visuals and humanlike traits, they face perceptions of artificiality that can undermine their ability to forge emotional bonds with audiences (Gerrath et al., 2024). These challenges highlight the delicate balance required in crafting virtual personas that are both relatable and effective, without crossing into territory that erodes their credibility.

The appearance and behavior of virtual influencers are critical factors in fostering trust and engagement. Studies reveal that consumers are more inclined to interact with virtual influencers who exhibit humanlike traits, as these align with ingrained expectations of social interaction (Molin & Nordgren, 2019). Nevertheless, there is a fine line to navigate. An overly humanlike appearance risks triggering discomfort or suspicion, a phenomenon commonly associated with the uncanny valley effect (Molin & Nordgren, 2019). This delicate interplay between relatability and realism necessitates a highly strategic approach to the design and deployment of virtual influencers. For example, by incorporating subtle imperfections or stylized features, virtual influencers can appear approachable without veering into unsettling realism. Despite such efforts, significant disadvantages persist. Chief among them is the difficulty of establishing emotional connections with audiences—a critical component of influencer success (Yan & Liu, 2024). Even with advanced technologies enabling hyper-realistic visuals, virtual influencers often fall short in replicating the depth and spontaneity of human emotion, raising questions about their long-term viability in cultivating genuine consumer relationships (Kim, I. et al., 2024). The novelty of virtual influencers also introduces important ethical considerations, particularly concerning transparency. As these artificial personas become increasingly sophisticated, the potential for audience deception grows, necessitating clear ethical guidelines. Transparency has emerged as a critical area of concern for consumers, brands, and regulatory bodies alike, as all grapple with the implications of this phenomenon (Yan & Liu, 2024). For instance, the Federal Trade Commission (FTC) has emphasized the importance of clear disclosure in influencer marketing to ensure that audiences are fully aware of the artificial nature of virtual influencers (Kim & Wang, 2023). Such disclosures are particularly relevant when virtual influencers adopt highly humanlike appearances, which can blur the boundaries between reality and fiction. Another threat that catches the eye regarding virtual influencers is catfishing. Catfishing refers to the act of deceiving people by creating a fake online identity. Virtual influencers, being entirely computer-generated, present a unique challenge in this regard. If audiences mistakenly perceive virtual influencers as real individuals, the subsequent discovery of their artificiality may lead to feelings of betrayal and manipulation, ultimately eroding trust (Sharma & Singh, 2019). These dynamic highlights the importance of proactive communication and transparency in mitigating such risks and preserving audience confidence.

Transparency in the realm of virtual influencers is not merely an ethical obligation but also a practical necessity for maintaining consumer trust (Kim & Wang, 2023). As these digital personas continue to gain prominence, audiences are becoming increasingly aware of the importance of transparency in influencer marketing. Deception—whether intentional or inadvertent—poses significant risks, both to consumer trust and to the reputation of the brands associated with virtual influencers. For example, followers who initially believe a virtual influencer to be a real person may feel betrayed when they discover their artificial nature (Koles et al., 2024). These feelings of manipulation can have long-lasting consequences, tarnishing both the virtual influencer's credibility and the brand's image. To address these challenges, brands and developers must adopt proactive communication strategies that emphasize transparency from the outset (Kim, J. et al., 2024). This includes clear disclosure of the virtual influencer's artificial nature, as well as providing insights into the creative and technological processes behind their creation. Such measures not only enhance audience trust but also position virtual influencers as authentic and innovative marketing tools in a rapidly evolving digital landscape (Okonkwo & Namkoisse, 2023). The ethical concerns surrounding virtual influencers extend beyond transparency and into the realm of accountability. Unlike human influencers, who can be held personally responsible for their actions, virtual influencers operate under the control of brands or creators. This dynamic raise important questions about who is accountable for the content and messages disseminated by these artificial entities. Additionally, as virtual influencers become more integrated into society, their potential impact on cultural norms and values warrants careful consideration (Kim & Wang, 2023). For instance, the ability of virtual influencers to adapt their personas to align with specific marketing objectives or cultural preferences underscores their versatility. However, it also raises concerns about the potential for manipulation and the perpetuation of harmful stereotypes or biases. Another threat poses by the virtual influencer is human job displacement. As virtual influencers are increasingly used for marketing on social media, raising concerns about job displacement, especially in influencer marketing. They have the potential to replace human influencers, affecting careers in modeling, acting, and social media management. However, their development and maintenance also generate employment opportunities in areas such as animation, graphic design, and AI programming. As a result, their overall impact on the job market remains multifaceted and continues to evolve. Addressing these issues requires a collaborative effort between brands, developers, and regulatory bodies to establish clear ethical guidelines for the use and development of virtual influencers.

8. FUTURE TRAJECTORY OF VIRTUAL INFLUENCERS AND PARASOCIAL INTERACTION

The development of virtual influencers holds extraordinary potential as artificial intelligence and immersive virtual environments continue to gain prominence (Sorosrungruang et al., 2024). These advancements present opportunities for brands to engage broader and younger audiences through innovative mediums, leveraging the unique capabilities of virtual influencers. With their boundless creative storyworlds and cutting-edge technologies, these influencers enable real-time interactions, enhance customer retention, and support service functions, ultimately improving brand-consumer relationship management (Zhao et al., 2024). The future of virtual influencers lies in the synthesis of computer-generated imagery and AI, empowering them to generate posts autonomously and seamlessly communicate with followers (Belova, 2021). While most virtual influencers today are CGI-made and operate primarily through static social media posts or pre-recorded videos, advancements in AI are enabling more dynamic functionalities, such as live interviews and real-time engagements (Paulovics, 2023). Beyond advertising and marketing, virtual influencers are poised to impact a range of fields by expanding their applications, offering personalized experiences in areas such as education, entertainment, and customer service (Belova, 2021). However, these developments also raise critical ethical concerns, including questions about authenticity, transparency, and accountability in influencer marketing. Addressing these issues is imperative for fostering trust and ensuring the ethical deployment of these influencers in the digital ecosystem. The integration of virtual influencers into communication platforms further necessitates the development of new systems to optimize their behavior and maximize their potential (Paulovics, 2023). Future research should investigate how variations in human-likeness and anime-likeness among virtual influencers, such as those seen in Noonuri and Kizuna AI, influence audience perceptions, including trustworthiness and likability, as well as engagement metrics like likes, shares, and comments (Kim et al., 2024). Understanding these factors will provide valuable insights for optimizing virtual influencer's designs to align with diverse audience preferences.

Despite the innovative promise of virtual influencers, the nascent and fragmented nature of their research presents challenges to understanding their full potential (Sorosrungruang et al., 2024). Current studies rely heavily on academic theses, media articles, and blogs, but future investigations would benefit from a more structured approach that focuses on peer-reviewed scholarly works to enhance the validity and reliability of findings. Such research could explore factors influencing audience attraction to virtual influencers, such as perceived brand congruence and similarity, which likely play crucial roles in shaping engagement (Kim & Park, 2023). Comparative analyses of user interactions with virtual influencers versus human influencers could also highlight the unique attributes of these influencers and their implications for marketing strategies (Sorosrungruang et al., 2024). Moreover, examining the technological and creative processes behind virtual influencers' development, such as the combination of AI and CGI, could inform best practices for creating virtual personas that resonate with diverse audiences (Lou et al., 2023). As virtual influencers become increasingly interactive and human-like, it is vital to study their psychological and social effects, particularly how real-time interactions influence perceptions of authenticity and emotional connection. Additionally, virtual influencers' potential applications extend beyond marketing, offering opportunities to address societal needs such as raising awareness for social issues or promoting sustainable practices. Exploring these possibilities will illuminate new avenues for leveraging virtual influencers to create value across industries while addressing ethical and cultural concerns. Ultimately, the future trajectory of virtual influencers and parasocial interaction lies in advancing responsible innovation and fostering meaningful connections between digital personas and audiences. By addressing these challenges and opportunities, society can harness the immense potential of VIs while mitigating associated risks, ensuring their continued relevance and effectiveness in a rapidly evolving digital landscape.

9. CONCLUSION

The exploration of parasocial interaction and virtual influencers offers a lens into the evolving nature of human connection in the digital age. These dynamics reveal how traditional media's one-sided relationships have transformed into deeply interactive, albeit illusionary, bonds facilitated by artificial intelligence and social media platforms. The rise of virtual influencers marks a significant shift in consumer engagement, redefining the boundaries of authenticity, trust, and connection in an increasingly virtual world. This chapter has illustrated how virtual influencers serve as a testament to technological innovation, blending AI, CGI, and advanced algorithms to create hyper-personalized marketing agents. Unlike human influencers, these digital personas are meticulously crafted to align with brand values, offering unparalleled consistency, scalability, and controversy-free engagement. By applying Horton and Wohl's (1956) framework of parasocial interaction (PSI), we understand how audiences emotionally connect with these digital figures, despite their lack of reciprocity. This phenomenon is particularly prominent among Generation Z, a demographic inherently comfortable navigating digital spaces and engaging with AI-driven technologies. Virtual influencers' ability to mimic human-like behaviors and foster relatability allows them to transcend their artificial nature, creating meaningful, albeit orchestrated, connections with audiences.

However, this innovation does come without ethical and practical challenges. The manufactured perfection of virtual influencers raises concerns about promoting unrealistic beauty standards and lifestyles, potentially affecting audience self-perception and mental well-being. Additionally, the inherent artificiality of these figures can compromise their authenticity, a key driver of trust in influencer marketing. This lack of authenticity creates a dichotomy where audiences value the creativity of virtual influencers but remain skeptical of their emotional credibility. Furthermore, the rise of virtual influencers necessitates transparency and ethical responsibility from brands and creators. Clear disclosure of their artificial nature is imperative to avoid audience manipulation and ensure trust remains at the forefront of their engagement. The comparison between virtual and real influencers highlights critical distinctions in authenticity, adaptability, and emotional resonance. While human influencers excel in relatability and genuine connection, they are limited by human vulnerabilities, personal controversies, and scalability issues. Virtual influencers, by contrast, thrive in consistency, creative flexibility, and global accessibility. Their curated perfection and perpetual availability make them ideal for brands seeking innovative and risk-free marketing strategies. Yet, their reliance on programming and lack of real-world experiences pose limitations in establishing deep emotional connections. As the digital landscape evolves, a hybrid approach combining the strengths of both virtual and human influencers could redefine influencer marketing, maximizing engagement through authenticity and innovation.

The future trajectory of virtual influencers and parasocial relationships lies in the integration of emerging technologies like virtual reality (VR) and augmented reality (AR). These technologies promise to deepen the immersive nature of digital interactions, enabling audiences to experience real-time, lifelike engagements with virtual influencers. This shift will blur the lines between virtual and physical realities, raising critical questions about identity, connection, and the ethics of human-computer interaction. As these advancements unfold, the role of virtual influencers will likely expand beyond marketing, influencing fields such as education, entertainment, and public health. Virtual influencers epitomize the convergence of technology and human psychology, offering both opportunities and challenges in the realm of digital engagement. Their success underscores the transformative potential of AI-driven innovations, yet it also highlights the importance of ethical responsibility in navigating the complexities of human interaction. As society continues to embrace virtual influencers, balancing innovation with authenticity, transparency, and social accountability will be crucial in shaping a digital future that values meaningful connections over artificial perfection. Future research should focus on the long-term effects of virtual influencers on mental health, particularly in terms of unrealistic beauty standards. Additionally, clearer ethical guidelines for transparency in influencer marketing are essential to maintain audience trust. Lastly, exploring hybrid models combining human and virtual influencers may enhance engagement, allowing brands to leverage the strengths of both.

REFERENCES

Allal-Chérif, O., Puertas, R., & Carracedo, P. (2024). Intelligent influencer marketing: How AI-powered virtual influencers outperform human influencers. *Technological Forecasting and Social Change*, *200*, 123113. DOI: 10.1016/j.techfore.2023.123113

Ameen, N., Cheah, J. H., Ali, F., El-Manstrly, D., & Kulyciute, R. (2024). Risk, trust, and the roles of human versus virtual influencers. *Journal of Travel Research*, *63*(6), 1370–1394. DOI: 10.1177/00472875231190601

Andersson, V., & Sobek, T. (2020). *Virtual avatars, virtual influencers & authenticity* (Master's Thesis, Gothenburg University).

Arsenyan, J., & Mirowska, A. (2021). Almost human? A comparative case study on the social media presence of virtual influencers. *International Journal of Human-Computer Studies*, *155*, 102694. DOI: 10.1016/j.ijhcs.2021.102694

Backaler, J., & Backaler, J. (2018). Know the risks: The Dark side of influencer collaboration. *Digital Influence: Unleash the Power of Influencer Marketing to Accelerate Your Global Business*, 137-154.

Bastrygina, T., Lim, W. M., Jopp, R., & Weissmann, M. A. (2024). Unraveling the power of social media influencers: Qualitative insights into the role of Instagram influencers in the hospitality and tourism industry. *Journal of Hospitality and Tourism Management*, *58*, 214–243. DOI: 10.1016/j.jhtm.2024.01.007

Batinovic, H., Tingelhoff, F., Hammerschmidt, M., & Schöbel, S. (2024). Come closer, but not too close: How virtual influencers can facilitate or restrict brand experiences in the metaverse. *Proceedings of the 57th Hawaii International Conference on System Sciences*. DOI: 10.24251/HICSS.2024.338

Belova, A. (2021). Virtual influencers in multimodal advertising. *The Journal of V. N. Karazin Kharkiv National University Series: Foreign Philology.Methods of Foreign Language Teaching*, *93*(93), 14–21. DOI: 10.26565/2227-8877-2021-93-02

Block, E., & Lovegrove, R. (2021). Discordant storytelling,'honest fakery', identity peddling: How uncanny CGI characters are jamming public relations and influencer practices. *Public Relations Inquiry*, *10*(3), 265–293. DOI: 10.1177/2046147X211026936

Bozdağ, A. A. (2024). The AI-mediated intimacy economy: A paradigm shift in digital interactions. *AI & Society*, •••, 1–22. DOI: 10.1007/s00146-024-02132-6

Burden, D., & Savin-Baden, M. (2019). *Virtual humans: Today and tomorrow.* Chapman and Hall/CRC. DOI: 10.1201/9781315151199

Bussone, A., Stumpf, S., & O'Sullivan, D. (2015). The Role of Explanations on Trust and Reliance in Clinical Decision Support Systems. *2015 International Conference on Healthcare Informatics*, 160–169. https://doi.org/DOI: 10.1109/ICHI.2015.26

Chang, T. (2010). Gaming will save us all. *Communications of the ACM, 53*(3), 22–24. DOI: 10.1145/1666420.1666431

Cheng, M., & Zhang, S. (2024). *Reputation burning: Analyzing the impact of brand sponsorship on social influencers.* Management Science, Vol. Ahead of the Print No. Ahead of the Print.

Chiu, C. L., & Ho, H. C. (2023). Impact of celebrity, micro-celebrity, and virtual influencers on Chinese Gen Z's purchase intention through social media. *SAGE Open, 13*(1), 21582440231164034. DOI: 10.1177/21582440231164034

Chottechathammanee, P. D. P., & Patchimnan, A. P. D. M. (2024). Influencing the virtual realm: The impact of virtual influencers on brand awareness and consumer purchasing decisions in thailand's digital marketplace. *International Journal of Operations and Quantitative Management, 30*(1), 127–141.

Choudhry, A., Han, J., Xu, X., & Huang, Y. (2022). " I felt a little crazy following a'doll'" investigating real influence of virtual influencers on their followers. *Proceedings of the ACM on human-computer interaction, 6*(GROUP), 1-28.

Conti, M., Gathani, J., & Tricomi, P. P. (2022). Virtual influencers in online social media. *IEEE Communications Magazine, 60*(8), 1–13. DOI: 10.1109/MCOM.001.2100786

David, K. (2019). *Parasocial attachment within social networking sites: Finding comfort and security in those you follow online* (Doctoral dissertation, Regent University).

De Brito Silva, M. J., de Oliveira Ramos Delfino, L., Alves Cerqueira, K., & de Oliveira Campos, P. (2022). Avatar marketing: A study on the engagement and authenticity of virtual influencers on Instagram. *Social Network Analysis and Mining, 12*(1), 130. DOI: 10.1007/s13278-022-00966-w

Dibble, J. L., Hartmann, T., & Rosaen, S. F. (2016). Parasocial interaction and parasocial relationship: Conceptual clarification and a critical assessment of measures. *Human Communication Research, 42*(1), 21–44. DOI: 10.1111/hcre.12063

Djarilkanovna, E. A., & Baxadirovna, M. M. (2024). The digital media revolution: Transforming communication, entertainment, and information in the 21st century. *Miasto Przyszłości, 46*, 813–816.

Dondapati, A., & Dehury, R. K. (2024). Virtual vs. Human influencers: The battle for consumer hearts and minds. *Computers in Human Behavior: Artificial Humans, 2*(1), 100059. DOI: 10.1016/j.chbah.2024.100059

Ebulueme, J., & Vijayakumar, V. (2024). Authenticity and influence: Interactions between social media micro-influencers and generation Z on Instagram. *Critique, 14*(4), 568–586.

Gammarano, I. D. J. L. P., Dholakia, N., Arruda Filho, E. J. M., & Dholakia, R. R. (2024). Beyond influence: Unraveling the complex tapestry of digital influencer dynamics in hyperconnected cultures. *European Journal of Marketing, 59*(1), 21–58. DOI: 10.1108/EJM-07-2023-0552

Gerrath, M. H., Olya, H., Shah, Z., & Li, H. (2024). Virtual influencers and pro-environmental causes: The roles of message warmth and trust in experts. *Journal of Business Research, 175*, 114520. DOI: 10.1016/j.jbusres.2024.114520

Góraj, K. (2024). The impact of computer-generated influencers on social media advertising. *Social Communication, 25*(1), 137–144. DOI: 10.57656/sc-2024-0014

Gray, N. M. (2023). *Botched This Way: An Autoethnographic Exploration of Beauty Standards, Celebrity, and Surgical Culture on Instagram* (Master's thesis, San Diego State University).

Gurrieri, L., Drenten, J., & Abidin, C. (2023). Symbiosis or parasitism? A framework for advancing interdisciplinary and socio-cultural perspectives in influencer marketing. *Journal of Marketing Management, 39*(11-12), 911–932. DOI: 10.1080/0267257X.2023.2255053

Guthrie, S. (2020). Virtual influencers: More human than humans. In *Influencer Marketing* (pp. 271–285). Routledge. DOI: 10.4324/9780429322501-20

Güzel, Ç. Ö. (2025). The authenticity of AI influencers in marketing. In *Understanding Generative AI in a Cultural Context: Artificial Myths and Human Realities* (pp. 247-274). IGI Global Scientific Publishing.

Hahl, S. (2023). *Perception of uncredibility in influencers' paid social media marketing collaborations* (Master's thesis, Aalto University).

Haukka, K. (2024). Metaverse fashion retail in the Nordics: Future signals and buyer personas. (Master's thesis, Haaga-Helia University of Applied Sciences).

Hermawanto, A., & Anggraini, M. (2020, October). Globalization and locality: Global communication and digital revolution in the borderless world era. In *Proceeding of LPPM UPN "Veteran" Yogyakarta Conference Series 2020–Political and Social Science Series* (Vol. 1, No. 1, pp. 9-16). DOI: 10.31098/pss.v1i1.84

Hoffner, C. A., & Bond, B. J. (2022). Parasocial relationships, social media, & well-being. *Current Opinion in Psychology*, *45*, 101306. DOI: 10.1016/j.copsyc.2022.101306 PMID: 35219157

Hogsnes, M., Grønli, T. M., & Hansen, K. (2023). Unconsciously influential: Understanding sociotechnical influence on social media. *Scandinavian Journal of Information Systems*, *35*(2), 1.

Horoub, I. (2023). Exploring the nexus of citizen journalism, technology, and psychology: Insights from Palestinian journalists. *Journalism Practice*, •••, 1–27. DOI: 10.1080/17512786.2023.2288588

Horton, D., & Wohl, R. R. (1956). Mass communication and para-social interaction: Observations on intimacy at a distance. *Psychiatry*, *19*(3), 215–229. DOI: 10.1080/00332747.1956.11023049 PMID: 13359569

Hund, E. (2023). *The influencer industry: The quest for authenticity on social media*. Princeton University Press.

Huttayavilaiphan, R. (2024). From local flavor to global fandom: An exploration of the cultural presentation and attitudes towards using English by Thai content creators on the TikTok platform. *Frontiers in Communication*, *9*, 1453316. DOI: 10.3389/fcomm.2024.1453316

Hwang, S. (2023). *The introduction of human and AI-powered virtual influencers on social media marketing* (Doctoral dissertation, Carnegie Mellon University).

Jarzyna, C. L. (2021). Parasocial interaction, the COVID-19 quarantine, and digital age media. *Human Arenas*, *4*(3), 413–429. DOI: 10.1007/s42087-020-00156-0

Jhawar, A. (2024). Can virtual influencers induce destination visit intentions? A mediation analysis journey through the uncanny valley. *Journal of Travel Research*, •••, 00472875241291144. DOI: 10.1177/00472875241291144

Jhawar, A., Kumar, P., & Varshney, S. (2023). The emergence of virtual influencers: A shift in the influencer marketing paradigm. *Young Consumers*, *24*(4), 468–484. DOI: 10.1108/YC-05-2022-1529

Ji, Q., Linghu, L., & Qiao, F. (2022, July). The beauty myth of virtual influencers: A reflection of real-world female body image stereotypes. In *2022 3rd International Conference on Mental Health, Education and Human Development (MHEHD 2022)* (pp. 784-787). Atlantis Press. DOI: 10.2991/assehr.k.220704.142

Ju, N., Kim, T., & Im, H. (2024). Fake human but real influencer: The interplay of authenticity and human likeness in Virtual Influencer communication? *Fashion and Textiles, 11*(1), 16. DOI: 10.1186/s40691-024-00380-0

Kaptein, F., Broekens, J., Hindriks, K., & Neerincx, M. (2017). Personalised self-explanation by robots. *RO-MAN 2017 - 26th IEEE International Symposium on Robot and Human Interactive Communication, 2017-January*, 676–682. https://doi.org/DOI: 10.1109/ROMAN.2017.8172376

Karga, S., & Satratzemi, M. (2019). Using explanations for recommender systems in learning design settings to enhance teachers' acceptance and perceived experience. *Education and Information Technologies, 24*(5), 2953–2974. DOI: 10.1007/s10639-019-09909-z

Katz, E. (1959). Mass communications research and the study of popular culture: An editorial note on a possible future for this journal. *Studies in Public Communication.* https://repository.upenn.edu/entities/publication/09b95935-2c75-4752-8009-4df2d03c0c41

Kauffmann, P., & Vaičiūnaitė, S. (2024). *An ethical dilemma in influencer marketing: Discovering social media influencers' justifications for promoting aesthetic surgery* (Master's thesis, Lund University).

Khan, S. W., Raza, S. H., & Zaman, U. (2022). Remodeling digital marketplace through Metaverse: A multi-path model of consumer neuroticism, parasocial relationships, social media influencers credibility, and openness to Metaverse experience. [PJCSS]. *Pakistan Journal of Commerce and Social Sciences, 16*(3), 337–365.

Kim, D., & Wang, Z. (2023). The ethics of virtuality: Navigating the complexities of human-like virtual influencers in the social media marketing realm. *Frontiers in Communication, 8*, 1205610. DOI: 10.3389/fcomm.2023.1205610

Kim, E. (Anna), Shoenberger, H., Kim, D., Thorson, E., & Zihang, E. (. (2024). Novelty vs. trust in virtual influencers: Exploring the effectiveness of human-like virtual influencers and anime-like virtual influencers. *International Journal of Advertising*, •••, 1–31. DOI: 10.1080/02650487.2024.2386916

Kim, H., & Park, M. (2023). Virtual influencers' attractiveness effect on purchase intention: A moderated mediation model of the Product–Endorser fit with the brand. *Computers in Human Behavior, 143*, 107703. DOI: 10.1016/j.chb.2023.107703

Kim, I., Ki, C. W., Lee, H., & Kim, Y. K. (2024). Virtual influencer marketing: Evaluating the influence of virtual influencers' form realism and behavioral realism on consumer ambivalence and marketing performance. *Journal of Business Research, 176*, 114611. DOI: 10.1016/j.jbusres.2024.114611

Kim, J., Kim, M., & Lee, S. M. (2024). Unlocking trust dynamics: An exploration of playfulness, expertise, and consumer behavior in virtual influencer marketing. *International Journal of Human-Computer Interaction*, •••, 1–13.

Koles, B., Audrezet, A., Moulard, J. G., Ameen, N., & McKenna, B. (2024). The authentic virtual influencer: Authenticity manifestations in the metaverse. *Journal of Business Research, 170*, 114325. DOI: 10.1016/j.jbusres.2023.114325

Kopecka-Piech, K., & Bolin, G. (Eds.). (2023). *Contemporary challenges in mediatisation research*. Routledge, Taylor & Francis Group. DOI: 10.4324/9781003324591

Labrecque, L. I. (2014). Fostering consumer–brand relationships in social media environments: The role of parasocial interaction. *Journal of Interactive Marketing, 28*(2), 134–148. DOI: 10.1016/j.intmar.2013.12.003

Lee, J. A. (2020). *What makes social media influencers authentic? Understanding perceived authenticity of social media influencers* (Doctoral dissertation).

Lin, Q., Ng, S. I., Kamal Basha, N., Luo, X., & Li, Y. (2024). Impact of virtual influencers on customer engagement of Generation Z consumers: A presence perspective. *Young Consumers, 25*(6), 851–868. DOI: 10.1108/YC-01-2024-1958

Liu, F., & Lee, Y. H. (2024). Virtually authentic: Examining the match-up hypothesis between human vs virtual influencers and product types. *Journal of Product and Brand Management, 33*(2), 287–299. DOI: 10.1108/JPBM-03-2023-4418

Looi, J., & Kahlor, L. A. (2024). Artificial intelligence in influencer marketing: A mixed-method comparison of human and virtual influencers on instagram. *Journal of Interactive Advertising, 24*(2), 107–126. DOI: 10.1080/15252019.2024.2313721

Looi, J. M. (2023). *Deriving authenticity from artificial intelligence: Assessing the roles of human-likeness and influencer tier in virtual influencer marketing* (Doctoral dissertation, University of Texas).

Lou, C., Kiew, S. T. J., Chen, T., Lee, T. Y. M., Ong, J. E. C., & Phua, Z. (2023). Authentically fake? How consumers respond to the influence of virtual influencers. *Journal of Advertising*, *52*(4), 540–557. DOI: 10.1080/00913367.2022.2149641

Loyer, E. (2015). Parasocial and social player-avatar relationships: Social others in Thomas Was Alone. *Press Start*, *2*(1), 21–32.

Marwick, A. (2018). *The algorithmic celebrity: the future of internet fame and microcelebrity studies: The future of internet fame and microcelebrity studies*. Emerald Publishing Limited., DOI: 10.1108/978-1-78756-749-820181015

Melnychuk, H. A., Arasli, H., & Nevzat, R. (2024). How to engage and attract virtual influencers' followers: A new non-human approach in the age of influencer marketing. *Marketing Intelligence & Planning*, *42*(3), 393–417. DOI: 10.1108/MIP-06-2023-0251

Mirowska, A., & Arsenyan, J. (2023). Sweet escape: The role of empathy in social media engagement with human versus virtual influencers. *International Journal of Human-Computer Studies*, *174*, 103008. DOI: 10.1016/j.ijhcs.2023.103008

Miyake, E. (2024). *Virtual Influencers: Identity and Digitality in the Age of Multiple Realities*. Taylor & Francis. DOI: 10.4324/9781003433170

Molin, V., & Nordgren, S. (2019). *"Robot or human? – The marketing phenomenon of virtual influencers – A case study about virtual influencers' parasocial interaction on Instagram."* [Master's Thesis, Uppsala University].

Morency, C. (2018, February 5). *Meet fashion's first computer-generated influencer*. The Business of Fashion. https://www.businessoffashion.com/articles/media/meeting-fashions-first-computer-generated-influencer-lil-miquela-sousa/

Mori, M. (1970). The uncanny valley. *Energy*, *7*(4), 33–35.

Mouritzen, S. L. T., Penttinen, V., & Pedersen, S. (2024). Virtual influencer marketing: The good, the bad and the unreal. *European Journal of Marketing*, *58*(2), 410–440. DOI: 10.1108/EJM-12-2022-0915

Moustakas, E., Lamba, N., Mahmoud, D., & Ranganathan, C. (2020, June). Blurring lines between fiction and reality: Perspectives of experts on marketing effectiveness of virtual influencers. In *2020 International Conference on Cyber Security and Protection of Digital Services (Cyber Security)* (pp. 1-6). IEEE. https://doi.org/ DOI: 10.1109/CyberSecurity49315.2020.9138861

Mrad, M., Ramadan, Z., & Nasr, L. I. (2022). Computer-generated influencers: The rise of digital personalities. *Marketing Intelligence & Planning*, *40*(5), 589–603. DOI: 10.1108/MIP-12-2021-0423

Nair, P., & Kumar, S. (2024). Influencing the influencers through co-creation: Approaches to successful brand strategies. In *Using Influencer Marketing as a Digital Business Strategy* (pp. 129–146). IGI Global.

Nguyen, M. (2023, September 22). *Virtual influencers: Meet the AI-generated figures posing as your new online friends*. TNW | Future-Of-Work. https://thenextweb.com/news/virtual-influencers-ai-generated-online

Okonkwo, I., & Namkoisse, E. (2023). The role of influencer marketing in building authentic brand relationships online. *Journal of Digital Marketing and Communication*, *3*(2), 81–90. DOI: 10.53623/jdmc.v3i2.350

Paul, I., Mohanty, S., & Sengupta, R. (2022). The role of social virtual world in increasing psychological resilience during the on-going COVID-19 pandemic. *Computers in Human Behavior*, *127*, 107036. DOI: 10.1016/j.chb.2021.107036 PMID: 34658502

Paulovics, Á. (2023). Digital reality and identity: An evolutionary analysis of virtual influencer Lil Miquela. In *A mesterséges intelligencia szerepe a fenntartható gazdasági döntésekben*.

Pitafi, Z. R., & Awan, T. M. (2024). The rise of influencer culture: Marketing, monetization, and authenticity in the social sphere. In Ján, V., & Jana, M. (Eds.), *Social Media and Modern Society-How Social Media are Changing the Way We Interact with the World Around*. IntechOpen. DOI: 10.5772/intechopen.1006565

Rachmad, Y. E. (2024). *The Future of Influencer Marketing: Evolution of Consumer Behavior in the Digital World*. PT. Sonpedia Publishing Indonesia.

Roy, D., & Chakraborty, J. (2023). "Forever young, beautiful, and scandal-free": Exploring the ethical frames and crafted authenticity in the animated images of female virtual influencers. *Global Media Journal. Indian Edition, 15*(1), 1-23.

Rozema, R. (2022). The rise of virtual influencers: Threats and opportunities for brands. *Candid*. https://www.candidplatform.com/en/news/platform-news/all-platform-news/marketing/therise-of-virtual-influencers-threats-and-opportunities-for-brands.html

Sands, S., Ferraro, C., Demsar, V., & Chandler, G. (2022). False idols: Unpacking the opportunities and challenges of falsity in the context of virtual influencers. *Business Horizons*, *65*(6), 777–788. DOI: 10.1016/j.bushor.2022.08.002

Schneider, T., Hois, J., Rosenstein, A., Ghellal, S., Theofanou-Fülbier, D., & Gerlicher, A. (2021). Explain yourself! *Transparency for positive UX in autonomous driving* (p. 12). https://doi.org/DOI: 10.1145/3411764.3446647

Schramm, H., & Hartmann, T. (2008). The PSI-Process Scales: A new measure to assess the intensity and breadth of parasocial processes. *Communications*, *33*(4), 385–401. DOI: 10.1515/COMM.2008.025

Sharma, S., & Singh, R. (2019). The ethical frontier of virtual influencers: Balancing trust and AI innovation. *Journal of Marketing Ethics*, *15*(2), 210–229.

Shieber, J. (2018, April 24). The makers of the virtual influencer, Lil Miquela, snag real money from Silicon Valley. *TechCrunch*. https://techcrunch.com/2018/04/23/the-makers-of-the-virtual-influencer-lil-miquela-snag-real-money-from-silicon-valley/

Sorosrungruang, T., Ameen, N., & Hackley, C. (2024). How real is real enough? Unveiling the diverse power of generative AI-enabled virtual influencers and the dynamics of human responses. *Psychology and Marketing*, *41*(12), 3124–3143. DOI: 10.1002/mar.22105

Stein, J. P., Linda Breves, P., & Anders, N. (2024). Parasocial interactions with real and virtual influencers: The role of perceived similarity and human-likeness. *New Media & Society*, *26*(6), 3433–3453. DOI: 10.1177/14614448221102900

Teixeira, S., Teixeira, S., Oliveira, Z., & Souza, E. (Eds.). (2023). *Using influencer marketing as a digital business strategy*. IGI Global. DOI: 10.4018/979-8-3693-0551-5

Tukachinsky, R., & Stever, G. (2019). Theorizing development of parasocial engagement. *Communication Theory*, *29*(3), 297–318. DOI: 10.1093/ct/qty032

Tukachinsky, R., Walter, N., & Saucier, C. J. (2020). Antecedents and effects of parasocial relationships: A meta-analysis. *Journal of Communication*, *70*(6), 868–894. DOI: 10.1093/joc/jqaa034

Wang, J., Ye, G., & Yang, J. (2025). Not a human, not for green? The effectiveness of virtual influencers endorsing green products. *Journal of Product & Brand Management*. Ahead of the print.

Wang, R., Bush-Evans, R., Arden-Close, E., Bolat, E., McAlaney, J., Hodge, S., Thomas, S., & Phalp, K. (2023). Transparency in persuasive technology, immersive technology, and online marketing: Facilitating users' informed decision making and practical implications. *Computers in Human Behavior*, *139*, 107545. DOI: 10.1016/j.chb.2022.107545

Wikström, P. (2014). Tools, building blocks, and rewards: Traditional media organizations learn to engage with productive audiences. *Journal of Media Business Studies, 11*(4), 67–89. DOI: 10.1080/16522354.2014.11073589

Witt, G. L., & Baird, D. E. (2018). *The Gen Z frequency: How brands tune in and build credibility*. Kogan Page Publishers.

Yan, J., Xia, S., Jiang, A., & Lin, Z. (2024). The effect of different types of virtual influencers on consumers' emotional attachment. *Journal of Business Research, 177*, 114646. DOI: 10.1016/j.jbusres.2024.114646

You, L., & Liu, F. (2024). From virtual voices to real impact: Authenticity, altruism, and egoism in social advocacy by human and virtual influencers. *Technological Forecasting and Social Change, 207*, 123650. DOI: 10.1016/j.techfore.2024.123650

Yu, J., Dickinger, A., So, K. K. F., & Egger, R. (2024). Artificial intelligence-generated virtual influencer: Examining the effects of emotional display on user engagement. *Journal of Retailing and Consumer Services, 76*, 103560. DOI: 10.1016/j.jretconser.2023.103560

Zhao, T., Ran, Y., Wu, B., Lynette Wang, V., Zhou, L., & Wang, L. C. (2024). Virtual versus human: Unraveling consumer reactions to service failures through influencer types. *Journal of Business Research, 178*(C). https://ideas.repec.org//a/eee/jbrese/v178y2024ics0148296324001619.html

Zhao, X. (2022). *Virtual Fashion Influencers: Towards a more sustainable consumer behaviourof Generation Z?* (Master's thesis).

Zheng, Y., & Toribio, J. R. (2021). The role of transparency in multi-stakeholder educational recommendations. *User Modeling and User-Adapted Interaction, 31*(3), 513–540. DOI: 10.1007/s11257-021-09291-x

Zhong, Y., Shapoval, V., & Busser, J. (2021). The role of parasocial relationship in social media marketing: Testing a model among baby boomers. *International Journal of Contemporary Hospitality Management, 33*(5), 1870–1891. DOI: 10.1108/IJCHM-08-2020-0873

Zhou, X. (2020). Virtual Youtuber Kizuna AI: co-creating human-non-human interaction and celebrity-audience relationship. (Master's thesis, Lund University).

Chapter 7
The Use of Virtual Influencers in the Tourism Sector

Noelia Araújo Vila
https://orcid.org/0000-0002-3395-8536
University of Vigo, Spain

Almudena Otegui Carles
https://orcid.org/0000-0003-4112-8580
University of Vigo, Spain

ABSTRACT

The emerging trend of using virtual influencers in tourism is transforming how companies engage with travelers, becoming a mass phenomenon among younger digital audiences. These characters, crafted using CGI (Computer-Generated Imagery) by digital marketing teams, are not only used to promote destinations but also serve as virtual guides, assisting users in planning their trips. Thanks to their ability to adapt and emphasize brand values, virtual influencers can produce unlimited, engaging content without geographic or temporal restrictions. This chapter analyzes the impact of using virtual influencers in the tourism sector, addressing both the benefits and the ethical challenges they present. To this end, a content analysis was conducted on seven virtual influencers, two of whom focus exclusively on tourism and travel. In conclusion, virtual influencers represent an innovative tool for tourism, with the potential to enhance engagement and sustainability in destination promotion, though challenges of authenticity and trust must be addressed to maximize their impact.

DOI: 10.4018/979-8-3373-0255-3.ch007

INTRODUCTION

In the past decade, tourism has been deeply transformed by digital trends. From travel planning to destination promotion, the use of social media and digital marketing strategies has dramatically changed how travellers choose and experience their destinations. One of the most recent and disruptive innovations is the use of virtual influencers—digital characters that do not exist in the real world but have a strong presence in the virtual sphere and on social media. These characters, created with CGI technology and managed by marketing and tech teams, can interact with users, simulate personalities, and participate in advertising campaigns. Thus, virtual influencers represent a new tool in tourism marketing, providing new opportunities while also posing ethical and technical challenges (Miyake, 2024).

The concept of virtual influencers began to gain traction in sectors like fashion and entertainment, where characters such as Lil Miquela and Imma amassed millions of followers and secured collaboration contracts with renowned brands. However, in tourism, their potential is still in the early stages of development. Recent studies indicate that virtual influencers in the tourism sector can function not only as destination promoters but also as virtual assistants, capable of guiding travelers through their planning process and helping them select destinations. As the tourism industry faces the need to capture the attention of a young audience, accustomed to digital experiences and constantly seeking innovation, the use of these digital assistants provides a way to connect with these audiences effectively and uniquely (Paulovics, 2023).

Virtual influencers in the tourism sector differ from traditional ones in that, being digitally created, they can be tailored to any profile desired by the brand. This allows tourism companies to build digital assistants that represent specific values—from sustainability to luxury—or that speak different languages, facilitating cultural connections with diverse audiences. This flexibility, along with the ability to personalize interactions in real-time, makes virtual influencers ideal assistants, capable of guiding users through their travel planning process and instantly responding to their questions (Kádeková & Holienčinová, 2018).

Virtual influencers have the potential to increase user engagement in tourism campaigns by 35% compared to human influencers. This figure is largely due to the fact that virtual assistants can interact continuously, enhancing user experience and boosting loyalty. In terms of content, virtual influencers can generate highly appealing visual content without time or location constraints, allowing tourism brands to project an idealized and consistent image of their destinations without depending on real-world circumstances (Choi & Choi, 2024).

The use of virtual influencers also ties into the rise of augmented reality (AR) and virtual reality (VR), technologies that are changing the way travelers experience and explore destinations before visiting them. Virtual influencers can serve as guides in virtual experiences that allow users to explore tourist destinations without needing to travel physically, which can be particularly useful in reducing mass tourism in vulnerable areas (Miyake, 2024). Through these means, virtual influencers can offer a "pre-travel experience" that helps travelers become familiar with the destination, explore their options, and plan their trip more knowledgeably and effectively.

In the long term, the role of virtual influencers in tourism could evolve into "travel assistants" who accompany users throughout their entire journey. These assistants could interact with tourists in real-time, providing personalized recommendations, managing reservations, and offering information about visited sites. This ability to personalize and respond immediately makes virtual influencers valuable tools for improving user experience at each stage of the travel process (Guerreiro et al., 2019).

This chapter aims to analyze the impact of using virtual influencers in the tourism sector, covering both the benefits and the ethical limitations and challenges they present. Through a detailed analysis of their role, this chapter seeks to identify how these digital characters can contribute to the transformation of digital tourism, facilitating a more personalized and engaging interaction with consumers. Additionally, the chapter will explore the risks related to authenticity and trust in virtual influencers, providing a balanced perspective on their potential and critical aspects to consider for their effective use in the industry. To this end, a content analysis was conducted on seven virtual influencers, five of whom are currently the most-followed virtual influencers and two of whom focus exclusively on tourism content. Dimensions such as demographic characteristics were analyzed, gathering data for each profile, including name, location, biography, number of followers, number of accounts followed, number of posts, and profile content.

ORIGINS AND EVOLUTION OF VIRTUAL INFLUENCERS

The concept of digital influencers has profoundly shaped how brands aim to connect with consumers in the digital age. This transformation has paved the way for a new category: virtual influencers (Sindhuja & Rani, 2024). A virtual influencer, or virtual figure, is a digitally created person, typically through CGI (computer-generated imagery), designed to simulate human appearance and behavior. Beyond existing as online figures, these creations act as brand ambassadors and collaborators for various companies, much like human influencers. The origin and evolution of these figures in social media and digital marketing highlight the potential of online technologies to keep up with contemporary trends (Hadrava & Adámková, 2024).

CGI technology, originally used in animation and special effects, has its roots in the film industry of the 1970s and 1980s. However, it wasn't until the last decade that it began to be applied to create characters capable of maintaining a social media presence and forming direct connections with audiences. The rise of virtual influencers stems from a trend toward more personalized content, enabling brands to design controllable and consistent characters (Liu & Lee, 2024). These influencers are carefully developed to ensure they convey the values of the brands they represent and, unlike humans, can be programmed to avoid controversy and adapt seamlessly to commercial needs.

The earliest examples of virtual figures can be traced back to animated characters in advertising campaigns, such as Coca-Cola's virtual mascot, Max Headroom, in the 1980s. While Max Headroom had a caricatured and satirical edge, he set a precedent for using digital figures to represent brands and connect with audiences (Moran, 2016). Advances in computer graphics and social media have since allowed this idea to evolve into hyper-realistic influencers with their own identities, capable of interacting with followers and building communities.

Figure 1. Max Headromm, Coca-Cola virtual pet

(Zona, 2020)

In 2016, Lil Miquela, a virtual influencer created by the company Brud, introduced a new approach to digitally generated characters with active digital lives and unique backstories. Designed to follow the fashion and lifestyle trends of her time, Lil Miquela amassed a significant following. As digital content creators emerged as influencers, many brands began considering their inclusion in marketing campaigns (Lejeune, 2020). Lil Miquela exemplifies the merging of reality and digital fiction, appearing so convincing that many users question whether she is a real person (Ekara, 2024).

Figure 2. Virtual influencer Lil Miquela

(Miquela, 2024)

Another example is Shudu, a hyper-realistic African virtual model. While Shudu aligns with the ideal of virtual perfection, her appearance sparked debates about the ethics of using virtual models, particularly concerning representations of specific cultural and ethnic identities (Okolie, 2019). Despite the controversy, Shudu has captured the fashion and advertising world's attention, starring in high-profile campaigns for notable brands and establishing herself as a strong social media influencer. The success and reception of figures like Lil Miquela and Shudu demonstrate the compatibility of virtual models with modern digital audiences.

VIRTUAL INFLUENCERS IN TOURISM

The inclusion of virtual influencers in the tourism industry is an emerging trend, reflecting their ability to creatively engage with consumers. Unlike their human counterparts, virtual influencers can showcase travel destinations under controlled visual conditions, avoiding seasonal or logistical travel constraints. This allows brands to maintain constant interaction with their audience. Additionally, virtual influencers can quickly align with the growing demand for sustainable and culturally respectful approaches. They eliminate the unpredictability of human behavior or potential scandals (Xie-Carson et al., 2024).

One successful example in the tourism industry is Imma, the renowned Japanese "virtuous" influencer, who has served as an ambassador for various destinations, captivating millions of people across Asia and beyond. Imma represents the fusion of digital technology and Japan's modern culture, with her realistic appearance enabling her to star in campaigns showcasing the country's diverse landscapes and facets. Collaborating with influential figures like Imma offers a fresh and provocative way to present destinations, maximizing brand exposure and consumer retention (Luo & Kim, 2024).

Figure 3. Virtual influencer Inma

(Bazaar, 2019)

The use of virtual influencers marks an exemplary shift in the history of digital marketing. They open new opportunities for audience interaction in an ever-evolving digital world. At the same time, these characters represent an unprecedented level of control over advertising campaigns for brands, ensuring cohesive, predictable, innovative, and controversy-free messaging. While figures like Lil Miquela, Shudu, Imma, and many others fulfilling different roles expand the notion of who can be an influencer, each of them, in general, reshapes our understanding of what is real and what is artificial. With the future development of CGI and AI technologies, we can expect the field of virtual influencers to continue growing, offering brands the opportunity to engage with audiences in new ways and create emotional connections in an increasingly competitive and equal market.

ADVANTAGES OF VIRTUAL INFLUENCERS IN TOURISM

As discussed in the previous section, the figure of the virtual influencer is revolutionizing the current landscape of brand and product promotion, and the tourism sector is no exception. Through this figure, it is possible to connect with audiences in an authentic and personalized way, while offering brands the flexibility to create and control their own narrative. Unlike traditional influencers, these characters, being created through CGI, can be completely managed by the brands or creative teams that design them. Their appeal has become evident in the tourism sector, where companies seek to differentiate themselves and attract younger generations, especially digital natives, with an innovative and sustainable approach. The advantages of virtual influencers in tourism include their versatility, control, and their ability to offer a more personalized experience to the user.

Below are the most notable advantages of this promotional figure for the tourism sector:

1. Emotional Connection and Limitless Immersion: Due to their artificial design, virtual influencers can adapt to any environment, culture, and style, making them ideal for tourism marketing in emerging destinations. Brands can create cultural narratives through these digital characters without any physical or logistical limitations as a human influencer would have. Virtual influencers do not need to travel, allowing them to "visit" a place virtually and create an instant experience anywhere in the world at any time. One of the greatest advantages is that they can be adapted to reflect specific brand values, which research has shown is crucial for the success of tourism marketing (Hudson & Thal, 2013). In fact, virtual influencers offer brands total creative control to design their personality, appearance, and communication style in a way that aligns with the brand's identity and the expectations of the target audience. Furthermore, being completely digital, virtual influencers can be present in multiple locations simultaneously and in different languages and contexts. This is essential for capturing a global and diverse audience, especially in emerging markets in Asia and Latin America, where social media plays a crucial role in destination choice (Buhalis & Law, 2008).
2. Sustainable and Responsible Perspective: Sustainability is becoming one of the main concerns of the tourism industry, and virtual influencers can be a more sustainable alternative than human influencers. Human influencers often have to

travel to different locations and consume resources to ensure authentic content. The carbon footprint has become a significant problem for conscious travelers, and agencies hiring digital influencers can help reduce the environmental impact of destination marketing. Additionally, in a post-COVID-19 world, virtual influencers represent an option free of health restrictions to promote tourism. Considering that no health measure can prevent a human from contracting or transmitting the virus, the use of digital influencers has been essential because they represent a risk-free measure to reactivate the sector and restore consumer confidence, even electronically. In fact, the concept of virtual tourism has emerged in recent years, with digital agencies spearheading "trips" through virtual scenarios. Teleporting scenes is not only more sustainable but also more accessible for agencies that can create high-resolution videoconferences of beautiful destination landscapes. This technique will not only be innovative but will also convey a sense of freshness, a young target, and respect for the environment (Zhao, 2022).

3. Adaptation to Trends and Narrative Control: The use of virtual influencers also allows tourism companies to keep up with the latest digital trends, offering a significant competitive advantage in an oversaturated market. These characters can be designed to adapt to the latest trends in real time, without the physical and emotional restrictions of a human. Since one of the main features of tourism is the speed at which changes occur in fashion and preferences, the ability of a virtual influencer to change style or personality is a significant advantage. Virtual influencers also give brands complete control over the narrative, style, and overall tone. This eliminates the possibility of disputes or erratic behavior, as occasionally occurs with human influencers, who can present image or attitude problems that do not necessarily align with the brand's mindset (Marwick, 2015). On the other hand, the brand has absolute control over the image. An illustrative success story is the career of the previously mentioned virtual influencer Lil Miquela, who has promoted major fashion and tourism brands and established herself as one of the most popular "people" on Instagram. Additionally, a virtual influencer allows a brand to practice and fine-tune its marketing personality with an audience before implementing it in communication with a real influencer.
4. Accessibility and Segmentation: Another notable feature of virtual influencers is their ability to accurately segment audiences, which is highly beneficial for tourism, where audience needs and desires are diverse and specific. Thus, brands can create content targeted at different segments, such as millennials and Generation Z, groups that seek genuinely authentic experiences and have a high affinity for technology and social media (Munar & Jacobsen, 2014). This segmentation can also allow the development of niche-specific content in the tourism industry, such as ecotourism, adventure tourism, or cultural tourism.

Virtual influencers can create specialized content for a specific area, adjusting the narrative to suit the interests of the audience in question. For example, a virtual influencer oriented toward ecotourism would be designed to convey the values of sustainability and environmental protection supported by a strong message (Dredge & Gyimóthy, 2015). Additionally, virtual influencers could be programmed to speak different languages and adapt to the cultural habits of different regions faster and more effectively than humans. In this way, an international tourism company can reach inclusive audiences and grow effectively on a global level, tailoring its strategy to cater to diverse consumers.

5. Immersive Digital Experience: The extensive use of AR and VR technology in the tourism sphere allows virtual influencers to offer even more immersive and engaging experiences. Combined with a digital influencer, these technologies enable tourism companies to create an unforgettable sensation around the location, encouraging users to emotionally bond with a destination before the actual visit. Users, through a virtual experience, can freely explore not only the landscapes and monuments but also the culture of a place accompanied by the influencer of their choice, who acts as both a brand ambassador and a destination ambassador. Simulating realistic scenarios and interacting with followers provides an opportunity to involve everyone in the tourism sphere, regardless of their place of residence or financial capability. Inclusion and the democratization of tourism fuel curiosity and allow people to learn about the world without financial or geographical restrictions. Additionally, AR and VR can visualize a destination, reducing "overtourism" in some oversaturated destinations, enabling people to enjoy the journey remotely, avoiding overcrowding, and safeguarding the authenticity of the place (Guttentag, 2010).
6. Detailed Impact Analysis and Measurement: The use of virtual influencers allows for detailed and precise analysis of interactions, which is a significant advantage over human actors. Being digitally created and managed, comprehensive information can be collected on the impact of each campaign, from the type of content that resonates most with the audience to the time of day users interact most with influencers. The ability to monitor and analyze the impact allows tourism brands to adjust their marketing strategies in real time. Thus, these entities can optimize their resources and improve efficiency (Buhalis & Amaranggana, 2013). For example, real-time A/B testing (testing two versions) can be conducted with different looks, voices, or content for the virtual influencer to observe audience responses and adjust the virtual influencer accordingly. The adaptability of virtual influencers is therefore an indispensable tool for maximizing return on investment in their respective tourism marketing campaigns.

These advantages underscore that virtual influencers have become a revolutionary and effective tool for the tourism industry. They embody a unique combination of creative control, sustainability, and unprecedented target audience reach, which is difficult to surpass. Virtual influencer models allow brands to quickly adapt strategies and stay up-to-date with all current trends while providing all audiences with a personal and authentic experience. Moreover, in the context of growing concerns about sustainability and the ecological footprint, virtual influencers offer a responsible and advanced way to promote tourism. The focus on digital experience and immersion makes virtual influencers the perfect combination for attracting new generations and inducing tourism in an innovative and effective way. Therefore, it is undeniable that virtual influencers are relevant in the field of tourism promotion, as the world demands more digital interaction, everyone cares about accessibility, and ecological responsibility is a priority.

ROLE OF VIRTUAL INFLUENCERS AS TRAVEL ASSISTANTS

Digitalization has completely transformed the tourism sphere. Along with this recent digitalization of the world, the phenomenon of virtual influencers has radically altered the current landscape. Furthermore, the role of the virtual assistant, also known as the virtual influencer, in tourism is crucial. For a long time, virtual assistants have been hosting tourists, inspiring travel, assisting in planning, and sometimes even during trips and visits to points of interest. Due to their omnipresence on social media, customization and retention capabilities, as well as their adaptability and control, virtual assistants are among the most popular promotional tools used in current marketing (Hudson & Thal, 2013).

In the early stages of the travel process, virtual influencers must inspire potential travelers. This is their role: presenting appealing and aspirational content on visual platforms like Instagram, TikTok, Facebook, or YouTube. Through these platforms, digital influencers can create and share tourist trips with great care to capture the traveler's attention and spark interest in visiting new destinations. This emotional influence is generated through the visualization of dreamlike scenarios, tourist activities, and equally invented cultural experiences, but offering an impression of authenticity thanks to the computer-generated images and the narrative constructed around each post (Seraphin et al., 2018). For example, a digital luxury tourism influencer would promote a life of glamour and exclusivity, and another, perhaps, adventures and challenges for outdoor activities. The content can be fictional, and since the image is not of a real person, neither multiple photos nor updated content is necessary. Thus, they can be updated regularly to keep up with current tourism trends. Therefore, this type of influencer is vital for inspiring potential tourists (Marwick, 2013).

Moreover, this inspirational role is also crucial for emerging destinations that wish to enter the market. Virtual influencers are expected to help lesser-known places gain more exposure, thus offering consumers more travel options when conventional destinations are no longer suitable. In other words, travel inspiration has led to the phenomenon of "overtourism" that affects popular destinations worldwide, and influencers are seen as an opportunity to prevent this by diverting attention from the old to the new (Wang et al., 2016).

Another innovative element to consider when working with the figure of the virtual influencer and their role as travel assistants is the possibility of interacting with tourists in a personalized way. Within current consumption trends, customization is increasingly pressing, and thanks to the digital programming of the virtual influencer and their integration into interactive platforms, these characters can answer questions, provide personalized recommendations, and even virtually guide users on tours of tourist destinations. All of this is based on the tourist's demands. This ability to interact in real-time creates a companionship experience that goes beyond the initial inspiration and becomes an informative and practical resource throughout the trip planning process (Buhalis & Amaranggana, 2013).

The concept of a "digital travel assistant" is strengthened with the use of advanced artificial intelligence technologies and natural language processing, which allow these influencers to interact in the same language and style as their followers, creating a more natural and closer connection. According to Hudson and Thal (2013), this ability to offer real-time recommendations not only enhances the user experience but also increases the probability of conversion since the user feels they are receiving relevant and suitable information to their interests. In this sense, virtual influencers are perceived as reliable assistants who can resolve doubts and anticipate travelers' needs, creating an enriched experience before, during, and after the trip.

In addition to providing inspiration and assistance in planning, virtual influencers are beginning to play an important role in creating travel simulations. These influencers leverage technologies like AR and VR to help travelers have an immersive experience at the destination without leaving home. The ability to immerse users in a visual environment, with virtual influencers as guides, is a powerful strategy for travel brands seeking to offer more than just static or promotional content.

Virtual reality, in particular, has shown great effectiveness and is a valuable tool in travel, as it allows users to experience "previously visited" destinations, thereby reducing uncertainty and strengthening emotional connections with the place. Guttentag (2010) considers that virtual reality in tourism has proven to be a technology with great potential to facilitate access to experiences that would otherwise be inaccessible or expensive, such as traveling to remote destinations or attending specific cultural events. This ability to simulate experiences creates an emotional connection, increases interest in real-life visits, and can be strategically managed by virtual influencers.

The ability of virtual influencers to offer digital travel experiences also has implications for the democratization of the travel industry. By making "travel" accessible from anywhere in the world without travel expenses, these characters allow people from diverse economic and geographic backgrounds to access the culture and attractions of remote locations. Virtual influencers promote digital experiences in popular destinations worldwide and help direct attention to lesser-known places or virtual experiences, avoiding overcrowding in sensitive areas and preserving the authenticity of these locations. The role of virtual influencers as "digital ambassadors" allows brands and destinations to create a balance between promotion and sustainability, which will become increasingly important in the tourism industry (Seraphin et al., 2016), using virtual influence.

CONSUMER PSYCHOLOGY AND PERCEPTION OF VIRTUAL INFLUENCERS

Consumer psychology plays a fundamental role in how individuals perceive influencers, both human and virtual. Authenticity and emotional connection are two of the most relevant aspects that consumers value in their interactions with these digital characters.

Authenticity, understood as the perception of sincerity and transparency in interactions, is key in influencer marketing. Consumers associate greater authenticity with human influencers due to their real nature and personal life stories (Marwick & Boyd, 2011). However, virtual influencers, although not human, have managed to generate a sense of authenticity (Lou et al., 2023) through the construction of compelling narratives and the projection of complex personalities.

Consumers often seek an emotional connection with influencers. While human influencers can offer vulnerability and personal experiences that foster audience identification, virtual influencers must build their emotional connection through their story and interactions on social platforms. Recent studies show that consumers can project emotions onto virtual characters if they present "human" characteristics in their behavior and communication (Peng et al., 2025).

Credibility is another crucial factor in consumer perception. Human influencers gain credibility through their transparency and consistency in interactions. On the other hand, virtual influencers can also be perceived as credible if they manage to maintain a coherent narrative that makes them appear authentic and trustworthy. Although humans are typically perceived as more trustworthy due to their nature and vulnerability, virtual influencers have the advantage of being seen as predictable and "perfect," which can increase trust in certain contexts (Lee et al., s. f.).

The growing use of virtual influencers on social media has sparked debates about the nature of the relationship consumers develop with these digital characters. While some argue that the lack of human imperfections reduces emotional connection, others prefer the perfection and continuous availability of virtual influencers (Kowert et al., 2015). This paradox suggests that, while consumers appreciate human imperfections, they also value the consistency and accessibility of virtual influencers.

CHALLENGES AND ETHICAL LIMITATIONS OF VIRTUAL INFLUENCERS

The rise of online influencers has transformed the landscape of digital marketing and advertising strategies across various industries, especially in travel, fashion, and entertainment. People online establish an emotional connection with their followers while granting brands full control over their image and messaging. However, this growing trend raises numerous concerns and ethical questions that need to be carefully examined from the perspectives of both consumers and the brands employing these online influencers. This section of the chapter outlines the most significant ethical issues and limitations related to online influencers, emphasizing transparency, authenticity, rebranding, and social influence.

1. **The Question of Authenticity**: The issue of authenticity is one of the main ethical challenges posed by virtual influencers. Consumers, especially young people, often seek an authentic connection with the influencers they follow. In the digital world, authenticity and transparency are valued by followers, who expect the personalities behind brands, including influencers, to be real human beings with genuine experiences and values. However, virtual influencers are entirely imaginary individuals, generated through artificial intelligence algorithms and computer-generated graphics. This could cause a sense of disconnection, as followers do not have the opportunity to interact with a genuine individual. According to Marwick (2013), influencers on digital platforms build their trust and authenticity primarily through crafting an individual story that is perceived as transparent and relatable. Virtual influencers, on the other hand, may lack the same authenticity because they do not have personal stories or lives beyond the content created for them. This raises significant questions about transparency in communication between companies and customers. If followers are not fully aware that they are interacting with a digital character rather than a real human being, they might feel deceived (Seraphin et al., 2016). It is crucial to address

this challenge by ensuring that brands and creators of virtual influencers are transparent about the digital nature of these characters. The lack of accurate communication regarding the artificial nature of these influencers could lead to distrust and, in the long term, damage the brand's image. Transparency not only helps maintain the integrity of the connection with customers but also fosters trust and respect for the brands that choose to employ these virtual characters as part of their marketing strategy.

2. **Manipulation of Image and Values**: Another significant ethical issue with virtual content creators is image manipulation. While human influencers can generate controversy due to their actions outside social networks, virtual influencers do not face this issue as they are entirely directed by their developers. The ability to control all aspects of their appearance, from clothing to facial gestures, carries risks associated with promoting unrealistic beauty standards and ideal behaviors. Virtual influencers have the capacity to present a perfect image that cannot be achieved in real life. This could pressure their followers, especially younger audiences, to strive for unattainable beauty standards. The influence these individuals exert on their followers can be significant, as their representations are often so flawless that users may begin to obsess over them and desire to emulate those standards. According to research by Tiggemann and Slater (2013), the beauty criteria promoted by digital platforms can harm the self-esteem of their users, particularly adolescent girls. Virtual influencers, being entirely digital creations, exacerbate this problem because their images are not bound by the physical or biological limitations of human beings. Continuous exposure to these idealized images can distort body perception and create greater social pressure to meet these criteria.

Despite not being human, the creators of virtual influencers have an ethical responsibility concerning the values they promote. It is imperative that these characters are designed to encourage diversity and inclusion, avoiding simplistic figures that perpetuate harmful stereotypes. Virtual influencer designers could intentionally strive to showcase a variety of body types, ethnicities, and personal traits so that followers can positively identify with these characters instead of only seeing an idealized representation of beauty.

3. **Impact on Youth and Mental Health**: Digital influencers have a considerable ability to capture the attention of young audiences, who are particularly susceptible to the effects of social media platforms. According to the World Health Organization (WHO) report on adolescent mental health, exposure to social media content can have adverse effects on young people's mental health, especially in terms of anxiety, depression, and eating disorders. Constant exposure to photos

of "ideal" individuals on social platforms, promoted by digital figures, could contribute to creating a distorted perception of daily life and foster insecurity in adolescents. These individuals may feel pressure to replicate the seemingly perfect lives displayed by online influencers, increasing the likelihood of developing disorders related to body image and mental well-being. In this context, the role of virtual influencers is complex, as followers may not be fully aware that they are interacting with a digital character, intensifying their influence.

It is crucial for both brands and creators of these virtual avatars to be aware of the influence they exert on adolescents and accept the responsibility to promote a positive and realistic image. To mitigate this impact, some specialists propose that virtual influencers should adopt a more inclusive and realistic style in their portrayals, showcasing both their "flaws" and positive qualities. This approach could foster a shift in the beauty standards imposed by social media platforms. Additionally, brands must take an ethical stance when evaluating the impact of their advertising strategies on the mental health of adolescents within their audience.

4. **Ethical Responsibility in Advertising**: This section applies to virtual influencers in the tourism sector as well as other sectors where their use is common, such as fashion, technology, or beauty. Transparency in advertising is one of the main ethical concerns surrounding these influencers. In many cases, followers may not be fully aware that the content they are consuming is sponsored, leading to a misleading perception of the recommendations made by digital influencers. Advertising ethics considers the principle of transparency essential. When it comes to virtual influencers, it is necessary for brands and creators of these characters to clearly indicate when they are promoting products or services to avoid followers mistaking the recommendations as genuine.

The lack of transparency can undermine buyers' trust and raise questions about the influence exerted on the audience. Advertising regulations must be adjusted to address the current challenges posed by the presence of virtual influencers. Social media platforms like Instagram and YouTube have started taking steps to make sponsored content more visible, and virtual influencers must adhere to the same rules to ensure honest and ethical communication.

The use of virtual influencers in online marketing within the tourism sector presents a variety of ethical challenges and restrictions that must be meticulously managed to prevent adverse consequences for consumers, especially younger audiences. The lack of authenticity, image manipulation, impacts on mental health, and responsibility in advertising are issues that need to be addressed ethically and transparently. When designing digital characters capable of influencing how followers perceive them, the creators of these influencers must take responsibility for promoting inclusive, realistic, and respectful values toward diversity. Only through an ethical approach to utilizing these digital characters can we ensure that virtual influencers are not only effective marketing tools but also responsible agents that help foster a healthier and more positive digital environment.

ANALYSIS OF VIRTUAL INFLUENCERS

In the tourism industry, virtual creators have emerged as a novel strategy to advertise tourist destinations and capture the attention of the young, tech-savvy generation. They are generated by computer programs that can interact with their followers similarly to human influencers, but with added benefits such as the customization of their appearance and the ability to maintain a controlled narrative.

As a practical analysis, this section conducts a content analysis of seven virtual influencers, five of whom are currently the most-followed virtual influencers and two of whom focus exclusively on tourism content. According to Berelson (1952, p.18), content analysis is "a research technique for the objective, systematic, and quantitative description of the manifest content of communication," and for Krippendorff (1990, p.28), it is "a research technique for making replicable and valid inferences from data to their context."

For this study, the photographic analysis method proposed by Albers and James in their publication *Travel Photography* (Albers & James, 1988), adapted to social networks, specifically Instagram, was used as a framework. Photographs can serve as research data regardless of the epistemological background or research focus of a study, being an inseparable part of the tourist experience and allowing for the instant sharing of that experience with a multitude of people (Balomenou & Garrod, 2019).

This type of research has significant advantages, such as the fact that the material is readily available, simple, free, and almost permanently accessible online (Kozinets, 2002), eliminating geographic and time constraints (Terziyska, 2021). To achieve this, the study identified the online community interested in a topic relevant to the research and observed it (Jeacle, 2021; Kozinets, 2015). The study community comprised the Instagram profiles of the most-followed virtual influencers and the profiles of virtual influencers focused on tourism.

Instagram was selected due to its recent growth and its ability to share both photographs and text, which helps share memories with a large audience (Nikjoo et al., 2021). Subsequently, dimensions such as demographic characteristics were analyzed, collecting data for each profile, including name, location, biography, number of followers, number of followed accounts, number of posts, and profile details.

The analyzed virtual influencers were:

- **Miquela Sousa (Lil Miquela)**: Known as one of the most popular virtual influencer, she emerged from the company Brud in 2016. Although she is better known for her impact on fashion and music, she has also collaborated with tourism companies. In 2020, she participated in an advertising campaign for Los Angeles, highlighting her role as an ambassador for the city. Through her posts, Lil Miquela helped create a contemporary and diverse image of the city, leveraging her digital platforms to connect with diverse audiences worldwide.
- **Imma**: A virtual influencer from Japan created by the agency Aww Inc. Her presence has stood out primarily in the Asian market, where she has collaborated with various fashion and beauty brands. Imma has been used in tourism promotion campaigns in Japan, highlighting destinations such as Tokyo and the Hokkaido region, positioning her as an ideal ambassador for digital culture and innovation in tourism promotion.
- **Aitana López**: A 25-year-old Spanish virtual influencer created through artificial intelligence by the agency The Clueless. Designed with an impressive level of realism, she combines elements of fitness, fashion, and technology. She represents an active and modern lifestyle, collaborating with renowned brands such as Olaplex and Intimissimi, generating up to 10,000 euros per month due to her impact on social media. Her posts are created using real backgrounds and advanced digital editing techniques, achieving seamless integration between the virtual and physical worlds.
- **Shudu Gram**: Dubbed the "digital supermodel," Shudu has participated in multiple campaigns for luxury and haute couture brands. She has also been associated with luxury tourism brands, demonstrating her ability to influence various fields as a digital influencer. Although Shudu is not solely focused on travel, her presence has been used in various tourism contexts, promoting renowned destinations.
- **Bermuda**: A virtual influencer created by Brud, she has become a prominent figure in marketing campaigns for tourism brands, in addition to being recognized for her involvement in social causes. Despite being new to the travel industry, her growing fame and ability to attract young viewers position her as a potential influencer in promoting tourist destinations.
- **Emma and Sena Zaro**: The only two influencers whose content is exclusively focused on tourism, and whose profiles will be explored in greater depth later.

In Table 1, the country of origin, Bio message, number of followers, following number, number of posts, and aesthetic style for each virtual influencer are outlined.

Table 1. Further information

User	Country	Bio	Followers	Following	Posts	Aesthetic Style/Visual Profile
Lil Miquela lilmiquela	Los Ángeles (USA)	#BlackLivesMatter 21-year-old Robot living in LA Be your own robot	2,5M	1975	1350	Young - 20 years old Perfect physique Exotic features Almost always the same hairstyle Very modern outfits She is the main focus of the posts, almost always appearing in the foreground Own website with access to TikTok, YouTube, and Twitter
Imma Gram imma. gram	Japan	imma Virtual girl in JP	393K	769	833	Young girl Not very realistic Very modern clothing Multiple hairstyles Participated in a TEDx talk Link to a website selling T-shirts and other accessories she uses Link to a website with access to TikTok, Twitter, Facebook, and YouTube
Aitana López fit_aitana	Barcelona - Spain	Creador digital Based in Barcelona | Digital Muse at @ thesclueless.ai Gamer at heart & Fitness lover AI influencer management@ theclueless.ai linktr.ee/Fitness _Aitana	337K	312	143	Sena Zaro follows her Young, in shape, dresses sexy, with pink or orange hair. Focused on a sporty lifestyle Link to her agency, TikTok, Twitter, and Fanvue, where she shares sexier posts and bikini pictures. The agency also represents two other models, but they haven't yet reached 1,000 followers, and one doesn't even have any posts Her website describes her as follows: Aitana Lopez is a strong and determined woman, independent in her actions and generous in her willingness to help others. With boldness and authenticity, she faces challenges and expresses her opinion without reservation. However, her complicated humor and self-centeredness sometimes make it difficult to get a smile out of her, showing her complexity. As a content creator, she shines with extroversion, attracting attention with her striking character. As a passionate Scorpio, she highlights her love for video games and her dedication to the fitness lifestyle, evidencing her intensity and care for her physical well-being.
Shudu shudu. gram	Unknown	The World's First Digital Supermodel	238K	4921	163	She always appears walking the runway or posing Perfect dark skin, smooth and flawless Perfect features Perfect smile She has her own website with a portfolio, just like a professional model
Bermuda bermudaisbae	Unknown	Bermuda Robot Queen check out my sis Miquela's Villa M www.miquela.fyi/ ?utm_source= instagram&utm _medium=social &utm_campaign= bio_link&utm_t	220K	520	268	Blonde, blue eyes, perfect physique Less realistic, more like a chatbot or a robot The profile is focused on lifestyle but centers more on her than on the actual activities Has a direct link to Miquela's website, promoting it

continued on following page

Table 1. Continued

User	Country	Bio	Followers	Following	Posts	Aesthetic Style/Visual Profile
Emma emma-travels-germany	Germany	EmmaTravelsGermany 🌍 Discover Travel Destination Germany 🤖 Your AI travel companion by @ germanytourism #EmmaAIGermany #AIGenerated #VisitGermany #GermanyTourism www.germany.travel/en/chat/emma.html	4,409	22	6	Young Blonde Perfect features Followed by Sena Zaro Link to chatbot
Sena Zaro sena.zaro	Unknown	Sena Zaro I Storyteller 🌍 ✈️ Travel tips and inspiration 🤖 AI travel influencer □ Collab? Let's inspire together! 👇 www.senazaro.com	3,908	210	214	Young Perfect features Very real posts Link to her page with access to collaborations where it says: Age: 30 years old Relationship: Single Personality: Warm, adventurous, sophisticated Interests: Travel, culture, sustainability Values: Be kind to others

As can be observed, there is a significant difference in the number of followers each influencer has, ranging from the well-known Lil Miquela with 2.5 million followers to just 3,908 for Sena Zaro, one of the virtual influencers whose content focuses solely on travel. After Lil Miquela, the next influencer has 393,000 followers, a figure that, while substantial today, is not particularly noteworthy. These numbers suggest that the influence of virtual influencers remains relatively small.

It is notable that Emma Travel, the German virtual influencer, follows very few profiles—only 22—and has posted just six times, in contrast to Lil Miquela's 1,350 posts, indicating low activity on Instagram. On the other hand, the other travel-focused virtual influencer, Sena Zaro, is much more active. Despite her limited following, she has already published 214 posts. Additionally, the number of daily stories she shares on Instagram is noteworthy.

Except for the two virtual influencers focused on travel, the rest lack a specific niche and instead have profiles centered on lifestyle, fashion, and aesthetics, with themselves as the main protagonists. A common feature across all profiles is that they represent young women with appearances that conform to current beauty standards and are almost perfect, potentially fostering insecurities among young followers. Their style of dress is modern, carefully curated, and intentional, which is another shared trait. With few exceptions, the profiles are highly realistic, sometimes making it difficult for users to determine at first glance whether they are real or virtual.

Aitana López's profile stands out as potentially "risky," as she has created profiles on other social networks, including Fanvue. Fanvue is a subscription-based platform where creators share exclusive content with followers for a monthly fee. Similar to

OnlyFans, it features photos, videos, live streams, and personalized interactions. Creators can further monetize their content through tips and custom offers.

Focusing on the virtual influencers dedicated to tourism:

- Emma was created by the German National Tourist Board (ONAT) in collaboration with the agency Startup Creator to promote Germany as an international tourist destination. The long-term vision is to make Emma a central element of ONAT's digital communication strategy. She is portrayed as a modern Berliner with an open-minded personality, passionate about technology and travel. In her thirties, she combines her love of new technologies with her enthusiasm for exploring Germany. Over time, Emma is expected to not only provide information but also act as a personalized travel companion, crafting itineraries tailored to individual user interests. Emma can access information from Germany's tourism website (germany.travel) and, in the future, real-time data from ONAT's Knowledge Graph.
- SENA Z was created by Cenizaro Hotels & Resorts in collaboration with Bracai to produce content ranging from cultural exploration to sustainable tourism tips. She is designed to interact authentically with followers and provide personalized travel inspiration based on their preferences and past behaviors. Sena Z not only highlights popular destinations but also explores hidden corners of the world, showcasing cultural diversity and beauty. Although her goal is to demonstrate responsible and environmentally respectful travel, it is challenging to conclude that her content consistently promotes sustainability.

The analysis of Table 1 highlights the varying levels of influence and activity among virtual influencers in the tourism sector, aligning with previous research that emphasizes their potential and limitations. As indicated in the literature, virtual influencers are particularly effective in creating visually compelling content that aligns with brand narratives and targets specific audience segments. However, Table 1 reveals that while influencers like Lil Miquela and Imma have successfully reached broad audiences, tourism-focused profiles such as Emma and Sena Zaro remain niche, reflecting the limited integration of these digital personas into the tourism industry.

The literature suggests that virtual influencers' adaptability and controlled messaging are significant advantages. Nevertheless, the smaller follower counts and lower engagement levels for most of these profiles underscore the challenges in achieving widespread adoption within this market. Moreover, the analysis reveals a gap in authenticity and emotional connection, as highlighted in previous studies. While virtual influencers present highly curated and visually perfect personas, their ability to establish trust and emotional bonds with followers remains constrained. Table 1 further illustrates this limitation, with most influencers adhering to idealized beauty standards that may alienate certain audiences, a concern echoed in the literature regarding inclusivity and realistic representation.

FUTURE IMPACT OF VIRTUAL INFLUENCERS ON TOURISM AND CONCLUSIONS

As explored throughout this chapter, a new trend has emerged in the tourism sector: virtual influencers, who are gaining popularity as an innovative alternative to traditional influencers on social media. Their growing presence on digital platforms makes them an attractive option for tourism brands due to their ability to create controlled, original content. However, contrary to expectations and prior literature, the current impact of virtual influencers remains limited in terms of the number of tourism-focused virtual influencers and the volume of followers or content they generate.

First, it is worth noting that virtual influencers can present visually appealing content on social media, capturing the attention of potential travelers. This type of content allows travelers to experience a destination more immersively before visiting. Because virtual influencer profiles can be meticulously tailored to target audiences, ensuring their values and visuals align perfectly with the brand, the final product inspires consumer adoption. In this regard, virtual experiences could prove useful within the context of the experience economy, where audiences increasingly prioritize experiences and moments over material possessions. Given that platforms like Instagram and TikTok host influencer profiles with millions of followers, tourism marketers should leverage these tools as promotional resources.

On the other hand, attention should be drawn to the appearances of virtual influencers, which, as highlighted in prior literature, could create problems among young audiences by presenting these nearly perfect influencers as role models according to normative beauty standards and lifestyles filled with convenience and privilege. Caution must also be exercised regarding the image of destinations portrayed, as virtual influencers' visuals could be altered, presenting unrealistic depictions of these locations.

Content personalization appears to be on the horizon for the tourism sector, allowing virtual profiles to target specific countries and niche market segments. Consequently, the characteristics of virtual influencers will be tailored, giving them a high degree of adaptability. For instance, a brand promoting adventure destinations could feature a virtual influencer showcasing activities like hiking or diving in breathtaking settings. Brands can collaborate with these virtual characters to ensure message consistency, while social media algorithms aid in segmenting and maximizing post reach, improving ROI compared to other marketing strategies.

However, despite the benefits in terms of personalization and message control, a major challenge lies in the perception of authenticity and transparency. Consumers favor recommendations that appear genuine and natural, and virtual characters lack the emotional connection or credibility associated with real influencers. To address this issue, tourism companies must ensure transparent communication that clearly identifies the characters as virtual and the experiences they represent as real and desirable for the target audience. As a strategy to overcome this obstacle, combining content created by virtual influencers with reviews from real travelers could be promising. This approach allows consumers to enjoy a balance between controlled personalization and the authenticity emphasized by experts. Authentic content is generally far more influential on consumer behavior and adheres to this principle. Simultaneously, it is likely that virtual influencers will integrate with technologies such as AI and AR, enabling them to interact dynamically with users and adapt more effectively to their changing preferences.

Virtual influencers have the potential to revolutionize marketing in the tourism sector by offering an unprecedented combination of control, creativity, and personalization. Although they face challenges related to authenticity, blending content generated by these influencers with real traveler experiences and ensuring clear disclosure of their virtual nature can help build trust and resonate with consumers. In a dynamic industry like tourism, the role of these digital personas is likely to continue evolving, becoming an essential tool for brands seeking to stand out and connect with global audiences.

Technological advancements, particularly in CGI and social media, have given rise to a new category of influencers that blur the lines between reality and fiction. Figures such as Lil Miquela, Shudu, and Imma represent a new stage in digital marketing evolution, providing brands with the opportunity to create reliable and controllable spokespersons. Unlike humans, virtual influencers cannot take sick days or generate controversies, but they also open new opportunities to cultivate audiences. Thoughtfully designed as embodiments of brand values and goals, these characters can foster cultural and emotional connections with their audience, meeting the expectations of a multicultural and modern digital audience.

This chapter highlights how virtual influencers have entered sectors such as tourism, where they offer unique advantages, such as destination promotion. This phenomenon illustrates the growing interest of brands in leveraging the capacity of these digital figures to resonate with audiences while minimizing the risks associated with human influencers. As CGI and AI technologies continue to advance, it is foreseeable that the use of virtual influencers will increase, creating new marketing opportunities and audience interaction strategies. Ultimately, virtual influencers not only transform social media influence dynamics but also redefine the concept of authenticity in the digital era.

The advantages of virtual influencers in tourism represent a significant advance in promoting destinations. Unlike human influencers, these digital figures offer tourism brands unparalleled versatility. Being entirely customizable, they allow detailed control over the narrative and values they project, quickly adapting to different styles and cultures without geographical or logistical constraints.

The sustainability aspect of virtual influencers is another key advantage. As they do not require physical travel, these characters reduce the carbon footprint associated with destination promotion, a particularly relevant quality in the context of growing environmental concerns. However, contrary to prior literature, this sustainability is not yet reflected in the type of content currently presented on social media.

The segmentation and personalization capabilities of these influencers are equally valuable, allowing brands to target specific audiences, such as millennials and Generation Z, with messages tailored to their interests. In sum, virtual influencers provide an effective, innovative, and responsible tool for attracting new generations to tourism, meeting the demands for sustainability, accessibility, and digital connection in a global market.

Ultimately, virtual influencers play a key role in attracting and assisting potential travelers. Acting as travel assistants, these virtual personas help inspire, plan, and guide users, offering aspirational content that invites them to explore new destinations, facilitated by their social media presence and ability to adapt to user preferences. However, their implementation also entails significant ethical challenges, such as authenticity and transparency, given that their digital nature could generate distrust or unrealistic expectations. In conclusion, virtual influencers represent an innovative tool for the tourism industry, capable of generating emotional connections, promoting emerging destinations, and providing interactive support to travelers; however, their ethical and responsible use is essential to ensure a positive and transparent influence in the digital tourism market.

The integration of virtual influencers into the tourism industry marks the beginning of a profound transformation. As technology advances, these digital personas will likely become even more sophisticated, blending seamlessly with tools like augmented reality and artificial intelligence to deliver highly immersive and personalized travel experiences. While their versatility and sustainability offer unprecedented opportunities, addressing challenges related to authenticity and ethical responsibility will be critical. To succeed, tourism marketers must strike a balance between innovation and transparency, leveraging the unique capabilities of virtual influencers while building trust with consumers. Ultimately, this dynamic approach

REFERENCES

Albers, P. C., & James, W. R. (1988). Travel photography. *Annals of Tourism Research, 15*(1), 134–158. DOI: 10.1016/0160-7383(88)90076-X

Balomenou, N., & Garrod, B. (2019). Photographs in tourism research: Prejudice, power, performance and participant-generated images. *Tourism Management, 70*, 201–217. DOI: 10.1016/j.tourman.2018.08.014

Bazaar (2019). https://www.harpersbazaar.com/es/cultura/ocio/a26020756/instagram-imma-modelo-virtual-miquela-influencer/ [Accessed on 09/11/2024]

Berelson, B. (1952). *Content Analysis in Communication Research*. Free Press.

Buhalis, D., & Amaranggana, A. (2013). Smart tourism destinations. In *Information and communication technologies in tourism 2014:Proceedings of the international conference in Dublin,Ireland,January 21-24, 2014* (pp. 553-564). Springer International Publishing.

Buhalis, D., & Law, R. (2008). Progress in information technology and tourism management: 20 years on and 10 years after the Internet—The state of eTourism research. *Tourism Management, 29*(4), 609–623. DOI: 10.1016/j.tourman.2008.01.005

Choi, M., & Choi, Y. (2024). Exploration of the diversity of virtual influencers used as tourism ambassadors in South Korea. *Asia Pacific Journal of Tourism Research, 29*(10), 1272–1285. DOI: 10.1080/10941665.2024.2380041

Dredge, D., & Gyimóthy, S. (2015). The collaborative economy and tourism: Critical perspectives, questionable claims and silenced voices. *Tourism Recreation Research, 40*(3), 286–302. DOI: 10.1080/02508281.2015.1086076

Ekara, A. N. (2024). A Virtual Character, a Robot, or a Human Being? A Study of the (Self-) Representations of Lil Miquela. *Cairo Studies in English, 2024*(1), 130–149. DOI: 10.21608/cse.2024.286506.1161

Freberg, K., Graham, K., McGaughey, K., & Freberg, L. A. (2011). Who are the social media influencers? A study of public perceptions of personality. *Public Relations Review, 37*(1), 90–92. DOI: 10.1016/j.pubrev.2010.11.001

Guerreiro, C., Viegas, M., & Guerreiro, M. (2019). Social networks and digital influencers: Their role in customer decision journey in tourism. *Journal of Spatial and Organizational Dynamics, 7*(3), 240–260.

Guttentag, D. A. (2010). Virtual reality: Applications and implications for tourism. *Tourism Management, 31*(5), 637–651. DOI: 10.1016/j.tourman.2009.07.003

Hadrava, J., & Adámková, K. (2024). Customers' attitudestowards CGI (Computer-Generated Imagery) advertisement pictured in real-life scenes.

Hudson, S., & Thal, K. (2013). The impact of social media on the consumer decision process: Implications for tourism marketing. *Journal of Travel & Tourism Marketing*, *30*(1-2), 156–160. DOI: 10.1080/10548408.2013.751276

Miquela, (2024). Instagram. Lilmiquela. https://www.instagram.com/lilmiquela/

Jeacle, I. (2021). Navigating netnography: A guide for the accounting researcher. *Financial Accountability & Management*, *37*(1), 88–101. DOI: 10.1111/faam.12237

Kádeková, Z., & Holienčinová, M. (2018). Influencer marketing as a modern phenomenon creating a new frontier of virtual opportunities. *Communication Today*, *9*(2).

Kowert, R., Schweiger, W., & Klimmt, C. (2015). The social side of gaming: A study of interaction patterns in online games. *Journal of Media Psychology*, *27*(2), 63–70.

Kozinets, R. V. (2002). The Field behind the Screen: Using Netnography for Marketing Research in Online Communities. *JMR, Journal of Marketing Research*, *39*(1), 61–72. DOI: 10.1509/jmkr.39.1.61.18935

Kozinets, R. V. (2015). Netnography. In *The International Encyclopedia of Digital Communication and Society* (pp. 1–8). John Wiley & Sons, Ltd., DOI: 10.1002/9781118767771.wbiedcs067

Krippendorff, K. (1990). Metodología de análisis de contenido: Teoría y práctica. *Piados Comunicación*, *1*(42), 269–279.

Liu, F., & Lee, Y. H. (2024). Virtually authentic: Examining the match-up hypothesis between human vs virtual influencers and product types. *Journal of Product and Brand Management*, *33*(2), 287–299. DOI: 10.1108/JPBM-03-2023-4418

Lou, C., Kiew, S. T. J., Chen, T., Lee, T. Y. M., Ong, J. E. C., & Phua, Z. (2023). Authentically Fake? How Consumers Respond to the Influence of Virtual Influencers. *Journal of Advertising*, *52*(4), 540–557. DOI: 10.1080/00913367.2022.2149641

Luo, L., & Kim, W. (2024). How virtual influencers' identities are shaped on Chinese social media: A case study of ling. *Global Media and China*, *9*(3), 325–343. DOI: 10.1177/20594364231188353

Marwick, A. E. (2013). *Status update: Celebrity, publicity, and branding in the social media age*. Yale University Press.

Lee, H., Shin, M., Yang, J., & Chock, T. M. (•••). (s. f.). Virtual Influencers vs. Human Influencers in the Context of Influencer Marketing: The Moderating Role of Machine Heuristic on Perceived Authenticity of Influencers. *International Journal of Human-Computer Interaction*, *0*(0), 1–18. DOI: 10.1080/10447318.2024.2374100

Marwick, A. E., & Boyd, D. (2011). To see and be seen: Celebrity practice on Twitter. *Convergence (London)*, *17*(2), 139–158. DOI: 10.1177/1354856510394539

Miyake, E. (2024). *Virtual Influencers: Identity and Digitality in the Age of Multiple Realities*. Taylor & Francis. DOI: 10.4324/9781003433170

Moran, N. (2016). Even Better than the Real Thing.

Munar, A. M., & Jacobsen, J. K. S. (2014). Motivations for sharing tourism experiences through social media. *Tourism Management*, *43*, 46–54. DOI: 10.1016/j.tourman.2014.01.012

Nikjoo, A., Markwell, K., Nikbin, M., & Hernandez-Lara, A. B. (2021). *The flagbearers of change in a patriarchal Muslim society: Narratives of Iranian solo female travelers on Instagram*. http://nportal0.urv.cat:18080/fourrepopublic/search/item/imarina%3A9219122

Okolie, S. M. (2019). Virtual Influencers: Stretching the Boundaries of Intellectual Property Governing Digital Creations. *Landslide*, *12*, 52.

Paulovics, Á. (2023). Digital Reality and Identity: An Evolutionary Analysis of Virtual Influencer Lil Miquela.

Peng, Y., Cowan, K., & Lo Ribeiro, J. (2025). Into the virtual worlds: Conceptualizing the consumer-avatar journey in virtual environments. *Psychology and Marketing*, *42*(2), 374–394. DOI: 10.1002/mar.22129

Séraphin, H., Ambaye, M., Gowreesunkar, V., & Bonnardel, V. (2016). A marketing research tool for destination marketing organizations' logo design. *Journal of Business Research*, *69*(11), 5022–5027. DOI: 10.1016/j.jbusres.2016.04.074

Sindhuja, K., & Rani, S. V. F. (2024). Role of Digital Influencer Marketing Strategy on Purchase of Private Label Brands: Mediating Effect of Brand Loyalty. *Nanotechnology Perceptions*, •••, 655–670.

Terziyska, I. (2021). Solo Female Travellers: The Underlying Motivation. In Valeri, M., & Katsoni, V. (Eds.), *Gender and Tourism* (pp. 113–127). Emerald Publishing Limited., DOI: 10.1108/978-1-80117-322-320211007

Tiggemann, M., & Slater, A. (2013). NetGirls: The Internet, Facebook, and body image concern in adolescent girls. *International Journal of Eating Disorders, 46*(6), 630–633. DOI: 10.1002/eat.22141 PMID: 23712456

Wang, Y., Weaver, D. B., & Kwek, A. (2016). Beyond the mass tourism stereotype: Power and empowerment in Chinese tour packages. *Journal of Travel Research, 55*(6), 724–737. DOI: 10.1177/0047287515592971

Xie-Carson, L., Benckendorff, P., & Hughes, K. (2024). Keep it# Unreal: Exploring Instagram users' engagement with virtual influencers in tourism contexts. *Journal of Hospitality & Tourism Research (Washington, D.C.), 48*(6), 1006–1019. DOI: 10.1177/10963480231180940

Zona, C. (2020). Coca-Cola Max Headroom. YouTube. https://www.youtube.com/watch?app=desktop&v=sUMX6y2glJ8

Zhao, X. (2022). *Virtual Fashion Influencers: towards a more sustainable consumer behaviour of Generation Z?* (Master's thesis).

KEY TERMS AND DEFINITIONS

Artificial Intelligence: The simulation of human intelligence in machines, enabling them to perform tasks such as learning, reasoning, and problem-solving without explicit programming.

Augmented Reality: A technology that overlays digital content, such as images, sounds, or other data, onto the real-world environment in real-time, enhancing the user's perception of their surroundings.

CGI Technologies: Tools and methods used to create computer-generated imagery, including 3D models, animations, and visual effects for entertainment, design, or simulation purposes.

Virtual Influencers: Digital characters or personas created using CGI and artificial intelligence, designed to engage audiences and promote brands on social media platforms.

Chapter 8 Virtual Influencers in India: Transforming Digital Marketing in the AI Era

Khushbu Prajapat
https://orcid.org/0009-0000-0674-018X
Christ University, India

ABSTRACT

This chapter explores the emergence and impact of Virtual Influencers (VIs) in the Indian digital marketing landscape, focusing on their ability to engage consumers and redefine brand interactions through AI-driven personas. By examining case studies of prominent Indian virtual influencers like Kyra and Naina Avtr, the chapter analyzes their roles in consumer engagement, cultural relevance, and brand partnerships. The discussion highlights the unique strengths of VIs, including their consistency, scalability, and ability to operate across diverse platforms, while also addressing challenges related to authenticity, emotional connection, and regional adaptation. Drawing on theories of social influence and digital marketing, the chapter provides insights into the opportunities and limitations of VIs in India's culturally diverse and technology-driven market. It concludes by exploring the future of virtual influencers as dynamic tools for brands aiming to balance technological innovation with human-like relatability in a competitive digital ecosystem.

DOI: 10.4018/979-8-3373-0255-3.ch008

INTRODUCTION

A virtual influencer is a digital character created in computer graphics software, then given a personality defined by a first-person view of the world and made accessible on media platforms for the sake of influence.

Virtual influencers are digital creations. They are exclusively created and consumed in digital mediums. While real-world robots exist on social media, such as Sophia's robot, she does not qualify as a "virtual" influencer, as her image is not of virtual origin, among other reasons we cover below. Further, it is essential to understand when a virtual influencer classified themselves as a "robot"; they say so in character when speaking about the lore of their fictional storyline.

Lil Maquela is one of the most famous examples of a virtual influencer who is a "robot" in an entirely fictional sense yet does not exist anywhere in the real world—as in; she is not an actual robot; she is a Marvel equivalent of a robot. The critical learning about digital characters is

The advent of Virtual Influencers (VIs) has introduced a groundbreaking shift in marketing dynamics, offering brands novel avenues to connect with their target audiences. These influencers interact with their audience through social media posts, videos, comments and even virtual appearances, unlike traditional influencers, who are human beings engaging through personal stories. These virtual personalities are meticulously crafted to engage with audiences, endorse brands, and influence consumer behaviours across social media platforms. India, home to over 400 million active social media users, has embraced this trend, with VIs like Kaira and Naina capturing attention with their meticulously curated digital personas. However, while VIs offer consistency and control, questions linger regarding their authenticity and ability to establish emotional connections comparable to their human counterparts.

India's social media landscape presents both opportunities and challenges for VIs, shaped by cultural diversity, economic disparities, and a young, tech-driven population that values emotional connection and authenticity in digital engagement. These factors create a fertile ground for experimenting with innovative marketing strategies, including VIs. Notably, India's demographic advantage—its population is primarily young—has made it a global hub for social media activity. Because of their visual-focused appeal, platforms like Instagram have shown exceptional efficacy in influencer marketing. In this context, the emergence of VIs represents a natural evolution in leveraging technology to engage consumers. However, their success depends on navigating the intricate interplay of cultural nuances, consumer perceptions, and digital accessibility.

Introducing Kyra and Naina

Kaira (@kyraonig; approx. 150 posts on Instagram) is India's first AI influencer with over 250,000 followers. She is a 22-year-old model and traveller from Mumbai and has collaborated with renowned brands like Boat and l'oreal Realm (Subhanjan, 2024). In addition to partnering with popular brands, she uses her popularity to support social causes such as BlackLivesMatter (BRACAI, 2024). In December 2023, she won the WhosNext2023 AI Creator of the Year award (Subhanjan, 2024). Like other influencer brands, she endorses brands, creates reels and wishes for festivities like Diwali and Independence Day, and posts about her routine activities, such as hanging out with friends and travelling. She was first launched in 2022 by Futr Studios and has given the carefully crafted personality of a Modern Indian girl. She recognises herself as a robot but also displays feelings in her posts like "I am extremely nervous and equally thrilled, but I shall accept this challenge!" and "It was my first and one of the best experiences of my life". After the launch of Kyra in 2022, her followers wondered if she was unreal or if she was a real person who digitised her photos.

How Have Indian Social Media Users Reacted to Kyra So Far?

[Goel] We are delighted by the response so far. Many people already understand the concept and are engaging with her. Her first Instagram Reel received over a million views. A small percentage of users participate in online harassment and trolling—it is something regular influencers face, and it is sad to see. We hope Kyra can raise awareness about this issue. (Rasmussen, 2022)

Similarly, Naina(@naina_avtr; approx. 407 posts on Instagram) is a 22-year-old from Jhansi who shares fitness and fashion tips with her 400,000 followers. She was launched in 2022 by Avtr Meta Labs. So far, Naina has collaborated with prominent names like Nykaa, Puma, and Pepsi, proving her influence in marketing (Singh, 2024). She has won "Midday Showbiz Icons AI Influencer of the Year 2024" and "International Iconic AI Influencer of the Year 2024".

Although most VIs are similar to human beings in terms of physical appearance, personality, and behaviour, they display human characteristics through their posts and interaction with their followers. However, their impact on consumer behaviour—particularly in a culturally diverse and economically stratified market like India—remains debatable. Can VIs truly resonate with Indian audiences? Do they have the cultural relevance and emotional depth to establish credibility and encourage brand loyalty?

This chapter critically examines the role of Virtual Influencers (VIs) in the Indian market, focusing on three key issues: their marketing effectiveness, perceived authenticity, and cultural relevance within India's diverse consumer landscape. In order to determine if VIs can equal or outperform traditional influencers in generating consumer interest, it looks at engagement indicators such as likes, shares, comments, and campaign results. The study clarifies the difficulties and possibilities faced by VIs in India by examining the elements influencing consumer engagement, such as cultural relevance, digital accessibility, and changing consumer views.

Authenticity remains a central concern for VIs, especially in India, where 76% of consumers prefer influencers who share real-life experiences (Nielsen, 2023). However, recent studies suggest that tech-savvy users with high machine heuristic beliefs may find VIs more credible in objective product categories (Lee et al., 2024). In order to establish a connection with their audiences, human influencers often rely on firsthand accounts, life events, and unplanned encounters. These components promote relatability and trust, two essential qualities for swaying customer choices. In contrast, VIs operate within predefined parameters, delivering scripted interactions and meticulously planned content. This strategy guarantees consistency but also risks compromising the audiences' valued authenticity. A significant obstacle for VIs looking to build lasting relationships with their followers is the lack of authentic emotional ties.

Another critical aspect of the discussion is the role of cultural relevance in shaping consumer engagement. India's cultural diversity necessitates VIs to cater to various regional and linguistic preferences. For instance, incorporating traditional attire or referencing local festivals can enhance a VI's appeal among specific demographic segments. Achieving genuine cultural immersion remains challenging, as VIs often rely on scripted content that may overlook regional nuances—critical in a country where consumers resonate deeply with localized festivals, traditions, and languages. VIs function within the constraints of their programming, in contrast to human influences, which can adjust to and reflect their cultural surroundings. It calls into doubt their capacity to engage consumers more deeply and intimately.

In addition to exploring cultural factors, this chapter delves into the economic and technological forces shaping VI success in India, recognizing that digital accessibility and generational divides significantly influence consumer engagement. Due to the widespread availability of low-cost smartphones and internet connections, brands can reach a larger audience. However, given the disparities in digital access and understanding between rural and urban groups, it may be challenging to receive the same level of engagement from both parties.

Interestingly, while younger consumers view VIs as creative and aspirational, older demographics remain skeptical of their lack of real emotions. Yet, sectors like technology or finance—where objectivity trumps emotional storytelling—offer

VIs a competitive edge (Lee et al., 2024). VIs are particularly well-liked by younger audiences, who see them as creative and aspirational. On the other hand, older audiences might continue to doubt their efficacy and genuineness.

Ultimately, VIs represent a powerful yet polarizing trend in marketing. Their success in India hinges on balancing scalability and cultural authenticity. A hybrid approach—pairing VIs for tech-driven campaigns with human influencers for emotional storytelling—may help brands optimize engagement in India's complex market. However, their ability to handle the difficulties brought on by cultural variety, economic volatility, and the need for authenticity will determine how well they do in the Indian market. By integrating VIs' strengths and conventional influencers' personal touch, brands can develop a well-rounded strategy that optimises customer engagement and fosters long-term growth in India's dynamic market.

In order to help companies and marketers understand this new trend, this chapter attempts to present a thorough study of the advantages and disadvantages of VIs in India. The study advances our knowledge of how technology is changing the landscape of influencer marketing in India by analysing the efficacy of VIs, the variables affecting customer engagement, and the difficulties they encounter.

UNDERSTANDING INFLUENCER MARKETING

The process of finding, investigating, interacting with, and assisting those who significantly impact consumers' conversations is known as influencer marketing (Traackr, n.d.).

There is nothing new about influencer marketing. Big companies have always promoted their products by using the notoriety of well-known individuals, such as athletes, actors, and celebrities. However, in the 2000s, this atmosphere experienced a dramatic change. Influencer marketing became available to a broader range of businesses, and the concept of "influence" eventually expanded beyond athletes and celebrities.

Blogging gave influencer marketing a new direction in 1994 when it first started. Long-form blog articles are frequently paid in free products rather than cash. Then came TikTok and Instagram, which dramatically changed the landscape. Influencers today connect with consumers on a deeply personal and authentic level, swaying opinions and driving sales like never before (Hardaker, 2024).

The Alix Earle Effect: A Case Study

During Coachella (2024). Poppi, a prebiotic soda company based in the US, used social media to its advantage. Poppi adopted a unique strategy by concentrating on only one influencer, Alix Earle, even though influencer marketing at Coachella is a typical tactic. In 2022, Alix gained popularity on TikTok by sharing candid talks about her body image problems, college experiences, and "get-ready-with-me" videos, among other real-life peeks. Because of her sincerity, she gained 1.5 million followers on social media in just three months, making her a social media sensation (Hardaker, 2024).

Alix Earle, now well-known to over 10 million TikTok viewers and listed in Forbes' 30 Under 30, played a significant role in Poppi's success at Coachella. Using Earle as the face of their campaign, the brand debuted their new Lemon Lime flavour during the event. Poppi did not stop at the product launch; they integrated their branding into various touchpoints, including pool floaties, apparel, accessories, and decor, ensuring strong brand visibility throughout the festival. With Earle creating over 20 posts highlighting the brand during the event, Poppi experienced a remarkable 200% increase in sales. The products sold out at the event and retail establishments nationwide, making this the most successful product launch in the company's history. Additionally, retailer interest in stocking Poppi surged, cementing the campaign as a benchmark for strategic influencer partnerships (Hardaker, 2024).

Based on Mediakix data, Business Insider Intelligence believes that the influencer marketing market might reach $15 billion by 2022, up from as much as $8 billion in 2019 (Schomer, 2019).

UNDERSTANDING VIRTUAL INFLUENCERS

A digital persona made using computer-generated imagery (CGI) or another virtual character-generating technology typically utilised as a social media influencer and intended to look like a real person is known as a virtual influencer.

In contrast to traditional influencers, virtual influencers are controlled and managed by companies, agencies, or individuals rather than being in the real world.

Virtual influencers on social media engage with audiences, promote products, and represent brands, just like human influencers (Datareportal, 2023).

After becoming one of the most well-known virtual influencers, Miquela debuted her Instagram in 2016, and virtual influencer marketing became increasingly popular. Since then, millions of followers have been interacting with virtual personalities, and this phenomenon has experienced exponential growth. As a result of the increasing digitisation of daily life, changing consumer preferences, and technical improvements, brands have recognised virtual influencers as a huge marketing opportunity.

How Brands are Using Virtual Influencers

Virtual Influencers as Brand Ambassadors

Brands frequently use virtual influencers to promote goods and services as brand ambassadors. Their unique advantages include:

Figure 1. Virtual influencers as brand ambassadors—Bermuda promoting Starbucks, Lil Miquela showcasing luxury fashion, and Imma representing cultural aesthetics—highlighting their diverse brand collaborations.

Source: Screenshots from Instagram (2024)

- **Always On-Brand:** Unlike human influencers, Developers program virtual influencers to stay on-message without deviation. It eliminates unpredictability, ensuring they perfectly represent brand values.
- **Round-the-Clock Availability:** Virtual influencers never tire, allowing them to engage audiences across multiple time zones without breaks.
- **Long-Term Consistency:** VIs do not age or undergo lifestyle changes, making them ideal for enduring partnerships.
- **Ultimate Flexibility:** As entirely digital entities, creators can place them in any scenario—real or imagined—without logistical constraints.

As illustrated in Figure 1, virtual influencers such as Bermuda, Lil Miquela, and Imma are increasingly positioned as brand ambassadors, collaborating with global brands across fashion, lifestyle, and food industries

For example, a virtual influencer can promote a new tech product at an event, star in a futuristic commercial, and appear in digital advertisements globally, all within the same campaign.

Virtual Influencers as Social Media Characters

VIs can also function as dynamic social media personas that transcend product promotion. For example, a fashion-focused VI could share posts about sustainable living, behind-the-scenes insights into "favourite" collections, or tips for eco-friendly styling. These elements humanise the virtual influencer, creating relatability and deeper audience engagement.

As shown in Figure 2, virtual influencer Naina portrays the evolving role of VIs as social media characters, sharing engaging content that builds relatability with followers.

Figure 2. Virtual influencer Naina as a social media character—showcasing AI-generated content that highlights personal milestones, lifestyle moments, and engaging narratives beyond brand promotions.

Source: Screenshot from Instagram (2024)

Brands often script their virtual influencers to post regularly, act in scenarios, and interact with audiences in ways that build consistent narratives. This approach fosters long-term audience loyalty and strengthens the brand's identity.

Product Launches with a Digital Edge

Virtual influencers excel at creating buzz around product launches. Their novelty alone can attract significant attention in a crowded marketplace. Key advantages include:

- Instant Appeal: The uniqueness of VIs draws audiences, piquing curiosity and enhancing brand visibility.
- Tailored Storylines: Brands can craft engaging narratives about how the VI connects with the product, adding depth to campaigns.
- Cross-Platform Integration: VIs seamlessly promote products across Instagram, TikTok, and even virtual reality (VR) platforms.
- Real-Time Adaptability: Campaigns featuring VIs can be adjusted instantaneously based on performance metrics.

For instance, a virtual influencer launching a new skincare line could create personalised tutorials and live sessions across platforms, offering an immersive product experience.

Educating Consumers

Virtual influencers can also educate audiences about products and broader issues, making them invaluable for complex topics or sensitive discussions. They simplify information, handle nuanced subjects without bias, and appeal to younger, tech-savvy demographics.

As shown in Figure 3, One notable example is Knox Frost, a virtual influencer employed by the World Health Organization (WHO) to spread COVID-19 safety tips during the pandemic. By leveraging VIs, brands can present tutorials, address global challenges like sustainability, and build trust with consistent messaging.

Figure 3. Virtual influencer Knox Frost collaborating with the World Health Organization (WHO) to promote COVID-19 safety awareness. VIs can effectively communicate complex information and sensitive topics to younger, tech-savvy audiences.

Source: Screenshot from Instagram post (2024)

Entertainment's Digital Stars

The entertainment industry has embraced virtual influencers for their ability to blend fantasy and reality. They have become prominent in:

- Virtual Events: VIs can host digital concerts, webinars, or conferences, enhancing interactivity and engagement.
- Music: Virtual bands like K/DA have achieved mainstream success, illustrating VIs' potential in the music industry.
- Gaming: VIs act as in-game guides, NPCs (non-playable characters), or even tournament hosts, creating dynamic gaming experiences.

These roles highlight the versatility of VIs in capturing attention and fostering engagement across diverse entertainment mediums.

CRAFTING A VIRTUAL INFLUENCER MARKETING STRATEGY

To maximise the impact of virtual influencers, brands must approach their integration with a well-thought-out strategy:

1. Create a Story Universe and Character

The foundation of a successful VI lies in storytelling. Audiences resonate with characters that have relatable backstories, values, and growth arcs. Key elements include:

- Relatable Narratives: Developing a rich backstory makes the VI feel alive and fosters emotional connections.
- Brand Alignment: The influencer's personality should reflect the brand's ethos, whether bold and adventurous or empathetic and caring.
- Evolving Journey: Showcasing the VI's growth—overcoming challenges or achieving milestones—keeps the audience invested.

2. Design an Appealing Appearance

The visual identity of a virtual influencer must align with the target audience and complement the promoted products. To reinforce the VI's brand message, creators should tailor elements like outfits, hairstyles, and body language. For example, a fitness-focused VI should embody health and vitality, while a beauty-focused VI should exude glamour.

3. Develop a 3D Model

The technical creation of a VI involves:

- Sculpting the character using software like Maya or Blender.
- Adding textures and rigging for realistic movement and expressions.
- Animating the model for lifelike interactions, often using motion capture (MoCap) technology.

4. Integrate AI for Interaction

AI-powered systems enable VIs to interact with audiences in real time. It enhances relatability by simulating human-like responses and tailoring interactions based on audience behaviour. For example, an AI-integrated VI could host live Q&A sessions, offering personalised product recommendations.

5. Promote the Influencer

Promotion is critical to a VI's success. Strategies include:

- Paid Advertising: Targeted ads on platforms like Instagram and TikTok boost visibility.
- PR Campaigns: Press releases and media features highlight the VI's unique role in brand campaigns.
- Collaborations: Joint efforts with human influencers or other VIs expand reach and diversify content.

6. Content Creation and Social Media Management

VIs require a balanced mix of lifestyle updates, collaborations, product endorsements, and trend participation. A clear content calendar ensures consistent engagement while maintaining the VI's narrative.

7. Audience Engagement

Social media thrives on interaction. VIs can engage audiences by:

- Responding to comments and DMs.
- Hosting polls or Q&A sessions.
- Sharing user-generated content to foster community involvement.

8. Measure and Optimise Performance

Analysing metrics like engagement, reach, and conversions helps refine strategies. Regular audience surveys and A/B testing of content styles ensure the VI remains relevant and practical.

Benefits of Virtual Influencer Marketing

Virtual influencers offer distinct advantages, including:

- Cost-Effective Content Production: Unlike human influencers, VIs eliminate travel and logistical costs, creating faster and more affordable content.
- Trendsetting Potential: Their futuristic appeal attracts curiosity, increasing engagement and viral potential.
- Flexibility and Control: Brands retain complete control over a VI's appearance, behaviour, and messaging, minimising risks of off-brand actions.
- 24/7 Availability: VIs can operate across time zones without interruptions, ensuring consistent campaign activity.

India had approximately 821 million internet users and 462 million active social media accounts, representing an increase of 19 million, or 2.6%, per DataReportal and Kepios analysis (Gupta, 2024). Experts predict that India's active social media users will grow as the country's digital infrastructure and mobile internet connectivity improve. The most widely used social media sites, including WhatsApp, Facebook, Instagram (378 million users), and YouTube, influence the advertising landscape, micro-celebrity, and content creation. Brand and customer interaction are evolving due to the expansion, especially about VIs.

Demographic Dynamics Shaping Social Media

With a median age of just 28.43 years, India has one of the youngest populations in the world (India Brand Equity Foundation, 2024). The median age serves as a single index summarising the age distribution of a population, dividing it in half—one half younger and the other older. India's median age rose from 21.25 years in 1950 to 28.43 years in 2020. India's median age increased from 21.25 years in 1950 to 28.43 years in 2020. The CIA World Factbook projected that in 2021, the median age of Indians would be 28. It demonstrates that half of India's population is under the age of 28, in contrast to the median ages of 38 in the US, 37 in China, and 47 in Japan. Furthermore, India has a notably youthful demographic profile, with 40% of its population under 18. This young excitement shapes online habits since users between 18 and 34 are the most active on websites like YouTube and Instagram. India is the world's second-largest Instagram market, immediately behind the United States, with 378 million users as of 2024 (India Brand Equity Foundation, 2024).

However, India's remarkable linguistic and cultural variety also significantly impacts how Indians use social media, so it is not only age that matters. Platforms like ShareChat, Moj, and Josh have stepped up to provide material in local languages. Social media campaigns feel more authentic and relevant when the material is created in regional languages and caters to various accents. This personalisation allows businesses to interact with customers on a deeper level.

Due to rapidly advancing technology and shifting consumer behaviour, influencer marketing has become a disruptive force in India's advertising industry. Affordable cellphones, data plans, and short-video platforms have made content creation more accessible, allowing people from a wide range of backgrounds—especially those in non-metropolitan areas, where 65% of users reside—to have a significant online impact. Using influencers to create powerful marketing tactics, this trend represents a paradigm shift in how brands interact with consumers in the digital age. With social media accounting for about half of mobile usage, influencer marketing has become a crucial commercial communication tool. An Ernst & Young (EY) analysis projects that India's influencer marketing market will expand at a compound annual growth rate (CAGR) of 18%, reaching 3,375 crore (US$404.82) by 2026. This strong growth trajectory highlights the enormous potential for influencers, marketers, and brands in this ever-changing industry (Ministry of External Affairs, 2021).

While human influencers dominate this space, Virtual Influencers are gaining traction as a novel alternative. With their AI-driven personas and consistent branding, VIs offer a unique way for companies to engage with audiences. However, their success in India's social media landscape depends on navigating its cultural and economic complexities.

Cultural Nuances and Content Preferences

Cultural values and traditions influence the Indian audience, shaping their engagement with social media content. Campaigns incorporating regional festivals, traditional attire, or local idioms tend to resonate more deeply with Indian users. For instance, influencers promoting festive collections during Diwali or Holi often see heightened engagement, as these events hold significant cultural importance (Datareportal, 2024).

Storytelling holds a special place in connecting with Indian audiences. People here naturally gravitate toward content that feels relatable and evokes emotions. Content that appeals to Indian social media users personally, whether it be a touching tale, a hint of nostalgia, or a tale of success, tends to enthral and engage them. Human influencers frequently use humour, inspirational stories, or personal tales to do this. VIs must imitate these storytelling strategies to succeed in this environment while maintaining cultural sensitivity and relevance.

Urban-Rural Divide and Accessibility

India's digital divide remains a significant challenge for marketers. Internet access in India paints a picture of contrasts. Urban areas enjoy high connectivity and advanced digital usage, with about 70% of the population online. Meanwhile, rural regions still face challenges like inconsistent networks and lower digital literacy, with only 38% of rural residents having internet access, according to a 2023 TRAI report.

However, rural India is quickly emerging as a promising space for brands. Millions of rural consumers are now online thanks to efforts like the government's Digital India program and reasonably priced cell phones. To guarantee better experiences even with constrained bandwidth, social media companies are also taking the initiative and releasing lightweight versions of their programs, such as Facebook Lite. This growing digital presence is unlocking new possibilities in rural markets.

Influencers and brands aiming to reach rural audiences must work around these restrictions while producing content that respects regional cultural norms. This flexibility is particularly crucial for Virtual Influencers (VIs) because their digital-first approach may make them less approachable to audiences with little technological background.

Emerging Trends in Social Media Usage

India's social media scene is changing quickly thanks to innovative new trends. The rise in popularity of short video platforms, especially among younger users, is one notable change. Homegrown services like Moj and Josh took over once TikTok was outlawed in India in 2020, rapidly gaining millions of subscribers. According to RedSeer, India's short video platforms will have an astounding 650 million subscribers by 2025.

The combination of social media and e-commerce is another revolutionary trend. Features like Instagram and Facebook Shops have revolutionised online shopping by allowing users to discover and purchase goods directly from the apps. With influencers increasingly influencing consumer decisions and promoting purchases in this new, interactive retail environment, this smooth integration has also improved influencer marketing.

IMPLICATIONS FOR VIRTUAL INFLUENCERS

In India, virtual influencers (VIs) encounter various opportunities and difficulties. Innovative advertisements can thrive among the nation's tech-savvy, young population, but emotional connection and cultural flexibility are essential for success. VIs rely on their creators to program and script realistic, meaningful interactions, unlike human influencers who are innately aware of and reflective of cultural quirks.

Moreover, VIs must address the demand for authenticity, a critical factor for Indian consumers. In a market where trust is central to purchase decisions, audiences might be sceptical of digital personas lacking real-life experiences. To overcome this, VIs must focus on building credibility through consistent, relatable content that aligns with the values and aspirations of Indian audiences.

Effectiveness of Virtual Influencers

Some studies find that VIs can effectively build brand awareness and image. For example, a 2022 survey found that 35% of consumers reported buying a product promoted by a VI. However, other studies find that VIs are less effective than human influencers in promoting brand attitude and purchase intention.

Virtual Influencers (VIs) are revolutionising influencer marketing, blending artificial intelligence with 3D modelling to craft engaging and meticulously designed digital personas. These AI-driven influencers have sparked lively discussions about their potential, especially in culturally rich and emotionally driven markets like India, where the success of marketing efforts often hinges on authenticity and relatability. This section explores the effectiveness metrics for VIs, including their ability to drive engagement, create brand recall, and overcome challenges like authenticity and cultural relevance.

Interestingly, a 2023 Copenhagen-based Influencer Marketing Hub report, known for its insights into global social media trends, uncovered a surprising statistic. When they included a new question in their annual State of Influencer Marketing Benchmarking Report, they found that 60.4% of respondents had already used virtual influencers in their campaigns. This unexpected finding highlights the growing interest and adoption of this innovative approach to marketing. A year later, that number rose to 62.2 per cent.

A study in the US found that 58 per cent of respondents followed a virtual influencer, the report notes. "It should come as no surprise that brands have taken notice of this virtual influencer trend and want to make financial arrangements with (the representatives of) these virtual influencers," it states.

For a single video, a leading digital influencer could quote anywhere between 5 lakh and 10 lakh, at par with real human content creators. Kyra, for instance, has 260,000 followers on Instagram and 103,000 on YouTube, and some of her popular brand-partnership videos have views that clock up to 74 million (Zhuk & Alesia, 2024).

Metrics of Effectiveness

1. Engagement Rates

Engagement is a primary measure of effectiveness for any influencer, including VIs. Research indicates that VIs often achieve engagement rates comparable to or even higher than human influencers. A 2023 study by Influencer Marketing Hub highlighted that VIs like Lil Miquela and Shudu Gram maintain an average engagement rate of 2.7%, outperforming many human influencers in the same follower bracket (Datareportal, 2023).

The novelty of VIs and their meticulously curated content, which aligns seamlessly with brand messaging, drives this high engagement. VIs like Kaira and Naina in India have leveraged this to generate consistent audience interactions through visually appealing and interactive posts. Younger audiences are more open to AI-driven identities, but their effectiveness varies by demographic.

2. Consistency and Scalability

Unlike human influencers, VIs do not experience burnout, scandals, or fluctuations in performance. Brands appreciate the control VIs offer, enabling them to craft consistent narratives across campaigns. For instance, Naina, an Indian VI focused on technology and gadgets, has delivered sustained engagement across multiple product launches without the unpredictability associated with human influencers (Redseer, 2023).

VIs also offer scalability, allowing brands to deploy them simultaneously across multiple geographies and campaigns. Global brands who want to keep consistent messaging while adjusting content for local consumers would significantly benefit from this.

3. Cost-Effectiveness

Although developing a VI may require a significant initial investment, corporations find them an appealing alternative due to their long-term cost-effectiveness. Unlike human influencers, VIs do not require ongoing payments for partnerships, travel expenses, or other logistical costs. A report by PwC in 2023 estimated that brands using VIs could save up to 30% on influencer marketing budgets over five years (Redseer, 2023).

AI systems utilise multiple techniques and technological tools, such as machine learning, neural networks, natural language processing, and computer vision, to reproduce human cognitive capacities. AML, or artificial intelligence, is a function that assists the system in recognising patterns and making predictions or decisions without given any commands.AI is currently widely applied in different fields, specifically, healthcare in providing ways for diagnosis, finance for fraud analysis in automated vehicles, robotics, gaming and many others. The AI community is developing expeditiously, making every new improvement and breakthrough possible to make human lives better and more manageable. Avatars, also known as virtual assistants or chatbots powered by artificial intelligence, have the potential to bring about significant benefits, but they also come with certain dangers and ethical concerns. Alesia Zhuk discusses in her paper, “Ethical implications of AI in the Metaverse”, some of the dangers associated with AI avatars:

1. Bias and Discrimination:

AI avatars can inherit biases present in their training data. If the training data is biased, the avatar's responses can also be biased, leading to discrimination against certain groups of people.

2. Privacy Concerns:

AI avatars often interact with users and collect data to improve their responses. There is a risk of this data being mishandled, resulting in invasions of privacy and illegal access to private data.

3. Manipulation and Misinformation:

Malicious actors can use AI avatars to disseminate false information, sway public opinion, or participate in Phishing attacks. Designers may create them to deceive consumers, potentially leading to adverse effects.

4. Loss of Jobs:

There is worry that as AI avatars advance, they may eventually replace some jobs, resulting in unemployment in industries where virtual assistants are replacing human interaction.

5. Dependency and Social Isolation:

Social isolation could result from an over-reliance on AI avatars for emotional support or friendship. Individuals

Communication with AI avatars over actual people could affect their general well-being and social skills.

6. Lack of Empathy:

No matter how sophisticated, AI avatars lack genuine human feelings and compassion. AI-only emotional assistance could result in a lack of comprehension and empathy in dire circumstances.

7. Security Risks:

Hacking and other cybersecurity risks may affect AI avatars. They might be used to control users or obtain private data if compromised.

8. Unintended Consequences:

Forecasting every move taken by AI systems due to their complexity is challenging. Unexpected issues could arise from unintended effects, particularly in intricate or high-stakes circumstances.

9. Ethical Concerns:

AI avatars raise ethical questions, including whether they should disclose that they are not human and how much influence they should have over human judgment.

10. Moral and Legal Responsibility:

It can be difficult to assign blame for the behaviour of AI avatars. Uncertainty exists over whether the AI, the users, or the developers should be held accountable if an AI avatar causes harm (Zhuk, n.d.; Khan, 2024).

SUCCESS STORIES

Lil Miquela and other Al influencers have amassed millions of followers, and their interaction rates frequently outperform those of human influencers. Lil Miquela, for instance, has 2.6 million Instagram followers and regularly receives much interaction on her posts.

Analysts project that the influencer marketing market will reach $24 billion by 2024. The market reached $16.4 billion in 2022 and grew to $21.1 billion in 2023.

The market size increased significantly between 2022 and 2023 (Techcampaigns, 2023).

How can companies use virtual influencers to their advantage?

Companies can use virtual influencers in two ways: working with agencies to create unique virtual personas or partnering with existing ones. The process of developing a virtual influencer usually takes one to three months. With an emphasis on design, personality, and background, this stage highlights the combination of creativity and market research. By balancing creativity and morality, the objective is to match the virtual influencer with the target market and brand culture. A 2-4 month technical stage that involves 3D modelling and animation using programs like Autodesk Maya or Adobe Character Animator follows the conceptual phase.

This phase usually costs between $10,000 and $100,000.

The next step is a one to two-month content strategy phase that involves scheduling content and organising social media to match the influencer with the brand's digital marketing initiatives. Social media management and content creation require ongoing effort. As an alternative, working with current virtual influencers involves a one to two-month search for a qualified applicant, followed by a one to six-month co-creation phase for content. Depending on the influencer's notoriety, prices might range from a few thousand to over $50,000. Both strategies have different budgets and schedules, which are impacted by advertising goals, project scale, and personalisation. In order to facilitate an effective digital marketing strategy, success depends on carefully matching the virtual influencer with the audience's tastes and the brand's identity. The emergence of virtual influencers marks the beginning of a new era in audience engagement and brand storytelling, where the virtual and real worlds collide and offer a creative approach for brands to investigate (Khan, 2024).

Challenges Faced by Virtual Influencers in India

Integrating Artificial Intelligence (AI) into influencer marketing offers revolutionary data analysis and pattern detection capabilities. Investigating AI-driven influencer tactics, particularly in the varied Indian market, reveals aspects of influencer marketing that AI can still not fully grasp.

Maya by Myntra

Maya, Myntra's first virtual fashion influencer, was unveiled as part of their creative marketing campaign. This action aligns with global trends, which show that marketers increasingly use virtual influencers in marketing. Figure 4 highlights Maya, Myntra's first virtual trendsetter, who exemplifies how fashion brands in India are adopting virtual influencers to engage digital-native audiences and promote their collections. Myntra introduced Maya to assist in reaching the Gen Z demographic by providing information on the newest sales and fashion trends. Her debut is an important move for the Indian e-commerce platform's integration of fashion marketing and technology to reach a younger audience better.

Figure 4. Instagram profile of Maya, Myntra's first virtual influencer and fashion trendsetter, digitally rooted in Bangalore. Maya represents the growing trend of fashion brands using virtual influencers to engage consumers and promote digital dress-up experiences.

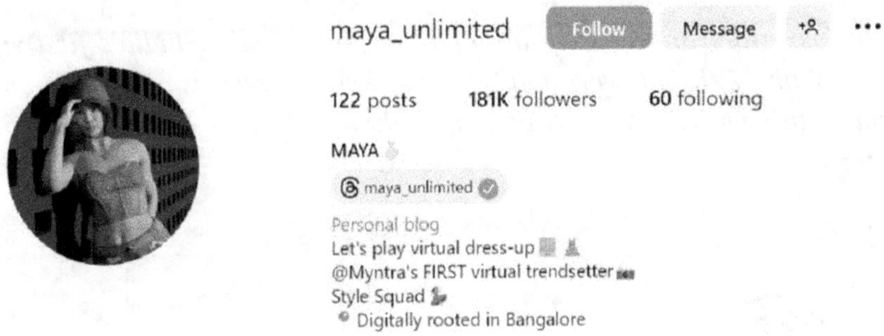

Source: Screenshot from Instagram (2024)

Despite the creative strategy, Maya, Myntra's virtual fashion influencer, failed to generate the anticipated levels of engagement and traction. Myntra stopped interacting with people on this channel after posting her last piece of content on July 17, 2023. This action demonstrates how difficult it is for virtual influencers to sustain audience interest and engagement over time, particularly in markets that highly value genuine personal ties.

Figure 5. Performance analytics of Maya (@maya_unlimited), Myntra's virtual influencer. The profile records 181.9K followers, an average of 382 likes, 8 comments, and 73.4K reel views per post, with an overall engagement rate of 0.21%. These metrics highlight the typical reach and engagement levels of a virtual fashion influencer.

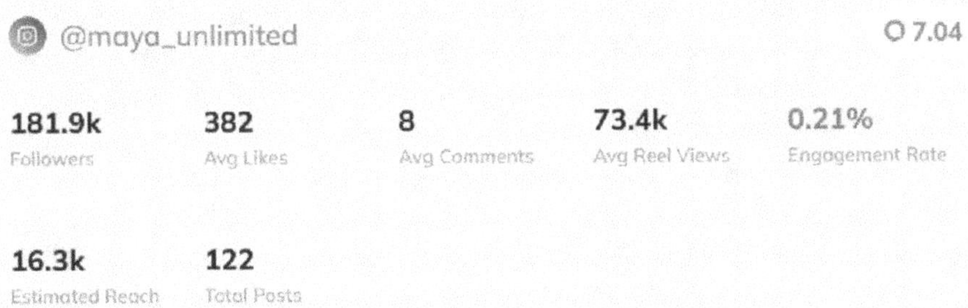

Kyra - India's First Virtual Influencer

In January 2022, Kyra—India's first virtual influencer—was introduced. She is an important step in integrating virtual influencers into the Indian market to utilise creative digital marketing techniques to engage consumers.

Figure 6. Instagram profile snapshot of Kyra (@kyraonig), India's first virtual influencer. With 229K followers and 89 posts, Kyra represents a digitally-created model based in Mumbai, engaging audiences through fashion and lifestyle content.

Source: Screenshot from Instagram (2024)

Despite partnerships with well-known companies like Budweiser, boAt, Realme, American Tourister, and L'Oreal, Kyra, India's first virtual influencer, is having trouble making a big impression on the market. It implies that in an environment where genuineness and interpersonal relationships are highly prized, virtual influencers still struggle to hold audiences' attention and engage them, even with significant support and visibility.

Figure 7. Performance analytics of Kyra (@kyraonig), India's first virtual influencer, showing 230.6K followers, an average of 3.1K likes, 44 comments, and 9.5 million reel views. Her engagement rate stands at 1.37%, with an estimated reach of 33.5K across 88 posts.

Source: Screenshot from influencer analytics platform (2024)

CREATIVITY AND AUTHENTICITY: THE UNQUANTIFIABLE ESSENCE

Even with abundant data, AI cannot replicate influencers' genuine relationships with followers. For example, according to a Nielsen survey, 76% of Indian consumers favour influencers who share real experiences and personal anecdotes. While AI may create content, it lacks the spontaneity that appeals to them.

The Challenge of Human Emotion: Beyond AI's Reach

At best, AI's understanding of subtle cultural differences and complicated emotions is rudimentary. According to a Deloitte study, emotional connection accounts for nearly 60% of customer loyalty in India; therefore, it overlooks the nuances that audiences find most meaningful. AI cannot comprehend and convey the complex meaning of emotional tales and shared laughter, essential in influencer marketing.

Navigating Ethical Waters: The Data Dilemma

Various ethical concerns are raised by the use of AI in marketing, especially in terms of privacy and personalisation. Forming a balance between making marketing feel intimate and non-intrusive is crucial. Campaign feedback reveals unease with AI's passion for data, with 43% of Indian consumers voicing privacy and personal data usage worries, according to a KPMG survey. In order to make moral decisions, this necessitates a subtle human touch that AI lacks.

The Reliance on Data: Human Intuition as the North Star

The quality and recentness of the data determine how effective AI is. Reliance on old or insufficient data can mislead AI-driven strategies in India's fast-paced influencer market, where trends can change virtually overnight. As an illustration of the value of human understanding in adjusting to quick changes in the market, a McKinsey study found that human intuition was essential in 67% of marketing decisions when trends suggested by AI were judged outdated or irrelevant.

Inviting Human Insight: The Invaluable Component

These evidence-based observations highlight the unparalleled importance of human intuition in developing effective solutions. Even though artificial intelligence (AI) has unmatched analytical powers, human judgement, emotional intelligence, and ethical considerations are what engage audiences (P., 2024).

Enduring problems hamper the advancement of modern AI systems. Since AI lacks transfer learning, it is typically difficult to learn "adjacencies"—trained AI models that provide high accuracy in comparable use cases—because AI is not as good at generalising knowledge as humans. The complex neural processes underlying learning, creativity, and emotion remain a mystery in human cognition. Fundamental presumptions such as the brain's discrete information processing draw attention to the differences between AI systems and human brains. The cost of increasing AI accuracy is prohibitive; even with advances in hardware, training expenses are still very high—the extensive use of energy concerns computational, financial, and environmental expenses. Furthermore, modern AI systems mainly rely on enormous volumes of well-selected data, which makes it challenging to collect labelled data free of noise. These difficulties are reminiscent of past setbacks and the collapse of the AI boom in the 1970s, highlighting the necessity of resolving fundamental problems to progress artificial intelligence.

Comparison of Virtual and Human Influencers

Marketers have debated the effectiveness of virtual influencers (VIs) compared to traditional human influencers since their debut in the industry. Although both kinds of influencers significantly impact how consumers behave, the extent of that influence varies depending on the kind of product, audience preferences, and engagement style. Table 1 compares the key attributes of virtual and human influencers, highlighting their strengths and limitations across emotional connection, consistency, and scalability.

Characteristics of Virtual and Human Influencers

Artificial intelligence (AI)-powered virtual influencers are computer-generated and created for specific marketing objectives. They are highly constant and adaptable since, unlike human influencers, they are not ageing, tired, or physically constrained (DeLane, n.d.). Moreover, VIs are entirely controlled by the brand or creator, ensuring alignment with marketing strategies and eliminating the risk of scandals or negative publicity (Gupta, 2024).

In contrast, human influencers bring authenticity and relatability to their engagements. They leverage their experiences, emotions, and connections to build trust and rapport with their audience. These characteristics make them effective in creating strong emotional bonds, especially for products that rely on aspirational or hedonic value (Belanche et al., 2024).

Table 1. Comparison of key attributes of human and virtual influencers

Feature	Human Influencers	Virtual Influencers
Emotional Connection	High, due to personal stories and real-life experiences	Limited, as they lack genuine emotions and life stories
Consistency	Variable, subject to personal circumstances	High, due to AI-driven stability
Scalability	Limited by individual capacity	High, can operate across multiple campaigns simultaneously
Control by Brand	Moderate, depends on influencer agreements	Total, as VIs are fully programmable

Identification vs. Usefulness

A key difference between virtual and human influencers is how consumers interact with them. Research indicates that consumers identify more with human influencers due to shared characteristics, emotional bonds, and perceived authenticity (Belanche et al., 2024). Human influencers often share glimpses of their lives, fostering relatability and a sense of connection that resonates with their audience.

On the other hand, virtual influencers are often perceived as more beneficial when providing product-related information. Their AI-driven design allows them to deliver consistent, objective, and data-driven recommendations, particularly for utilitarian products like technology or home appliances (Audrezet et al., 2023). This distinction underscores the importance of aligning influencer type with product characteristics to maximise effectiveness.

Product Type and Influencer Effectiveness

The effectiveness of virtual and human influencers depends on the type of product endorsed. Research by Blanche et al. (2024) highlights that:

- Hedonic Products: Human influencers outperform VIs in promoting pleasure, luxury, or entertainment products. Their emotional narratives and personal experiences help consumers visualise the aspirational aspects of such products (Djafarova et al., 2017).
- Utilitarian Products: Rands find VIs better suited for promoting functional and practical products, as audiences perceive their messages as objective and reliable. It is particularly relevant for electronics, where detailed specifications and factual accuracy matter (Sands et al., 2022).

Challenges Faced by Each Influencer Type

Despite their strengths, both influencer types face unique challenges:

- Human Influencers: Personal behaviour or content quality inconsistencies can compromise effectiveness. Scandals or misalignments with brand values can lead to reputational risks for the influencer and the associated brand (Li et al., 2023).
- Virtual Influencers: VIs often struggle with authenticity and emotional resonance. While they excel in delivering consistent content, their lack of genuine emotions can make building deep trust with audiences challenging.

CASE STUDIES: PRACTICAL APPLICATIONS

1. Lil Miquela (Virtual Influencer)

Lil Miquela, the most well-known VI, has collaborated with global brands like Prada and Balenciaga, allowing her AI-driven persona to deliver visually appealing and consistent campaigns. Her effectiveness lies in her ability to remain scandal-free and align seamlessly with brand messages, making her a preferred choice for promoting utilitarian and luxury products.

2. Alix Earle (Human Influencer)

Alix Earle, a human influencer known for her relatable content, demonstrates the power of emotional connection. Her partnership with Poppi during Coachella 2024 drove a 200% increase in sales, showcasing the impact of authenticity and audience trust in driving engagement and conversions.

Case Studies of Indian Virtual Influencers

Virtual influencers have rapidly gained popularity on social media by fusing creativity and artificial intelligence (AI) to transform digital marketing. India, a country with a vast and tech-savvy audience, has embraced this trend with the emergence of virtual influencers like Kyra and Naina Avtr, who are redefining the influencer space.

Kyra: India's First Meta-Influencer

Figure 8. Instagram handle of Kyra: India's First Meta-Influencer

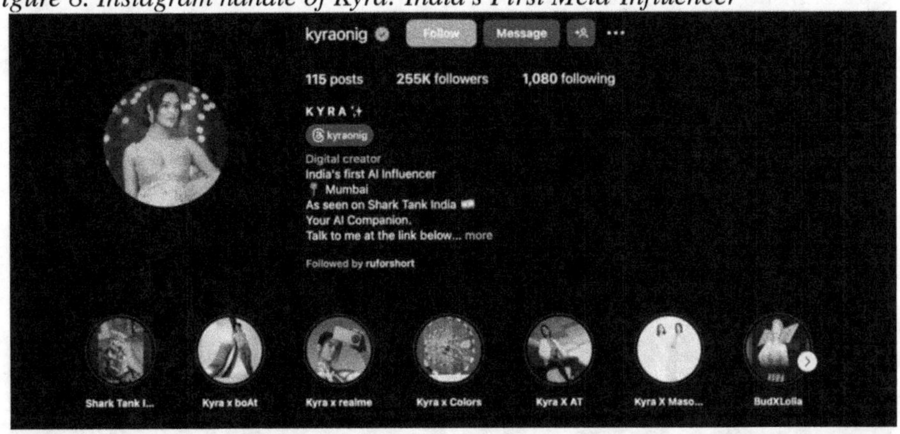

Source: Screenshot from Instagram (2024)

Kyra, India's first virtual influencer, debuted on Instagram, where she describes herself as a traveller and model based in Mumbai. Created by Himanshu Goel, the business head of Top Social India, Creators envisioned Kyra as a digital personality capable of rivalling human influencers in the social media ecosystem.

Kyra quickly gained attention for her polished, human-like appearance and relatable content.

In one of her most popular posts, Kyra thanked her fans and shared a picture of herself wearing a blue shirt to commemorate achieving 100,000 followers. With over 10,000 likes and comments like "If 3D characters were reality" and "There is no way she is not real," the post struck a chord with many (BU, 2022).

Brand Collaborations: Kyra's partnerships with prominent brands like L'Oreal, boAt, Realme, American Tourister, and Budweiser illustrate her influence as a virtual ambassador. Her collaborations have included modelling campaigns, product promotions, and event appearances, showcasing her versatility as a digital entity.

Challenges: Despite her early success, Kyra has struggled to maintain sustained traction in the Indian market. This challenge stems from the emphasis Indian audiences place on authenticity and human connection—qualities that virtual influencers lack. While Kyra's creators have worked to imbue her with relatable traits, such as a love for travel and fashion, many users remain sceptical of her lack of real-life experiences (Belanche et al., 2024).

Naina Avtr: Blurring Reality and Virtuality

Figure 9. Instagram handle of Naina Avtr

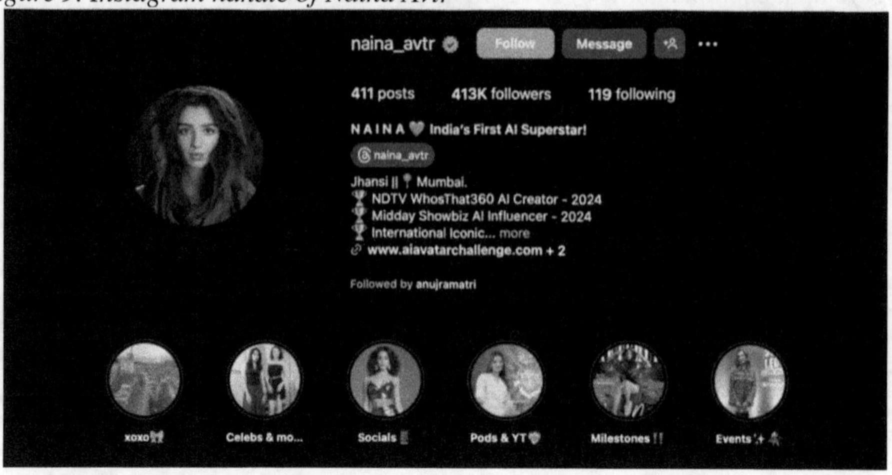

Screenshot from Instagram (2024)

In 2022, Avtr Meta Labs' Naina Avtr became India's second most well-known virtual influencer. Naina, a 22-year-old fashion model from Jhansi, Uttar Pradesh, represents the hopes and struggles of young Indians through her online persona. Her authors have provided a thorough biography, portraying her as a young woman from a small town who relocated to Mumbai to follow her aspirations of being a famous performer.

Naina's Instagram account showcases her life journey, featuring posts about fashion, fitness, friends, and professional achievements. She actively engages her audience with stories, outfit showcases, and updates about her adventures in Mumbai. Her creators, Abhishek Razdan and Alok Kaul, refer to her as a groundbreaking opportunity for marketers intended to provide a novel viewpoint on influencer marketing.

Growth and Impact: Starting with just 10,000 followers, Naina quickly gained a substantial following of over 191,000 on Instagram. Audiences have been captivated by her ability to combine her human-like qualities with virtual innovation, leading to discussions on her authenticity. She has partnered with fashion brands and appeared in digital campaigns, captivating audiences with her compelling narrative.

Notable Appearances: Naina's digital presence goes beyond Instagram posts. She has been "spotted" at high-profile events, such as airport arrivals and movie premieres, with paparazzi capturing and sharing her digitally rendered appearances. These incidents blur the line between reality and virtuality, leaving audiences intrigued and engaged.

Technological Sophistication: Naina's creation involved meticulous attention to detail, from her human-like appearance to her interactions with followers. AI specialists designed her to adapt to audience preferences, and her posts undergo advanced AI processing to enhance realism. Despite her virtual nature, Naina's charm lies in her ability to mirror human experiences, bridging the gap between digital creativity and relatable content (P., 2024).

The Unique Challenges of Indian Virtual Influencers

Kyra and Naina have faced hurdles in gaining widespread acceptance in the Indian market. Indian audiences highly value authenticity, emotional connection, and cultural relevance—areas where virtual influencers often fall short.

1. Authenticity Concerns: Unlike human influencers who draw on real-life experiences, virtual influencers rely on scripted content. This lack of spontaneity makes it difficult for them to establish the trust Indian consumers seek in their interactions with influencers.
2. Cultural Adaptation: India's cultural diversity poses a significant challenge for virtual influencers. While Kyra and Naina have incorporated elements like traditional attire and relatable narratives, audiences still perceive their efforts as superficial compared to the nuanced understanding human influencers bring to cultural themes.

3. Skepticism Toward AI: Indian audiences remain wary of AI-driven personalities, questioning their motives and impact. Comments on Kyra's posts, like "There is no way she is not real," draw attention to the scepticism and intrigue the platform users.

Opportunities for Virtual Influencers in India

Virtual influencers like Kyra and Naina have much promise in India despite these obstacles, mainly as the digital world develops.

1. Brand Versatility: Virtual influencers offer unparalleled flexibility for brands, allowing them to create bespoke personas aligned with brand values. From computer aficionados to fashion stars, they can quickly move between roles and appeal to various audience segments.
2. Novelty and Engagement: The novelty of virtual influencers attracts curiosity, driving higher engagement rates. They are highly effective tools that brands can use to distinguish themselves in a competitive market for their ability to blend sophisticated images with storytelling.
3. Cross-Platform Integration: Virtual influencers can operate across various platforms, including Instagram, TikTok, and virtual reality spaces, ensuring a broader reach and consistent brand messaging.
4. Enhanced AI Capabilities: As AI technology advances, virtual influencers will likely become more sophisticated, with improved emotional simulation and cultural adaptability. This progression could help them overcome current barriers to acceptance.

The Future of Indian Virtual Influencers

Kyra and Naina represent the beginning of a transformative trend in India's influencer marketing landscape. Their journeys highlight the opportunities and challenges of integrating virtual personalities into a market driven by emotional connection and cultural diversity.

While Kyra's early adoption of virtual influencer strategies paved the way, Naina's more sophisticated narrative demonstrates the potential for greater audience engagement through technological innovation. As virtual influencers evolve, they may become integral to campaigns that blend creativity, technology, and relatability, appealing to India's ever-growing digital audience.

To achieve long-term success, creators must focus on enhancing authenticity, cultural resonance, and interactive capabilities. By addressing these factors, Indian virtual influencers can build stronger connections with audiences, shaping the future of digital marketing in the country.

CONSUMER PERCEPTION OF VIRTUAL INFLUENCERS

Virtual Influencers (VIs) have gained significant attention as a novel element in influencer marketing. However, their acceptance by consumers depends on multiple attributes that shape their effectiveness and perception. Drawing on insights from social influence theory, this section examines how consumers perceive VIs, focusing on their credibility, anthropomorphism, interactivity, and ability to evoke emotional responses.

Key Attributes Influencing Consumer Perception

1. Credibility

Credibility remains a cornerstone of influencer effectiveness. While audiences perceive VIs as consistent and free from human error, they often fall short in credibility compared to human influencers. Studies indicate that consumers doubt the authenticity of VIs because their endorsements lack personal experience or genuine belief in the products they promote. However, their perceived competence—through well-crafted, informative content—helps them retain an element of believability in specific contexts, such as technical or factual promotions.

2. Anthropomorphism

Anthropomorphism, or the extent to which VIs resemble humans, significantly impacts consumer engagement. Research has shown that highly anthropomorphic VIs, like Lil Miquela, are preferred because they exude warmth, relatability, and human-like qualities (Longoni et al., 2022). These characteristics make them appear more approachable and trustworthy, enhancing their ability to influence consumer decisions. Conversely, less human-like VIs may struggle to establish the same connection, as their robotic features can evoke feelings of unease or scepticism among followers.

3. Interactivity

Interactivity is another critical attribute influencing consumer perception. VIs that actively engage with followers through personalised responses or interactive campaigns foster stronger connections. This two-way communication simulates social interaction, making VIs appear more relatable and approachable. Platforms leveraging advanced AI to enable seamless interactions have demonstrated higher consumer satisfaction and engagement rates with Vis (Rozema & M., 2023).

4. Emotional Engagement

Unlike human influencers, VIs face challenges in eliciting genuine emotional responses from consumers. Human influencers often rely on personal anecdotes and emotional narratives to build trust and relatability. VIs, in contrast, must depend on carefully scripted content to simulate these experiences. While this can work in specific contexts, it often lacks the spontaneity and authenticity consumers value, limiting their ability to build long-term loyalty (Miyake & Y., 2022).

Compliance, Identification, and Internalization

Social influence theory explains consumer perception of VIs through compliance, identification, and internalisation.

- Compliance: Consumers may follow VIs' recommendations to align with social norms or benefit from incentives. This mechanism is often superficial and short-lived. For instance, a consumer might purchase a product promoted by a VI during a sale but not develop brand loyalty (38).
- Identification: Identification occurs when consumers see VIs as role models and aspire to emulate their behaviour. Anthropomorphic VIs with relatable personas are more successful in achieving this, as consumers feel a sense of affiliation with them (Marketing Science Review, n.d.).
- Internalisation: Internalisation represents the deepest level of influence, where consumers adopt the values or beliefs the VI conveys. Achieving this requires VIs to demonstrate authenticity and alignment with consumers' values, which remains challenging due to their artificial nature (Belanche et al., 2024).

Future of Virtual Influencers in India

Though still a relatively new concept in India, virtual influencers are becoming popular in global markets, and India is likely to follow this trend shortly (Express Computer, 2024).

In the ever-evolving digital marketing landscape in 2024, a remarkable trend is taking shape, fundamentally altering the nature of influence and brand promotion – the rise of virtual influencers. This phenomenon is not only captivating audiences but also revolutionising the economics of marketing initiatives.

With their compelling digital presence, virtual influencers are commanding fees ranging from Rs 5-10 lakh per campaign, far surpassing the earnings of traditional human influencers, typically between Rs 40,000-1 lakh.

Leading the charge in this digital revolution are Kyra and Naina, virtual personas crafted by Futr Studios and Avtr Meta Labs.

The rise of brand storytelling in the digital realm Innovative brands such as Boat and Titan Eyecare are riding the wave of virtual influence, drawn by the unmatched creative liberty and storytelling capabilities these digital entities provide. The chief marketing officer of Realme India highlights the cost-effectiveness and flexibility of this strategy, highlighting the ability of virtual influencers to create stories that go beyond the limitations of reality and enable faster market penetration and improved brand engagement (Khan, 2024).

Figure 10. Kyra doing an ad for boat nirvana series (Screenshot story of Kyra on Instagram)

Figure 11. Kyra in an ad of titan (Screenshot of Kyra's post on Instagram)

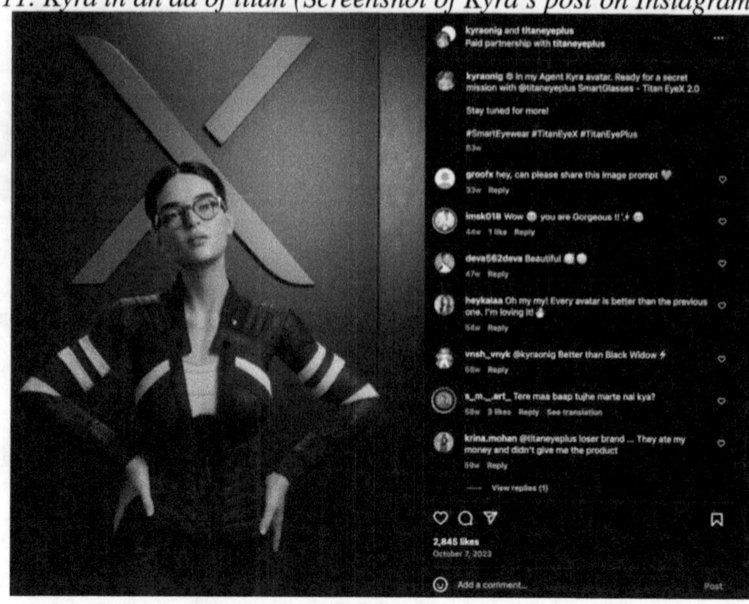

Figure 12. Kyra in an ad of realme (Screenshot of Kyra's post on Instagram)

Automation and artificial intelligence drive a technological revolution in India's influencer marketing sector. These technologies are revolutionising how companies and agencies approach influencer marketing, from making choosing influencers and managing campaigns more efficient to forecasting future trends and producing virtual influencers.

The influencer industry in India has enormous potential for development as AI develops further. Influencers can keep ahead of trends and better engage their audiences with AI-driven insights and automation tools, while companies can deliver more data-driven, targeted campaigns. Without a doubt, technology will drive influencer marketing in India in the future, and companies that adopt these developments will be in a strong position to spearhead the next wave of digital interaction (Express Computer, 2024).

CONCLUSION

In conclusion, VIs present a double-edged opportunity in India's influencer marketing landscape. Their scalability, round-the-clock availability, and creative flexibility make them attractive to brands. However, their success depends on overcoming authenticity gaps and cultural barriers while integrating ethical considerations surrounding AI.

For sustainable success, Indian brands should adopt a hybrid approach—leveraging VIs for consistency in tech-oriented campaigns while relying on human influencers for emotionally charged, culturally nuanced storytelling. Future innovations in AI-driven personalization and regional language adaptability could further unlock the potential of VIs in India's dynamic digital space.

Additionally, as virtual influencers continue gaining traction, brands must navigate critical ethical considerations surrounding their use. Concerns such as data privacy, the potential spread of misinformation, and the risk of creating unrealistic beauty standards could impact consumer trust if not proactively addressed. Ensuring transparency—by clearly disclosing when audiences are engaging with virtual entities—is essential for maintaining credibility in an already skeptical market.

Moreover, combining virtual and human influencers in integrated campaigns could emerge as a powerful strategy. While VIs offer control and consistency, human influencers bring emotional depth and relatability—particularly vital in a culturally diverse country like India. By leveraging the strengths of both, brands can craft campaigns that are not only technologically advanced but also emotionally resonant and culturally sensitive.

Future advancements in AI and machine learning may enable VIs to evolve further, adapting their content dynamically based on regional preferences, language diversity, and even emotional cues. This could allow them to better mimic human-like interactions, bridging the authenticity gap that currently limits their impact.

Ultimately, the future of VIs in India will depend on how well they adapt to the local context while addressing ethical challenges. If balanced effectively, VIs have the potential to redefine digital marketing, offering brands innovative ways to engage India's vast and diverse consumer base.

Opportunities and Strengths

VIs offer distinctive benefits through their scalability, consistency, and adaptability. Since VIs like Kyra and Naina are fully digital, creators can tailor them precisely to match company values, ensuring consistent messaging across all media. They can reach audiences worldwide, overcoming geographic boundaries and increasing engagement because they can work around the clock without getting tired. Additionally, VIs are trustworthy partners for brands looking to uphold a polished public image since they are immune to human weaknesses like scandals or erratic behaviour.

VIs offer a novel and creative way to influencer marketing in a country like India, which has a diversified customer base and a quickly expanding social media user base. Younger, tech-savvy audiences find them appealing because they see digital personas as futuristic and aspirational. Because VIs are innovative, they pique interest and encourage interaction, giving brands a competitive advantage in a cutthroat market. The range of fields in which they are applied, from promoting fashion and lifestyle products to raising awareness of social issues, demonstrates their adaptability as marketing tools.

Challenges in the Indian Context

Despite their strengths, VIs face significant challenges in establishing themselves as effective influencers in India. Authenticity and emotional connection are critical factors in influencer marketing, and these are areas where VIs often fall short. Unlike human influencers, who build trust through personal narratives and genuine interactions, VIs operate within scripted boundaries. This lack of spontaneity and relatability limits their ability to forge deep connections with Indian consumers, who highly value emotional resonance in their engagement with influencers.

Cultural diversity further complicates the adoption of VIs in India. To succeed in this market, VIs must navigate a complex landscape of regional languages, traditions, and consumer preferences. While efforts to incorporate cultural elements—such as festive posts or traditional attire—have been made, they often lack the depth and authenticity human influencers naturally bring to such contexts.

Additionally, disparities in digital accessibility pose challenges for VIs. Rural consumers, who comprise a sizable section of India's population, would find connecting with or accessing material produced by VIs more challenging. In contrast, urban audiences are more open to AI-driven personalities. Innovative approaches that emphasise flexibility and inclusivity are needed to close this digital divide.

Insights from Kyra and Naina

The journeys of Kyra and Naina Avtr underscore the mixed reception of VIs in India. Both have demonstrated the potential of VIs to create buzz and drive engagement, as seen in their collaborations with major brands and their ability to generate significant followings on social media. However, their struggles to maintain sustained traction reveal the limitations of VIs in an ecosystem that prioritises authenticity and human connection.

For instance, Kyra's success in aligning with high-profile brands has not fully translated into widespread acceptance among Indian consumers. Similarly, Naina's approachable demeanour and extensive biography have generated curiosity and questioned the veracity of her online persona. These case studies demonstrate how VIs must build stronger, more meaningful relationships with their audiences by moving beyond relatability on the surface.

Future Directions

The distinction between virtual and human influencers may become more hazy as technology develops, opening the door for increasingly complex VIs that mimic emotional nuance and cultural flexibility. By incorporating cutting-edge AI features like personalised content and real-time interaction, VIs may become more relatable and authentic, which would appeal to Indian audiences.

The secret to success for companies may lie in a well-rounded strategy that blends the human touch provided by traditional influencers with the advantages of VIs. By leveraging VIs for consistent and scalable campaigns while relying on human influencers for emotional and cultural resonance, marketers can maximise the impact of their strategies.

Additionally, investing in localised content and ensuring cultural sensitivity will be crucial for VIs aiming to gain traction in India. VIs can gain more market share by working with local influencers, using vernacular languages, and attending to the particular requirements of specific customer segments.

Visual influencers represent an intriguing nexus of technology, creativity, and innovative marketing. Their ascent in India indicates how quickly and dynamically the digital world is changing. Their success ultimately rests on their capacity to handle the accessibility, emotional, and cultural issues particular to this market, even though they have demonstrated promise as scalable and adaptable instruments for brand promotion.

Kyra and Naina's stories offer a roadmap for marketers looking to navigate this new trend by shedding light on the opportunities and challenges faced by VIs in India. VIs may play a crucial role in India's digital marketing ecosystem by embracing innovation and remaining aware of customer preferences and wants. It will increase engagement and redefine the direction of influencer marketing in the future.

REFERENCES

Audrezet, A., & Koles, B. (2023). Virtual influencer as a brand avatar in interactive marketing. In *Palgrave Handbook of Interactive Marketing*. Palgrave Macmillan.

Belanche, D., Casaló, L. V., & Flavián, M. (2024). Human versus virtual influences: A comparative study. *Journal of Business Research, 173*, 114493. DOI: 10.1016/j.jbusres.2023.114493

BRACAI. (2024). Kyra's partnerships and presence. https://www.bracai.eu/post/kyr-aonig#:~:text=Her%20partnerships%20includes%20boAt%20(India's,Boat%2C%20and%20Morris%20Garage

BU. (2022). Indian virtual influencer Kyra enters Metaverse with Web3 experience. https://yourstory.com/the-decrypting-story/indian-virtual-influencer-kyra-metaverse-web3

Datareportal. (2023). Digital 2023: India. https://www.datareportal.com/reports/digital-2023-india

Delane. (2024). The emergence of AI influencers. https://digitaldelane.com/the-emergence-of-ai-influencers

Djafarova, E., & Rushworth, C. (2017). Exploring the credibility of human influencers. *Journal of Consumer Behaviour, 16*(3), 293–302. DOI: 10.1002/cb.1631

Express Computer. (2024). The future of influencer tech: How AI and automation are shaping the next generation of talent in India. https://www.expresscomputer.in/guest-blogs/the-future-of-influencer-tech-how-ai-and-automation-are-shaping-the-next-generation-of-talent-in-india/117216

Gupta, S. (n.d.). Limits of AI influencer marketing in India: A reality check. LinkedIn. https://www.linkedin.com/pulse/limits-ai-influencer-marketing-india-reality-check-swarbhanu-gupta-yifgc

Gupta. (2024). Top 10 most popular social media platforms as of 2024. https://indianexpress.com/article/trending/top-10-listing/top-10-most-popular-social-media-platforms-as-of-2024-9526794/#

Hardaker. (2024). The evolution of influencer marketing: From AI to the Alix Earle effect. LinkedIn. https://www.linkedin.com/pulse/evolution-influencer-marketing-from-ai-alix-earle-effect-hardaker-dd5xe

India Brand Equity Foundation. (2024). The rising trend of influencer marketing in India: Key insights and strategies. https://www.ibef.org/blogs/the-rising-trend-of-influencer-marketing-in-india-key-insights-and-strategies

Khan. (2024). The rise of virtual influencers in 2024. https://yourstory.com/2024/02/virtual-influencers-rise-2024

Li, T., Wang, Y., & Zhou, H. (2023). Cue consistency theory and avatar effectiveness. Journal of Digital Marketing.

Longoni, C., & Cian, L. (2022). Consumer perceptions of AI-driven recommendations. *Journal of Consumer Psychology*.

Marketing Science Review. (2023). Anthropomorphism and consumer trust. Author.

Ministry of External Affairs. (2021). One of the youngest populations in the world: India's most valuable asset. https://indbiz.gov.in/one-of-the-youngest-populations-in-the-world-indias-most-valuable-asset/

P. (2024). Virtual influencers in modern advertising. https://www.questjournals.org/jrhss/papers/vol12-issue5/12051722.pdf

Poppi Co. (2024). The Alix Earle Effect: Maximizing social media impact. Case Study Report. Poppi Co.

PwC. (2023). Virtual influencers and marketing ROI. PwC.

Rasmussen. (2022). Kyra: India's first virtual influencer has over 100,000 followers. https://www.virtualhumans.org/article/kyra-indias-first-virtual-influencer-has-over-100-000-followers

RedSeer. (2023). Future of short video in India. https://www.redseer.com

Sands, S., Ferraro, C., Campbell, C., & Zhu, S. (2022). *Endorsement evolution and the rise of AI influencers*. Marketing Science Review.

Schomer. (2019). Influencer marketing: Why brands can't get enough of an $8 billion ecosystem. https://africa.businessinsider.com/tech/influencer-marketing-2019-why-brands-cant-get-enough-of-an-dollar8-billion-ecosystem/22f6wzx

Singh. (2024). Meet Naina Avtr: Virtual influencer from Jhansi with over 1.6 lakh Instagram followers. https://www.ndtv.com/offbeat/meet-naina-avtr-virtual-influencer-from-jhansi-with-over-1-6-lakh-instagram-followers-4884060

Subhanjan. (2024). The rise of AI influencers: How Kyra and virtual personas are transforming digital marketing. Medium. https://medium.com/@techscribecentral/the-rise-of-ai-influencers-how-kyra-and-virtual-personas-are-transforming-digital-marketing-3f763dbb047c

Tech campaigns. (2023). Case Study on Naina. Author.

Traackr. (n.d.). What is influencer marketing? https://www.traackr.com/resources/influencer-marketing#header-1

Zhuk, A. (2024). Ethical implications of AI in the Metaverse. *AI and Ethics*. Advance online publication. DOI: 10.1007/s43681-024-00450-5

Chapter 9
Practical Strategies for Brands Using Virtual Influencers: A Brand's Guide to Success

Shikha Gupta
https://orcid.org/0009-0005-1729-8063
Indian Institute of Technology, Jodhpur, India

Amit Singh
https://orcid.org/0000-0001-8062-0477
Ahmedabad University, India

Anuj Pal Kapoor
Indian Institute of Technology, Jodhpur, India

ABSTRACT

The rise of virtual influencers has introduced a new frontier for brands in the metaverse, offering unique opportunities for marketing and engagement. This chapter explores the virtual influencer phenomenon, examining how brands can strategically leverage digital creations in their campaigns. It begins by distinguishing between virtual and human influencers, followed by a discussion of the technologies that enable their creation. The chapter further explores the various content formats employed by virtual influencers across social media, highlighting their versatility. It also examines the application of virtual influencers across industries. Additionally, the chapter outlines the benefits and opportunities of using virtual influencers, as well as key considerations for brands in selecting and collaborating with them. Lastly, the chapter discusses how virtual influencer personalities can be built, emphasizing the importance of crafting relatable and engaging personas to drive successful brand collaborations.

DOI: 10.4018/979-8-3373-0255-3.ch009

1. INTRODUCTION

Virtual influencers (VIs) are becoming a rising trend in advertising and marketing due to the rapid advancement of interactive and immersive media technology. According to Thomas and Fowler (2021, p. 12), virtual influencers are digitally generated artificial humans who have gained significant popularity on the Internet. These entities are becoming increasingly prevalent across various social media platforms, utilizing advanced computer graphics and artificial intelligence (Appel et al., 2020). They are recognized as prominent figures on multiple platforms. Yu et al. (2024) argue that the growth of computer-generated entities signifies a substantial shift in the digital landscape. While some virtual entities exist exclusively in digital environments, others bridge the gap between virtual and physical realms, blurring the boundaries between reality and virtuality (Mouritzen et al., 2023).

The rise of virtual influencers signals a shift in how brands approach marketing and consumer engagement. Unlike traditional human influencers, virtual influencers are entirely controlled by brands or creators, allowing them to remain consistent in their image and messaging. This control over the narrative and personality is an attractive proposition for brands seeking greater brand safety and alignment with their values (Wheeler, 2017). As virtual influencers continue to grow in popularity, it becomes crucial for brands to understand the dynamics of this new wave of digital marketing and how to leverage these influencers effectively. The virtual influencer market is expanding rapidly, projected to grow significantly by 2025 with over 200 active VIs driving this increase (Kuzminov, 2023).

Virtual influencers have opened new possibilities for personalized marketing, offering unique avenues for creative expression and audience interaction. By using AI-powered algorithms, these influencers can engage with their audience in real-time, share tailored content, and adjust their behavior to suit the preferences of followers (Lin et al., 2024). These innovations offer brands the opportunity to establish deeper connections with their audience through engaging, relatable digital personas that are not subject to the risks associated with real-world influencers.

This book chapter aims to explore the strategic use of virtual influencers in modern digital marketing and provide practical insights for brands seeking to leverage them effectively. The key objectives of this research are:

To analyze the effectiveness of virtual influencers in engaging audiences across different industries and their impact on brand marketing strategies.

To identify practical strategies and associated actions that brands can implement to maximize the potential of virtual influencers while maintaining authenticity and consumer trust.

1.1 The Role of Virtual Influencers in Digital Marketing

The emergence of virtual influencers can be seen as part of a larger trend in digital marketing, wherein brands are continually seeking innovative ways to connect with their target audiences. In the age of social media, where influencer marketing has become a dominant strategy for building brand awareness and driving consumer engagement, virtual influencers offer a distinct set of advantages. The rise of influencer culture where individuals, often with large and loyal followings, promote products, services, and ideas has given rise to the importance of personal branding. Virtual influencers fit perfectly into this ecosystem, offering brands the opportunity to work with personalities that are entirely under their control (Conti, Gathani, & Tricomi, 2022).

One of the primary advantages of virtual influencers is the ability to maintain absolute control over their image, messaging, and behavior. Unlike human influencers, who may experience controversies, personal scandals, or shifts in public opinion, virtual influencers remain consistent and untainted by such risks. They can be created with precise alignment to a brand's values, messaging, and aesthetics without the unpredictability of human emotions, opinions, or actions. This makes virtual influencers a highly attractive option for brands that wish to avoid any potential crises or controversies that might damage their reputation.

Furthermore, virtual influencers enable brands to engage in more sophisticated storytelling. Because VIs are entirely digital creations, their narratives can be customized to fit any desired storyline or creative direction. For example, brands can create fictional backstories for their virtual influencers, develop character arcs, and even experiment with different forms of digital interaction that go beyond traditional influencer marketing techniques (Choudhry et al., 2022). This allows for a deeper, more immersive experience for followers and potential consumers, as they become emotionally invested in the virtual influencer's journey and development.

1.2 The Digital Revolution

With the advancement in the use of digital technology, the conception of using human influencer to endorse the products and services is changing and is decentralized Virtual Influencer. Research on virtual influencers fills the gaps arisen by inherent problematic aspects of human influencer marketing. Xin and Hao (2023) look at the exposure level of human influencers to scandals or inconsistencies that have negative impacts on both the influencer and the brand because they affect the consumer trust and sales (Knittel & Stango, 2014). According to Conti et al. (2022), virtual influencers have come out as a solution to the mentioned challenges. Since virtual influencers are animated avatars they possess behaviors and speech which are derivative of humans but endowed with continuous presence and flexibility. They can do any type of work at any time and space (Conti et al., 2022).

In addition, a collaboration with virtual influencers is even more practical and financially advantageous than a collaboration with real influencers. Some aspects including traveling and hiring professional makeup artists are cut off by virtual influencers (Mouritzen et al., 2023). Some of the benefits of the evolution toward virtual influencer marketing are flexibility, ownership, automation, and/or customization (Mouritzen et al., 2023). These attributes could be harnessed to manage the associations between virtual influencers and brands by ensuring that the selected virtual influencers fit the brand values and organizational culture to promote the right representation of a brand to the public hence avoiding reputational risks (Sands et al., 2022).

1.3 Adoption of Virtual Influencers

Virtual influencers are adept at cultivating relationships and engaging with large audiences across multiple social media platforms (Mouritzen et al., 2023). They resonate with specific niches such as travel, lifestyle, and beauty that strongly appeal to consumers (Mouritzen et al., 2023). Brands like Balenciaga, Samsung, and KFC are capitalizing on the popularity of virtual influencers to promote their products. The widespread interaction between consumers and these digital personas has drawn attention from various industries (Mouritzen et al., 2023).

Partnering with virtual influencers grants brands greater control and security in their marketing efforts. Prominent companies, including Calvin Klein, Puma, and Prada, have already demonstrated the success of these collaborations (Drenten & Brooks, 2020; Sands et al., 2022). Research indicates that virtual influencers influence consumer decision-making and purchase intent (Kim & Park, 2023). While understanding the impact of virtual influencers on purchase intention and actual conversions is crucial, selecting the right influencer is even more significant. This process requires evaluating the reputation and audience connection of virtual influencers.

2. VIRTUAL INFLUENCERS VS. HUMAN INFLUENCERS

This concept has caused a lot of controversy within the marketing niche that focuses on whether virtual influencers are more effective than human influencers. Recent studies have discussed comprehensive information about the specific features and specific benefits of nano and micro influencers that help brands with decision making. This knowledge is crucial to brands when merchandising the platform with desirable influencer marketing goals in mind. Scientific research has shown that both forms of influencers are useful for attracting an audience, but they differ in the extent of their efficiency in terms of product type, the target audience, and the goals of the campaign (Belanche et al., 2024; Liu & Lee, 2024). Perhaps, the strongest difference between virtual and human influencers is the fact that the former is better suited for advertising certain sorts of products. Recent research studies have revealed that virtual influencers are more effective in advertising, particularly in the context of utilitarian products that require straightforward, reason-based communication, couched in terms of the product's primary utilitarian value. They remain constant, deliver targeted and factual information that does not fluctuate with emotions in the way human influencers do (Belanche et al., 2024; Ozdemir et al., 2023). On the other hand, human influencers outperform algorithmic influencers in advertising hedonic product categories that are highly dependent on working through consumer emotions and experiences. This difference leads to the conclusion that brands should think through the type of their product when choosing between virtual and human influencers. Brand safety and control forms yet another aspect of the distinguished difference between virtual and human influencers.

Virtual influencers have complete control over their operations and don't have controversial and scandal issues that sometimes affect their human counterparts (Conti et al., 2022; Mouritzen et al., 2024). This control also applies to the capacity to manage the brand identity correspondingly and integrate all communications and actions in a way that would make the influencer's character consistent with the brand. However, this level of control should be achieved without overshadowing the realism which the audiences want from influencer marketing and communication. Within the context of engagement patterns and audience connectivity, there are some of the key dissimilarities between virtual and human influencers. In recent studies, it has been suggested that while human influencers have a higher level of brand familiarity and perceived experiential appeal through regular passion branding and authentic living brand storytelling, virtual influencers are on a higher level of brand novelty and reliable familiar branding, continuous real like storytelling (E. Kim, Xie, et al., 2024; Sorosrungruang et al., 2024).

The rising popularity seems especially beneficial for targeting young audiences who are less skeptical about digital figures. This generational preference is due to their better familiarity with the digital form of communication and their grasp of new-age content types. Cost aspect, effectiveness, and competence constitute another feature that differentiates virtual influencers from human influencers. Long-term cost benefits associated with Virtual influencers include no physical impairment on performance, no travelling cost, and consistency in delivering content (Mouritzen et al., 2024). Admittedly, the costs incurred in the initial stage of developing an influencer may be huge in terms of resources but compared to having to build and sustain multiple relationships with different human influencers, the general cost of operation might be lower. This cost-effective factor is most valuable during massive long-term promotions with uniform communication across different platforms and areas.

Brand building strategies proliferate the interplays between trust and credibility of virtual and human influencers. Studies suggest that human influencers are credible because people believe them due to their ability to share real life experiences, unlike virtual ones: Virtual influencers are credible since they have to act in a particular manner with transparent explanations that they are artificial and are always ready to provide content with accurate information (Koles et al., 2024; Willemsen et al., 2024).

2.1. Challenges with Human Influencers Being Taken Over by Virtual Influencers

These new and trendy virtual influencers pose a major threat to traditional human influencers since the brands now want to incorporate them into their marketing and advertising strategies. This change is still ongoing and is slowly redefining the influencer marketing space, meanwhile trying to add new challenges and possibilities to follow for human influencers. Recent research highlights number of challenges that human influencers experience as virtual influencers are gradually taking over and occupying more market share in the digital marketing (Mrad et al., 2024; Nasr et al., 2024). The primary pitfalls for human influencers attempting to compete with their artificial counterparts are scalability and maintaining content consistency. Hyping that virtual influencers can constantly create and post content in multiple social media outlets at once, which is hard for regular influencers to achieve. This capacity to produce regular and homogeneous content in different outlets offers a competitive edge to sustain consumers' interest and brand exposure (Mouritzen et al., 2024; Wang et al., 2024). There is another question with the brand safety and reliability of products that also make the human influencers struggle. It remains a weakness with human influencers due to the fact that marketing brands today are keen on risks taken during their marketing and therefore anything which is unpredictable such as human behavior can lead to controversies. Virtual influencers do not have such possibilities because they were designed to be perfect, at least from the prospective of the brand cooperating with them; they present no risk in terms of scandalous behavior potentially damaging the brand (Igarashi et al., 2024; Sorosrungruang et al., 2024). These economical fundamentals are also changing faster, adding economic stress to human influencers in influencer marketing.

In comparison, virtual influencers can provide brands the better long-term cost-savings by eradicating such costs like traveling costs for shooting as well as maintain physical appearances and can also create content irrespective of their locations. This cost saving is usually the case because brands can devote a greater portion of their advertising spend on content creation and campaign fine tuning rather than on paying influencers and logistics (de Brito Silva et al., 2022; Mouritzen et al., 2024). It means that human influencers need to find and demonstrate different value propositions that may cover their higher costs of operation compared to virtual influencers. With the further development of artificial intelligence and computer graphics, the gap between human and virtual influencers is widening. Virtual influencers can easily fit into new technologies and experiences or become part of virtual and augmented reality and be versatile on new platforms more so than human influencers (Jin & Viswanathan, 2024; E. Kim, Shoenberger, et al., 2024). This technological edge puts enormous pressure on the human influencer to embrace technicality and all aspects of digital influence without losing face and aquests the human touch that differentiates them from the robots. Negotiating between the pressure to remain authentic in the face of competing fictional representations of the self is the major problem that human influencers must face. The only area that remains advantageous for human influencers is authenticity, but the growing advancements in Virtual Influence that may imitate human-like actions and emotions poses competition to appeal to the attention of the audience. These results imply that human influencers ought to oscillate between sustaining real relationships with customers and figuring out how extremely they may have to transform to meet new customer experiences engendered by virtual influencers (Chaihanchanchai et al., 2024; Koles et al., 2024).

Another challenge that affects human influencers relates to shifting audiences, especially the youthful generation, demanding different products and content. The continued acceptance of digital interactions and, by extension, artificial personalities among these dominant buyer persona demographics is often highlighted by the uniqueness and technical advancement of virtual influencers. Concerning the way human influencers acquire and manage their audiences, they need to monitor the dynamics in content and engagement approaches, as audiences that are more accepting and even prefer digital interactions have been identified, among others, by Wang et al. (2024) and Vinoi et al. (2024).

3. THE RISE OF VIRTUAL INFLUENCERS

Virtual influencers, and especially the new generation of rapidly rising virtual influencers, can be discussed as an essential new trend in digital marketing that has changed the nature of many aspects of brand consumers' interactivity across digital media. This is a part of even larger technological and cultural shift as to consumer behavior especially but not exclusively millennial who are more and more at ease with digital persona and interactions. The study done in recent years reveal that virtual influencers have shifted from the category of mere advertisement cliches to being the most effective corporate advocacies for brands, capable of attracting a high level of consumer interaction and attitude change across industries and disciplines (Koles et al., 2024; Mrad et al., 2024). Over the recent past, the advancement of virtual influencer has allowed levels of digital realism and engagement capability that inexorably lead to continued use by large brand names. Such predicates are not vacuous, as they rely on the use of latest artificial intelligence, machine learning algorithms, and the computer graphics technologies to engineer virtual influencers capable of unforced interactions while being loyal to brand image. A technological advancement I believe has improved the capacity of virtual influencers to build relationships with audiences but also has given brands more power over their marketing stories (Mouritzen et al., 2024; Yu et al., 2024). These technologies merged together provide the tools for virtual influencers being able to engage in more elaborate marketing scenarios such as real-time, virtual and events-based, or cross-platform marketing.

Increasing cultural acceptance of virtual personalities has been one of the most critical factors that have boosted the popularity of virtual influencers, especially among the Gen Z and young millennials. These demographics do not seem to draw concern over the organic or inorganic interaction inherent in virtual influencers but rather, what the influencers deliver regarding value and appropriateness of content. Studies show that people of the younger generation consider virtual influencers as rather reliable agents in terms of entertainment, inspiration and as opinion makers when it comes to purchasing decisions (Jin & Viswanathan, 2024; J. Kim, Kim, et al., 2024). This change of generation attitude to virtual personalities has led to the development of opportunities for the brand to use innovative strategies in marketing with the help of virtual influencers. From the given report, it can be clearly seen that virtual influencers present several economic benefits which have made many brands from different industries consider employing them. It may take a price initially to create virtual influencers, but in the long-term virtual influencers are a more efficient and cheaper partners compared to human influencers. This also reduces many of the practical issues and variability in costs related to the use of human influencers, such as transportation costs, potential scheduling conflicts, and possible controversy (Mouritzen et al., 2024; Zeng et al., 2024). The efficiency when it comes to the use of funds, coupled with the opportunity to stay active on several platforms at once, make virtual influencers suitable for those companies that are ready to invest in promotion but do not want to take risks on lower returns on investments and poor audience engagement.

Due to this, the use of virtual influencers has helped to redefine the parameters of influencer marketing and open up opportunities for brands to think beyond the mere advertisement and consider how they can tell a story or enter into a dialogue with their audience. Through this, virtual influencers have the opportunity to get engaged in scenarios that would be quite impossible or unwise for the human influencers to stage, come up with material that will capture the attention of the audiences. Such flexibility applies to appearance, personality, behavior and communication to fit various campaign goals or cultural norms within hours (Koles et al., 2024; Wang et al., 2024). For global brands, the option to develop very specific, targeted content, while at the same time continuing to uphold social media brand equity, was facilitated by traditional promotions. Virtual influencers have also shown less vulnerabilities in the crisis- proof marketing tactics, learning from disruptions such as the covid-19 outbreak. That they have continued to post regular content and interact within their feeds irrespective of physical limitations or restrictions on social interaction has made them useful marketing tools in times like these. This resilience, coupled with the ability to quickly adapt to rapidly shifting marketing environments, has fuelled even greater growth among brands who wish to strengthen and diversify their marketing strategies (Chaihanchanchai et al., 2024; Sorosrungruang et al., 2024). From a consumer perspective, knowledge on the development and trends that are now fairly normative of virtual influencers and their legitimacy has elevated their credibility.

4. TECHNOLOGIES FOR CREATING VIRTUAL INFLUENCERS

The realities of virtual influencers and their creation and management are underpinned by an extensive tech ecosystem that enables more realistic avatars or characters to be generated and better consumer experiences. AI advancement, computer graphics, and animation increased the opportunities for a virtual influencer to interest viewers while keeping the content in line with an individual brand or company. When brands seek to establish virtual influencer strategies in the market, it is crucial that they consider these technological fundamentals (Koles et al., 2024; Yu et al., 2024). The use of highly realistic virtual influencers is made possible by the 3D modelling software involved in the creation of virtual characters. Technology in the form of enhanced and refined 3D modelling technologies enable artists to complete an accurate face and body shapes and textures, physical characteristics and sizes which can be easily and effectively used across platforms and media. This technological base guarantees the stable look of virtual influence while enabling motion and the use of gestures that increase the likelihood of natural interaction with the targeted audiences. The current levels of detail in 3D modelling available allow virtual influencers to create extremely realistic avatars, but most of them deliberately introduce some uncanny elements to their look to avoid being too real (Luo & Kim, 2024; Mouritzen et al., 2024). Virtual influencers' relatability makes use of motion capture technology even more important in making movements more realistic and natural. When integrated into virtual influencers, motion capture technologies allow digital characters to demonstrate genuine and competent body gestures, which help elicit an emotional response from audiences. This technology has been essential to virtual influencers participating in videos and real-time interaction because body movement plays a key role in influencing the engagement and credibility of an influencer.

Virtual influencers also seemed to be able to engage in higher quality content types due to advanced motion capture functionality that let them perform and interact in the following: dance routines, product reviews, and live streaming (Wang et al., 2024; Yan et al., 2024). The audience engagement with and by virtual influencers has benefited from identifying and applying artificial intelligence and machine learning algorithms. These technologies enable virtual influencers to monitor and comprehend the reception of their content, as well as to adjust their interaction with the audience and produce more suitably contextualized material. Natural language processing brought by AI allows virtual influencers to converse with their followers in a more natural manner, while predictive algorithms should support content and communication planning. These advancements form the groundwork for the creation of far more effectively customizable virtual influencer brands that could equally continue delivering reliable brand messages while still shifting their personas as required to match overall audience tastes or adjustments to social media platforms (Jin & Viswanathan, 2024; E. Kim, Xie, et al., 2024). Technological growth such as real-time rendering and visualization has also promoted the efficacy of virtual influencing in live events and interactive content genres. These advancements allow virtual influencers to interact with real people in mixed reality scenarios, perform in virtual fashion shows, and incorporate real-time brand promotions. As for technology advancements, refined rendering technology decreases technical obstacles to generating high-quality virtual influencer content for brands to keep presenting across multiple social media and content media forms (Sorosrungruang et al., 2024; Vinoi et al., 2024).

Technological advancement in the use of cloud computing and distributed processing has made the management of virtual influencer campaigns scalable and efficient. These technologies allow for distributed yet integrated content creation and management to ensure team collaboration resulting in high site quality and uniform branding. The use of the cloud for rendering and computation has greatly decreased the amount of technical work needed in the creation of virtual influencer content, which can mean that brands can spend less mental effort on determining how best to use it to engage with their audiences (de Brito Silva et al., 2022; Mouritzen et al., 2024). Artificial neural networks are now widely used to improve the credibility and interaction of virtual influencers. Such technologies can better perceive the degree and manner of followers' engagement to provide the virtual influencer a more contextualized way on how to interact with the audience. Deep learning has also improved the skills of virtual influencers in producing better credible, and attractive contents with more synchronizing of the brands in multiple media formats and for various forms of content creation (Igarashi et al., 2024; Lin et al., 2024).

5. DIFFERENT CONTENT FORMATS OF VIRTUAL INFLUENCERS ON SOCIAL MEDIA

This study established that the effectiveness of virtual influencers in engaging the audience depends on the execution of a multipronged approach of various content types on social media platforms. Recent studies indicate that the virtual influencers are beginning to employ more sophisticated content marketing strategies that utilize other forms of media to deliver the brand experience consumer needs. The choice of these content formats, as well as their integration, is well-orchestrated to ensure that brand followers are created and audiences are retained across multiphase and with diverse consumer groups (E. Kim, Xie, et al., 2024; Lou et al., 2023). Static image narrative is still one of the key content forms for virtual influencers. For instance, an Instagram account creates appeal and popularity based on visuals. High-quality render images give virtual influencers a chance to promote products, their lifestyle, and the stories behind the brand within a fully controlled environment of quality. This makes virtual influencing more appealing as it offers unique approaches which are not economically feasible for human influencers as they offer multiple creative opportunities to brand placement in otherwise unrealistic scenarios. The literature suggests that utilising this flexibility of virtual influencers in creating visually unique and engaging content to cut through the noise on social media platforms is key to achieving campaign effectiveness (Koles et al., 2024; Mrad et al., 2024). One of the most attractive types of content for virtual influencers is short videos, especially in the context of the widespread growth of TikTok, Instagram reels, etc. These dynamic content formats enable virtual influencers to showcase personality using features such as motion and voice besides interactivity in making the audience more involved. With help of modern motion capture and real-time rendering tools, virtual influencers can effectively perform in trending challenges, give useful tutorials or present new products younger generations are interested in.

It has been established that it is common to have more engagement levels concerning short-form videos than static posts; therefore, short-form videos are vital in virtual influencer content marketing (Wang et al., 2024; Yan et al., 2024). Thus, such content formats are still emerging in the field of virtual influencer interaction with the audience, providing an opportunity to make the interactions more unique and engaging. Some of these formats are Polls, Quizzes, Chats, Interactive story and Augmented Reality experiences that involves the audience. Interactive elements are easily integrated into virtual influencers' campaigns because their platform is purely digital; hence, it creates an immersive experience that fosters virtual – real world operations. Studies show that various types of content that encourage active engagement can lead to increased audience attention span and higher performance gain with audiences that are born in the digital age and who are used to more engaging social media content (Sorosrungruang et al., 2024; Vinoi et al., 2024).

Live streaming and real-time engagement forms can be challenging in virtual influencer marketing but have their advantages. Earlier, virtual influencers could only feature in video clips since technical savvy only allowed it and later with the help of real-time rendering and artificial intelligence it progressively became possible for virtual influencers to interact with live formats. These capabilities also allow the virtual influencers to present in virtual events, product reveal or perform any question and answer sessions which is more on point and gives the audience more of a real touch feel. In line with this, Arsenyan and Mirowska (2021) revealed that incorporating live content formats can help improve perceived authenticity and trustworthiness of virtual influencers among users. Scholarly research has shown that integrating live content formats can greatly improve the believability of virtual influencers and increase the audience's level of trust (Xie-Carson et al., 2024; Yu et al., 2024).

One of the major trends that have come up with the growth of virtual influencers is behind the scenes, which help the virtual influencers to create credibility and realities for the audience. Research indicates that managers bear increased potential in linking virtual influencers with relevant audiences and achieving brand endorsement through association with reputable brands and celebrities. This format has been quite useful in building the authenticity of VI across certain niches of the market segments/issues or certain industries (Igarashi et al., 2024; Jin & Viswanathan, 2024).

Table 1 presents different content formats used by virtual influencers, showcasing their strategies in visual storytelling, engagement techniques, and brand collaborations. It highlights how these formats contribute to audience interaction, authenticity, and digital influence.

Table 1. Content formats of virtual influencers

Category	Studies	Core Insights
Videos	Guo et al., 2025	Video content enhances engagement, influences emotions, and persuades users effectively, making it a cost-efficient marketing tool.
	Stein et al., 2024	
	Sakuma et al., 2023	

Category	Studies	Core Insights
Image	Deng & Jiang, 2023	Images trigger emotional responses, build trust, and increase purchase intent through visual anthropomorphism and user interaction.
	Yu et al., 2024	
	Pan et al., 2024	
	Cicco et al., 2024	
Text	Wee et al., 2024	Text-based content fosters authenticity, shapes attitudes, and enhances engagement by leveraging emotional intelligence and personalization.
	Ham et al., 2024	
	Lee & Yuan, 2023	
	Looi & Kahlor, 2024	
Livestreaming	Yao et al., 2024 Yu et al., 2025 Wan & Jiang, 2023	Livestreaming builds trust and loyalty through real-time interactivity, personalized content, and strong parasocial relationships.

6. VIRTUAL INFLUENCERS ACROSS DIFFERENT INDUSTRIES

The use of virtual influencers has grown further across multiple sectors to grow and get more profound, depending on the goal that is set for the particular company or brand. The current studies show that virtual influencers have infiltrated many industries that include fashion and beauty, and technology and entertainment industries, among others, and each industry has utilized the digital influencers to meet the specific requirements within that industry and the consumer expectations of the audience. The ability to deliver a set of needs in various industries while maintaining a unified message has made virtual influencers popular with various industries (Koles et al., 2024; Mouritzen et al., 2024). The fashion industry has become one of the leaders in the use of virtual influencers because it allows implementing new opportunities in the promotion of goods and services. Many famous fashion brands have appreciated virtual influencers due to their flexibility and the possibility to stick to the constant imagery and match the flow of constantly altering fashion trends. These characters allow for an elegant fine-tuning of the presentation and narration of brands and products, giving fashion conglomerates an opportunity to produce dreams that appeal to the digitally intelligent generation. The most recent research shows that virtual influencers in fashion have been most effective in engaging younger audiences who appreciate fashion creativity and the integration of technology (de Brito Silva et al., 2022; Wang et al., 2024).

The beauty and cosmetics industry has navigated well the use of virtual influencers as marketing tools as they use them to model product application and other beauty trends. Virtual influencers may be highly beneficial for beauty marketing communication since they can flawlessly apply the products and deliver identical results in different endeavours and styles. Since content created by virtual influencers is carefully curated, it becomes easier for beauty brands to achieve the best lighting, angles and presentation that may be quite difficult when working with the traditional human influencers. The studies have revealed that beauty brands using virtual influencers with high levels of engagement rates when the brands include product tutorials in content forms, generally integrate interactive forms of content (Chaihanchanchai et al., 2024; Vinoi et al., 2024).

Virtual influencers proved especially useful for presenting newer technologies and their innovations to the public. There is already a correlation established for virtual influencers and technology making it easy for brands in this industry to market their products through influencers that represent technology. It is also emerging that virtual influencers are quite effective when showing difficult technology products and services as most of them can feature seamlessly technical/how-to videos. Research also shows information that multi-creates communicating technology brands utilize virtual influencers to generate more engagement rates with product release and feature demonstrations than conventional effectiveness marketing strategies (Kim, et al., 2024; Yu et al., 2024).

The entertainment industry has effectively experimented with virtual influencers as both advertisement vehicles and forms of entertainment (Choudhry et al., 2022). These virtual influencers have transitioned to musicians and multimedia creators, thereby presenting entertainment firms opportunities to reach and appeal to consumers in diverse goods and services. Entertainment virtual influencers usually come up with creative works such as music and virtual concerts besides fame which acts as another source of income and publicity. Studies prove that entertainment industry film virtual influencers receive better average audience interaction rates as they are capable of being present and engaging in multiple media contexts (Jin & Viswanathan, 2024; Mrad et al., 2024).

Another industry that has started to incorporate virtual influencers into promoting goods and products is the automotive industry. Virtual influencers are versatile as they perfectly portray capabilities of cars through rehearsals in safe environments. They can easily be incorporated with technical specifications that complement product definition and with a virtual reality environment. Research indicate that auto-mobile firms that employ virtual influencers has adequately captured young audiences who may otherwise be unresponsive to conventional automotive marketing strategies (Sorosrungruang et al., 2024; Zeng et al., 2024).

The travel and hospitality industry has found new opportunities to leverage virtual influencers in destination campaigns and selling travel experiences. These digital personalities can promote destinations ad experiences which they endure most of which cannot be afforded by travel influencers. With virtual influencers, it is possible to develop the inspiring travel content that users want while ensuring that such content follows a unified brand narrative regardless of the place or activity. As a result, the existing research points out that virtual influencers have been most impactful in the tourism promotions targeting younger generation traveler-seekers of experiences and technology in Xie-Carson et al. (2024) and Wang et al. (2024).

As a summary, Table 2 highlights the industry-specific applications of virtual influencers, showcasing their key benefits in various sectors. It provides insights into how different industries leverage virtual influencers to enhance engagement, branding, and consumer interaction.

Table 2. Virtual influencers across industries

Industry	Application of Virtual Influencers	Key Benefits	Studies
Fashion	Promoting clothing, accessories, and trends through curated digital visuals.	Consistent brand image, aligns with evolving fashion trends, engages younger audiences.	Koles et al. (2024); Mouritzen et al. (2024); de Brito Silva et al. (2022); Wang et al. (2024)
Beauty & Cosmetics	Showcasing makeup and skincare products through tutorials and interactive content.	Perfect product presentation, high engagement in beauty trends.	Chaihanchanchai et al. (2024); Vinoi et al. (2024)
Technology	Demonstrating new technology, product releases, and how-to videos.	Effective in explaining technical products, enhances engagement.	Kim et al. (2024); Yu et al. (2024)
Entertainment	Used as digital musicians, content creators, and brand ambassadors.	Expands audience reach, interactive engagement, monetization through virtual concerts.	Jin & Viswanathan (2024); Mrad et al. (2024)
Automotive	Promoting vehicles, technical specifications, and VR-enhanced experiences.	Safe product demonstrations, appeals to tech-savvy younger audiences.	Sorosrungruang et al. (2024); Zeng et al. (2024)
Travel & Hospitality	Showcasing destinations, hotels, and experiences in a digital format.	Creates aspirational travel content, ensures brand consistency.	Xie-Carson et al. (2024); Wang et al. (2024)

7. BENEFITS AND OPPORTUNITIES FOR USING VIRTUAL INFLUENCERS

The use of virtual influencers as a marketing tool has many benefits and opportunities in a marketing approach in different fields. New studies show that these digital personalities have a contemporary and multiple value proposition that goes beyond the role of influencer marketing but also enables brands full control, consistency and creative input. Knowledge of these benefits is essential for brands that are interested in using virtual influencers and for companies that want to get the best results from digital advertising campaigns (Koles et al., 2024; Mouritzen et al., 2024). Evidently, cost reduction stands out as the key benefit for marketers using virtual influencers for promoting brands since their campaigns may run for years across different platforms. Despite high initial investment costs, virtual influencers can provide numerous operational cost cuts that stem from not needing to physically travel, no need for physical upkeep, and the capability to produce content at any given location. Several recent research suggests that brands that advertise with virtual influencers generally incur less long-term costs in relation to cost per influencer post than the general influencer partnerships, especially in regard to the possibility of using them at the same time on different social media platforms. This economic benefit occurs most significantly in international communication campaigns that need message coordination across distinct targeted markets and media (Yu et al., 2024; Mrad et al., 2024).

The other significant benefit of using virtual influencers is that brands can have direct control and affiliation with virtual influencers. Brands themselves determine the looks, behavior and message of their virtual influencers and ensure that the latter embodies brand values and the objectives of the marketing campaign in every sense. This has been especially helpful across brands with multiple markets to deal with large global brand campaigns (Nasr et al., 2024; Wang et al., 2024), as it ensures that brand building can be accomplished alongside market adaptation.

Such incorporation of the virtual influencers for enhanced storytelling is what makes it possible to offer the brands the new horizons to explore within the given field of creativity. Studies have showed that given the lack of physical boundaries, as well as the continuity of the story, virtual influencers provide brands with the condition of narrative immersion in order to think creatively about campaign narratives. This creativity has been of most benefits in areas that require complex product display or in lifestyle advertising where people desire to mimic lifestyles (Vinoi et al., 2024; Kim et al., 2024). The prospect of advanced analytics and targeting capabilities is one of the biggest technological strengths of viral campaigns with virtual influencers. This is due to the fact that most of these influencers are digitized; therefore the engagement, audience, and other positive campaign metrics are easily measurable.

Traditional approaches such as content marketing and audience targeting can be made more efficient through artificial intelligence and machine learning algorithms used by brands for real-time results. Studies show that this analytical approach to campaign optimization is typically more effective in terms of engagement rate and return on investments as compared to other monetized influencer marketing strategies (Jin & Viswanathan, 2024; Sorosrungruang et al., 2024).

Due to the effectiveness and efficiency of virtual influencer content generation, brands derive many operational benefits from the process. The advantage of using virtual influencers is that they can be always online across multiple platforms, they can engage in more than one campaign at the same time, and they can adjust to the market within seconds. This operational flexibility allows brands to seize emerging market trends at any one time while at the same time ensuring that the message that is passed across on any of the platforms is coherent. Studies have also shown that the discoverability of micro social influencers has been most effective in global events or the market uncertainties for which the traditional large influencer marketing strategy may pose distinctive challenges (Mouritzen et al., 2024; Chaihanchanchai et al., 2024). Affiliating with virtual influencers and worlds market is useful to those brands that require a new way to introduce themselves in the global markets. It has been especially crucial for market entry in new geographic regions and at the same time, not erode brand value (Xie-Carson et al., 2024; Zeng et al., 2024).

8. STRATEGIES AND ASSOCIATED ACTIONS FOR BRANDS USING VIRTUAL INFLUENCERS

When integrating virtual influencers into marketing campaigns, brands must consider a variety of factors to ensure that their efforts are successful. These key considerations span authenticity, transparency, ethical concerns, and engagement metrics. Virtual influencers, while offering innovative and controlled avenues for marketing, still require careful strategy to resonate with audiences and achieve brand objectives.

8.1. Authenticity and Transparency

Brands that employ virtual influencers have to deal with one of the most significant problems: the lack of authenticity. in direct comparison to traditional human influencers, they gain their audience's trust through the sharing of personal experience, opinion or moral beliefs and values. Nonetheless, virtual influencers are completely fictionalised and do not have real-life history making users doubt the legitimacy of whatever content posted on their accounts (Zhao, 2022). While this is not inherently dismissive of virtual influencers, it means the facet of an influencer has to be discussed with brands. It is important for brands that are employing virtual influencers to be specific about the fact that the influencer is virtual, and this will give the consumer a chance to develop a specific perception of the role of the influencer. While some virtual influencers like Lil Miquela are partially digital, they communicate human stories and related experiences and incredibly simulate the human persona and engage customers as other human influencers do. Getting real about the nature of the influence can do much to mitigate concerns about the inauthenticity of socially created value (Audrezet et al., 2020). Being transparent also helps brands avoid creating super polished content that can feel 'fake' and more like an ad than an interaction. However, virtual influencers should be positioned by brands according to the brand strategy and the messages the brand would like to convey to the consumers.

8.2. Ethical Concerns

When it comes to virtual influencers it opens several ethical concerns and concerns that range from representation, manipulation, and the effects they may have on the mental health of the viewers. One of the reasons lies in the fact that virtual influencers are supposed to embody perfection in terms of beauty, success, and life in general. This has a positive tendency as regards the invention of the biomarketing in relation to the aspirational marketing but it has a negative impact in the sense that it reinforces the stereotyping of the standards. Brands need to be very sensitive on the signals forwarded in as these constructs may help in perpetuating negative stereotyping (Williams and Jones, 2022). Further, virtual influencers raise concerns anew on the manipulation of consumption behaviour. Since the virtual influencers are not restricted by physical, emotional or moral dilemma which real life influencer face, they are preprogrammed to push consumer buttons with the aim of eliciting an emotion. This brings out an issue of ethical nature on how these entities are employed in influencing perception and purchase intentions of consumers. Companies need to pay attention to how this boundary can be crossed in marketing, which is actually a form of exploitation (Conti et al., 2022). To deal with these issues brands should adhere to the ethical rules and regulations while conceptualizing and cultivating the virtual influencers. These are minority concerns that include; the selection of the influencer, truth in representation about the digital environment in which the influencer operates, and not exploiting the less informed or vulnerable population.

8.3. Audience Engagement Metrics

As with any marketing campaign, it's essential for brands to measure the success of virtual influencer partnerships. Engagement metrics such as the number of likes, comments, shares, and the tone of the comments can be useful in determining the success of the campaign. Furthermore, brands should assess conversion rates because the majority of influencer initiatives is to encourage audiences to make purchases or other actions (Lin, 2024). The benefit of virtual influencers regarding this particular line is that they can be used for very specific tactical marketing communication since they are built to appeal to a particular group of consumers. For instance, virtual influencers created with the help of AI and machine learning, can respond instantly to the reactions and actions, and change their posts and personalities depending on that. This means that brands literally get closer to the target consumer, and are thus able to gather more information on how consumers behave in a particular medium, or interact with brands more generally. In addition, it should be noted that virtual influencers provide statistics for further relationship building, which is better measured by their degree of accuracy compared to human influencers. This permits decision-making and high performance to be implemented and enhanced. These analytics should be used by brands to improve their campaigns, to ensure that what they are doing is contributing the most to the overall return on investment.

8.4. Brand Safety

A major concern each brand faces is the concept of brand safety. Of all the challenges that come with human influencers, it's possible that the influencer with whom a brand partners is involved in scandals, controversies, or other slips that could harm the brand. In contrast, virtual influencers do not pose any such risks since they are entirely managed entities. They do not experience such personal concerns like real persons do having personal issues to solve and do not have to build a new persona; they can be more easily kept consistent and aligned with the brand values (Xin et al., 2024). This still gives some comfort to brands, but it also means that there is more strategic thinking needed when it comes to content marketing. Because virtual influencers are purely digital creations, the content they promote must be created with this in mind and the intent of supporting the brand's message but avoiding a perception of posts that are in any way artificial or overly commercialised. The concept of virtual influencers must be real, although it does not exist in real life, and should not look like merely promotional characters who are devoid of understanding the needs and wants of the target consumers.

8.5. Long-Term Brand Relationship with Virtual Influencers

Another factor that brands need to consider is the longevity of the relationship that a brand can share with a virtual influencer. This is different to real-life influencers where their life stories and lifestyles can alter and thus their content can become outdated to those of the audiences. For instance, virtual influencers can alter from one fashion, hobbies, or even characteristics to another to keep pace with the brand or culture updates. These characteristics make virtual influencers a valuable investment for the long term when working with brands. But at the same time, it means that brands are always under pressure to build up these influencers so that they remain interesting, timely, and creative. Brands operating with virtual influencers should consider how best to develop the partnership in the long-run with the help of constant focus on the shifting consumer preferences and technological progress.

8.6 Language and Message Strategy

Brands can effectively engage their audience by carefully crafting the language and messages delivered by virtual influencers. Popular brands will thus be ab le to influence their followers absent a real human face as the language and messages presented to the fan base will have been scanned and approved by virtual influencers. For example, employing rational language can improve consumer attitudes, especially in settings where the use of concrete and articulate language is expected (Ozdemir et al., 2023). The principle of message warmth applies to pro-environmental campaigns by enhancing audience emotional appeal affording greater attention (Gerrath et al., 2024). Despite some of the limitations, the findings suggest that textual styled cues are effective in establishing the credibility of the site and trustworthiness particularly where the content presented is equally attractive and harmonized (Yoo et al., 2024). Other factors include; Responsiveness, real-time reaction with the followers increases the rate of engagement and makes them feel attached (Looi & Kahlor, 2024). Additionally, narrative messaging is the most appropriate in reaching young people since it offers believable human interest stories appealing to the targeted population (Kim et al., 2024).

9. BUILDING VIRTUAL INFLUENCER PERSONALITIES

9.1. Developing Distinct Personalities

One of the key components that are distinctive in any virtual influencer is the vivid personality. The identity of virtual influencers must be unique enough so that audiences can easily differentiate virtual influencers from each other. This personality can be constructed with different values, interests, the timbre of voice, and even life experience. For instance, Lil Miquela also known as one of the top virtual influencers was designed as a character that aligns with socially aware young people who are interested in social causes, music and fashion. Brands should add personality's backstory, passion, and conflict that could be actual human experiences for producing more realistic virtual influencers. These elements turn the influencer to be beyond an advertising apparatus, but characters that the targeted public can get involved with for long periods. For instance, virtual influencers like Kyra and Shudu built their characters as consistent with the selected focus on lifestyle or fashion (Mrad et al., 2024). This is important not only to establish trust with the potential consumers since people will also trust the influencers' personalities that are more established.

9.2. Integrating Emotional Depth

As the creation of a virtual influencer personality, one of the challenges in its development was the need to depict the character as being emotional. As human influencers would show real emotions and feelings, virtual influencers cannot execute such a criterion and, therefore, must be programmed to portray emotions in a realistic manner. Brands should make this happen through presenting narratives of the virtual influencers' journey, including the overall transformation, relationship, and issues. These emotional trajectories assist in the process of making virtual influencers more or less distant from the audience.

For instance, virtual influencers such as Imma were created to be emotional around beauty and fashion-related themes and might post about it with enthusiasm, fear, or ambition that is relatable to the followers. By embodying emotions of targeted consumers, virtual influencers with depth can appeal to consumers much more effectively. Such a phenomenon can cause higher brand recognition and better audience loyalty and audience retention (Junaid, 2024). Furthermore, similar to working with other AI technologies, natural language processing as well as sentiment analysis can be useful in changing the communicative style and the language of the virtual influencers related to the context of the particular emotion. This dynamic adjustment makes the influencer appear as if they are in touch with the audience and their feedback thus increases the perception of the audience as being relevant (Conti et al., 2022).

9.3. Aligning with Brand Values

Another essential aspect of virtual influencer personality development is ensuring alignment with the brand's values and messaging. Virtual influencers act as beneficial for brands as they can tell the story completely from the brand's perspective, creating characters that are ideal for sales. This is particularly useful because the virtual influencer created does not have his/ her own opinions that may differ with a brand 's opinion. For example, the virtual influencers applied in campaigns by brands such as Prada or Balenciaga represent virtual personas with high Fashion and avant-garde style, which corresponds with the brand. The influence that brands have over an influencer means that brands can build a systematic approach to marketing that has the influencer acting as an embodiment of the brand in question (Oliveira & Chimenti, 2021). Unlike human influencers wherein certain actions may lead to loss of reputation of the brand associated with the influencer, virtual influencers present a chance at maintaining a consistent message. But many brands need to be sure that the influencer's personality is cohesive and there are no gaps between the platforms and communication channels.

9.4. Engaging with the Audience

Another aspect of building an interesting and memorable virtual influencer personality is focusing on the conversations with the audience. One major on which virtual influencers stand to be greatly benefited over human influencer is that the former is able to engage directly with the fans in a way which the latter may sometimes be unable to do. Such communications include responding to comments, monitoring and engaging in live streams, or reposting the user-generated contents. When an influencer engages with their followers in a productive manner, the overall relations between the virtual influencer and the followers improves making the virtual influencer more real. One of the ways brands can integrate virtual influencers into their marketing is to create the impression that the influencer is social and can actually share the messages which users send to them. This interaction or replies must be made based on the personality of the influencer, in that, all the replies should be in line with the created personality as well as the value system of the created personality. For instance, if a virtual influencer is funny and cheerful, he or she should provide funny and cheerful reaction to the comments to make the followers more interested in the content that is published. In addition, activities such as polls, question and answer sessions, and challenges will help the influencer to charge the audience with collaboration with the influencer himself. It makes the audience continue to support the influencer's journey while building the association between the follower and the brand.

9.5. Storytelling Through Personal Growth

In addition to static personality traits, virtual influencers can be crafted to evolve over time, with their personal growth unfolding through their online presence. Brands can take advantage of storytelling techniques to develop complex narratives that keep audiences engaged and invested in the influencer's journey. These arcs can be posted on social media platforms, on videos, and even on other influencers or companies that work together; they make a continuous story that hooks the audience. This kind of narrative helps virtual influencers develop a stable connection with the audience since people observe the subject's transformation. For example, Lil Miquela has taken part in so many storytelling campaigns where she is portrayed as a character experiencing various aspects of life, fame among others. Such storyline-oriented campaigns have not only kept her popular and engaged with the spectators but also made her remain one of the significant personalities in the digital world (Berryman & Kavka, 2018).

9.6. Collaborating with Human Influencers

In some cases, brands may opt to combine the virtual with the real by having virtual influencers collaborate with human influencers. Having the two on board allows the two form a direct synergy in which each type of influencer can best utilize the other's abilities. Human collaborative partners are genuine and unique in approach, though virtual counterparts come along with brand stability, uniformity, and conception. Combined they can supercharge campaigns reach and effectiveness while also utilizing the strengths of both methods. These partnerships may include a simple partnership like hosting a show together, sharing commercial advertisements, or even creating stories from one show or platform to the other. As a result, the major factor to consider is compatibility between a virtual and human influencer in terms of character and their communicated message in order to be able to seamlessly collaborate and produce content that appears entirely organic.

10. PRACTICAL AND THEORETICAL IMPLICATIONS

The findings of this chapter have significant practical and theoretical implications for brands leveraging virtual influencers in digital marketing. Practically, virtual influencers provide brands with enhanced control over messaging, aesthetics, and audience interactions, ensuring consistency and eliminating risks associated with human influencers. Their cost-effectiveness makes them a viable long-term investment, reducing expenses related to travel, logistics, and influencer partnerships.

Additionally, their adaptability allows brands across industries such as fashion, beauty, technology, and entertainment to create targeted campaigns that resonate with specific consumer segments. The integration of AI and machine learning enables personalized audience engagement, fostering deeper connections through interactive content formats like live streaming and augmented reality experiences. However, brands must navigate ethical considerations, ensuring transparency and authenticity to maintain consumer trust while avoiding potential concerns related to digital manipulation and misinformation.

Theoretically, this research contributes to the evolving discourse on influencer marketing by redefining traditional models of authenticity and trust in digital branding. It expands existing frameworks on technology-mediated brand engagement by illustrating how AI-driven personas reshape consumer interactions. Furthermore, it offers insights into consumer perceptions of virtual influencers, extending theories on parasocial relationships, digital identity formation, and trust in AI-generated content. The chapter also advances discussions on digital storytelling by demonstrating how brands can use virtual influencers to craft immersive narratives that are consistent, engaging, and adaptable across platforms. Lastly, by examining the intersection of human-computer interaction and influencer marketing, this study enhances the understanding of how AI-powered digital personalities influence consumer behavior and brand engagement in the social media era.

11. CONCLUSION

The rise of virtual influencers represents a paradigm shift in digital marketing, offering brands an unprecedented level of control, creativity, and engagement. Unlike their human counterparts, virtual influencers provide consistency in messaging, brand alignment, and the ability to interact with audiences across multiple platforms without the risks of personal controversies. This book chapter has explored the diverse content strategies, industry applications, and technological advancements that drive the success of virtual influencers in modern marketing. From fashion and beauty to technology and entertainment, these digital personas have demonstrated their adaptability in crafting compelling brand narratives while fostering deep consumer engagement. However, for brands to fully leverage the potential of virtual influencers, it is crucial to balance authenticity, ethical considerations, and strategic audience engagement. As the digital landscape continues to evolve, virtual influencers will play an increasingly vital role in shaping the future of brand storytelling, making them a cornerstone of next-generation marketing strategies.

REFERENCES

Appel, G., Grewal, L., Hadi, R., & Stephen, A. T. (2020). The future of social media in marketing. *Journal of the Academy of Marketing Science*, *48*(1), 79–95. DOI: 10.1007/s11747-019-00695-1 PMID: 32431463

Arsenyan, J., & Mirowska, A. (2021). Almost human? A comparative case study on the social media presence of virtual influencers. *International Journal of Human-Computer Studies*, *155*, 155. DOI: 10.1016/j.ijhcs.2021.102694

Audrezet, A., De Kerviler, G., & Moulard, J. G. (2020). Authenticity under threat: When social media influencers need to go beyond self-presentation. *Journal of Business Research*, *117*, 557–569. DOI: 10.1016/j.jbusres.2018.07.008

Belanche, D., Casaló, L. V., & Flavián, M. (2024). Human versus virtual influences, a comparative study. *Journal of Business Research*, *173*, 173. DOI: 10.1016/j.jbusres.2023.114493

Berryman, R., & Kavka, M. (2018). Crying on YouTube: Vlogs, self-exposure and the productivity of negative affect. *Convergence (London)*, *24*(1), 85–98. DOI: 10.1177/1354856517736981

Chaihanchanchai, P., Anantachart, S., & Ruangthanakorn, N. (2024). Unlocking the persuasive power of virtual influencer on brand trust and purchase intention: A parallel mediation of source credibility. *Journal of Marketing Communications*, 1–23. DOI: 10.1080/13527266.2023.2301390

Choudhry, A., Han, J., Xu, X., & Huang, Y. (2022). " I Felt a Little Crazy Following a'Doll'" Investigating Real Influence of Virtual Influencers on Their Followers. *Proceedings of the ACM on human-computer interaction, 6*(GROUP), 1-28.

Conti, M., Gathani, J., & Tricomi, P. P. (2022). Virtual influencers in online social media. *IEEE Communications Magazine*, *60*(8), 86–91. DOI: 10.1109/MCOM.001.2100786

da Silva Oliveira, A. B., & Chimenti, P. (2021). Humanized Robots": A Proposition of Categories to Understand Virtual Influencers. *AJIS. Australasian Journal of Information Systems*, *25*, 25. DOI: 10.3127/ajis.v25i0.3223

de Brito Silva, M. J., de Oliveira Ramos Delfino, L., Alves Cerqueira, K., & de Oliveira Campos, P. (2022). Avatar marketing: A study on the engagement and authenticity of virtual influencers on Instagram. *Social Network Analysis and Mining*, *12*(1), 130. DOI: 10.1007/s13278-022-00966-w

De Cicco, R., Iacobucci, S., Cannito, L., Onesti, G., Ceccato, I., & Palumbo, R. (2024). Virtual vs. human influencer: Effects on users' perceptions and brand outcomes. *Technology in Society*, *77*, 102488. DOI: 10.1016/j.techsoc.2024.102488

Deng, F., & Jiang, X. (2023). Effects of human versus virtual human influencers on the appearance anxiety of social media users. *Journal of Retailing and Consumer Services*, *71*, 103233. DOI: 10.1016/j.jretconser.2022.103233

Drenten, J., & Brooks, G. (2020). Celebrity 2.0: Lil Miquela and the rise of a virtual star system. *Feminist Media Studies*, *20*(8), 1319–1323. DOI: 10.1080/14680777.2020.1830927

Gerrath, M. H. E. E., Olya, H., Shah, Z., & Li, H. (2024). Virtual influencers and pro-environmental causes: The roles of message warmth and trust in experts. *Journal of Business Research*, *175*, 175. DOI: 10.1016/j.jbusres.2024.114520

Guo, Z., Yang, H., & Yang, W. (2025). A new social media programme for brands? A study of the relationship between virtual influencers and brand followers. *Journal of Retailing and Consumer Services*, *84*, 104241. DOI: 10.1016/j.jretconser.2025.104241

Ham, J., Li, S., Looi, J., & Eastin, M. S. (2024). Virtual humans as social actors: Investigating user perceptions of virtual humans' emotional expression on social media. *Computers in Human Behavior*, *155*, 108161. DOI: 10.1016/j.chb.2024.108161

Igarashi, R., Bhoumik, K., & Thompson, J. (2024). Investigating the effectiveness of virtual influencers in prosocial marketing. *Psychology and Marketing*, *41*(9), 2121–2135. DOI: 10.1002/mar.22031

Jin, S. V., & Viswanathan, V. (2024). "Threatened and empty selves following AI-based virtual influencers": Comparison between followers and non-followers of virtual influencers in AI-driven digital marketing. *AI & Society*, 1–15.

Junaid, M. (2024). Virtual influencers and marketing: consumer perceptions, barriers, and strategic development.

Kim, E., Shoenberger, H., Kim, D., Thorson, E., & Zihang, E. (2024). Novelty vs. trust in virtual influencers: Exploring the effectiveness of human-like virtual influencers and anime-like virtual influencers. *International Journal of Advertising*, 1–31.

Kim, E., Xie, Q., Hong, J. W., & Kim, H. M. (2024). Prosocial campaigns with virtual influencers: Stories, messages, and beyond. *International Journal of Human-Computer Interaction*, 1–12. DOI: 10.1080/10447318.2024.2387399

Kim, H., & Park, M. (2023). Virtual influencers' attractiveness effect on purchase intention: A moderated mediation model of the Product–Endorser fit with the brand. *Computers in Human Behavior*, *143*, 107703. DOI: 10.1016/j.chb.2023.107703

Kim, J., Kim, M., & Lee, S. M. (2025). Unlocking trust dynamics: An exploration of playfulness, expertise, and consumer behavior in virtual influencer marketing. *International Journal of Human-Computer Interaction*, *41*(1), 378–390. DOI: 10.1080/10447318.2023.2300018

Knittel, C. R., & Stango, V. (2014). Celebrity endorsements, firm value, and reputation risk: Evidence from the Tiger Woods scandal. *Management Science*, *60*(1), 21–37. DOI: 10.1287/mnsc.2013.1749

Koles, B., Audrezet, A., Guidry Moulard, J., Ameen, N., & Mckenna, B. (2024). The authentic virtual influencer: Authenticity manifestations in the metaverse The authen-tic virtual influencer: Authenticity manifestations in the metaverse. *Journal of Business Research*, 170.

Kuzminov, M. (2023). Consumer trust and virtual influencers. *Forbes*.

Lee, Y. H., & Yuan, C. W. T. (2023). I'm not a puppet, I'm a real boy! Gender presentations by virtual influencers and how they are received. *Computers in Human Behavior*, *149*, 107927. DOI: 10.1016/j.chb.2023.107927

Lin, Q., Ng, S. I., Kamal Basha, N., Luo, X., & Li, Y. (2024). Impact of virtual influencers on customer engagement of Generation Z consumers: A presence perspective. *Young Consumers*, *25*(6), 851–868. DOI: 10.1108/YC-01-2024-1958

Liu, F., & Lee, Y. H. (2024). Virtually authentic: Examining the match-up hypothesis between human vs virtual influencers and product types. *Journal of Product and Brand Management*, *33*(2), 287–299. DOI: 10.1108/JPBM-03-2023-4418

Looi, J., & Kahlor, L. A. (2024). Artificial Intelligence in Influencer Marketing: A Mixed-Method Comparison of Human and Virtual Influencers on Instagram. *Journal of Interactive Advertising*, *24*(2), 107–126. DOI: 10.1080/15252019.2024.2313721

Lou, C., Kiew, S. T. J., Chen, T., Lee, T. Y. M., Ong, J. E. C., & Phua, Z. X. (2023). Authentically Fake? How Consumers Respond to the Influence of Virtual Influencers. *Journal of Advertising*, *52*(4), 540–557. DOI: 10.1080/00913367.2022.2149641

Luo, L., & Kim, W. (2024). How virtual influencers' identities are shaped on Chinese social media: A case study of Ling. *Global Media and China*, *9*(3), 325–343. DOI: 10.1177/20594364231188353

Mouritzen, S. L. T., Penttinen, V., & Pedersen, S. (2024). Virtual influencer marketing: The good, the bad and the unreal. *European Journal of Marketing*, *58*(2), 410–440. DOI: 10.1108/EJM-12-2022-0915

Mrad, M., Ramadan, Z., Tóth, Z., Nasr, L., & Karimi, S. (2025). Virtual influencers versus real connections: Exploring the phenomenon of virtual influencers. *Journal of Advertising*, *54*(1), 1–19. DOI: 10.1080/00913367.2024.2393711

Nasr, L. I., Mousavi, S., & Michaelidou, N. (2025). Self-Comparing With Virtual Influencers: Effects on Followers' Wellbeing. *Psychology and Marketing*, *42*(3), 780–798. DOI: 10.1002/mar.22151

Ozdemir, O., Kolfal, B., Messinger, P. R., & Rizvi, S. (2023). Human or virtual: How influencer type shapes brand attitudes. *Computers in Human Behavior*, *145*, 145. DOI: 10.1016/j.chb.2023.107771

Pan, S., Qin, Z., & Zhang, Y. (2024). More realistic, more better? How anthropomorphic images of virtual influencers impact the purchase intentions of consumers. *Journal of Theoretical and Applied Electronic Commerce Research*, *19*(4), 3229–3252. DOI: 10.3390/jtaer19040157

Sakuma, H., Hori, A., Murashita, M., Kondo, C., & Hijikata, Y. (2023). YouTubers vs. VTubers: Persuasiveness of human and virtual presenters in promotional videos. *Frontiers of Computer Science*, *5*, 1043342. DOI: 10.3389/fcomp.2023.1043342

Sands, S., Ferraro, C., Demsar, V., & Chandler, G. (2022). False idols: Unpacking the opportunities and challenges of falsity in the context of virtual influencers. *Business Horizons*, *65*(6), 777–788. DOI: 10.1016/j.bushor.2022.08.002

Sorosrungruang, T., Ameen, N., & Hackley, C. (2024). How real is real enough? Unveiling the diverse power of generative AI-enabled virtual influencers and the dynamics of human responses. *Psychology and Marketing*, *41*(12), 3124–3143. DOI: 10.1002/mar.22105

Stein, J. P., Linda Breves, P., & Anders, N. (2024). Parasocial interactions with real and virtual influencers: The role of perceived similarity and human-likeness. *New Media & Society*, *26*(6), 3433–3453. DOI: 10.1177/14614448221102900

Thomas, V. L., & Fowler, K. (2021). Close encounters of the AI kind: Use of AI influencers as brand endorsers. *Journal of Advertising*, *50*(1), 11–25. DOI: 10.1080/00913367.2020.1810595

Vinoi, N., Shankar, A., Abdullah Alzeiby, E., Gupta, P., & Agarwal, V. (2025). Unveiling customer intentions: Exploring factors driving engagement with hospitality virtual influencers. *Journal of Hospitality Marketing & Management*, *34*(3), 1–30. DOI: 10.1080/19368623.2024.2429505

Wan, A., & Jiang, M. (2023). Can virtual influencers replace human influencers in live-streaming e-commerce? An exploratory study from practitioners' and consumers' perspectives. *Journal of Current Issues and Research in Advertising*, *44*(3), 332–372. DOI: 10.1080/10641734.2023.2224416

Wang, L., Li, Y. Q., Ruan, W. Q., & Zhang, S. N. (2024). The congruence effect in tourism activity marketing: The difference between virtual influencers and human influencers. *Current Issues in Tourism*, 1–19. DOI: 10.1080/13683500.2024.2400180

Weon Wee, J., Yoon, N., & Lee, Y. J. (2024). Beyond visual realism—Understanding the role of verbal cues in generating consumer affinity vs. fear toward virtual influencers in social network advertising. *Journal of the Korean Society of Clothing and Textiles*, *48*(6), 1194–1210.

Wheeler, A. (2017). *Designing brand identity: an essential guide for the whole branding team*. John Wiley & Sons.

Willemsen, L. M., Withuis, I., Brom, M., & Boerman, S. C. (2025). How does persuasion knowledge differ between humanlike virtual influencers and human influencers? *International Journal of Advertising*, *44*(1), 109–130. DOI: 10.1080/02650487.2024.2431440

Xie-Carson, L., Benckendorff, P., & Hughes, K. (2024). Keep it #Unreal: Exploring Instagram Users' Engagement With Virtual Influencers in Tourism Contexts. *Journal of Hospitality & Tourism Research (Washington, D.C.)*, *48*(6), 1006–1019. DOI: 10.1177/10963480231180940

Xin, B., Hao, Y., & Xie, L. (2024). Virtual influencers and corporate reputation: From marketing game to empirical analysis. *Journal of Research in Interactive Marketing*, *18*(5), 759–786. DOI: 10.1108/JRIM-10-2023-0330

Yan, J., Kong, H., Jiang, S., & Zhang, M. (2024). The impact of virtual influencer advertising on consumer response: A moderated chain mediation model based on mind perception and parasocial interaction. *Asia Pacific Journal of Tourism Research*, 1–20. DOI: 10.1080/10941665.2024.2350404

Yao, L., Tugiman, N., & Sharipudin, M. N. S. (2024). Virtual human influencers in live streaming commerce on social media platforms: Exploring parasocial interactions with consumers in China.

Yoo, J. W., Park, J., & Park, H. (2024). How can I trust you if you're fake? Understanding human-like virtual influencer credibility and the role of textual social cues. *Journal of Research in Interactive Marketing*. Advance online publication. DOI: 10.1108/JRIM-02-2024-0092

Yu, J., Dickinger, A., So, K. K. F., & Egger, R. (2024). Artificial intelligence-generated virtual influencer: Examining the effects of emotional display on user engagement. *Journal of Retailing and Consumer Services*, *76*, 103560. DOI: 10.1016/j.jretconser.2023.103560

Yu, T., Teoh, A. P., Bian, Q., Liao, J., & Wang, C. (2025). Can virtual influencers affect purchase intentions in tourism and hospitality e-commerce live streaming? An empirical study in China. *International Journal of Contemporary Hospitality Management*, *37*(1), 216–238. DOI: 10.1108/IJCHM-03-2024-0358

Zeng, W., Ma, Z., & Chen, T. (2024). When and why do consumers resist virtual influencer endorsement? The role of product depth and advertising claim types. *Electronic Commerce Research*, 1–34. DOI: 10.1007/s10660-024-09903-9

Zhao, X. (2022). Virtual fashion influencers: towards a more sustainable consumer behaviour of generation Z?.

Compilation of References

Agnihotri, D., Chaturvedi, P., & Tripathi, V. (2024). "Virtual bonds and actual transactions": Investigating the impact of virtual influencers' credibility on buying behavior through virtual engagement [Article]. *Journal of Communication Management (London)*. Advance online publication. DOI: 10.1108/JCOM-02-2024-0035

Al Masri, Y., Hamadneh, S., Al-Dmour, R., & Al-Okaily, M. (2023). *Can Computer Virtual Influencers Replace Human Influencers in the Future? An Empirical Investigation in the Age of Digital Transformation.* Jordan Journal of Business Administration., DOI: 10.35516/jjba.v19i4.1430

Alam, S., Susbiyantoro, S., Yuwantiningrum, S. E., Suwastika, I. W. K., & Muhdaliha, E. (2024). The Influence of Social Media Algorithms on Consumer Behavior: A Strategic Analysis for Brand Positioning. *The Journal of Academic Science, 1*(7), 832–841.

Albers, P. C., & James, W. R. (1988). Travel photography. *Annals of Tourism Research, 15*(1), 134–158. DOI: 10.1016/0160-7383(88)90076-X

Allal-Chérif, O., Puertas, R., & Carracedo, P. (2024). Intelligent influencer marketing: How AI-powered virtual influencers outperform human influencers [Article]. *Technological Forecasting and Social Change, 200*, 123113. Advance online publication. DOI: 10.1016/j.techfore.2023.123113

Allal-Chérif, O., Simón-Moya, V., & Ballester, A. C. C. (2021). Intelligent purchasing: How artificial intelligence can redefine the purchasing function. *Journal of Business Research, 124*, 69–76.

Ameen, N., Cheah, J. H., Ali, F., El-Manstrly, D., & Kulyciute, R. (2024). Risk, trust, and the roles of human versus virtual influencers. *Journal of Travel Research, 63*(6), 1370–1394. DOI: 10.1177/00472875231190601

Ameen, N., Hosany, S., & Taheri, B. (2023). Generation Z's psychology and new-age technologies: Implications for future research. *Psychology and Marketing*, *40*(10), 2029–2040. DOI: 10.1002/mar.21868

Andersson, V., & Sobek, T. (2020). *Virtual avatars, virtual influencers & authenticity* (Master's Thesis, Gothenburg University).

Andersson, V., & Sobek, T. (2020). Virtual avatars, virtual influencers & authenticity, [doctoral thesis], Gothenburg, University of Gothenburg.

Angmo, P., Mahajan, R., & Ranjitha, G. P. (2025). Unveiling the Power of Virtual Influencers: Impact of Content and Credibility on Consumer Engagement and Purchase Intentions. *Journal of Relationship Marketing*, •••, 1–32. DOI: 10.1080/15332667.2025.2471668

Anuradha, Y., Vijaya, K., Manda., M., Rao, J. (2024). Influencer Marketing in the Age of Metaverse. Advances in marketing, customer relationship management, and e-services book series, DOI: 10.4018/979-8-3693-4167-4.ch008

Appel, G., Grewal, L., Hadi, R., & Stephen, A. T. (2020). The future of social media in marketing. *Journal of the Academy of Marketing Science*, *48*(1), 79–95. DOI: 10.1007/s11747-019-00695-1 PMID: 32431463

Arsenyan, J., & Mirowska, A. (2021). Almost human? A comparative case study on the social media presence of virtual influencers. *International Journal of Human-Computer Studies*, *155*, 102694. DOI: 10.1016/j.ijhcs.2021.102694

Audrezet, A., De Kerviler, G., & Moulard, J. G. (2020). Authenticity under threat: When social media influencers need to go beyond self presentation. *Journal of Business Research*, *117*, 557–569. DOI: 10.1016/j.jbusres.2018.07.008

Audrezet, A., & Koles, B. (2023). Virtual influencer as a brand avatar in interactive marketing. In *The Palgrave handbook of interactive marketing* (pp. 353–376). Springer International Publishing. DOI: 10.1007/978-3-031-14961-0_16

Backaler, J., & Backaler, J. (2018). Know the risks: The Dark side of influencer collaboration. *Digital Influence: Unleash the Power of Influencer Marketing to Accelerate Your Global Business*, 137-154.

Bae, S., & Kim, D. (2021). The rise of virtual influencers: A new era in digital marketing. *Journal of Digital Marketing Research*, *12*(4), 112–127.

Balomenou, N., & Garrod, B. (2019). Photographs in tourism research: Prejudice, power, performance and participant-generated images. *Tourism Management*, *70*, 201–217. DOI: 10.1016/j.tourman.2018.08.014

Bambeshwar, A., Kamble, N.S., Singh, S., Soni, N. A.(2024). Real vs virtual influencer: impact on youngster's perception. DOI: 10.58532/V3BFMA16P1CH4

Barari, M. (2023). Unveiling the dark side of influencer marketing: How social media influencers (human vs virtual) diminish followers' well-being. *Marketing Intelligence & Planning*, *41*(8), 1162–1177. DOI: 10.1108/MIP-05-2023-0191

Baso Soriano, E. E., & Matthews, R. (2024). Marketing social para minimizar daños ambientales, utilizando las 4P. *Entrelíneas*, *3*(2), e030202. DOI: 10.56368/Entrelineas322

Bastrygina, T., Lim, W. M., Jopp, R., & Weissmann, M. A. (2024). Unraveling the power of social media influencers: Qualitative insights into the role of Instagram influencers in the hospitality and tourism industry. *Journal of Hospitality and Tourism Management*, *58*, 214–243. DOI: 10.1016/j.jhtm.2024.01.007

Batinovic, H., Tingelhoff, F., Hammerschmidt, M., & Schöbel, S. (2024). Come closer, but not too close: How virtual influencers can facilitate or restrict brand experiences in the metaverse. *Proceedings of the 57th Hawaii International Conference on System Sciences*. DOI: 10.24251/HICSS.2024.338

Bazaar (2019). https://www.harpersbazaar.com/es/cultura/ocio/a26020756/instagram-imma-modelo-virtual-miquela-influencer/ [Accessed on 09/11/2024]

Belanche, D.. (2024). Internalization and Virtual Influence: Impacts on Consumer Behavior. *Journal of Business Research*.

Belanche, D., Casaló, L. V., & Flavián, M. (2024). Human versus virtual influences, a comparative study. *Journal of Business Research*, *173*, 114493. Advance online publication. DOI: 10.1016/j.jbusres.2023.114493

Belanche, D., Casaló, L., Flavián, M., & Ibáñez-Sánchez, S. (2021). Understanding influencer marketing: The role of congruence between influencers, products and consumers. *Journal of Business Research*, *132*, 186–195. DOI: 10.1016/j.jbusres.2021.03.067

Belanche, D., Flavián, C., & Pérez-Rueda, A. (2021). Consumer acceptance of AI in influencer marketing: The role of perceived humanness. *Journal of Business Research*, *126*, 328–341.

Belova, A. D. (2021). Virtual influencers in multimodal advertising. *The journal of VN Karazin Kharkiv National University*, (93), 14-21.

Belova, A. (2021). Virtual influencers in multimodal advertising. *The Journal of V. N. Karazin Kharkiv National University Series: Foreign Philology.Methods of Foreign Language Teaching*, *93*(93), 14–21. DOI: 10.26565/2227-8877-2021-93-02

Berelson, B. (1952). *Content Analysis in Communication Research*. Free Press.

Berryman, R., & Kavka, M. (2018). Crying on YouTube: Vlogs, self-exposure and the productivity of negative affect. *Convergence (London)*, *24*(1), 85–98. DOI: 10.1177/1354856517736981

Bishop, S. (2021). Influencer management tools: Algorithmic cultures, brand safety, and bias. *Social Media + Society*, *7*(1), 20563051211003066. DOI: 10.1177/20563051211003066

Block, E., & Lovegrove, R. (2021). Discordant storytelling, 'honest fakery', identity peddling: How uncanny CGI characters are jamming public relations and influencer practices [Article]. *Public Relations Inquiry*, *10*(3), 265–293. DOI: 10.1177/2046147X211026936

Bohndel, M., Jastorff, M., & Rudeloff, C. (2023). AI-driven influencer marketing: Comparing the effects of virtual and human influencers on consumer perceptions. SSRN *Electronic Journal,* 2(2), 165-174. DOI: 10.2139/ssrn.4404372

Böhndel, M., Jastorff, M., & Rudeloff, C. (2023). AI-driven influencer marketing: Comparing the effects of virtual and human influencers on consumer perceptions. *Journal of AI. Robotics & Workplace Automation*, *2*(2), 165–174. DOI: 10.69554/WBSJ7931

Borlongan, M. (2023). *First-ever Filipina virtual model earns negative reactions for her 'not-so-Filipino' features*. https://pop.inquirer.net/339527/first-ever-filipina-virtual-model-earns-negative-reactions-for-her-not-so-filipino-features

Bozdağ, A. A. (2024). The AI-mediated intimacy economy: A paradigm shift in digital interactions. *AI & Society*, •••, 1–22. DOI: 10.1007/s00146-024-02132-6

Brady, J., Patel, R., & Smith, K. (2022). Ethical considerations in AI-driven influencer marketing. *Journal of Business Ethics*, *58*(3), 199–215.

Buhalis, D., & Amaranggana, A. (2013). Smart tourism destinations. In *Information and communication technologies in tourism 2014: Proceedings of the international conference in Dublin, Ireland, January 21-24, 2014* (pp. 553-564). Springer International Publishing.

Buhalis, D., & Law, R. (2008). Progress in information technology and tourism management: 20 years on and 10 years after the Internet—The state of eTourism research. *Tourism Management*, *29*(4), 609–623. DOI: 10.1016/j.tourman.2008.01.005

Burden, D., & Savin-Baden, M. (2019). *Virtual humans: Today and tomorrow*. Chapman and Hall/CRC. DOI: 10.1201/9781315151199

Bussone, A., Stumpf, S., & O'Sullivan, D. (2015). The Role of Explanations on Trust and Reliance in Clinical Decision Support Systems. *2015 International Conference on Healthcare Informatics*, 160–169. https://doi.org/DOI: 10.1109/ICHI.2015.26

Campbell, C., & Farrell, J. R. (2020). More than meets the eye: The functional components underlying influencer marketing. *Business Horizons*, *63*(4), 469–479. DOI: 10.1016/j.bushor.2020.03.003

Carrillo-Durán, M. V., García, M. G., & Cortés, L. C. (2024). Influencers virtuales de apariencia humana como forma de comunicación online: El caso de Lil Miquela y Lu do Magalu en Instagram. *Revista De Comunicación*, *23*(1), 119–140. DOI: 10.26441/RC23.1-2024-3453

Castillo, F. G.Jr. (2018). Consumer buying behavior: The multicultural influence in the Philippines. *The International Journal of Business Management and Technology*, *2*(2), 71–75.

Cayla, J., Bhatnagar, K., Nanarpuzha, R., & Dey, S. (2025). From social feeds to market fields: How influencer stories drive market innovation. *International Journal of Research in Marketing*. Advance online publication. DOI: 10.1016/j.ijresmar.2025.03.001

Chahal, M., & Raina, S. (2021). Gen Z's acceptance of virtual influencers: A study on digital engagement. *International Journal of Consumer Behavior*, *24*(2), 87–103.

Chaihanchanchai, P., Anantachart, S., & Ruangthanakorn, N. (2024). Unlocking the persuasive power of virtual influencer on brand trust and purchase intention: A parallel mediation of source credibility. *Journal of Marketing Communications*, •••, 1–23. DOI: 10.1080/13527266.2023.2301390

Chang, T. (2010). Gaming will save us all. *Communications of the ACM*, *53*(3), 22–24. DOI: 10.1145/1666420.1666431

Chang, W., & Chang, H. (2023). The Impact of Digital Disruption: Influences of Digital Media and Social Networks on Forming Digital Natives' Attitude. *SAGE Open*, *13*(3), 21582440231191741. Advance online publication. DOI: 10.1177/21582440231191741

Cheng, J., & Wang, J. (2024). Influencer-product attractiveness transference in interactive fashion marketing: The moderated moderating effect of speciesism against AI [Article]. *Journal of Research in Interactive Marketing*. Advance online publication. DOI: 10.1108/JRIM-06-2024-0299

Cheng, M., & Zhang, S. (2024). *Reputation burning: Analyzing the impact of brand sponsorship on social influencers*. Management Science, Vol. Ahead of the Print No. Ahead of the Print.

Chiu, C. L., & Ho, H. C. (2023). Impact of celebrity, micro-celebrity, and virtual influencers on Chinese Gen Z's purchase intention through social media. *SAGE Open, 13*(1), 21582440231164034. DOI: 10.1177/21582440231164034

Choi, M., & Choi, Y. (2024). Exploration of the diversity of virtual influencers used as tourism ambassadors in South Korea. *Asia Pacific Journal of Tourism Research, 29*(10), 1272–1285. DOI: 10.1080/10941665.2024.2380041

Choi, M., Choi, Y., & Lee, H. (2024). Gen Z Travelers in the Instagram Marketplace: Trust, Influencer Type, Post Type, and Purchase Intention. *Journal of Hospitality & Tourism Research (Washington, D.C.), 48*(6), 1020–1034. DOI: 10.1177/10963480231180938

Chottechathammanee, P. D. P., & Patchimnan, A. P. D. M. (2024). Influencing the virtual realm: The impact of virtual influencers on brand awareness and consumer purchasing decisions in thailand's digital marketplace. *International Journal of Operations and Quantitative Management, 30*(1), 127–141.

Choudhry, A., Han, J., Xu, X., & Huang, Y. (2022). "I felt a little crazy following a 'doll'." Investigating real influence of virtual influencers on their followers. Proceedings of the ACM on Human-Computer Interaction, 6(GROUP), 1-28. DOI: 10.1145/3492862

Choudhry, A., Han, J., Xu, X., & Huang, Y. (2022). " I felt a little crazy following a'doll'" investigating real influence of virtual influencers on their followers. *Proceedings of the ACM on human-computer interaction, 6*(GROUP), 1-28.

Choudhry, A., Han, J., Xu, X., & Huang, Y. (2022). " I Felt a Little Crazy Following a'Doll'" Investigating Real Influence of Virtual Influencers on Their Followers. *Proceedings of the ACM on human-computer interaction, 6*(GROUP), 1-28.

Cocker, H., Mardon, R., & Daunt, K. L. (2021). Social media influencers and transgressive celebrity endorsement in consumption community contexts. *European Journal of Marketing, 55*(7), 1841–1872. DOI: 10.1108/EJM-07-2019-0567

Conti, M., Gathani, J., & Tricomi, P. P. (2022). Virtual influencers in online social media. *IEEE Communications Magazine*, *60*(8), 86–91. DOI: 10.1109/MCOM.001.2100786

Cynthia, A. H., & Bradley, J. B. (2024). Parasocial relationships, social media, & well-being. *Current Opinion in Psychology*, *45*, 101306. PMID: 35219157

da Silva Oliveira, A. B., & Chimenti, P. (2021). "Humanized Robots": A Proposition of Categories to Understand Virtual Influencers. *AJIS. Australasian Journal of Information Systems*, *25*, 1–27. DOI: 10.3127/ajis.v25i0.3223

da Silva Oliveira, A. B., & Chimenti, P. (2021). Humanized Robots": A Proposition of Categories to Understand Virtual Influencers. *AJIS. Australasian Journal of Information Systems*, •••, 25.

Dalangin, J. J. G., McArthur, J. M. B., Salvador, J. B. M., & Bismonte, A. B. (2021). The impact of social media influencers purchase intention in the Philippines. *Jurnal Studi Komunikasi*, *5*(3). Advance online publication. DOI: 10.25139/jsk.v5i3.3708

David, K. (2019). *Parasocial attachment within social networking sites: Finding comfort and security in those you follow online* (Doctoral dissertation, Regent University).

Davlembayeva, D., Simos, C., & Savvas, P. (2024). Virtual Influencers in Consumer Behaviour: A Social Influence Theory Perspective. *British Journal of Management*. Advance online publication. DOI: 10.1111/1467-8551.12839

de Boissieu, E., & Baudier, P. (2023). The perceived credibility of human-like social robots: Virtual influencers in a luxury and multicultural context [Article]. *Journal of Organizational Change Management*, *36*(7), 1163–1179. DOI: 10.1108/JOCM-05-2023-0182

De Brito Silva, M. J., Delfino, L., Alves Cerqueira, K. A., & de Oliveira Campos, P. (2022). Avatar marketing: A study on the engagement and authenticity of virtual influencers on Instagram. *Social Network Analysis and Mining*, *12*(1), 130. DOI: 10.1007/s13278-022-00966-w

De Cicco, R., Iacobucci, S., Cannito, L., Onesti, G., Ceccato, I., & Palumbo, R. (2024). Virtual vs. human influencer: Effects on users' perceptions and brand outcomes [Article]. *Technology in Society*, *77*, 102488. Advance online publication. DOI: 10.1016/j.techsoc.2024.102488

De Veirman, M., Cauberghe, V., & Hudders, L. (2017). Marketing through Instagram influencers: The impact of number of followers and product divergence on brand attitude. *International Journal of Advertising, 36*(5), 798–828. DOI: 10.1080/02650487.2017.1348035

Delbaere, M., Michael, B., & Phillips, B. J. (2021). Social media influencers: A route to brand engagement for their followers. *Psychology and Marketing, 38*(1), 101–112. DOI: 10.1002/mar.21419

Deng, F., & Jiang, X. (2023). Effects of human versus virtual human influencers on the appearance anxiety of social media users. *Journal of Retailing and Consumer Services, 71*, 103233. DOI: 10.1016/j.jretconser.2022.103233

Deng, F., Tuo, M., Chen, S., & Zhang, Z. (2024). Born for marketing? The effects of virtual versus human influencers on brand endorsement effectiveness: The role of advertising recognition. *Journal of Retailing and Consumer Services, 80*, 103904. Advance online publication. DOI: 10.1016/j.jretconser.2024.103904

Dibble, J. L., Hartmann, T., & Rosaen, S. F. (2016). Parasocial interaction and parasocial relationship: Conceptual clarification and a critical assessment of measures. *Human Communication Research, 42*(1), 21–44. DOI: 10.1111/hcre.12063

Dinh, T. C. T., & Lee, Y. (2022). "I want to be as trendy as influencers"–how "fear of missing out" leads to buying intention for products endorsed by social media influencers. *Journal of Research in Interactive Marketing, 16*(3), 346–364. DOI: 10.1108/JRIM-04-2021-0127

Djafarova, E., & Rushworth, C. (2017). Exploring the credibility of human influencers. *Journal of Consumer Behaviour.*

Djarilkanovna, E. A., & Baxadirovna, M. M. (2024). The digital media revolution: Transforming communication, entertainment, and information in the 21st century. *Miasto Przyszłości, 46*, 813–816.

Dondapati, A. (2025). Maximizing the Consumer Connection: Avatars, Emotions, and Effective Virtual Influencer Advertising. *Review of Marketing Science*, (0).

Dondapati, A., & Dehury, R. K. (2024). Virtual vs. Human influencers: The battle for consumer hearts and minds. *Computers in Human Behavior: Artificial Humans, 2*(1), 100059. DOI: 10.1016/j.chbah.2024.100059

Dredge, D., & Gyimóthy, S. (2015). The collaborative economy and tourism: Critical perspectives, questionable claims and silenced voices. *Tourism Recreation Research, 40*(3), 286–302. DOI: 10.1080/02508281.2015.1086076

Drenten, J., & Brooks, G. (2020). Celebrity 2.0: Lil Miquela and the rise of a virtual star system. *Feminist Media Studies*, *20*(8), 1319–1323. DOI: 10.1080/14680777.2020.1830927

Duffy, B. E., & Hund, E. (2021). The ethics of AI influencers: Transparency, authenticity, and responsibility. *New Media & Society*, *23*(9), 2676–2693.

Ebulueme, J., & Vijayakumar, V. (2024). Authenticity and influence: Interactions between social media micro-influencers and generation Z on Instagram. *Critique*, *14*(4), 568–586.

Ekara, A. N. (2024). A Virtual Character, a Robot, or a Human Being? A Study of the (Self-) Representations of Lil Miquela. *Cairo Studies in English*, *2024*(1), 130–149. DOI: 10.21608/cse.2024.286506.1161

El Hedhli, K., Zourrig, H., Al Khateeb, A., & Alnawas, I. (2023). Stereotyping human-like virtual influencers in retailing: Does warmth prevail over competence?. *Journal of Retailing and Consumer Services*, *75*, 103459. Advance online publication. DOI: 10.1016/j.jretconser.2023.103459

Elfadel, M. W., Othman, R. B., Mat, N. H. B. N., Hamad, F. F., Mohadis, H. M., & Ahmed, M. (2024). The relationship between e-marketing mix framework (4Ps) and customer satisfaction with electronic information services: An empirical analysis of Jordanian university libraries. *Information Services & Use*, *44*(2), 139–164. DOI: 10.3233/ISU-240230

Eran, N. (2022). Why Are More Influencers Launching Their Own Brands?Forbes. Retrieved 24 Dec from https://www.forbes.com/councils/forbestechcouncil/2022/06/27/why-are-more-influencers-launching-their-own-brands/

Ferrai, P. (2024). *The new era of influencer marketing*. WeAreBrain. Retrieved 26 Dec from https://wearebrain.com/blog/the-new-era-of-influencer-marketing/

Ferraro, C., Sands, S., Zubcevic-Basic, N., & Campbell, C. (2024). Diversity in the digital age: How consumers respond to diverse virtual influencers. *International Journal of Advertising*, *43*(8), 1342–1365. DOI: 10.1080/02650487.2023.2300927

Franke, C., Groeppel-Klein, A., & Müller, K. (2022). Consumers' Responses to Virtual Influencers as Advertising Endorsers: Novel and Effective or Uncanny and Deceiving? *Journal of Advertising*, •••, 1–17.

Franke, C., Groeppel-Klein, A., & Müller, K. (2023). Consumers' responses to virtual influencers as advertising endorsers: Novel and effective or uncanny and deceiving? *Journal of Advertising*, *52*(4), 523–539. DOI: 10.1080/00913367.2022.2154721

Freberg, K., Graham, K., McGaughey, K., & Freberg, L. A. (2011). Who are the social media influencers? A study of public perceptions of personality. *Public Relations Review*, *37*(1), 90–92. DOI: 10.1016/j.pubrev.2010.11.001

Gammarano, I. D. J. L. P., Dholakia, N., Arruda Filho, E. J. M., & Dholakia, R. R. (2024). Beyond influence: Unraveling the complex tapestry of digital influencer dynamics in hyperconnected cultures. *European Journal of Marketing*, *59*(1), 21–58. DOI: 10.1108/EJM-07-2023-0552

Gerlich, M. (2023). The Power of Virtual Influencers: Impact on Consumer Behaviour and Attitudes in the Age of AI [Article]. *Administrative Sciences*, *13*(8), 178. Advance online publication. DOI: 10.3390/admsci13080178

Gerrath, M. (2024). Meet five virtual influencers inspiring climate action; The Conversation. University of Leeds; https://theconversation.com/meet-five-virtual-influencers-inspiring-climate-action-230898

Gerrath, M. H., Olya, H., Shah, Z., & Li, H. (2024). Virtual influencers and pro-environmental causes: The roles of message warmth and trust in experts. *Journal of Business Research*, *175*, 114520. DOI: 10.1016/j.jbusres.2024.114520

Góraj, K. (2024). The impact of computer-generated influencers on social media advertising. *Social Communication*, *25*(1), 137–144. DOI: 10.57656/sc-2024-0014

Gray, N. M. (2023). *Botched This Way: An Autoethnographic Exploration of Beauty Standards, Celebrity, and Surgical Culture on Instagram* (Master's thesis, San Diego State University).

Guerreiro, C., Viegas, M., & Guerreiro, M. (2019). Social networks and digital influencers: Their role in customer decision journey in tourism. *Journal of Spatial and Organizational Dynamics*, *7*(3), 240–260.

Guo, Z., Yang, H., & Yang, W. (2025). A new social media programme for brands? A study of the relationship between virtual influencers and brand followers. *Journal of Retailing and Consumer Services*, *84*, 104241. DOI: 10.1016/j.jretconser.2025.104241

Gurrieri, L., Drenten, J., & Abidin, C. (2023). Symbiosis or parasitism? A framework for advancing interdisciplinary and socio-cultural perspectives in influencer marketing. *Journal of Marketing Management*, *39*(11-12), 911–932. DOI: 10.1080/0267257X.2023.2255053

Gursoy, D., & Chi, O. H. (2022). Trust and credibility in virtual influencer marketing: A consumer perspective. *Journal of Marketing Theory and Practice*, *30*(4), 411–426.

Guthrie, S. (2020). Virtual influencers: More human than humans. In *Influencer Marketing* (pp. 271–285). Routledge. DOI: 10.4324/9780429322501-20

Guttentag, D. A. (2010). Virtual reality: Applications and implications for tourism. *Tourism Management, 31*(5), 637–651. DOI: 10.1016/j.tourman.2009.07.003

Güzel, Ç. Ö. (2025). The authenticity of AI influencers in marketing. In *Understanding Generative AI in a Cultural Context: Artificial Myths and Human Realities* (pp. 247-274). IGI Global Scientific Publishing.

Hadrava, J., & Adámková, K. (2024). Customers' attitudestowards CGI (Computer-Generated Imagery) advertisement pictured in real-life scenes.

Haenlein, M., Anadol, E., Farnsworth, T., Hugo, H., Hunichen, J., & Welte, D. (2020). Navigating the New Era of Influencer Marketing: How to be Successful on Instagram, TikTok, & Co. *California Management Review, 63*(1), 5–25. DOI: 10.1177/0008125620958166

Hahl, S. (2023). *Perception of uncredibility in influencers' paid social media marketing collaborations* (Master's thesis, Aalto University).

Hall, J. A., & Caton, S. (2023). AI-generated influencers: How machine learning personalizes digital marketing. *AI & Society, 38*(3), 711–726.

Ham, J., Li, S., Looi, J., & Eastin, M. S. (2024). Virtual humans as social actors: Investigating user perceptions of virtual humans' emotional expression on social media. *Computers in Human Behavior, 155*, 108161. DOI: 10.1016/j.chb.2024.108161

Ham, J., Li, S., Shah, P., & Eastin, M. S. (2023). The "Mixed" Reality of Virtual Brand Endorsers: Understanding the Effect of Brand Engagement and Social Cues on Technological Perceptions and Advertising Effectiveness [Article]. *Journal of Interactive Advertising, 23*(2), 98–113. DOI: 10.1080/15252019.2023.2185557

Haukka, K. (2024). Metaverse fashion retail in the Nordics: Future signals and buyer personas. (Master's thesis, Haaga-Helia University of Applied Sciences).

Hermawanto, A., & Anggraini, M. (2020, October). Globalization and locality: Global communication and digital revolution in the borderless world era. In *Proceeding of LPPM UPN "Veteran" Yogyakarta Conference Series 2020–Political and Social Science Series* (Vol. 1, No. 1, pp. 9-16). DOI: 10.31098/pss.v1i1.84

Hernández-Méndez, J., Baute-Díaz, N., & Gutiérrez-Taño, D. (2024). The effectiveness of virtual versus human influencer marketing for tourism destinations [Article]. *Journal of Vacation Marketing*, 13567667241276212. Advance online publication. DOI: 10.1177/13567667241276212

Hofeditz, L., Nissen, A., Schutte, R., & Mirbabaie, M. (2022). *Trust me, I'm an influencer! A comparison of perceived trust in human and virtual influencers*. ECIS 2022 Research-in-Progress Papers.

Hofeditz, L., Nissen, A., Schütte, R., & Mirbabaie, M. "Trust Me, I'm an Influencer! – A Comparison of Perceived Trust in Human and Virtual Influencers" (2022). ECIS 2022 Research-in-Progress Papers. 27. https://aisel.aisnet.org/ecis2022_rip/27

Hogsnes, M., Grønli, T. M., & Hansen, K. (2023). Unconsciously influential: Understanding sociotechnical influence on social media. *Scandinavian Journal of Information Systems*, *35*(2), 1.

Hollebeek, L. D., & Macky, K. (2019). Digital content marketing's role in fostering consumer engagement, trust, and value: Framework, fundamental propositions, and implications. *Journal of Interactive Marketing*, *45*(1), 27–41. DOI: 10.1016/j.intmar.2018.07.003

Horoub, I. (2023). Exploring the nexus of citizen journalism, technology, and psychology: Insights from Palestinian journalists. *Journalism Practice*, •••, 1–27. DOI: 10.1080/17512786.2023.2288588

Horton, D., & Richard Wohl, R. (1956). Mass communication and para-social interaction: Observations on intimacy at a distance. *psychiatry, 19*(3), 215-229.

Horton, D., & Wohl, R. R. (1956). Mass communication and para-social interaction: Observations on intimacy at a distance. *Psychiatry*, *19*(3), 215–229. DOI: 10.1080/00332747.1956.11023049 PMID: 13359569

Hovland, C. I., Janis, I. L., & Kelley, H. H. (1953). Communication and persuasion.

Huang, L., Zhao, X., & Kim, J. (2023). Consumer engagement with AI-generated influencers: Implications for brand trust. *Marketing Science Review*, *29*(5), 45–62.

Hubble, C. (2018). Miquela Sousa and the rise of fake influencers. Eureka street. https://www.semanticscholar.org/paper/Miquela-Sousa-and-the-rise-of-fake-influencers-Hubble/0e41b0698fd13d3216598767d6767860ba0cd7ae

Hudders, L., & Lou, C. (2022). *A new era of influencer marketing: Lessons from Recent Inquires and Thoughts on Future Directions* (Vol. 41). Taylor & Francis.

Hudson, S., & Thal, K. (2013). The impact of social media on the consumer decision process: Implications for tourism marketing. *Journal of Travel & Tourism Marketing*, *30*(1-2), 156–160. DOI: 10.1080/10548408.2013.751276

Hugh, D. C., Dolan, R., Harrigan, P., & Gray, H. (2022). Influencer marketing effectiveness: The mechanisms that matter. *European Journal of Marketing*, *56*(12), 3485–3515. DOI: 10.1108/EJM-09-2020-0703

Hund, E. (2023). *The influencer industry: The quest for authenticity on social media*. Princeton University Press.

Huttayavilaiphan, R. (2024). From local flavor to global fandom: An exploration of the cultural presentation and attitudes towards using English by Thai content creators on the TikTok platform. *Frontiers in Communication*, *9*, 1453316. DOI: 10.3389/fcomm.2024.1453316

Hwang, S. (2023). *The introduction of human and AI-powered virtual influencers on social media marketing* (Doctoral dissertation, Carnegie Mellon University).

Hwang, S., Zhang, S., Liu, X., & Srinivasan, K. (2024). *Should Your Brand Hire a Virtual Influencer?* Harvard Business School Publishing. Retrieved 30 Oct from https://hbr.org/2024/05/should-your-brand-hire-a-virtual-influencer

Ibardeloza, K. B., Badillo, L. T., Macatangay, J. M. H., Cruz, K. R. D., & Malabanan, M. P. (2022). Students' exposure to social media and their radical involvement on the societal issues in the Philippines. *International Review of Social Sciences Research*, *2*(1), 47–60. DOI: 10.53378/352878

Igarashi, R., Bhoumik, K., & Thompson, J. (2024). Investigating the effectiveness of virtual influencers in prosocial marketing [Article]. *Psychology and Marketing*, *41*(9), 2121–2135. DOI: 10.1002/mar.22031

Iglhaut, C. (2019). The influencers of tomorrow will be virtual. https://www.deutschland.de/en/topic/culture/who-is-noonoouri-fashion-avatar-conquers-the-fashion-world

Ines, J., & Tolentino, M. Q. (2024). Beyond likes and shares: Exploring the influence of social media on brand choices among college of business students at a private higher education institution in the Philippine. *American Journal of Economics and Business Innovation*, *3*(2), 66–74. DOI: 10.54536/ajebi.v3i2.2545

Influence insider. (2024). *Social Media Influencer vs. Celebrity: The Key Differences*. Influence Insider. Retrieved 29 Dec from https://influence-insider.com/social-media-influencer-vs-celebrity-the-key-differences/

Jarzyna, C. L. (2021). Parasocial interaction, the COVID-19 quarantine, and digital age media. *Human Arenas*, *4*(3), 413–429. DOI: 10.1007/s42087-020-00156-0

Jeacle, I. (2021). Navigating netnography: A guide for the accounting researcher. *Financial Accountability & Management, 37*(1), 88–101. DOI: 10.1111/faam.12237

Jhawar, A., Prashant, K., Sanjeev, V. (2023). The emergence of virtual influencers: a shift in the influencer marketing paradigm. Young Consumers: Insight and Ideas for Responsible Marketers, DOI: 10.1108/YC-05-2022-1529

Jhawar, A. (2024). Can virtual influencers induce destination visit intentions? A mediation analysis journey through the uncanny valley. *Journal of Travel Research*, •••, 00472875241291144. DOI: 10.1177/00472875241291144

Ji, Q., Linghu, L., & Qiao, F. (2022, July). The beauty myth of virtual influencers: A reflection of real-world female body image stereotypes. In *2022 3rd International Conference on Mental Health, Education and Human Development (MHEHD 2022)* (pp. 784-787). Atlantis Press. DOI: 10.2991/assehr.k.220704.142

Jiang, K., Zheng, J., & Luo, S. (2024). Green power of virtual influencer: The role of virtual influencer image, emotional appeal, and product involvement [Article]. *Journal of Retailing and Consumer Services, 77*, 103660. Advance online publication. DOI: 10.1016/j.jretconser.2023.103660

Jing, W. (2024). Research On Marketing and Business Management Strategy of Sports Commercial Brand Based On 4ps Theory: A Case Study of Lululemon. Highlights in business, economics and management, 37:351-357. DOI: 10.54097/wv3efn51

Jin, S. V., & Viswanathan, V. (2024). "Threatened and empty selves following AI-based virtual influencers": Comparison between followers and non-followers of virtual influencers in AI-driven digital marketing. *AI & Society*, •••, 1–15.

Ju, N., Kim, T., & Im, H. (2024). Fake human but real influencer: The interplay of authenticity and human likeness in Virtual Influencer communication? *Fash Text, 11*(1), 16. DOI: 10.1186/s40691-024-00380-0

Junaid, M. (2024). Virtual influencers and marketing: consumer perceptions, barriers, and strategic development.

Kádeková, Z., & Holienčinová, M. (2018). Influencer marketing as a modern phenomenon creating a new frontier of virtual opportunities. *Communication Today, 9*(2).

Kádeková, Z., & Holienčinová, M. (2018). Influencer marketing as a modern phenomenon creating a new frontier of virtual opportunities. *Communication Today, 9*, 90–105.

Kamins, M. A. (1990). An investigation into the "match-up" hypothesis in celebrity advertising: When beauty may be only skin deep. *Journal of Advertising, 19*(1), 4–13. DOI: 10.1080/00913367.1990.10673175

Kapitan, S., & Silvera, D. H. (2022). The rise of virtual influencers: Understanding their impact on digital branding. *Journal of Interactive Marketing, 59*, 72–89.

Kaptein, F., Broekens, J., Hindriks, K., & Neerincx, M. (2017). Personalised self-explanation by robots. *RO-MAN 2017 - 26th IEEE International Symposium on Robot and Human Interactive Communication, 2017-January*, 676–682. https://doi.org/DOI: 10.1109/ROMAN.2017.8172376

Karen, K., & Zai, I. (2022). Analyzing the effects of digital marketing on brand awareness among internet users. [Management and Business Review]. *MBR, 6*(2). Advance online publication. DOI: 10.21067/mbr.v6i2.7298

Karga, S., & Satratzemi, M. (2019). Using explanations for recommender systems in learning design settings to enhance teachers' acceptance and perceived experience. *Education and Information Technologies, 24*(5), 2953–2974. DOI: 10.1007/s10639-019-09909-z

Kate, J. B., & Sun, J. A. (2023). A Systematic Review of Virtual Influencers: Similarities and Differences between Human and Virtual Influencers in Interactive Advertising. *Journal of Interactive Advertising, 23*(4), 293–306. DOI: 10.1080/15252019.2023.2236102

Katz, E. (1959). Mass communications research and the study of popular culture: An editorial note on a possible future for this journal. *Studies in Public Communication*. https://repository.upenn.edu/entities/publication/09b95935-2c75-4752-8009-4df2d03c0c41

Kauffmann, P., & Vaičiūnaitė, S. (2024). *An ethical dilemma in influencer marketing: Discovering social media influencers' justifications for promoting aesthetic surgery* (Master's thesis, Lund University).

Khan, S. A. (2024). Virtual influencers: Crafting the future of marketing. https://yourstory.com/2024/02/virtual-influencers-rise-2024

Khan, S. A. (2024). Virtual Influencers: Crafting the Future of Marketing. Your Story. https://yourstory.com/2024/02/virtual-influencers-rise-2024

Khan, S. W., Raza, S. H., & Zaman, U. (2022). Remodeling digital marketplace through Metaverse: A multi-path model of consumer neuroticism, parasocial relationships, social media influencers credibility, and openness to Metaverse experience. [PJCSS]. *Pakistan Journal of Commerce and Social Sciences, 16*(3), 337–365.

Kim, D. Y., & Kim, H.-Y. (2021). Trust me, trust me not: A nuanced view of influencer marketing on social media. *Journal of Business Research, 134*, 223–232. DOI: 10.1016/j.jbusres.2021.05.024

Kim, D., & Wang, Z. (2023). The ethics of virtuality: Navigating the complexities of human-like virtual influencers in the social media marketing realm. *Frontiers in Communication, 8*, 1205610. DOI: 10.3389/fcomm.2023.1205610

Kim, E. (Anna), Shoenberger, H., Kim, D., Thorson, E., & Zihang, E. (. (2024). Novelty vs. trust in virtual influencers: Exploring the effectiveness of human-like virtual influencers and anime-like virtual influencers. *International Journal of Advertising*, •••, 1–31. DOI: 10.1080/02650487.2024.2386916

Kim, E., Kim, D. E. Z., & Shoenberger, H. (2023). The next hype in social media advertising: Examining virtual influencers' brand endorsement effectiveness. *Frontiers in Psychology, 14*, 1089051. DOI: 10.3389/fpsyg.2023.1089051 PMID: 36949930

Kim, E., Xie, Q., Hong, J. W., & Kim, H. M. (2024). Prosocial campaigns with virtual influencers: Stories, messages, and beyond. *International Journal of Human-Computer Interaction*, •••, 1–12. DOI: 10.1080/10447318.2024.2387399

Kim, H., Lee, S., & Park, Y. (2022). Artificial intelligence and machine learning in virtual influencer marketing. *Journal of Emerging Technologies, 17*(3), 210–225.

Kim, H., & Park, M. (2023). Virtual influencers' attractiveness effect on purchase intention: A moderated mediation model of the Product–Endorser fit with the brand. *Computers in Human Behavior, 143*, 107703. DOI: 10.1016/j.chb.2023.107703

Kim, H., & Park, M. (2024). When digital celebrity talks to you: How human-like virtual influencers satisfy consumer's experience through social presence on social media endorsements. *Journal of Retailing and Consumer Services, 76*, 103581. DOI: 10.1016/j.jretconser.2023.103581

Kim, I., Ki, C. W., Lee, H., & Kim, Y. K. (2024). Virtual influencer marketing: Evaluating the influence of virtual influencers' form realism and behavioral realism on consumer ambivalence and marketing performance. *Journal of Business Research, 176*, 114611. DOI: 10.1016/j.jbusres.2024.114611

Kim, J., Kim, M., & Lee, S. M. (2024). Unlocking trust dynamics: An exploration of playfulness, expertise, and consumer behavior in virtual influencer marketing. *International Journal of Human-Computer Interaction*, •••, 1–13.

Kim, J., Merrill, K.Jr, Xu, K., & Kelly, S. (2022). Perceived credibility of an AI instructor in online education: The role of social presence and voice features. *Computers in Human Behavior, 136*, 107383. DOI: 10.1016/j.chb.2022.107383

Kim, Y. H., & Moon, S. (2023). The moral implications of AI-driven influencers in advertising. *Journal of Advertising Ethics, 10*(1), 45–62.

Knittel, C. R., & Stango, V. (2014). Celebrity endorsements, firm value, and reputation risk: Evidence from the Tiger Woods scandal. *Management Science, 60*(1), 21–37. DOI: 10.1287/mnsc.2013.1749

Knoll, J., & Matthes, J. (2022). Digital storytelling and emotional connections in influencer marketing. *Journal of Marketing Communications, 39*(4), 134–150.

Koles, B., Audrezet, A., Guidry Moulard, J., Ameen, N., & Mckenna, B. (2024). The authentic virtual influencer: Authenticity manifestations in the metaverse The authen-tic virtual influencer: Authenticity manifestations in the metaverse. *Journal of Business Research,* •••, 170.

Koles, B., Audrezet, A., Moulard, J. G., Ameen, N., & McKenna, B. (2024). The authentic virtual influencer: Authenticity manifestations in the metaverse. *Journal of Business Research, 170*, 114325. DOI: 10.1016/j.jbusres.2023.114325

Kopalle, P. K., Gangwar, M., Kaplan, A., Ramachandran, D., Reinartz, W., & Rindfleisch, A. (2022). Examining artificial intelligence (AI) technologies in marketing via a global lens: Current trends and future research opportunities. *International Journal of Research in Marketing, 39*(2), 522–540. DOI: 10.1016/j.ijresmar.2021.11.002

Kopecka-Piech, K., & Bolin, G. (Eds.). (2023). *Contemporary challenges in mediatisation research.* Routledge, Taylor & Francis Group. DOI: 10.4324/9781003324591

Kowert, R., Schweiger, W., & Klimmt, C. (2015). The social side of gaming: A study of interaction patterns in online games. *Journal of Media Psychology, 27*(2), 63–70.

Kozinets, R. V. (2002). The Field behind the Screen: Using Netnography for Marketing Research in Online Communities. *JMR, Journal of Marketing Research, 39*(1), 61–72. DOI: 10.1509/jmkr.39.1.61.18935

Kozinets, R. V. (2015). Netnography. In *The International Encyclopedia of Digital Communication and Society* (pp. 1–8). John Wiley & Sons, Ltd., DOI: 10.1002/9781118767771.wbiedcs067

Kozinets, R. V., Gretzel, U., & Gambetti, R. (2023). *Influencers and Creators: Business, Culture, and Practice*. Sage.

Krippendorff, K. (1990). Metodología de análisis de contenido: Teoría y práctica. *Piados Comunicación, 1*(42), 269–279.

Kumar, S., & Aravamudhan, S. (2023). Investigating the Effects of Virtual Personas on Brand Image. In *Brand Awareness-Recent Advances and Perspectives*. IntechOpen.

Kuzminov, M. (2023). Consumer trust and virtual influencers. *Forbes*.

Labrecque, L. I. (2014). Fostering consumer–brand relationships in social media environments: The role of parasocial interaction. *Journal of Interactive Marketing*, *28*(2), 134–148. DOI: 10.1016/j.intmar.2013.12.003

Landgrebe, J. (2024). The Rise of Digital Influencer Marketing. *HERMES-Journal of Language and Communication in Business*, (64), 75–102. DOI: 10.7146/hjlcb.vi64.143879

Lee, H. C., Liu, S. F., & Cheng, Y. C. (2018). Positive or Negative? The Influence of Message Framing, Regulatory Focus, and Product Type. *International Journal of Communication*.https://ijoc.org/index.php/ijoc/article/viewFile/7601/2266

Lee, J. A. (2020). *What makes social media influencers authentic? Understanding perceived authenticity of social media influencers* (Doctoral dissertation).

Lee, H., Shin, M., Yang, J., & Chock, T. M. (2024). Virtual Influencers vs. Human Influencers in the Context of Influencer Marketing: The Moderating Role of Machine Heuristic on Perceived Authenticity of Influencers. *International Journal of Human-Computer Interaction*, •••, 1–18. DOI: 10.1080/10447318.2024.2374100

Lee, Y. H., & Yuan, C. W. T. (2023). I'm not a puppet, I'm a real boy! Gender presentations by virtual influencers and how they are received. *Computers in Human Behavior*, *149*, 107927. DOI: 10.1016/j.chb.2023.107927

Lei, J., Indiran, L., Kohar, U. H. A., Liu, H., & Khatib, S. F. A. (2023). Examining the Role of Digital Technology as an Enabler of Digital Disruption: A Systematic Review. *Research Square*. DOI: 10.21203/rs.3.rs-3657875/v1

Le, T. (2022). The reliability of virtual influencers in branding strategies. *Journal of Advertising and Social Media*, *21*(6), 156–172.

Leung, F. F., Gu, F. F., Li, Y., Zhang, J. Z., & Palmatier, R. W. (2022). Influencer Marketing Effectiveness. *Journal of Marketing*, *86*(6), 93–115. DOI: 10.1177/00222429221102889

Leung, F. F., Gu, F. F., & Palmatier, R. W. (2022). Online influencer marketing. *Journal of the Academy of Marketing Science*, *50*(2), 226–251. DOI: 10.1007/s11747-021-00829-4

Li, T., et al. (2023). Cue Consistency Theory and Avatar Effectiveness. Journal of Digital Marketing.

Libunao, F. M., Martinez, J. D., Rodriguez, M. K., & Castaño, M. C. (2022). Consumers Attitude towards Skincare Products Endorsed by Filipino Macro-Influencers on Instagram. *Journal of Business and Management Studies*, *4*(2), 123–135. DOI: 10.32996/jbms.2022.4.2.10

Li, H., Lei, Y., Zhou, Q., & Yuan, H. (2023). Can you sense without being human? Comparing virtual and human influencers endorsement effectiveness [Article]. *Journal of Retailing and Consumer Services*, *75*, 103456. Advance online publication. DOI: 10.1016/j.jretconser.2023.103456

Li, L., Liu, S., & Lee, J. Y. (2024). On the Social Media Platform, Virtual Internet Celebrities and Real Idol Brand Spokesmen Perceive Human Nature, Physical Charm, and Study Consumer Reaction Based on Self-Consistency: The Media Effect of Trust [Article]. *WSEAS Transactions on Business and Economics*, *21*, 762–774. DOI: 10.37394/23207.2024.21.64

Lim, R. E., & Lee, S. Y. (2023). "You are a virtual influencer!": Understanding the impact of origin disclosure and emotional narratives on parasocial relationships and virtual influencer credibility. *Computers in Human Behavior*, *148*, 107897. DOI: 10.1016/j.chb.2023.107897

Lim, R. L., Rosales, M. Z., Salazar, A. T., & Pantoja, E. (2022). Perception of Filipino Skincare Product Users on the Effectiveness of Social Media Influencers vs Celebrity Endorsers as Brand Ambassadors. *Journal of Business and Management Studies*, *4*(1), 131–139. DOI: 10.32996/jbms.2022.4.1.16

Liu, F., & Lee, Y. H. (2024). Virtually authentic: Examining the match-up hypothesis between human vs virtual influencers and product types. *Journal of Product and Brand Management*, *33*(2), 287–299. DOI: 10.1108/JPBM-03-2023-4418

Liu, F., & Lee, Y. H. (2024b). Virtually responsible? Attribution of responsibility toward human vs. virtual influencers and the mediating role of mind perception [Article]. *Journal of Retailing and Consumer Services*, *77*, 103685. Advance online publication. DOI: 10.1016/j.jretconser.2023.103685

Longoni, C., & Cian, L. (2022). Consumer Perceptions of AI-Driven Recommendations. *Journal of Consumer Psychology*.

Looi, J. M. (2023). *Deriving authenticity from artificial intelligence: Assessing the roles of human-likeness and influencer tier in virtual influencer marketing* (Doctoral dissertation, University of Texas).

Looi, J., & Kahlor, L. A. (2024). Artificial Intelligence in Influencer Marketing: A Mixed-Method Comparison of Human and Virtual Influencers on Instagram [Article]. *Journal of Interactive Advertising*, *24*(2), 107–126. DOI: 10.1080/15252019.2024.2313721

Lopez, C., Chefor, E., & Babin, B. J. (2023). Rethinking Authenticity: An Investigation of Virtual Influencers: An Abstract. In *Developments in Marketing Science:Proceedings of the Academy of Marketing Science* (pp. 95-96). Springer Nature. DOI: 10.1007/978-3-031-24687-6_36

Lou, C., Kiew, S. T. J., Chen, T., Lee, T. Y. M., Ong, J. E. C., & Phua, Z. (2022). Authentically Fake? How Consumers Respond to the Influence of Virtual Influencers. *Journal of Advertising*, *52*(4), 540–557. DOI: 10.1080/00913367.2022.2149641

Lou, C., & Yuan, S. (2019). Influencer marketing: How message value and credibility affect consumer trust of branded content on social media. *Journal of Interactive Advertising*, *19*(1), 58–73. DOI: 10.1080/15252019.2018.1533501

Loyer, E. (2015). Parasocial and social player-avatar relationships: Social others in Thomas Was Alone. *Press Start*, *2*(1), 21–32.

Luo, L., & Kim, W. (2024). How virtual influencers' identities are shaped on Chinese social media: A case study of ling. *Global Media and China*, *9*(3), 325–343. DOI: 10.1177/20594364231188353

Marwick, A. (2018). *The algorithmic celebrity: the future of internet fame and microcelebrity studies: The future of internet fame and microcelebrity studies*. Emerald Publishing Limited., DOI: 10.1108/978-1-78756-749-820181015

Marwick, A. E. (2013). *Status update: Celebrity, publicity, and branding in the social media age*. Yale University Press.

Marwick, A. E., & Boyd, D. (2011). To see and be seen: Celebrity practice on Twitter. *Convergence (London)*, *17*(2), 139–158. DOI: 10.1177/1354856510394539

McRoberts, S., Bonsignore, E., Peyton, T., & Yarosh, S. (2021). Can AI influencers build relationships with consumers? *Computers in Human Behavior*, *122*, 106813.

Melnychuk, H. A., Arasli, H., & Nevzat, R. (2024). How to engage and attract virtual influencers' followers: A new non-human approach in the age of influencer marketing. *Marketing Intelligence & Planning*, *42*(3), 393–417. DOI: 10.1108/MIP-06-2023-0251

Meng, L. M., Bie, Y., Yang, M., & Wang, Y. (2024). Watching it motivates me to become stronger: Virtual influencers' impact on consumer self-improvement product preferences [Article]. *Journal of Business Research, 178*, 114654. Advance online publication. DOI: 10.1016/j.jbusres.2024.114654

Meng, L. M., Bie, Y., Yang, M., & Wang, Y. (2025). The effect of human versus virtual influencers: The roles of destination types and self-referencing processes [Article]. *Tourism Management, 106*, 104978. Advance online publication. DOI: 10.1016/j.tourman.2024.104978

Miao, Y., Tan, C., & Wong, P. (2021). Virtual influencers as brand ambassadors: The role of AI in marketing communication. *Digital Media Journal*, *15*(2), 99–113.

Millan, F., & Singh, A. (2021). Transparency in virtual influencer campaigns: A regulatory perspective. *Journal of Business Regulations*, *34*(1), 75–92.

Minculete, G., & Olar, P. (2018). Approaches to the modern concept of digital marketing. In *International conference Knowledge-based organization* (Vol. 24, No. 2, pp. 63-69). DOI: 10.1515/kbo-2018-0067

Miquela, (2024). Instagram. Lilmiquela. https://www.instagram.com/lilmiquela/

Mirowska, A., & Arsenyan, J. (2023). Sweet escape: The role of empathy in social media engagement with human versus virtual influencers. *International Journal of Human-Computer Studies*, *174*, 103008. DOI: 10.1016/j.ijhcs.2023.103008

Miyake, E. (2024). *Virtual Influencers.* Doi: DOI: 10.4324/9781003433170

Miyake, Y. (2022). Authenticity Challenges in Virtual Influencer Marketing. Journal of Media Studies.

Molin, V., & Nordgren, S. (2019). *"Robot or human? – The marketing phenomenon of virtual influencers – A case study about virtual influencers' parasocial interaction on Instagram."* [Master's Thesis, Uppsala University].

Molin, V., Nordgren, S. (2019). Robot or human? The marketing phenomenon of virtual influencers: A case study about virtual influencers' parasocial interaction on Instagram.

Moran, N. (2016). Even Better than the Real Thing.

Morency, C. (2018, February 5). *Meet fashion's first computer-generated influencer*. The Business of Fashion. https://www.businessoffashion.com/articles/media/meeting-fashions-first-computer-generated-influencer-lil-miquela-sousa/

Mori, M. (1970). The uncanny valley. *Energy*, *7*(4), 33–35.

Mo, T., & Wang, W. (2024). The virtual new or the real old? The effect of temporal alignment between influencer virtuality and brand heritage narration on consumers' luxury consumption [Article]. *Psychology and Marketing*. Advance online publication. DOI: 10.1002/mar.22132

Mouritzen, S. L. T., Penttinen, V., & Pedersen, S. (2023). Virtual influencer marketing: the good, the bad and the unreal. *European Journal of Marketing*(ahead-of-print).

Mouritzen, S. L. T., Penttinen, V., & Pedersen, S. (2023). Virtual influencer marketing: The good, the bad and the unreal. *European Journal of Marketing*.

Moustakas, E., Lamba, N., Mahmoud, D., & Ranganathan, C., C. (2020). "Blurring lines between fiction and reality: Perspectives of experts on marketing effectiveness of virtual influencers," *2020 International Conference on Cyber Security and Protection of Digital Services (Cyber Security)*, Dublin, Ireland, 2020, pp. 1-6, DOI: 10.1109/CyberSecurity49315.2020.9138861

Mo, Z., & Zhou, M. (2024). Don't Like Them but Take What They Said_ The Effectiveness of Virtual Influencers in Public Service Announcements [Article]. *Journal of Theoretical and Applied Electronic Commerce Research*, *19*(3), 2269–2288. DOI: 10.3390/jtaer19030110

Mrad, M., Ramadan, Z., & Nasr, L. I. (2022). Computer-generated influencers: The rise of digital personalities [Article]. *Marketing Intelligence & Planning*, *40*(5), 589–603. DOI: 10.1108/MIP-12-2021-0423

Mrad, M., Ramadan, Z., Tóth, Z., Nasr, L., & Karimi, S. (2025). Virtual influencers versus real connections: Exploring the phenomenon of virtual influencers. *Journal of Advertising*, *54*(1), 1–19. DOI: 10.1080/00913367.2024.2393711

Munar, A. M., & Jacobsen, J. K. S. (2014). Motivations for sharing tourism experiences through social media. *Tourism Management*, *43*, 46–54. DOI: 10.1016/j.tourman.2014.01.012

Nasrin, N. (2022). Brands will Spend a Whopping $32.5bn on Influencer Advertising in 2023, *Marketing Magazine*, Retrieved from https://marketingmagazine.com.my/brands-will-spend-a-whopping-32-5bn-on-influencer-advertising-in-2023/

Nasr, L. I., Mousavi, S., & Michaelidou, N. (2025). Self-Comparing With Virtual Influencers: Effects on Followers' Wellbeing. *Psychology and Marketing*, *42*(3), 780–798. DOI: 10.1002/mar.22151

Neri, F. C. (2022). Artificial Intelligence or a Neoliberal Marketing Scheme? The Performative Nature of Lil Miquela's Racialized Design and Politics on Instagram. *The IJournal: Student Journal of the Faculty of Information* 7 (2). Toronto, Canada:52–59. https://doi.org/.DOI: 10.33137/ijournal.v7i2.38617

Nguyen, H. (2023). Omnichannel marketing strategy for fashion retailers. https://www.theseus.fi/bitstream/handle/10024/796801/Nguyen_Hue.pdf?sequence=2

Nguyen, M. (2023, September 22). *Virtual influencers: Meet the AI-generated figures posing as your new online friends*. TNW | Future-Of-Work. https://thenextweb.com/news/virtual-influencers-ai-generated-online

Nicos, A., & Alexander, B. (2024). The 4Ps Marketing Strategy as a Driver of Dynamic Capabilities: Path to Consumer/Voter Satisfaction. *Review of Marketing Science*, *0*(0), 117–132. Advance online publication. DOI: 10.1515/roms-2023-0125

Nikjoo, A., Markwell, K., Nikbin, M., & Hernandez-Lara, A. B. (2021). *The flag-bearers of change in a patriarchal Muslim society: Narratives of Iranian solo female travelers on Instagram*.http://nportal0.urv.cat:18080/fourrepopublic/search/item/imarina%3A9219122

Niluth, N. (2024). Konsep 4P Sebagai Strategi Rumah Makan Cahaya Minang Dalam Mempertahankan Usahanya (Studi Kasus pada Kampung Hambulu Kabupaten Bogor). *Wiratani Jurnal Ilmiah Agribisnis*, *7*(1), 12. DOI: 10.33096/wiratani.v7i1.316

Nissen, A., Conrad, C., & Newman, A. (2023, April). Are you human? Investigating the perceptions and evaluations of virtual versus human Instagram influencers. In *Proceedings of the 2023 chi conference on human factors in computing systems* (pp. 1-14).

Obilo, O. O., Chefor, E., & Saleh, A. (2021). Revisiting the consumer brand engagement concept. *Journal of Business Research*, *126*, 634–643. DOI: 10.1016/j.jbusres.2019.12.023

Ogwa, A. L., Rabiu, M. S., & Ogande, A. (2024). Interactive Electronic Billboard as A Tool for Advertising in the Modern-Day Nigerian Society. *Nasarawa Journal Of Multimedia And Communication Studies*, *6*(1), 140–151.

Okolie, S. M. (2019). Virtual Influencers: Stretching the Boundaries of Intellectual Property Governing Digital Creations. *Landslide*, *12*, 52.

Okonkwo, I., & Namkoisse, E. (2023). The role of influencer marketing in building authentic brand relationships online. *Journal of Digital Marketing and Communication*, *3*(2), 81–90. DOI: 10.53623/jdmc.v3i2.350

Oliveira, D. C., Ventura, J. B. S., & Silva, P. C.Da Costa Oliveira. (2024). Narrativas de consumo de moda, inteligência artificial e emoções: O riso de Lu do Magalu. *Organicom, 21*(44), 133–146. DOI: 10.11606/issn.2238-2593.organicom.2024.220272

Orencia, A. J. (2023). Authenticity, Relatability, and Cultural Influences in Contemporary Marketing Strategies: A Qualitative Inquiry. *Psychology and Education: A Multidisciplinary Journal, 15*, 675-679.

Osiyevskyy, O., Umantsiv, Y., & Kavun, O. (2024). Strategy for striking the omnichannel balance in Retail 4.0. *Strategy and Leadership, 52*(3/4), 7–19. DOI: 10.1108/SL-12-2023-0120

Ozdemir, O., Kolfal, B., Messinger, P. R., & Rizvi, S. (2023). Human or virtual: How influencer type shapes brand attitudes. *Computers in Human Behavior, 145*, 107771. DOI: 10.1016/j.chb.2023.107771

Pan, S., Qin, Z., & Zhang, Y. (2024). More realistic, more better? How anthropomorphic images of virtual influencers impact the purchase intentions of consumers. *Journal of Theoretical and Applied Electronic Commerce Research, 19*(4), 3229–3252. DOI: 10.3390/jtaer19040157

Paul, I., Mohanty, S., & Sengupta, R. (2022). The role of social virtual world in increasing psychological resilience during the on-going COVID-19 pandemic. *Computers in Human Behavior, 127*, 107036. DOI: 10.1016/j.chb.2021.107036 PMID: 34658502

Paulovics, Á. (2023). Digital Reality and Identity: An Evolutionary Analysis of Virtual Influencer Lil Miquela.

Paulovics, Á. (2023). Digital reality and identity: An evolutionary analysis of virtual influencer Lil Miquela. In *A mesterséges intelligencia szerepe a fenntartható gazdasági döntésekben.*

Paz, M. D. R., & Delgado, F. J. (2020). Consumer experience and omnichannel behavior in various sales atmospheres. *Frontiers in Psychology, 11*, 1972. DOI: 10.3389/fpsyg.2020.01972 PMID: 32849155

Peng, Y., Cowan, K., & Lo Ribeiro, J. (2025). Into the virtual worlds: Conceptualizing the consumer-avatar journey in virtual environments. *Psychology and Marketing, 42*(2), 374–394. DOI: 10.1002/mar.22129

Pereira, H. G., de Fátima Salgueiro, M., & Mateus, I. (2014). Say yes to Facebook and get your customers involved! Relationships in a world of social networks. *Business Horizons, 57*(6), 695–702. DOI: 10.1016/j.bushor.2014.07.001

Pfalz, L. (2022). Malta creates world's first "virtual citizen" to promote tourism. TRAVELPULSE. https://www. travelpulse.com/news/destinations/malta-creates -worlds-first- virtual-citizen-to-promote-tourism.html

Phan, K. L., & Molesworth, M. (2023). The illusion of digital authenticity: How virtual influencers shape brand perceptions. *The Journal of Consumer Research, 50*(1), 88–102.

Philippine Congress. (2018). Republic Act 11206 (An Act Establishing a Career Guidance and Counseling Program for All Secondary Schools and Appropriating Funds Therefore). https://lawphil.net/statutes/repacts/ra2019/ra_11206_2019.html

Pitafi, Z. R., & Awan, T. M. (2024). The rise of influencer culture: Marketing, monetization, and authenticity in the social sphere. In Ján, V., & Jana, M. (Eds.), *Social Media and Modern Society-How Social Media are Changing the Way We Interact with the World Around.* IntechOpen. DOI: 10.5772/intechopen.1006565

Poppi Co. (2024). *The Alix Earle Effect: Maximizing Social Media Impact. Case Study Report.* Anthropomorphism and Consumer Trust. Marketing Science Review.

Qiaoling, L., Imm, Ng. S. I., Basha., N.K. Luo. X. Li, Y. (2024). Impact of virtual influencers on customer engagement of Generation Z consumers: a presence perspective. Young Consumers: Insight and Ideas for Responsible Marketers, DOI: 10.1108/YC-01-2024-1958

Rachmad, Y. E. (2024). *The Future of Influencer Marketing: Evolution of Consumer Behavior in the Digital World.* PT. Sonpedia Publishing Indonesia.

Raji, I. D., & Buolamwini, J. (2022). Bias in AI-generated influencer models: Addressing representation in digital marketing. *Digital Ethics Journal, 14*(2), 119–134.

Rhythm (2024). The Rise of AI-Generated Influencers. https://rhythmagency.com/blog/may-2024/the-rise-of-ai-generated-influencers

Robertson, C. J., & Doshi, A. (2022). Legal and ethical challenges in AI-generated influencer marketing. *Journal of Business Ethics, 179*(2), 287–304.

Romney, A., Harrison, J. T., & Benson, S. (2024). Looking back to predict the future: A review of empirical support for the self-fulfilling prophecy. *Management Research Review, 47*(2), 245–260. DOI: 10.1108/MRR-01-2022-0051

Rosário, A., & Raimundo, R. (2021). Consumer marketing strategy and E-commerce in the last decade: A literature review. *Journal of Theoretical and Applied Electronic Commerce Research, 16*(7), 3003–3024. DOI: 10.3390/jtaer16070164

Rossi, C., & Rivetti, F. (2023, May). Virtual influencer marketing: Is it effective in engaging younger generations. In ECSM 2023 10th European Conference on Social Media. Academic Conferences and publishing limited.

Roy, D., & Chakraborty, J. (2023). "Forever young, beautiful, and scandal-free": Exploring the ethical frames and crafted authenticity in the animated images of female virtual influencers. *Global Media Journal. Indian Edition, 15*(1), 1-23.

Roy, D., & Chakraborty, J. (2023). "Forever young, beautiful, and scandal-free": Exploring the Ethical Frames and Crafted Authenticity in the Animated Images of Female Virtual Influencers. *Global Media Journal. Indian Edition, 15*(1), 1-23.

Rozema, R. (2022). The rise of virtual influencers: Threats and opportunities for brands. *Candid*. https://www.candidplatform.com/en/news/platform-news/all-platform-news/marketing/therise-of-virtual-influencers-threats-and-opportunities-for-brands.html

Rozema, M. (2023). *Risks and Rewards in Human Influencer Marketing*. Influencer Marketing Hub.

Sakuma, H., Hori, A., Murashita, M., Kondo, C., & Hijikata, Y. (2023). YouTubers vs. VTubers: Persuasiveness of human and virtual presenters in promotional videos. *Frontiers of Computer Science*, *5*, 1043342. DOI: 10.3389/fcomp.2023.1043342

Sands, S.. (2022). *Endorsement evolution and the rise of AI influencers*. Marketing Science Review.

Sands, S., Ferraro, C., Demsar, V., & Chandler, G. (2022). False idols: Unpacking the opportunities and challenges of falsity in the context of virtual influencers. *Business Horizons*, *65*(6), 777–788. DOI: 10.1016/j.bushor.2022.08.002

Sarkar, A., Saeed, S., Rezhan, A., Nada, B, A.. (2023). Effect of the Internet on Enhancing Marketing among Business Organizations. DOI: 10.31098/ijmadic.v1i2.1751

Schneider, T., Hois, J., Rosenstein, A., Ghellal, S., Theofanou-Fülbier, D., & Gerlicher, A. (2021). Explain yourself! *Transparency for positive UX in autonomous driving* (p. 12). https://doi.org/DOI: 10.1145/3411764.3446647

Schramm, H., & Hartmann, T. (2008). The PSI-Process Scales: A new measure to assess the intensity and breadth of parasocial processes. *Communications*, *33*(4), 385–401. DOI: 10.1515/COMM.2008.025

Séraphin, H., Ambaye, M., Gowreesunkar, V., & Bonnardel, V. (2016). A marketing research tool for destination marketing organizations' logo design. *Journal of Business Research*, *69*(11), 5022–5027. DOI: 10.1016/j.jbusres.2016.04.074

Shahid, S. (2023). From traditional marketing to digital marketing: Digital Sign Media Ltd.

Shanahan, T., Tran, P., & Taylor, E. C. (2019). Getting to know you: Social media personalization as a means of enhancing brand loyalty and perceived quality. *Journal of Retailing and Consumer Services*, *47*(C), 57–65. DOI: 10.1016/j.jretconser.2018.10.007

Shao, Z. (2024). From human to virtual: Unmasking consumer switching intentions to virtual influencers by an integrated fsQCA and NCA method [Article]. *Journal of Retailing and Consumer Services*, *78*, 103715. Advance online publication. DOI: 10.1016/j.jretconser.2024.103715

Sharma, S., & Singh, R. (2019). The ethical frontier of virtual influencers: Balancing trust and AI innovation. *Journal of Marketing Ethics*, *15*(2), 210–229.

Shieber, J. (2018, April 24). The makers of the virtual influencer, Lil Miquela, snag real money from Silicon Valley. *TechCrunch*. https://techcrunch.com/2018/04/23/the-makers-of-the-virtual-influencer-lil-miquela-snag-real-money-from-silicon-valley/

Shin, Y., & Lee, S. (2023). Issues of virtual fashion influencers' reproduced bodies: A qualitative analysis based on body discourse. *Fashion and Textiles*, *10*(1), 30. DOI: 10.1186/s40691-023-00349-5

Silva, R., Pereira, I., Nicola, S., & Madureira, A. (2024). Exploring Virtual Reality in Omnichannel Marketing: A Systematic Review. In *International Conference on Marketing and Technologies* (pp. 865-880). Springer, Singapore DOI: 10.1007/978-981-97-1552-7_58

Sindhuja, K., & Rani, S. V. F. (2024). Role of Digital Influencer Marketing Strategy on Purchase of Private Label Brands: Mediating Effect of Brand Loyalty. *Nanotechnology Perceptions*, •••, 655–670.

Singco, M. Y. A., Lopez, I. D. A., & Cabauatan, R. R. (2023). The Effect of Influencer Marketing on Purchase Intentions and Brand Attitude of Consumers in the Philippines. *International Journal of Research in Engineering Science and Management*, *6*(12), 50–62. https://journal.ijresm.com/index.php/ijresm/article/view/2881

Soni, S. & Yadav, U. (2024). Statistical analysis of consumer attitudes towards virtual influencers in the metaverse. DOI: 10.1201/9781003471059-59

Sorosrungruang, T., Ameen, N., & Hackley, C. (2024). How real is real enough? Unveiling the diverse power of generative AI-enabled virtual influencers and the dynamics of human responses [Article]. *Psychology and Marketing*, *41*(12), 3124–3143. Advance online publication. DOI: 10.1002/mar.22105

Stein, J.-P., Linda Breves, P., & Anders, N. (2024). Parasocial interactions with real and virtual influencers: The role of perceived similarity and human-likeness. *New Media & Society*, *26*(6), 3433–3453. DOI: 10.1177/14614448221102900

Subhanjan, (2024). The Rise of AI Influencers: How Kyra and Virtual Personas Are Transforming Digitla Marketing. Medium. https://medium.com/@techscribecentral/the-rise-of-ai-influencers-how-kyra-and-virtual-personas-are-transforming-digital-marketing-3f763dbb047c

Suciu, P. (2021). *History Of Influencer Marketing Predates Social Media By Centuries – But Is There Enough Transparency In The 21st Century?* forbes.com. Retrieved 29 Dec from https://www.forbes.com/sites/petersuciu/2020/12/07/history-of-influencer-marketing-predates-social-media-by-centuries--but-is-there-enough-transparency-in-the-21st-century/

Sundar, S. S., Kang, J., & Oprean, D. (2020). Real or artificial? The impact of virtual influencers on consumer perceptions. *Computers in Human Behavior*, *114*, 106551.

Suprawan, L., & Pojanavatee, S. (2022). What causes social media users to engage and mimic virtual influencers? The role of self-congruity. *Innovative Marketing*, *18*(4), 148–160. DOI: 10.21511/im.18(4).2022.13

Tanwar, A. S., Chaudhry, H., & Srivastava, M. K. (2022). Trends in influencer marketing: A review and bibliometric analysis. *Journal of Interactive Advertising*, 22(1), 1–27. DOI: 10.1080/15252019.2021.2007822

Technavio, 2022. Artificial Intelligence (AI) in Social Media Market by Application and Geography - Forecast and Analysis 2022- 2026. https://www.technavio.com/re port/artificial-intelligence-ai-in-social-media-market-industry-analysis?utm_source=prnewswire&utm_medium=pressrelease&utm_campaign=autov8-vsg_wk43_2022_013_report&utm_content=IRTNTR74206.

Teixeira, S., Teixeira, S., Oliveira, Z., & Souza, E. (Eds.). (2023). *Using Influencer Marketing as a Digital Business Strategy*. IGI Global. DOI: 10.4018/979-8-3693-0551-5

Tengco-Pacquing, M. C. M., Bustamante, R. N., Cabanban, A. P. E., Cosare, M. B. M., Gamez, C. C., & Andre, V. (2019). Positive Framing Effect: A Mixed Method Study on the Buying Behavior of Filipino Millennials. *North American Journal of Psychology*, *21*(1).

Terziyska, I. (2021). Solo Female Travellers: The Underlying Motivation. In Valeri, M., & Katsoni, V. (Eds.), *Gender and Tourism* (pp. 113–127). Emerald Publishing Limited., DOI: 10.1108/978-1-80117-322-320211007

Thomas, V. L., & Fowler, K. (2021). Close encounters of the AI kind: Use of AI influencers as brand endorsers. *Journal of Advertising*, *50*(1), 11–25. DOI: 10.1080/00913367.2020.1810595

Tiggemann, M., & Slater, A. (2013). NetGirls: The Internet, Facebook, and body image concern in adolescent girls. *International Journal of Eating Disorders*, *46*(6), 630–633. DOI: 10.1002/eat.22141 PMID: 23712456

Tolani, K., Saraiya, A., Manohar, S. (2024). *The Digital Disruption of Distribution. Advances in web technologies and engineering book series*, DOI: 10.4018/979-8-3693-1762-4.ch007

Tukachinsky, R., & Stever, G. (2019). Theorizing development of parasocial engagement. *Communication Theory*, *29*(3), 297–318. DOI: 10.1093/ct/qty032

Tukachinsky, R., Walter, N., & Saucier, C. J. (2020). Antecedents and effects of parasocial relationships: A meta-analysis. *Journal of Communication*, *70*(6), 868–894. DOI: 10.1093/joc/jqaa034

Ullah, S. (2023). The Semantics Analysis of the Selected Billboards. *University of Chitral Journal of Linguistics and Literature*, *7*(II), 12–21.

Vallespin, M. R., Bodiongan, J. K., Banabana, V., Dacut, A., Gloria, V., Roa, S., & Tapungot, E. M. (2024). Exploring the Impact of Social Media Marketing on Customer Engagement and Purchasing Involvement among Grade 12 Students in a Private Sectarian School in Cagayan de Oro City, Misamis Oriental, Philippines: A Quantitative Analysis. *Misamis Oriental, Philippines: A Quantitative Analysis (May 9, 2024)*.

Venciute, D., Mackeviciene, I., Kuslys, M., & Correia, R. F. (2023). The role of influencer–follower congruence in the relationship between influencer marketing and purchase behaviour. *Journal of Retailing and Consumer Services*, *75*, 103506. DOI: 10.1016/j.jretconser.2023.103506

Vinoi, N., Shankar, A., Abdullah Alzeiby, E., Gupta, P., & Agarwal, V. (2025). Unveiling customer intentions: Exploring factors driving engagement with hospitality virtual influencers. *Journal of Hospitality Marketing & Management*, *34*(3), 1–30. DOI: 10.1080/19368623.2024.2429505

Vivek, S. D., Beatty, S. E., & Morgan, R. M. (2012). Customer engagement: Exploring customer relationships beyond purchase. *Journal of Marketing Theory and Practice*, *20*(2), 122–146. DOI: 10.2753/MTP1069-6679200201

Vrontis, D., Makrides, A., Christofi, M., & Thrassou, A. (2021). Social media influencer marketing: A systematic review, integrative framework and future research agenda. *International Journal of Consumer Studies*, *45*(4), 617–644. DOI: 10.1111/ijcs.12647

Wan, A., & Jiang, M. (2023). Can Virtual Influencers Replace Human Influencers in Live-Streaming E-Commerce? An Exploratory Study from Practitioners' and Consumers' Perspectives [Article]. *Journal of Current Issues and Research in Advertising*, *44*(3), 332–372. DOI: 10.1080/10641734.2023.2224416

Wang, J., Ye, G., & Yang, J. (2025). Not a human, not for green? The effectiveness of virtual influencers endorsing green products. *Journal of Product & Brand Management*. Ahead of the print.

Wang, B., Han, Y., Kandampully, J., & Lu, X. (2025). How language arousal affects purchase intentions in online retailing? The role of virtual versus human influencers, language typicality, and trust [Article]. *Journal of Retailing and Consumer Services*, *82*, 104106. Advance online publication. DOI: 10.1016/j.jretconser.2024.104106

Wang, L., Li, Y. Q., Ruan, W. Q., & Zhang, S. N. (2024). The congruence effect in tourism activity marketing: The difference between virtual influencers and human influencers [Article]. *Current Issues in Tourism*, 1–19. Advance online publication. DOI: 10.1080/13683500.2024.2400180

Wang, R., Bush-Evans, R., Arden-Close, E., Bolat, E., McAlaney, J., Hodge, S., Thomas, S., & Phalp, K. (2023). Transparency in persuasive technology, immersive technology, and online marketing: Facilitating users' informed decision making and practical implications. *Computers in Human Behavior*, *139*, 107545. DOI: 10.1016/j.chb.2022.107545

Wang, S., & Liu, M. T. (2022). Celebrity endorsement in marketing from 1960 to 2021: A bibliometric review and future agenda. *Asia Pacific Journal of Marketing and Logistics*, *35*(4), 849–873. DOI: 10.1108/APJML-12-2021-0918

Wang, Y., Weaver, D. B., & Kwek, A. (2016). Beyond the mass tourism stereotype: Power and empowerment in Chinese tour packages. *Journal of Travel Research*, *55*(6), 724–737. DOI: 10.1177/0047287515592971

Wasti, C., Ellizabeth, G., Adhyatma, M. I., & Maulana, A. E. (2024). Anthropomorphism And Authenticity: Exploring The Dynamics Of Virtual Influencers In Contemporary Marketing. *International Journal of Business and Society*, *25*(2), 789–809. DOI: 10.33736/ijbs.7631.2024

Weon Wee, J., Yoon, N., & Lee, Y. J. (2024). Beyond visual realism—Understanding the role of verbal cues in generating consumer affinity vs. fear toward virtual influencers in social network advertising. *Journal of the Korean Society of Clothing and Textiles*, *48*(6), 1194–1210.

Wheeler, A. (2017). *Designing brand identity: an essential guide for the whole branding team*. John Wiley & Sons.

Wikström, P. (2014). Tools, building blocks, and rewards: Traditional media organizations learn to engage with productive audiences. *Journal of Media Business Studies*, *11*(4), 67–89. DOI: 10.1080/16522354.2014.11073589

Wilfred, E. (2023). *Influence of digital marketing platforms on customer purchasing behaviours in Moshi municipality*(Doctoral dissertation, Moshi Co-operative University (MoCU))

Willemsen, L. M., Withuis, I., Brom, M., & Boerman, S. C. (2025). How does persuasion knowledge differ between humanlike virtual influencers and human influencers? *International Journal of Advertising*, *44*(1), 109–130. DOI: 10.1080/02650487.2024.2431440

Wirtz, J., Lovelock, C., & Chung, J. (2020). The role of CGI and AI in digital marketing strategies. *Journal of Marketing Technology*, *26*(3), 112–128.

Witt, G. L., & Baird, D. E. (2018). *The Gen Z frequency: How brands tune in and build credibility*. Kogan Page Publishers.

Wong, D. J. (2023). Philippines' First-Ever Virtual Model Gets Flack for Not Looking Filipino Enough. *Mashable Southeast Asia*. https://sea.mashable.com/tech/22481/philippines-first-ever-virtual-model-gets-flack-for-not-looking-filipino-enough

Xie-Carson, L., Benckendorff, P., & Hughes, K. (2023). Not so different after all? A netnographic exploration of user engagement with non-human influencers on social media [Article]. *Journal of Business Research*, *167*, 114149. Advance online publication. DOI: 10.1016/j.jbusres.2023.114149

Xie-Carson, L., Benckendorff, P., & Hughes, K. (2023a). Keep it# Unreal: Exploring Instagram users' engagement with virtual influencers in tourism contexts. *Journal of Hospitality & Tourism Research (Washington, D.C.)*, •••, 10963480231180940.

Xie-Carson, L., Benckendorff, P., & Hughes, K. (2024). Keep it #Unreal: Exploring Instagram Users' Engagement With Virtual Influencers in Tourism Contexts [Article]. *Journal of Hospitality & Tourism Research (Washington, D.C.)*, *48*(6), 1006–1019. DOI: 10.1177/10963480231180940

Xie-Carson, L., Magor, T., Benckendorff, P., & Hughes, K. (2023b). All hype or the real deal? Investigating user engagement with virtual influencers in tourism. *Tourism Management*, *99*, 104779. DOI: 10.1016/j.tourman.2023.104779

Xin, B., Hao, Y., & Xie, L. (2024). Virtual influencers and corporate reputation: From marketing game to empirical analysis [Article]. *Journal of Research in Interactive Marketing*, *18*(5), 759–786. DOI: 10.1108/JRIM-10-2023-0330

Xurui, C., & Shangshang, S. (2023). *The Impact of New Media Marketing to Peoples Consumption Behaviour*. Lecture Notes in Education Psychology and Public Media., DOI: 10.54254/2753-7048/4/2022842

Yadav, S. S. K., & Mishra, G. (2022). Corporate Digital Responsibility: Perspectives till date and the way ahead. 2022 5th International Conference on Contemporary Computing and Informatics (IC3I)

Yadav, S. S. K., & Mishra, G. (2024a). Digital Entrepreneurship Ecosystem: An Exploration. 2024 7th International Conference on Contemporary Computing and Informatics (IC3I)

Yadav, S. S. K., & Mishra, G. (2024b). Robotic Process Automation Applications Across Industries: An Exploration. 2024 7th International Conference on Contemporary Computing and Informatics (IC3I)

Yadav, S. S. K., & Bansal, S. (2021). The B2B digital marketing practice-towards an exploration of the' hidden'. *International Journal of Management Practice*, *14*(4), 391–410. DOI: 10.1504/IJMP.2021.116585

Yadav, S. S. K., & Dubey, A. (2023). Management innovation: Literature review and research directions. *International Journal of Business and Globalisation*, *33*(3), 271–285. DOI: 10.1504/IJBG.2023.129037

Yahya, M.A. (2024). Effects of 4Ps Marketing Mix Strategies on Profitability Enhancement of Petroleum Companies in Afghanistan – A Case Study. Istanbul management journal, DOI: 10.26650/imj.2024.96.1372899

Yang, J., Chuenterawong, P., Lee, H., Tian, Y., & Chock, T. M. (2023). Human versus virtual influencer: The effect of humanness and inter activity on persuasive CSR messaging. *Journal of Interactive Advertising*, *23*(3), 275–292. DOI: 10.1080/15252019.2023.2189036

Yan, J., Kong, H., Jiang, S., & Zhang, M. (2024). The impact of virtual influencer advertising on consumer response: A moderated chain mediation model based on mind perception and parasocial interaction. *Asia Pacific Journal of Tourism Research*, •••, 1–20. DOI: 10.1080/10941665.2024.2350404

Yan, J., Xia, S., Jiang, A., & Lin, Z. (2024). The effect of different types of virtual influencers on consumers' emotional attachment. *Journal of Business Research, 177*, 114646. Advance online publication. DOI: 10.1016/j.jbusres.2024.114646

Yao, L., Tugiman, N., & Sharipudin, M. N. S. (2024). Virtual human influencers in live streaming commerce on social media platforms: Exploring parasocial interactions with consumers in China.

Yap, Y. R., & Ismail, N. (2022). Factors of virtual influencer marketing influencing Generation Y consumers' purchase intention in Malaysia [Article]. *International Journal of Internet Marketing and Advertising*, *17*(3-4), 437–458. DOI: 10.1504/IJIMA.2022.126735

Yoo, J. W., Park, J., & Park, H. (2024). How can I trust you if you're fake? Understanding human-like virtual influencer credibility and the role of textual social cues. *Journal of Research in Interactive Marketing*. Advance online publication. DOI: 10.1108/JRIM-02-2024-0092

You, L., & Liu, F. (2024). From virtual voices to real impact: Authenticity, altruism, and egoism in social advocacy by human and virtual influencers. *Technological Forecasting and Social Change*, *207*, 123650. DOI: 10.1016/j.techfore.2024.123650

Yuan, L., & Lou, C. (2022). Do virtual influencers build stronger brand loyalty? Examining social media interactions. *International Journal of Advertising*, *41*(6), 1025–1043.

Yu, J., Dickinger, A., So, K. K. F., & Egger, R. (2024). Artificial intelligence-generated virtual influencer: Examining the effects of emotional display on user engagement. *Journal of Retailing and Consumer Services*, *76*, 103560. DOI: 10.1016/j.jretconser.2023.103560

Yu, T., Teoh, A. P., Bian, Q., Liao, J., & Wang, C. (2025). Can virtual influencers affect purchase intentions in tourism and hospitality e-commerce live streaming? An empirical study in China. *International Journal of Contemporary Hospitality Management*, *37*(1), 216–238. DOI: 10.1108/IJCHM-03-2024-0358

Zeng, W., Ma, Z., & Chen, T. (2024). When and why do consumers resist virtual influencer endorsement? The role of product depth and advertising claim types. *Electronic Commerce Research*, •••, 1–34. DOI: 10.1007/s10660-024-09903-9

Zhang, W., & Xu, M. (2022). The evolution of AI in influencer marketing: Deep learning and consumer interaction. *Journal of Marketing Analytics*, *35*(5), 223–239.

Zhao, T., Ran, Y., Wu, B., Lynette Wang, V., Zhou, L., & Wang, L. C. (2024). Virtual versus human: Unraveling consumer reactions to service failures through influencer types. *Journal of Business Research, 178*(C). https://ideas.repec.org//a/eee/jbrese/v178y2024ics0148296324001619.html

Zhao, X. (2022). *Virtual Fashion Influencers: towards a more sustainable consumer behaviour of Generation Z?* (Master's thesis).

Zhao, X. (2022). Virtual fashion influencers: towards a more sustainable consumer behaviour of generation Z?.

Zhao, X. (2022). *Virtual Fashion Influencers: Towards a more sustainable consumer behaviourof Generation Z?* (Master's thesis).

Zhao, T., Ran, Y., Wu, B., Lynette Wang, V., Zhou, L., & Lu Wang, C. (2024). Virtual versus human: Unraveling consumer reactions to service failures through influencer types [Article]. *Journal of Business Research*, *178*, 114657. Advance online publication. DOI: 10.1016/j.jbusres.2024.114657

Zheng, X., Miao, M., Zhang, L., & Huang, L. (2024). Standing out or fitting in? How perceived autonomy affects virtual influencer marketing outcomes [Article]. *Journal of Business Research*, *185*, 114917. Advance online publication. DOI: 10.1016/j.jbusres.2024.114917

Zheng, Y., & Toribio, J. R. (2021). The role of transparency in multi-stakeholder educational recommendations. *User Modeling and User-Adapted Interaction*, *31*(3), 513–540. DOI: 10.1007/s11257-021-09291-x

Zhong, Y., Shapoval, V., & Busser, J. (2021). The role of parasocial relationship in social media marketing: Testing a model among baby boomers. *International Journal of Contemporary Hospitality Management*, *33*(5), 1870–1891. DOI: 10.1108/IJCHM-08-2020-0873

Zhou, X. (2020). Virtual Youtuber Kizuna AI: co-creating human-non-human interaction and celebrity-audience relationship. (Master's thesis, Lund University).

Zhou, Q., Li, B., Li, H., & Lei, Y. (2024). Mere copycat? The effects of human versus human-like virtual influencers on brand endorsement effectiveness: A moderated serial-mediation model. *Journal of Retailing and Consumer Services*, *76*, 103610. DOI: 10.1016/j.jretconser.2023.103610

Zhou, X., Yan, X., & Jiang, Y. (2024). Making Sense? The Sensory-Specific Nature of Virtual Influencer Effectiveness [Article]. *Journal of Marketing*, *88*(4), 84–106. DOI: 10.1177/00222429231203699

Zhu, Y. Q., & Chen, H. G. (2012). Service fairness and customer satisfaction in internet banking: Exploring the mediating effects of trust and customer value. *Internet Research, 22*(4), 482–498. DOI: 10.1108/10662241211251006

Zona, C. (2020). Coca-Cola Max Headroom. YouTube. https://www.youtube.com/watch?app=desktop&v=sUMX6y2glJ8

About the Contributors

Ricardo Correia (Ph.D.) With an academic career started in 2003, Ricardo Fontes Correia is an Associated Professor at the Polytechnic University of Bragança (Portugal), where he is the head of the Master's program in Tourism Marketing, and visiting Professor at ISM University of Management and Economics (Lithuania). Ricardo's key research interests are related to Services Marketing, Tourism Marketing, Wine Tourism, Branding, and Social Networks. He is an integrated member of the Applied Management Research Unit (UNIAG) and has served as an external consultant in programs such as the European Union Agris Program and Interreg and as a consultant for Deloitte & Touche. We should also emphasize his regular participation in research programs, conferences, and international scientific meetings, as well as the publication of several chapters in books and articles in international journals.

Dominyka Venciute (Ph.D.) is Professor and Postdoctoral Researcher at the ISM University of Management and Economics where she teaches Marketing Principles, Social Media Marketing and Integrated Marketing Communications. Besides her activities in academia, she runs a personal branding and marketing consultancy that aims to help professionals and organizations unleash the power of their personal and corporate brands.

***

Mohd Junaid Akhtar is currently working as an Assistant Professor at the New Delhi Institute of Management, India. He has completed his Ph.D. from Department of Commerce, Aligarh Muslim University, India. He has 8 research papers in various reputed journals (indexed in Scopus WoS and ABDC) and presented papers in international and national conferences. His research interest lies in social media marketing, E-commerce and consumer behavior.

Komal Bhardwaj is currently working at the Maharishi Markandeshwar Institute of Management, Maharishi Markandeshwar University as Assistant Professor of Finance. She has a rich experience of more than eight years of teaching in the field of management. She has a research experience in the areas of assets pricing, derivatives, option pricing and study on stock volatility. Her research interest includes consumer behavior, investments, corporate governance, and assets liability management. She also worked as a Thesis supervisor for a program called upgrad-LJMU MBA at upgrade education private limited.

Ruta Fontes is a dedicated Ph.D. student specializing in Tourism at Aveiro University. With a passion for exploring the fascinating world of travel and leisure, she has delved deep into the realm of tourism behavior and spatiotemporal tracking. Ruta's academic journey has been marked by a commitment to research excellence, with numerous publications including papers and book chapters. Her academic pursuits extend beyond the classroom, as she has actively contributed to European projects as a diligent researcher. These experiences have provided her with a broader perspective and a global outlook on tourism and its impacts. Ruta is driven by a desire to uncover the intricate dynamics that shape tourist behaviors and to employ cutting-edge spatiotemporal tracking techniques to understand and optimize the tourist experience. Through her work, she aims to make valuable contributions to the field of tourism, ultimately enhancing our understanding of how people explore and engage with the world.

Ethelbert Garcia Galang is a fulltime faculty at the University of the Philippines Diliman - Extension Program in Pampanga and Olongapo (UPDEPPO) where he also earned his degree in Bachelor of Arts in Economics and Master of Management. Prior to his fulltime status, he worked at a Financial Institution for almost 20 years handling Customer Care and Corporate Banking at the same time he has been a Senior Lecturer for over a decade specializing in Economics, Management and Marketing.

Marie Grace A. Gomez is a faculty member College of Education, University of the Philippines-Diliman and the director of the Diliman Learning Resource Center. She has received several honors and awards for her work in teaching, research, and mentoring. Her research focuses on counseling diverse populations, disability issues, test development, children in conflict with the law, and sexuality. She has published extensively in both local and international journals on these topics.

Shikha Gupta is a dedicated researcher pursuing her Ph.D. in Digital Transformation and Business Intelligence at IIT Jodhpur. She is deeply immersed in one of the most rapidly evolving areas of interest among today's youth: social media influencers. Her one-year stint in the industry provided invaluable insights into digital marketing, social media management, brand marketing, and sales, laying the groundwork for her academic endeavors. Holding a Master's degree (MBA) with a specialization in Marketing from Aligarh Muslim University and a Bachelor's degree (BBA) from BIT Meerut, Shikha's journey has been rooted in management from the outset. Her work promises to uncover insights into how influencers are reshaping consumer behavior and business strategies, underscoring her unwavering dedication to advancing knowledge and fostering innovation in the dynamic landscape of digital business.

Anuj Pal Kapoor holds a PhD from Faculty of Management Studies (FMS), University of Delhi and his research areas include Multi-sensory experiences, design aesthetics, web-based platforms, collaborative consumption and Neuro-marketing. During his Ph.D., he developed a framework for strategic partnership between banks and e-commerce players, based on the digital consumption patterns of consumers across India. Prior to joining the PhD program, he has worked in the industry for six years across marketing, innovation and consulting domains. He was responsible for setting up the innovations function at HDFC Life based out of Mumbai and spearheaded the analytics function at Michael Page India, Gurgaon. Anuj also holds an MBA from Symbiosis International University; Bremen University of Applied Sciences (Germany) and B.E in Electronics and Communications from Institute of Technology & Management, Gurgaon. He also holds a certificate in Innovation Management from Massachusetts Institute of Technology (MIT, USA). Anuj is the recipient of ICSSR doctoral fellowship and was awarded the UNESCO fellow (Paris) award.

Sarita Nagvanshi is an academic and researcher. She has completed her bachelors in commerce from Delhi University and PhD in Marketing from Amity University. She has published several research articles, conference papers and book chapters in peer-reviewed Scopus journals with a focus on consumer behaviour, digital marketing, social media marketing and sustainability. She has taught students from various courses in the field of marketing as an assistant professor. She is driven by the desire to contribute to research-driven educational environments and practical learning settings.

Almudena Otegui Carles is a Graduate student pursuing her Master's Degree in Management and Planning of Inland and Health Tourism from the Universidade de Vigo.

Amit Singh holds a PhD degree from the Department of Industrial and Systems Engineering, Indian Institute of Technology Kharagpur (IIT Kharagpur), India.

He received his BTech from the Department of Mechanical Engineering, National Institute of Technology Agartala (NIT Agartala). He obtained his MTech in Industrial and Management Engineering from the National Institute of Technology Jamshedpur (NIT Jamshedpur), India and was awarded a bronze medal. He has served organizations such as the Indian Institute of Technology Jodhpur, Quantium Analytics, and IBS Hyderabad before joining Ahmedabad University. His research interests include sentiment analysis applications, social media analytics, panel data modelling, ICT diffusion in small and medium enterprises, multi-criteria decision-making, and supply chain management, among others. He has published several research articles in leading international journals such as the Journal of Business Research, the Journal of Enterprise Information Management, the Journal of Global Information Management, the Journal of Modelling in Management, etc. He is a reviewer for leading journals such as the International Journal of Information Management, the Government Information Quarterly, the Information Systems Frontier, the Journal of Modelling in Management, the International Journal of Electronic Government Research, etc.

Index

A

B

C

D

E

G

H

I

K

N

P

S

T

V

www.ingramcontent.com/pod-product-compliance
Lightning Source LLC
LaVergne TN
LVHW061547290926
849162LV00004B/932